HERITAGE OF HARMONY
An Insight into Medieval India

HERITAGE OF HARMONY
An Insight into Medieval India

Dr. Ajeet Jawed

GYAN PUBLISHING HOUSE
NEW DELHI-110002

Heritage of Harmony : An Insight into Medieval India

(History, Religion)

Rs. 790

ISBN: 81-212-0817-3

Published in 2002 in India by
Gyan Publishing House
5, Ansari Road, Darya Ganj, New Delhi-110002
Phones : 3282060, 3261060, Fax (011) 3285914
E-mail : gyanbook@vsnl.com
Website : http://www.gyanbooks.com

Laser Typesetting at: Sharma Graphic, New Delhi
Printed at: Mehra Offset Press, New Delhi

Contents

Contents

Preface

Our country has had a glorious past and a rich heritage. For centuries people lived together in peace and harmony. Religion in India was never the cause of conflict or discord among the people. Hinduism and Islam, the two different creeds were not hostile to each other, instead they acted and reacted upon each other and gave rise to new religions and numerous sects. Though the rulers of the medieval period were Muslims yet India never became a Muslim country. We all know about Akbar, but others, even his predecessors were no less hetter than Akbar. In the peaceful environments people worked together in making India a land of prosperity and wonder. However, most of the works written on Medieval India by the British and the communal minded Hindu as well as Muslim historians tell a different story. According to them Medieval period was dark ages, full of oppression, atrocities, injustices and exploitation of the non-Muslims at the hands of the Muslim rulers. Instead of amity, there was disharmony, discord, distrust disunity and divisions and India was lagging behind in every field. They have completely ignored the bright side of the picture of the Medieval India in order to suit their own vested interest. The distortion has been given such a wide currency that it is now accepted as actual historical fact by the general public.

The aim of the present work is to place the picture of India's past as it really was and to restore the perspective which had been deliberately distorted. For this work, considerable research has been done. Numerous works written on medieval India along with original source material has been utilised.

I must acknowledge my debt of gratitude to the authorities and staff of National Archives of India Library, Nehru Memorial Museum and Library, Central Secretariat Library, Arts Library Delhi University, Hardayal Library and Satyawati College Library for providing me facilities for research work. I am also thankful to Miss Madhuri and Swarnjit Kaur of Central Secretariat Library and Mukesh Manas, lecturer in Hindi Department, Satyawati College Mrs. Manjeet H. Singh for helping me in different ways.

I am obliged to my friend Kumkum Roy, Reader at J.N.U for through the script and giving me her valuable suggestions. I also express my gratitude to my husband Dr. M.A. Jawed and my children Amit, Aseem, Bulbul and Saba, whose cooperation made my work easier. I am also thankful to Gyan Publishing House for Publishing my work.

Dr. Ajeet Jawed

1

Interaction Between Hinduism and Islam : Rise of Sufi and Bhakti Movements

Islam appeared on the Indian scene in the 7th century in a peaceful manner. The Arab traders from Iraq settled down in the southern region and carried mercantile activities. They traded in spices, ivory and gems and through them India was linked with other parts of the world. At that time, the Arabs monopolized all seafaring trade between East and West. As trade proved highly profitable, the Indian rulers provided the Arabs all facilities, protection and patronage.

The Arabs had also brought with them their faith, i.e., Islam which rapidly made inroads and was well received by the people of the land .The Hindu rulers respected Islam and allowed the Arabs to erect their mosques and propagate their religion. The Zamorin of Calicut even went so far as to encourage conversions to Islam. He ordered that in every family of fishermen in his kingdom one or more of the male members should be brought up as Mohammedan. He wanted them to man Arab ships on which he depended for aggrandizement. The native converts received the same consideration and respect as foreign merchants even though before their conversion they belonged to the lowest grades of Indian society. This encouraged further conversions. The Hindu rulers also allowed Arabs to marry Indian women and very soon an Indo-Arabian community came into existence.[1] Thus the mundane motives of Indian rulers were responsible for the rapid spread of Islam in India.

Besides economic gains, the simplicity of the new religion also had great appeal, which worked for its popularity. Merchants, travellers and scholars who visited India, as early as the Arab merchants, settled in the country, testify in their writings appreciation of Islam by the Hindu Kings. Sulaiman, an Arab merchant, who was in India in the 9th century stated that the Indian Rajas were well disposed towards Islam and none liked the Arabs more than the Vallabhi king of Gujarat. Buzurg bin Shahryar writes that the king Mahrug of Alor in Kashmir in the 9th century had the Quran translated into Hindi and used to listen to the translation read to him every day. Masudi, the famous historian, who travelled in Western India, in the beginning of the 10th century, found Islam flourishing on the West Coast. He writes that the Vallabhi ruler of western India showed great respect to Islam and protected the interests of the Muslims in his realm.[2] The king of Malabar, the last of the Cheraman Perumal kings, converted himself to Islam and went to Arabia where he died four years later.3 The memory of the event was kept alive in Malabar by the Zamorin, who at the time of his installation to the throne dressed like a Musalman and occupied the throne only as viceroy awaiting the return of the converted ancestor from Arabia. The Maharajas of Travancore also received their sword of kingship with the word; "I will keep this sword until the uncle who has gone to Mecca returns"[4] The Vijaynagar kings also patronised Islam and occasionally invited Muslim generals to witness Hindu festivals at Vijaynagar. Muslims were designated as Mappilla, a title of honour. A Muslim could be seated by the side of the Nambudari Brahmin while a Nayar could not. The religious head of Mappillas, the Thangal, was allowed to ride in a palanquin along side the Zamorin.[5]

In all the states of Malabar, Muslims formed a very strong community and received fair and liberal treatment from Hindu rulers. They held important posts and were trusted and respected. In Fakanar (a place in south Canara), the thirty war ships of the Raja were in the charge of a Muslim commander. In the city of Calicut, trade and commerce were in the hands of Muslims. Ibrahim, a merchant from Bahrain, was the head of the merchants in the town. He was the chief officer in the customhouse with whom, foreign merchants and captains negotiated. The judge of Calicut was also a Muslim. Ibn Battuta, an African traveller, writes that a Muslim named Misqal "possessed great riches and many ships for trading purposes in India and China and Fars"[6] Muslims were trusted and were given high positions in the state administrations by the Hindu Rajas.They were also recruited in the army in large numbers. The ruler of

Somnath had a large number of Muslim officers. So complete was the identity of interest that Indian Muslims along with Hindus resisted waves of Muslim invasions. The army of Malik Kafur was opposed by Raja Vir Ballal who included in his contingent 20,000 Muslims. By the 10th century, Muslims had spread over the whole coast and in a comparatively short time acquired considerable influence both in society and politics in the southern India.[7]

In northern India, Muslim Arabs first entered from the west. They appeared as invaders and although after the conquest of the Sind they could not make any advance into India from that direction, their merchants, missionaries and saints visited the country, travelled freely and settled in towns. Thus before the invasion of Mohammed Ghori, India was already familiar with Muslims and their religion.

The Sufi Movement

With the establishment of the Delhi Sultanate in1206 Muslims became a ruling power. Following in the train of invaders were men of peace who preached love and harmony and worked in a big way to bring Islam and Hinduism closer to each other. Usually they were individuals endowed with piety and religious zeal. They wandered from place to place, intermingled with the people and propagated their teachings. However, Indian conditions, ideas and attitudes deeply influenced these saints and Indianised their outlook. In course of time, they discarded orthodox Islam and preached Islam which had an Indian flavour. They studied Hindu scriptures, learnt local languages, interacted with the native saints and incorporated many local beliefs, and practices in their own Faith. They were called Sufi and the religion they preached came to be known as Sufism, which profoundly influenced the entire country.

Sufism, in the words of Dr. Tara Chand "was a religion of intense devotion, love was its passion; poetry, song and dance its worship and passing away in God its ideal"[8] The Sufis worked not only on the spiritual plane but also for removing feelings of enmity and exclusiveness and sought to restructure society on the principles of amity and brotherhood. They opposed orthodoxy, denounced hypocrisy and emphasised on equality of all men and the essential unity of all religions. They learnt local languages, identified with the common masses and worked to alleviate them from suffering and distress. Service of the needy and oppressed was the cardinal principle of their discipline. They taught their disciples to cultivate the virtues of humility, goodwill, tolerance and forgiveness. Their simplicity, devotion, catholicity and kindness led a large number of people to become their disciples and to accept their creed. The mystical philosophy of the Sufis suggested an easy approach to God. Their Khanqhas (communes) were the place where salvation could be achieved. Its doors were open for all irrespective of race, religion, caste or creed. The Sufis laid emphasis more on the spirit of the religion rather than on the formal theology. The devotees assembled at these Khanqahs and spent whole night chanting the praises of God along with their saints. With the passage of time, the prestige and influence of the saints increased tremendously and the Indian converts outnumbered the immigrants.[9]

Sufis were revered like gods during their lifetime and after their death tombs were raised in their honour which became places of pilgrimage for the followers. Sufis settled in different parts of the country were the harbingers of Hindu Muslim unity, as they believed that all were the loved-ones of the same God.

Sufi in Punjab

There are many illustrious names in the long list of Sufis who settled in Punjab. Among the earliest was Ali Mukhdum Hujwiri (A.D 1092) who, because of his great generosity came to be known as Data Ganj Baksh, i.e., God's treasure house. Members of all the communities, commoners and kings alike, venerated the tomb of Data Ganj Baksh.Sayyid Ahmed Sultan Sakhi Sarwar, popularly known as Lakhi Data, too had a vast following of both Hindus and Muslim.[10]

The most important name in Punjab, however, is that of Shaikh Fariduddin Masud Ganj-e-Shakar (d.1265), popularly known as Baba Farid. He was a descendent of a royal family of Afghanistan and his family had settled down in Multan. Sufi philosophy deeply influenced him. He gave up his estate and wealth and became a disciple of Khwaja Qutbuddin Chisti and settled at Ajodhan now known as Pakpattan (in Pakistan).[11]

He preached his philosophy in Punjabi language in the form of dohas. He said;

"Farida Sakkar Khand nibat garh Makhiyu Manjha dudh
Sabey bastu mithian rub na puja tudh"[12]

(Sugar, honey candy molasses and milk, all are sweet but none of these can be compared with the sweetness of the name of the

Lord.)

He pointed out to his disciples that there was no need to search for God as He is everywhere and within everyone.

His teachings exercised great influence and his fame reached far and wide. About 134 of his hymns included in the Sikh holy book Adi Granth bears evidence to the veneration that was accorded to him by the non Muslims.[13] People in thousands used to come to pay their respect and seek his blessings. How deep was the reverence of the people for him was manifested when he visited Delhi to meet saint Qutbuddin. A vast stream of devotees flowed unabated towards him throughout his period of stay in Delhi. In 1253 when Sultan Nasiruddin marched towards Uch and Multan, soldiers of his army thronged in the streets and bazaars of Ajodhan to pay their respect to the saint in such a manner that there was virtually a stampede and his disciples had to throw a cordon round him to save him from possible injury.[14]

Baba Farid had intimate relations with a number of yogis who too paid frequent visits to his place called Jamat-Khana. Baba led a life of poverty and starvation and had a great aversion to the company of the rich. He instructed his disciples: "Pay particular attention to my advice. Do not make friends with kings and nobles. Consider their visit to your home as fatal" (for your spirit) While advising his chief disciple Sheikh Nizamuddin Auliya, Baba Farid said; "The main purpose in this (path of sufism) is the concentration of heart which can be achieved only by the abstinence of the prohibited means of livelihood and association with the kings"[15] Sultans like Balban and Alauddin had great respect for him. Once when Ala-ud-din sought his advice Baba Farid replied: "O Sultan! I refuse to help thee by giving advice in the governance of the country. We saints are concerned with the eternal country of the soul we do not interfere with your worldly affairs"[16]

Sheikh Ibrahim was the 11th successor to the spiritual *gaddi* of Baba Farid He was intimately associated with Baba Nanak, the first Guru of the Sikhs. Baba Nanak used to visit his place frequently and had religious discourses with him.[17]

Another divine of Lahore was Mian Mir (1550-1636) He had a large following all over the country. He did not lay emphasis on the propagation of Shariat as on the prayers, meditation and penance. Emperor Jahangir wrote in his autobiography about him as:

'Truly he is the beloved of God. In sanctity and purity of soul, he hath no equal in this age."Jahangir used to visit him and received religious instructions from him.[18] People from far off places flocked to Lahore to seek Mian Mir's blessings and guidance. His catholicity and kindness won him respect and reverence from Hindus and Muslims alike He was the personal friend of the 5th Guru of the Sikhs, Guru Arjun. Mian Mir also laid the foundation stone of the Golden Temple at Amritsar.

Sultan Baba another Sufi saint of Punjab shared the same creed. He believed in the oneness of God and asked his disciples to give up sectarian attitude and worship the Almighty. He used to say;

I am neither a Hindu nor a Muslim,
I am neither a Mullah nor a Qazi,
My heart does not fear death,
Nor does it long for paradise,
Oh God give me your vision,
Everything else is false.[19]

Mullah Shah Badakshani (d.1661) was revered by many. He had studied the Hinduism also. In his opinion all religions were alike as all suggest the way leading to the same God. Among his large number of followers was Prince Dara Shikoh and his sister Jahanara who believed in the unity of God.[20] The most noted Sufi saint of Punjab, however is Bulle Shah. He was born in 1680 A D in Kasur He passed his early days in the company of Sufi saints and Vedantists. When he grew up he became the disciple of Shah Inayat, another reputed saint known for his liberal views. Bulle Shah believed in the philosophy of love and devotion through which God can be realized and salvation attained. He stated:

I know not who I am
Neither I am a believer resting in the mosque
Nor a kafir seated in the Temple
I am neither pure nor a sinner,
Neither I am a Pharaoh nor a Moses
Nor can ye find me when you seek me in the Vedas

Bulle Shah pointed out that his path was the true path in the realization of one Supreme Being;

O Bulla, intoxicate thy self with the wine of divine love
Men will slander you and call you a hundred names,
When they abuse you with the name of kafir,
Say, yes friend, you are right.[21]

He revered Lord Krishna as much as Prophet Mohammed and wrote many verses in his praise. He says,

In Brindavavan you grazed the cattle, invading Lanka.
You made the sound of victory;
You again came as the pilgrim of Mecca;
You made wonderful changes of form;
What are you hiding yourself from now?[22]

Bulla's verses in the Punjabi dialect captured the minds of all the people of Punjab. He roamed the region preaching his viewpoint.[23]

Bulla shah lived in a period of great turmoil. Emperor Aurangzeb's polices were producing disharmony and conflict. But orthodoxy had no place in Bulla's philosophy. He fearlessly preached that there was no difference between the Quran and the Puran. The fanatic Haji was as much the target of his denunciation as the Pandit. He met Guru Gobind Singh and admired his religion and his God as the Universal deity.[24] His religious catholicity won him place in every heart of the Punjabis. Both Hindu and Muslim sang his Sufi songs with equal fervour. (Even today his songs are popular in both India as well in Pakistan In Raj Kapoor's film Bobby, Bulla's song 'Beshak Mandir Masjid dha de Bulle Sha Ye kahta "won the hearts of millions)

Ajmer

Khwaja Moinuddin Chishti (d.1236) was a great Sufi saint of Ajmer He enjoyed immense popularity and had numerous followers all over the country. It is said that when Moinuddin settled down in Ajmer, the high caste priests demanded of Prithviraj the ruler of Ajmer, to banish the Khwaja from the region. The king sent Shadi Dev (or Shadi Ram) the chief priest of a temple where the king along with his courtiers used to offer worship, to persuade the Khwaja to leave the place. Legend relates that in approaching the Khwaja, the priest was so much impressed by the saint's spirituality that he embraced Islam and became a disciple of the Khwaja.[25]

Moinuddin preached peace, harmony and co-existence and commanded great respect from all the people irrespective of their religion. He laid great emphasis on service to mankind. When asked about the highest form of devotion to God he replied: "It was nothing but redressing the misery of those in distress.fulfilling the needs of the helpless and feeding the hungry." He asked his disciples to develop "river like generosity sun like affection and earth like hospitality" He believed in the equality to all men, the essential unity of all religions and freedom from all religious prejudices.[26]

In times of difficulties and strains, kings and common people sought his guidance and blessings. After his death, his Dargah became a pilgrimage for the devotees.[27]

Delhi

Khwaja Qutbuddin Bakhtiar Kaki (d.1236) was the spiritual master of Baba Farid. He was immensely popular among the people of Delhi and his ideas were a happy blend of Upanishadic philosophy and the holy thoughts of the Prophet. He himself lived in highly impoverished circumstances but did not accept any office or gifts from the rulers. He enjoined the king Iltutmish who had very high regard for the saint;

"O ruler of Delhi, it is incumbent on thee to be good to all poor people, mendicants, darveshes and helpless folk. Treat all men kindly and strive for their welfare. Every one who thus behaves towards his subjects is looked after by the Almighty and all his enemies turn into friends"[28]

Iltutmish wanted Qutb Sahib to be the spiritual head of the state but the saint declined. Once Qutb Sahib decided to leave Delhi for Ajmer, the public of Delhi flocked to him imploring the saint not to leave them. Iltutmish himself followed the crowd of the people.[29]

Qutb Sahib died in 1235. He was buried at Mahrauli near Delhi. Sultan Iltutmish built Qutb Minar in his memory and named it after him.[30] All the sultans and the Mughal emperors revered him. Emperor Shah Alam prayed him as God.[31]

However, the most popular Sufi saint of Delhi, was Nizamuddin Aulia. (d.1325) His broad outlook and humanitarianism attracted both Hindus and Muslims alike. Service to humanity, in his opinion was the true means to achieve spiritual salvation as well as worldly happiness.

Saint Nizamuddin was the successor of Baba Farid and like him had intimate contacts and high regard for the Yogis and other Hindu saints. He had seen the reign of seven sultans succeeding one after another on the throne of Delhi; but like his master he never visited the Darbar of any one of them.

Nizamuddin's Khanqah was open to all and the influence of his creed spread fast. Ziauddin Barani an orthodox historian as well as noble and contemporary of the saint writes:

"Khwaja Nizam-ud-din had opened wide his door and admitted all sorts of people -nobles, plebeians, rich and poor, learned and illiterates, free men and slaves. People refrained from many improper things because they considered themselves disciples of the Khwaja. The general public showed an inclination to religion and prayer. There was no quarter of the city in which a gathering of the pious was not held every month.

People in large number flocked to his meetings for guidance solace and help. His khanqah became a great centre of learning. The presents in cash and kind, which he got, were passed on to meet the expenses of langar (free kitchen) which he maintained. He had given strict orders that whatever was received during a single day must be spent by the same evening. Thousands of poor and needy were fed daily at his kitchen. But the saint himself fasted most of the days and in the evening he ate only a half bread with some boiled vegetables."[32]

He taught tolerance, compassion and respect for other faiths. One of his favourite sayings was "Nothing will bring greater reward on the day of judgement than bringing happiness to the hearts of men"[33] His increasing influence and popularity aroused the wrath of the orthodox ulemas. They disapproved of his practices and denounced his views. At their insistence sultan Ghiasuddin Tughlaq had him brought before a tribunal of 53 theologians. But they all pronounced in favour of the saint. They even refrained from forbidding the musical and mystical preaching for which above all, the saint was reproached.[34] The Sheikh was so popular with the people that sultan Alauddin began to entertain the suspicion about his influence and authority in society Sultan Muhammad bin Tughlaq had a profound respect for the saint and used to visit him to solicit his blessings .He even carried the coffin of the saint when the latter departed from this world.[35]

Amir Khusrau one of his illustrious disciples revered him like God and wrote verses in his praise.[36]

Amir Khusrau carried forward the message of harmony and won a special place in the hearts of the people forever. He studied Hinduism and admired the devotion and practices of its followers. He opined;

Nist Hindu archi ki dinar chamne
Hast bast jay ba qarare chaman

(Though Hindu is not like me in religion, he believes in the same thing as I do,) Again;

Ay Kizi but tana ba Hindu bar!

Ham az way amuz para stishgar !

(O you sneer at the idolatry of the Hindu learn also from him how worship is done).[37]

Nizamuddin's idea kept on inspiring the future Sufis. Among them was saint Bawri Saheb. He was the Guru of Bir Saheb a Hindu saint, who again was the Guru of the great mystic Yari Saheb. Like his Gurus Yari Saheb was free from all kinds of sectarianism. In his verses he mentioned the name of Allah with that of Rama and Hari.[38]

Sarmad, the famous sufi martyr of Delhi of the 17th century enjoyed immense hold over the masses of Delhi. He belonged to the universal order of pantheist. He used to say "I obey the Quran; I am a Hindu priest and a monk; I am a Rabbi Jew, I am an infidel and I am a Muslim"[39]

In his view, God was One and was everywhere and could be realized only through true devotion.

"Few can distinguish between the Lover, the idolater and the trickster

The dwellers in the Kaba, the Mosque and the Chapel of course cannot recognize

Enter thou realm of unity and watch oneness prevailing all round

Discriminate the rose from the thorn, and the lover from the Beloved, if you can."[40] Again he says;

In one place He takes the form of black stone

And in other He becomes the idol of a Hindu (Black stone or Sang-i- Aswad of KABA that the pilgrims kiss or touch at the time of pilgrimage. The stone is believed to have come down from the heaven at the time of construction of Kaba by Abraham.)[41]

Drunk with divine love and ecstasy he lost self-consciousness and turned a nudist. When Emperor Aurangzeb castigated him about this Sarmad replied:

One who gave you the kingly throne? Provided me with all means of vescation; he grants dress to the sinful to hide their sins,But to the sinless He only gives the garment of nudity"[42]

Sarmad had studied Jewish scriptures (the Book of Moses), the New Testament and all other books on Christianity and the Quran but found his God in a boy named Abhay Chand. He worshipped him as holiness incarnate:

In this great monastery old and round,

Is Abhay Chand my God? Whom have I found?[43]

Fearlessly, he preached his ideas, which later cost him his life. Among his large following in Delhi, was Prince Dara Shikoh, the elder son of Shah Jahan. To his followers Sarmad revealed;

"One who comprehends the secrets of the truth
Has become vaster than the vast Heaven,
Mulla says 'Ahmad ascended to heaven;
Sarmad says, nay heaven came down to Ahmad"[44]

Sarmad's preaching and popularity greatly annoyed and unnerved the orthodox Mulla and their puritan Emperor Aurangzeb who beheaded him for blasphemy.[45]

People did not forgive Aurangzeb for Sarmad's execution. Sarmad's verses and quatrains were therefore, treated as instances of Gods grace and mercy and much care was taken to record and preserve them He has ever since been regarded as a martyr Shahid Sarmad.

Sind

Sind produced many prominent Sufi saints whose preaching brought the people on a common spiritual platform. Feelings of good will, fraternity, mutual respect and co- operation made Sind a land of harmony and peace.

The first noted Sufi saint of the region was Qazi Kadan. Most of his verses, which have been recovered from Bhagat Haridas Mutt in Haryana, clearly reflect the catholicity of his views. His God was not in Books. He found him everywhere. He used to say;

"Jogi jagayas sutto huyus ninda mein"(the yogi woke me up when Iwas fast asleep.)

Qazi Kadan influenced and inspired many saints all over the country most important among them was a Hindu saint Dadu Dayal.46

Shah Abdul Karim (1536-1623) was another popular saint of Sind He received his first religious inspiration from a Vaishnavite saint who initiated him in to the mysteries of OM This symbol served as a beacon light to him. For him there was no difference between Allah and Rama. He worshipped both and was revered by both Hindu and Muslim masses.[47]

Shah Inayat, a highly respected Sufi of Sind, also known as Bin Sir Saint (beheaded), preached the religion of love. He had a large number of followers including Bulle Shah, an illustrious Sufi saint and poet of Punjab. Thousands of devotees used to gather at his place to pay their respect and to get his blessings and direction. When the Hindus of Sind, under the oppression of the Kalhora kings were fleeing, it was he who sheltered many such fugitive families in his own hermitage. His Faith, that God is not the property of any particular sect finally led to his execution by a fanatic.[48]

Shah Abdul Latif (1689-1752) was one of the greatest Sufi saints of Sind. He was a son of a saint named Shah Karim. His zeal to realize God made him spend three years visiting holy places from Hinglez to Dwarka His Risalo is a sacred work revered by both Hindu and Muslims alike. He condemned the hypocrisy of the orthodoxy of both the communities. He said to Muslims:

"Faith does not consists in saying the Kalma with evils in your heart, you are a devil and not a Mussalman"

Likewise he asked the Hindus:

" Don't call yourself a Hindu, you don't deserve your janeo The Tilak behoves only those who are true to God"[49]

He was a symbol of the unity between Hindus and Muslims. He wore black dress during Muharrum, and draped himself as a Yogi in Bhagwa. Atal and Chanchal, two singers from Delhi, played music in his Khanqah, despite orthodoxy's displeasure.[50]

His God was everywhere and one could realize Him only through devotion. He said:

"To be one with Him
Set aside the chapters of Shariah and be fakir "

He says added:

"When truth is one and the Beloved (God) the same
Why should man fight over the means"?

To him the land of Sind was sacred He pointed out:

"Those who get acquainted with Ganja Hills
Become saints, forsaking all books and scriptures."[51]

When Shah Latif decided to leave this world "he wore a black, somber garment and went to a solitary chamber. He remained there for twenty -one days and took occasionally a few morsel of food. On the morning of the twenty -first day, he came out and took a bath. Then he lay down and pulled a sheet over himself. He asked his faqirs to play music and sing devotional songs. There was music and song for three days and Lo! Latif the Lord was absorbed in Love".[52]

His popularity and influence went on increasing even after his death .His shrine at Bhit became a weekly meeting place for both Hindus and Muslims of either sex for a spiritual communion.[53]

Sind, the land of Sufi saints, produced another Sufi saint named Abdul Wahab (1739-1829) popularly known as Sachal Sarmast-the true intoxicated one. Like Shah Latif, Sarmast too was an aspirant of Hindu -Muslim unity and did not believe in any specific creed. He used to say:

"I am neither a Mulla nor a Brahmin, nor even a page of the Quran .Not for me the Scripture or the Gita. I am neither east nor west, neither earth nor sky. I am a Jogi"[54]

Again he says:

"We became neither Sheiks nor Makhdum,

Neither Qazis nor Mullas, nor Pirs; We devised no such hypocritical creeds

We learnt only the art of God's love" [55]

He blamed both Mulla and Pundit for creating divisions on every ground:

"It is religions

Which have misled the people in the country, The Sheikhdom and Pirdom

Some people bend in Mosque and others bow in temples

But the pseudo- wise don't come near by love" [56]

He reveals:

"O Sadhu, the Lord is one beyond doubt

He enjoys the scene everywhere and is king at all points.

Sometimes he will read the Hindu Scriptures, sometimes the Quran

He can be Jesus as well as Mohammed and even Hanuman. He can create bewilderment for His ownself for his Lila" [57]

He prescribed to the Sikhs that their God was not different. He is one and the same Almighty.

"O Granthi, chant the Japji verses,

And you will meet the Guru;

Use the knife of love, cut off hatred and intolerance,

On you're both left and right he is one and the same Satguru".[58]

At the beat of a drum and the pull of a string, he would stand up, his hair on end and dance. He preached love, amity and harmony. Although the British annexation was decades away, Sarmast could predict the havoc they would create .He enjoined both the Hindus and the Muslims to unite to prevent such a catastrophe: "Time has come to overcome these divisions. Be quick to eschew all fruitless and graceless controversies. Let Hindu and Muslim co-mingle in love. Let it not be too late to save the situation. If action is not taken in time, these foreigners will leave behind heaps of corpses "[59]

Kashmir

No region of the country remained unaffected by Sufism. The influence of Sufis had spread everywhere In Kashmir, the founder of the Sufi movement was Syed Ali Hamdani, affectionately known by Kashmiris as Shah-e- Hamdan .He held liberal views and was revered by both Hindu and Muslim. Sultan Qutbuddin was one of his disciples Once Syed Saheb gave the Sultan a cap which, out of respect, the Sultan wore always under his crown. The subsequent Sultans followed the same practice until the cap was buried with the body of Fath Shah according to the latter's will. Lalleshwari or Lalla, a well-known Bhaktini of Kashmir had intimate association with the saint and like him preached the religion of love and devotion.[60]

Deccan

In Deccan, a Sufi saint Baba Sharfuddin was deeply respected by both the Hindus and the Muslims of the region. He lived a secluded life in prayers and meditation on a Pahadi Shareef or Holy Hill. He served the people of the area, teaching the local villagers universal brotherhood, healing their soul with holy ministrations and their bodies with herbs and natural remedies. Whenever they came to him with a problem, he would suggest "go and pray at your temple" which they did and the problem was solved. The villagers loved him; all strata of society called him Maha Dev He died at the age of one hundred years in 1286. He went down into the village on that day. 'A corpse lies at the top of the hill' he told the people. 'I need help to bury it.' The villagers were only too happy to oblige and followed him at a respectful distance. Near the summit they lost sight of the aged holy man. There they found a corpse. The body was covered with a shroud. Immediately they dug a grave and when they removed the cloth to bathe the body before the burial, the villagers made a startling discovery. It was the saint whom they loved and adored, the one who, minutes earlier, had led them up the hill to his own corpse and funeral. A shrine was built in his memory and it became a place of pilgrimage for the commoners and the kings. Sixth Nizam, Mahboob Ali Pasha and his nobles too used to visit his shrine for the blessings of the saint. The Nizam often sat in meditation at the shrine and was said to be in spiritual rapport with the saint. Even today pilgrims of all religions climb the one hundred and thirty two steps to pay their respects, to pray and seek solace.[61]

Hazrat Khwaja Gesu Daraz (1321-1422), was a popular Sufi saint. He had studied Hindu scriptures and had high admiration for Hindu philosophy. His ideas were a blend of Hinduism and Islam and his teachings exercised great influence over the masses as well as the ruling classes. Bahmani kings followed his discourses on religion and mysticism. When the saint died, the then Sultan Firoz went along with his nobles to pay his respects. The Bahmani Sultan Ahmad 1 was his devotee and built a magnificent tomb of the saint at Gulbarga. Ibrahim Adilshah II too revered his name and wrote verses in his praise.[62]

The Khwaja was very fond of music and because of his influence music festivals became popular all over Deccan to the chagrin of the of the orthodox ulema.[63]

Hazrat Gesu Daraz insisted upon his disciples that the greatest worship was to do justice to everyone. He used to say:

"Look the tree stands erect in the Scorching heat but it provides shade to others. Wood burns itself to provide comfort to others. It is thus natural that a man should undertake pain in order to provide pleasure to others."[64]

The United Province

In United Provinces, Sheikh Wali Mohammad Nazir gave the message of harmony. With guitar in his hands, the Sufi sang in praise of God in the suburbs of Agra in Akbarabad. It was his belief that God was one and could be realized only through devotion and meditation Nazir was a devotee of Lord Krishna. He says:

Lucky he is. His wail is heard. He comes,
Who can doubt his realization, the very picture of
Shri Krishna, floats before his eyes as he sings.[65]

Another mystic, Sabjani used to venerate both the Mosques and the temples of idols. In the temple he used to perform in accordance to the customs of Hindus, the puja and the dandut but in the Mosque he prayed like a Muslim. He never gave preference to one creed over the other.[66]

Thus, Sufism, slowly but surely became a most popular creed, It was a unique blend of Islam, Vedanta and Humanism, which flourished on the Indian soil and acquired deep roots. It opposed the rigidity of both Islam and Hinduism and preached the philosophy of love and service to the mankind. The Sufis were not only respected but also revered like God by their followers. A large number of people became convert to Sufi creed. Not only the common man sought the blessings and guidance of the Sufi saints, the kings too turned to them for the fulfillment of their ambitions and aspirations. History, from the beginning of the Sultanate to the end of the Mughal rule, makes it amply clear that rulers allowed the sufis to preach their ideas which were not only not completely in accordance with the Quran but some of which violated its injections. Most of the rulers themselves were their disciples and took their counsel, revered their names, and built magnificent tombs in their memory and participated in their Urs as devotees. Hindu rulers too held these saints in high esteem. Shivaji, revered saint Baba Yakut of Kelsi.His grandfather had great faith in a saint Shah Sharif of Ahmad Nagar. In honour of the saint he gave his sons the name of Shahji and Sharifji.Mahadji Sindhia and his son Daulat Rao were followers of Mansur Shah Sindhia used to visit the tomb of the saint before launching their military expeditions.[67] Hindu rajas like Ajit Singh and Jagat Singh visited the Dargah of Saint Moinuddin Chisti and gave liberal grants for the maintenance of the Dargah.[68] When Hemu started his campaign against Akbar, he made it a point to pay a visit to the tomb of Hazrat Qutubuddin Bakhtiar Kaki.[69] Emperor Humayun too had deep respect for the Sufis. Once Humayun,s life was saved by a water-carrier. He rescued the drowning monarch in a river and brought him safely to the bank. The Emperor then asked his deliverer what his name was. He said it was Nizam. "To me" said the emperor, in the exuberance of his gratitude, "thou art as Nizam Aulia, and thou shalt be placed on my throne." Humayun kept his word and placed his rescuers on the throne for a day when he regained his kingdom.[70] Akbar visited the shrine of Mionuddin Chishti and resolved that if he was blessed with a son he would go on foot from Agra to his blessed Mausoleum, a distance of 140 kms. When Jodhabai became pregnant Akbar in order to ward off evil spirit, sent her to the monastery, built by Sheikh Salim and there Jahangir was born on August 30,1569. Akbar built on the spot a city of gardens and palaces, naming it Fatehpur and made it the residence of the Court. Akbar named his son Salim, out of reverence for the saint. He used to call him Sheikhu Baba. In accordance with his resolve, he also went to Ajmer from Agra barefooted, each day walking a distance of 10 to12 kos. Jahangir and Shahjahan went to the shrine of the saint barefooted to offer prayers after becoming emperors. On Jahangir's order, a book on the history of Sufism was also written. Prince Dara himself wrote biographies of hundred and seven saints in his work Sakawat-al-Auliya.[71] Even Aurangzeb made it a point to meet the visiting Sufis and to go the Mazars of well-known saints. In 1686-1687, before proceeding to Golkunda, Aurangzeb went to Gulbarga and stayed for a week at the Mausoleum of the Chishti saint Gesu Daraz.[72] Nizam-ul-Mulk was a disciple of a Sufi saint called Hazarat Nizamuddin Aurangabadi. The Nizam wanted to keep his control in Deccan. He visited the saint who offered Nizam a plate of Kulchas. The Nizam ate seven. When he was going to depart Hazarat Nizamuddin prophesied "As you have eaten seven Kulchas, so your dynasty will rule for seven generations." In 1724 Nizam declared himself the Governor of the six Deccan provinces. For his flag, Nizam-ul-Mulk chose a Kulcha set on a yellow background. This remained the flag of all his successors.[73]

The reason of increasing popularity of the Sufis was not only their liberal ideas and outlook but also their humanist attitude. Many of them, who distanced themselves from the rulers, led a life of poverty but always served the downtrodden. They stood on the side of the people and had the courage to criticize and persuade the rulers to act fairly and justly with their subjects. Sheikh Sadruddin interceded with Timur on behalf of the Hindu ruler of Bhatner.[74] A Sufi Saint remonstrated Sikandar Lodi, against his prohibition of pilgrimages. "Wretch", cried he, drawing his sword, "do you defend idolatry!" "No", replied he, "but I maintain that kings ought not to prosecute their subjects" Sikandar was appeased.[75] Once Sikandar Lodi, stationed at Delhi as the deputy of his father, thought of looting the Hindu temples at Kurukshetra. Before taking action, he however consulted Mian Abdullah Ajudhani who advised against it. This enraged the prince so much that he charged the saint with supporting idolaters and threatened to begin by killing him. The saint said that he was prepared for it. This silenced Sikandar and he bowed to his Fatwa.[76] Mulla Abul Hakim gave ruling against the conversion of a Jain temple into a Mosque by Prince Aurangzeb.[77] The well-known saint Sheikh Kalimullah objected to Aurangzeb being called as Zinda Pir. He held orthodox Mullas to ridicule and accused Aurangzeb of hypocrisy.[78] Shah Abdul Rahim, Abdul Latif and Sheikh Burhan opposed Aurangzeb's fanaticism. Sarmad too condemned

Aurangzeb's orthodoxy and lust for power, which cost him his life. Rishi Bhakta, Pir of Kashmir admonished Aurangzeb (when he was in Kashmir in 1663) for killing Sarmad. It so happened that Aurangzeb after killing the saint could not eat. Whenever he was eating his meals, blood came before his eyes. He requested the Pir to explain why this was so. Rishi Pir told him that it was the blood of innocent Sarmad whom he had put to death. He asked Aurangzeb to remember the contents of the two following Persian couplets:

Lay not the hand in disapproval on anything you see, be it good, be it bad;

To call the handiwork faulty is to find fault with the craftsman.

Though there are different religions, none is forbidden:

The gardener has flowers of different colours in the flower -bed"

Rishi Pir then invoked the spirit of Sarmad and beseeched him to excuse Aurangzeb. Thereafter the emperor no longer saw blood in his food. Rishi Pir also advised him that he should earn his own daily bread by some honest manual labour and not to take anything for his own food from the public treasury. Thenceforth the emperor began to work during his leisure hours as a scribe of the Quran and whatever money he received for the copies he lived thereon.[79]

The Sufis at times advised the rulers to ameliorate the conditions of the poor. Once Aurangzeb visited Abdul Latif, a Sufi saint of Burhanpur and offered him income of a few villages for the expenses of the monastery, the latter refused and said "I am placed under obligation when the king grants me villages; but Iam not under obligation when God gives me food." He asked Aurangzeb "Receive only half of the revenue which you obtain from your subjects and take less than even half from the hard -working and helpless peasants.... Administer justice to the oppressed in such a way that no one will be deprived of his right. Don't allow the weak to be oppressed by the tyrants"[80] The Sufis helped all, whosoever approached them in time of need. Once Raja Govind Dev Maratha, defeated by Muhammad Gangu Bahmani, son of Allauddin Hasan Gangu Bahmani, fled to the abode of Shah Imamuddin. The Saint advised him not to shut himself in the fort, but to repair himself along with his wife and children to Gujarat. The Raja accepted his advice and stayed with him under his protection till his wife and children joined him, whereupon the saint laid his hand on the head of each member of the family and prayed for their safe journey and their future happiness. When the king Muhammad Gangu came to know about this, he became angry with the saint; but the saint did not care for his anger and said that his doors were open for everyone.[81]

The catholicity and humanistic attitude of the Sufis thus worked in a big way in bringing the two communities closer to each other. They were the harbinger of a new era wherein both Hindu and Muslim joined together in chanting prayers in praise of one Almighty who was both Allah and Ram. Not only illiterate and ignorant were influenced but the learned, like Brahmins, too did not remain unaffected. Many of them took to ways and practices of the Sufis. They used to read and revere the Quran. Instead of being clean shaved, the Brahmins started growing beard, walking with a big stick, reading Persian and reciting Masnawi.

Khanqahs of Sufis were the centres not only for congregations but also a place of promoting integration. Disciples and devotees of Sufis, irrespective of race, religion, region and caste, travelled together sat and ate together in the free kitchens of Sufis. This interaction developed brotherly feelings. They not only discussed but started sharing their happiness and sorrow and visiting each other's houses, participating in the family functions as well. Disharmony and distrust disappeared, amity, goodwill, mutual-respect and mutual understanding ushered in, which made India, a land of peace and harmony.

Bhakti Movement

Interaction between Hinduism and Islam led to a powerful spiritual movement all over the country. It gave rise to a liberal religious movement in the form of Bhakti, which made a rapid progress and swept the entire country 14th century onwards. The movement drew both the Hindu and Muslim in its fold and sought to reconstruct the Indian society by synthesizing Hinduism and Islam to ensure the communal goodwill and to create an environment of tolerance and co-operation.

Bhakti like Sufism, was the religion of love and devotion .It was brought about by Hindu saints who had great respect for Islam and were impressed by its simplicity and insistence on oneness of God. Besides its ideals of human equality and universal brotherhood influenced them greatly. Their close interaction with the Sufis and their own study of Hindu scriptures convinced them that God is one and all divisions are artificial. They attempted to reform and reconstruct the Hindu society in the light of new principles. Bhakti movement had, thus both social and religious dimensions The saints sought to bring the two communities spiritually closer by incorporating all that was good in both the religions and discarding all that obstructed or stood in the way of the well being of the people. They boldly criticised the ritualism, sectarianism and hypocrisy of their age and preached universal love. They explained in popular language and by means of homely simile, the great spiritual truths, which they realized and the vision of God they had experienced.

The spirit of Bhakti was not confined to any particular region but was at work all over the country. There was Ramanuja in South, Ramananda in U.P., Chaitanya in Bengal, Kabir and Nanak in the North, Mirabai and Dadu in Rajasthan, Tukaram and Namdeva in Maharashtra, Vallabhswami in Telangana, Lalleshwari in Kashmir and Eknath in Deccan. The main point of the teachings of Bhaktas was that God called Ram by the Hindus and

Rahim by the Muslims was one and the only way to approach Him was through meditation, devotion, singing of hymns and doing good deeds.

Like Sufis, the Bhakta's preaching attracted devotees from all the communities. Besides numerous Hindus, the Bhaktas had a large number of Muslim disciples and some of the Bhaktas were also Muslims.This intermingling of the two communities, ushered a new epoch on the spiritual plane.

Namdev

The bhakti movement gained strength in Maharashtra in the 13th century. Namdev was the first Marathi exponent of the Bhakti cult. It is said that in his youth Namdev was a robber and once killed 84 soldiers. He was suddenly converted to spiritual life, when he heard the piteous cries and curses of the helpless wife of a victim.[82]

Namdev declared that both Hindus and Muslims were blind in insisting upon worshipping in temples and mosques while he for his worship needed neither temple nor mosque. He said:

Hindu andha Turku kana1 duhante gyani syana 11
Hindu puje dehura 1 Mussalman masit
Namo soi sevya I jahan dehura na masit 11
(The Hindu is blind: the Turk is half-blind,
But one who knows is wiser than either,
The Hindu worship in temple and

The Muslim in mosque; Nama worships the same God (but)
Neither in temple nor mosque)[83]

Namdev openly preached to Brahman:

"A stone deity and his mock devotee can never save each other such Gods have been destroyed by the Turks in hundreds and thrown in to rivers. Still they lacked even the capacity to cry" [84]

Masse irrespective of caste or creed flocked to his place and listened to his preaching. Among his disciples were a few Muslims converted to Hinduism.[85]

Tukaram

Another Bhakt of Maharashtra who emphasized the oneness of God and rapprochement between the Hindus and the Muslims was saint Tukaram (1408-1469). He was a contemporary of Shivaji and wielded a great influence on him and the people of Maharashtra.

Tukaram's teachings are in the form of Abhangs, which were sung and are still sung with devotion. He attempted to reconcile between Hindu-Muslim Faiths as is indicated in the following Abhang:

'First among the great names is Allah, never forget to respect it,
Allah is verily one; the Prophet is verily one
These thou art one, there Thou art one,
O! friend.
There is neither I nor thou"[86]

Again:

O friend! Meditate on Allah who is in the guise of of all, says Tuka;
The man who understands this becomes a Darwish"[87]

Chaitanya

In Bengal the bhakti school was represented by Shri Chaitanya (1485-1533). He came in touch with many Sufi-saints and was deeply impressed by their thought. He too carried forward the spirit of devotion to God and service to mankind. He proclaimed the universal brotherhood and asked both the Brahmins and the Maulvis to give up their petty pride and to lead the people on the true path for the realization of the One Supreme Being. His was a movement against all externalism whether Hindu or Muslim He said:

"You wander aimlessly;
Mandir Mandir, Masjid Masjid;
Oh my teacher,

What a headache it is
The foolish, while weeping look at me.[88]

Chaitanya, a great devotee of Krishna, created a great awakening in Bengal. Devotees both Hindus and Muslims thronged to his place and joined him in chanting hymns in praise of Shri Krishna. Under his influence, many Muslims accepted Vaishnava Faith and became Hindus.These Muslims were not only common people but were also from wealthy and learned classes. On his way from Birindaban to Kashi alone Chaitanya converted ten Pathan Vairagis.[89] In Bengal, the two wealthy Muslims Sakar Malik and Dabir Khan who were in the service of a Muslim king Husain Shah of Gaud left their position and Faith and joined Chaitanya assuming the names of Sanatana and Rupa. Chaitanya sent both of them to Birindaban, the place associated with Krishna and asked them to write books about Vaishnavism. It was mainly due to the efforts of these two disciples and their followers that Birindaban soon grew up to be the centre of most the magnificent temples of India.[90]

Yasaraj Khan a state official of Husain Shah too became a devotee of Krishna and Sang Krishnamangla. Mahatma Haridas, son of Malai Kazi was a Muslim Vaishnava saint. He asked the orthodox mulla:

"I know not how your God is; the mulla cries out loudly for Him inside the Mosque: Is your Lord deaf"[91] Haridas belonged to Chaitanya's inner circle and preached his cult in the city and suburbs. The intermingling of Sufis and Chaitanya's philosophies gave rise to Baul songs, which were sung and are still sung with devotion by both Hindus and Muslims.

Eknath

In the Deccan saint Eknath was the pioneer of the Bhakti movement. He was an officer in the fort of Daulatabad under the Sultan. Though he was a Brahmin yet he ignored all caste restrictions and served the "poorest, the lowliest and the lost" with equal love and humility. His liberal ideas and outlook made him a reverential figure and won him disciples from different creeds, classes and communities. Thursday being regarded sacred by him, his Muslim masters declared that a holiday.[92]

Ramananda

Ramananda (1299-1410) and his disciple Kabir (led the cult of Bhakti in northern India. Ramananda wandered all over the country for the realization of God. It is related that he came into contact at

Benaras with learned Muslim scholars and Sufis and was thus able to formulate his theology.[93] It was based on bhakti or faith in God. He renounced the rigidity of Hindu rituals and allowed Hindus of lower castes to join him in worshipping the Supreme Being. He partook food with everyone including Muslims and admitted even women in his order.[94] His disciples took the name of Avdhuts, the detached and regarded themselves free from all sorts of social customs. Ramananda imparted devotional knowledge to everyone irrespective of his or her caste or creed. Consequently the movement of Bhakti spread rapidly. "Stray references to Muslims becoming Hindus are no doubt met in early periods but under the influence of this movement, this trend seems to have gained momentum" writes Radhakamal Mukerjee in "The Culture and Arts of India" According to Bhavisya Purana, many Muslims became Vaishnavas, "with the tulsi rosary on their necks, the name of Rama on their tongues and Vaishnava insignia on their foreheads."[95]

Ramananda envisaged Ramrajya, the kingdom of God on earth, based on equality of man so far totally unknown to Hinduism. It caught the imagination of common masses who in large number became his followers. Among them was a Muslim weaver Kabir, who it is said was a Hindu by birth.

Kabir

Bhakt Kabir has been described by W.W. Hunter as the Indian Luther of the 15th century. Although brought up in a Muslim family, Kabir acquired the knowledge of Hindu sacred scriptures. Ramananda was his Guru. Kabir says "I was revealed in Kasi and was awakened by Ramananda."[96] Kabir also remained in spiritual communion with a Muslim Sufi Sheikh Taqi of Allahabad In one of his verses, Kabir refers to Sheikh Taqi in these words; "My Haj is on the bank of the Gomati where dwells my Pir wearing a yellow robe"[97]

It is said that Kabir besought Sheikh to bestow upon him such blessings that he might be enabled to remove those differences of belief that separated Hindus from Muslims. Sheikh Taqi regretted that this was beyond his power but said that he would bring it about that both Hindus and Muslims should regard Kabir with reverence.[98] Kabir merged his Vaishnava concept of Bhakti with Sufi devotion to Allah he admired all that was good in both the religions and condemned all that was dogmatic. A weaver by profession, Kabir wove his cloth and while he did so, he sang his ideas in verses as:

"If God is within the Mosque, then to whom does this world outside belong?

If Ram be within the image which you find in your Pilgrimage
Then who is there to know what happens without?
Hari is in the East, Allah is in the West: look within
Your heart to find both Rahim and Ram!
All men and women in the world are His living forms
Kabir is the child of Allah Ram; He is my Guru
He is my Pir.[99]

Kabir realized that there is one God with different names. He asked the people not to fight in the name of God. Instead all should join together in worshipping the Almighty. He formed the two words Allah and Ram into a compound.

He is one; there is no second,
Ram, Khuda, Shakti, Siva are one,
By the one name I hold fast
Kabir proclaims this aloud.[100]

He stated that both Hindus and Muslims were children of the same God and "in all vessels, whether Hindu or Mussalman, there is one soul Allah Ram; my illusion has disappeared, there is no difference between Hindu and Mussalman". He also said, "The Hindus and Turks have one path which the true teacher has pointed out"[101]

He criticized both Brahmin and Sheikh for preaching hatred in the name of religion. He asked the people not to pay any heed to their preaching and not to fight, as Kaba was as sacred as Kashi. Kabir asked both Hindu and Mussalman to have reverence for all living creatures and to abstain from bloodshed. He used to say:

"Brother! From where have the two masters of the universe come? Tell me who has invented the name of Allah Ram Kesav, Hari and Hazrat? It is to show to the world that two different signs are made; One is called Nimaz while the other is termed puja. Mahadev and Muhammad are one and the same. What is Hindu? What is Turk? Both inhabit the same earth. One reads the Veda and the other Quran and the khutba. One is Maulana and the other Pandit. Earthen vessels have different names, although they are made from the same earth. Kabir says both are misled, none have found God"[102]

By means of ramanis, sabads and sakhis Kabir imparted religious instructions to his disciples.

To Muslims he said:

Adam, who was first, did not know
Whence came mother Eve?
Then there was no Turk nor Hindus;
No blood of the mother, no seed of the father
Then there were no cows, no butchers;
Who pray cried ' In the name of God'?
Then there was no race, no caste;
Who made Hell and Paradise.[103]

Kabir's preaching immensely popularized the Bhakti movement. However, his ideas annoyed both the Pandits and the Qazis as Kabir boldly pointed out:

"They fast all day, at night they slaughter the cow
Here murder their devotion; how can this please God?"[104]

If Kabir cricised the Muslims for performing sunnat (circumcision), and practice of Namaz (prayers) and Roza (fast) he equally condemned the Hindus idolatry, caste and customs. No wonder that both the Hindu and Muslim orthodox joined together against Kabir and made complaint against him to Sultan Sikandar Lodi on the ground of heresy. Kabir explained to Lodi "Those only are Pirs who recognise the pains of others, those who cannot are kafirs"[105] Kabir expressed his happiness at both Brahmins and Qazis uniting together against him. He said:

'Today indeed my mission is fulfilled. I have caused the Hindus and the Muslims to come together in the court of the king. If they could do so in the Court of an earthly King, and out of hatred, how glorious would be the day when they would join together in the heavenly Court of the King of Kings and from love instead of hatred"[106]

The Sultan, it is said, was immensely pleased. He did not find any thing blasphemous in the teachings of Kabir and dismissed the plaint.

The masses, however, held him in high esteem and followed his instructions. He was called Pir Kabir by the Muslims and Bhagat Kabir by the Hindus. His numerous disciples were called as Kabirpanthis. (In the Census Report of 1901 the number of Kabirpanthis excluding the figures of both United Provinces and Punjab was 843,171) Kabir died at Maghar. His disciples urged him to die at Kasi as it was believed that those who died in Kasi would immediately enter into the presence of Ram while those who died at Maghar would return to this world and assume the form of ass. Kabir rebuked them and said, "Is the power of Ram so limited that he cannot save his servant because he prefers to die outside Kasi, the city of Shiva?"[107]

It is said that when Kabir died both the Hindus and Muslims claimed his body; the Hindus wanted to cremate it with Hindu rites and the Muslims were desirous of burying the Pir according to the Muslim coustom. But when they actually rushed to take charge of the earthly remains of the saint, both discovered only a heap of flowers under the shroud. (There are two shrines of Kabir in Banaras one is in the custody of Hindus and the other in the hands of Muslims. One Bijli khan got erected the tomb of Kabir at Maghar in 1450).

Baba Nanak sounded the echo of unity in the northwest. He regarded Kabir his spiritual guru and carried forward Kabir's message i.e., spirit of bhakti and turned it into a whirlwind.

Baba Nanak

Baba Nanak was deeply inspired and influenced by Kabir and like him sought the unification of the Hindus and Muslims by wiping out communal consciousness from their minds. He preached love, harmony, devotion, oneness of God and in the process gave rise to a new religion Khalsa Panth i.e. Sikhism. Kabir's teachings were incorporated in to the new religion as has been said "Kabir panth ab bhayo Khalsa"

Baba Nanak was born at Talwandi, a village in Lahore in 1469 AD. A Muslim lady called Daulton was his midwife. The family priest gave him the name Nanak common to both Hindus and Muslims. He learned and Sanskrit from a pundit and Persian from mullah Qutubuddin.[108]

It is said that Nanak studied the scriptures of both Islam and Hinduism. He was a pupil of one Seid Hussain and he passed his early life in the company of this Muslim devotee from whom he imbibed the general essentials of Islam.[109]

The religion of Islam and its philosophy greatly coloured Nanak's thinking. Doçtor Tarachand writes;

"How deep Guru Nanak's debt is to Islam, it is hardly necessary to state, for it is so evident in his words and thoughts. Manifestly he was steeped in Sufi lore and the fact of the matter is, that it is much harder to find how much exactly he drew from the Hindu scriptures."[110]

(As time passed Sikhism became a full-fledged religion almost on the pattern of Islam. It has a prophet Guru Nanak, a book-Guru Granth Saheb and a church Gurudwara for the sangat that is devotees. Amritsar became the Mecca of the Sikhs.)

Guru Nanak revered Prophet Mohammed and made it a practice in his leisure hours to translate literally and make notes and extracts of the moral maxims of Islam.[111] Like Kabir Nanak too frequented the company of Muslim Sufi saints. Prominent amongst them were shah, Bu Ali Qalandar of Panipat, Pir Makhdum Bahauddin Zakaria of Multan, Sheikh Sharaf. Sheikh Ibrahim and Miyan Mitha.[112]

Nanak carried the beads or the tasbih of the Muslims in his hands and wore the sacred thread zunnar round his neck. He also went to Mecca and performed the Haj. He wore blue dress, the Quran under his arm, a small jug for ablutions and carried a prayer-mat with him.[113]

His janam sakhis (biographies) declared that the first words Guru Nanak uttered after his revelations were "there is no Hindu, there is no Mussalman." All have a common father and same blood is running in their veins. Nanak taught that "religion does not consist in mere words; he who looks on all men as equals is truly religious...those who love the Lord loves everybody"[114] Nanak's teachings made tremendous impact on both Hindus and Muslims and a large number of them became his disciples. The two disciples who always accompanied him were Balla, a Hindu and Maradana, a Muslim musician.

Nanak had intimate relations with Sheikh Farid II. He travelled with the Sheikh for ten years and the two taught the people the spiritual way.[115] Both made efforts to evolve a meeting ground between Hindus and Muslims. It was on account of their mutual efforts that the festival of Basant Panchami came to be celebrated jointly by the Hindus and Muslims.[116] His instructions for the Muslims were:

"Make kindness thy mosque, sincerity thy prayer carpet
What is just and lawful thy Quran
Modesty thy circumcision, civility thy fasting
So shall thou be a Mussalman
Make right conduct thy Qaba, truth thv spiritual guide
Good work thy creed and thy prayer,
The will of God thy rosary and God will preserve thine honor O Nanak"[117]

Because of his non-sectarian views Baba Nanak became extremely popular and his influence spread rapidly in the entire region. His bhakti drew nearer both the Hindus and Muslims.[118]

They accepted his faith and became his disciples. Like Kabir, he was also called Guru of Hindus and Pir of Muslims. Baba Nanak Shah fakir "Hindu ka Guru Mussalman ka Pir" He was also called reverentially Hazrat Baba Nanak.[119]

Nanak preached a message of tolerance and trust amongst the different communities. He asked the rulers to be kind and just and not to oppress the masses but to serve them. He asked Sikander Lodi to shed fanaticism and to serve the people who are the creation of God.[120] It is also said that he went to Turkey and interviewed the Sultan of Turkey. He admonished him for oppressing the innocent. This had great effect on the Sultan and he discontinued tyranny and became a changed person.[121]

Both kings and commoners revered him. Not without reason did both the Hindus and Muslims claim his body. The Hindus wanted to cremate him whereas the Muslims wanted their Wali to be buried. Both covered Guru Nanak's body with flowers and as the old chronicle says "the flowers of both remained green".

Dadu

Like Nanak, Dadu (1544-1603) too was deeply influenced by Kabir and regarded him his Guru. He was a disciple of a Sufi saint Sheikh Budhan. Though born in a Brahmin family Dadu worshiped no God or Goddess nor did he take to fasting or pilgrimages. He believed in one God who was the father of all the people Hindus or Muslims. He rejected the authority of scriptures holy to the Hindu or Muslim, denounced all rituals and founded a Brahma society, which admitted devotees irrespective of any discrimination.. The place where all the devotees gathered after the day's work for adoration of the Supreme Being was called Alakh-Dariba (the place of All Mighty). Not only the common people but the learned people like Qazi Kadam, Sheikh Farid ji, Qazi Mohammad, Sheikh Bahawad and Rajjab also attended the religious gatherings and chanted hymns in praise of one God.[122]

Dadu says about his God:

"no Hindu I am, nor yet a Mussalman
I follow none of the six systems; I worship the Merciful
Dadu belongs to neither faction; he is the devotee of Allah Ram
He who is without form or limitation the same is my Guru".[123]

Dadu pointed out the futility of hatred and emphasised on goodwill towards every creature. He preached;

"Worship the divine spirit and bear hatred towards none,
In worship thou wilt find peace, in hatred sorrow,
In every man is One Spirit, whether he be Hindu or Mussalman,
Both brethren have alike hands and feet, both have ears,
Both brethren have eyes, be thy Hindus or Musalmans,
When thou lookest in the mirror of doubt, there appears to be two;
When error is dispelled and doubt resolved there is no other.
To whom then wilt thou bear enmity, when there is no other?
Why give pain to any when the indwelling Rama is in every man." [124]

Dadu made clear to his devotees that there was only one God though his names were many:

"The one invisible Ilahi art thou,
Thou art Rama and Rahim
Thou art beautiful master (malik)
The names are Keshav and Kareem
What is the panth (sect) of Brahma, Vishnu and Mahesh, which is the din (faith of Mohammed)
And what is the way of Gabriel, the one Allah is there Pir and Murshid (perceptor and director).[125]

Dadu's advocacy of oneness of all and his relentless efforts in uprooting all noxious practices earned him the wrath of the orthodoxy of the day. They argued with him that salvation of man was not possible by following the universal path of his, which was devoid of all distinctions. To them Dadu replied:

"Great nature itself and all great men are on my side. What cult do they pursue earth and sky,
Water and wind, day and night, sun and moon?
What creed was followed by Mohammed, tell me or by Gabriel
To what sect did they belong? Who but Allah was their Guru and Saint?
The invisible God alone is the world teacher, there is none else.[126]

Both Hindu and Muslim orthodox then complained to Raja Man Singh against Dadu's teaching but the former didn't find any fault.[127]

Dadu's sayings (bani) resounded in Rajasthan and a large number of people accepted his faith. Dadu not only admitted Muslims to his order but many gurus of his sect were Muslims. One of them was Rajjab who revered his master Dadu and carried the message of bhakti in different corners of the country. Rajjab says:

"This universe is the Veda, the creation is the Quran, the pundits and the qazis are indeed deceived when they think that the whole world is encompassed within the leaves of their dry books. The heart of the worshipper is the page on which the story of the universal

truth is being written in letters of life. When all these hearts unite in the vast universe of man there you will find all Vedas and Quran. This is the living Veda, the living Quran; study that, why do you waste your time over the dead books.[128]

Dadu's bhakti was a religion of love and service to mankind. His followers called Dadu panthis did not believe in scriptures but prayed to the Supreme Being who was formless and Almighty. Theologically, they are alike the Kabir panthis but they follow the practice of exposing their dead like the Persians. The dead are neither buried nor cremated but are cast out in the jungle. Dadu panthi says that it is good that the wild animals should eat upon the dead and satisfy their hunger. Dadu himself had directed his disciples to leave his body in jungle. After his death in 1660, his body was taken to a hill in a palanquin. They placed the bier on the high crest and covered his body with a white sheet and returned. It is said that when the devotees were watching, the palanquin disappeared.[129]

Lallayogeshari

Lallayogeshari, popularly known as Lal Ded by the people of Kashmir, preached Bhakti in the 14th century. (Her real name was Padmavati. It is interesting to know the origin of the appellation of Lal Ded. She was a yogini and owing to yogic exercises, it is said her abdomen had projected and enlarged so much that it answered the purpose of loin cloth. At this stage she tore away her garments and moved about nakedly. Hence Lal Ded).[130]

She was greatly influenced by Sufi philosophy. Tradition relates that she was not only contemporary but also a friend of the Sufi saint Sayyid Ali Hamdani, popularly known as Shah Hamdam.[131] Lalla like other Bhakts, believed in One God and universal brotherhood. She illustrated the fundamental unity by the analogy of ice, snow and water, which though seemingly different are yet the same in essence. All religions, she believed, were one in essence and that the difference of caste, creed, birth and position were superficial. She debunks idol-worship, animal sacrifice, and pilgrimage to holy places.

She asked both Hindus and Muslims to shed fanaticism and live like brothers. She imparted her ideas to the general masses in

Kashmiri language. She preached;

"Shiv Chuy thali thali roza,
Me zan Hindu ta Mussalman
Turk ay chuk pan panun parzanav
Say chay Sahibas sato zaniy za

(Shiva pervades the whole universe; do not differentiate between Hindu and Muslim. If you are intelligent, recognise thyself.)[132]

Lalla went about dancing in spiritual ecstasy pouring out her poetry. She had a large number of disciples and was equally revered by both Hindus and Muslims. She was called Aarifa Bibi with affection by the Muslim Her sayings constitute nearly half of the numerous proverbs and wise sayings, current in Kashmiri language.

Bhakti movement was thus a progressive socio-religious movement. It attacked religious rigidities, social inequalities and feelings of exclusiveness. Sectarianism, intolerance, ill will, enmity or conflict had no place in it. It was truly national as it encompassed not only Hindus belonging to different castes but also had a large number of Muslims. They all joined together, forgetting differences of all kind in the prayers of One Supreme Being.who was both Ram and Rahim. Muslims like their Hindu brethren invoked.

Almighty's name as Thakur (Lord) Dhani (rich) and Kartar (master) etc. Many Muslims became the devotees of Rama and Krishna and some also became convert to the new creed. Though their number was not very large yet it reflected the harmonious co-existence and the readiness of the masses to follow, revere and worship one God.

Syncretic Cults

Centuries of contacts between the two communities gradually led to the emergence and evolution of many popular cults. They were the mixtures of both Hinduism and Islam. Love, harmony and peace were the cardinal principles of these cults.

Islam and Hinduism were two different religions. However, the quest of knowing the unknown Supreme Being led the saints of the two communities to study the scriptures of the two religions. This, in turn made them critically examine their own religion in the light of their newly acquired knowledge, and in this process they evolved new cults which provided them spiritual satisfaction and revealed a new path for the realization of God. They formulated their own philosophies, beliefs and practices and kept doors of their sects open for all irrespective of caste, creed, race and religion. Numerous sects founded by Hindu as well as Muslim saints came in to existence and flourished during the entire Muslim rule and worked in a big way in integrating the people of India on both spiritual and social plane.

Kartabhajas

It was founded by Samarnpal, known as Karta Baba. The sect first arose in the district of Nadia but spread rapidly in other districts of Bengal. The sect believed in One God, and emphasized Hindu Muslim unity. It believed in equality and was against any kind of discrimination. All its members used to eat together and regarded Friday as sacred and spent it in religious meditations. No outward adherence to the sect was required. A Hindu could retain his sacred thread and a Muslim was not required to shave on becoming a member of this sect. The Kartabhajas paid equal respect to and sang the names of Kali, Krishna and Allah.[133]

The sect had not only a large number of Muslim members, it also placed them as the head of Preaching Centres and the devout Hindu followers took the left-overs of their food[134]

Lingayats

The Lingayat sect emerged in the south in the 12th century. Its founders are believed to be three, named Basav, Channa Vasav, and Ekant Rammaya. It is a Shaiva sect. They believed in One God whom they call Par Shiva who manifests himself as the world teacher Allama Prabhu. Basava the originator of this movement is supposed to be an incarnation of Allama Prabhu. As the Muslims have their Char Pirs (the four masters), so the Lingayats, too have Char Aradhyas (the four to be adored). The Lingayat's ceremony of initiation is exactly like that of Sufis.

The Lingayats believed in Vedas but not in idol-worship and the hegemony of the Brahmins:

"O Brahman listen to me!
In all this blessed land
There is but one great caste,
One tribe and one brotherhood.
One God doth dwell above
And He hath made us one
In birth and frame and tongue"[135]

An untouchable can be admitted into their fold just like a

Brahmin. There are no sacrifices, fasts or pilgrimages for a Lingayat. Marriage is voluntary and the consent of the bride is necessary. Child marriage is forbidden., divorce and widow-remarriage is permitted. The dead are buried and not cremated. There are no after-death ceremonies

like Hindus. They believed that adherence to their Faith will save them from the cycle of rebirth. They are strictly vegetarian and believe in non-violence. They hold that God and Love are one and the same and desired mankind to live in peace, considering love as God [136]

The Husaini Brahmin

Khwaja Moin-ud-din Chishti formed the Husaini Brahmin Sect. The Husaini Brahmins are Hindus. They believed in Atharv-Veda and narrate the story of Hazarat Imam Husain. They observe fast during the Hindu Shivratri and Muslim Ramzan. They give feasts for the Muslim Id and the Hindu Ramnavmi.The men mark their forehead with Tilak but wear the Muslim dress and the women put on the Hindu vermilion dot on their forehead.

They have adopted many Muslim practices and beliefs and are special devotees of the shrine of Khwaja Moinuddin Chisti.[137]

Vairagies

Vairagi sect admits both the Hindus and Muslims but regard their path as different from Vedas and Quran. They denounce the world and worship Vishnu, Rama and Krishna. They always put round their neck rosaries of Tulsi. They hold that Bismillah means

Vishnu. Not only a good majority of common Muslims but also some wealthy people like Mirza Saleh and Mirza Haider joined this sect and became Vairagis.[138]

Vaishnavas

This sect was very popular among the Muslims. They hurt no living being and avoided fellowship with men of other creeds whether Hindu or Muslims They prayed five times a day with their face towards east and repeated the names of God, all the angels and the Prophets. They do not cremate but bury their dead.[139]

Yogi Sect

This sect too includes both Hindus and Muslims.The Muslim devotees like their Hindu brothers wear the ocher robe of Hindu ascetics and their presence is indispensable in many Hindu ceremonies. The Yogis, chiefly Muslims compose songs and lyrics in praise of God and they are known in the northwest region of India as Bhartharis.[140]

Babalalis

Baba Lal founded Babalalis sect in 1625 at Dehanpur, near Sirhind. He held similar views to those of Kabir and Dadu. He too emphasized harmony, tolerance and co-operation. He used to quote Hafiz in his preaching:

"The object of all religions is alike,
All men seek their beloved.
What is the difference between prudent and wild?
The entire world loves dwelling
Why talk of a Mosque or a Church"? [141]

The liberality and depth of his idea and simplicity of his life influenced Hindus and Muslims alike and many became his followers. Prince Dara Shikoh was also his disciple and had met him many a time and obtained instructions on religion.

Chhajjupanthi

Chhajjupanthi sect was founded by Chhajju Bhagat of Lahore, in times of Aurangzeb, reveals a curious combination of Hindu Muslim creeds. The people of Punjab held Chajju Bhagat in high esteem. Both Hindus and Muslims flocked to his place for spiritual guidance. It was said of him:

"Jo sukh Chajju de Chaubare,
Na Ballakh na Bukhare"[142]

(The spiritual satisfaction one gets at Bhagat Chajju's place, cannot be acquired even at Ballakh or Bukhara.)

Saint Paltoo too preached same message that:

"The Rama is in the East and Khuda in the West,
Who then lives in the north and south?
Where is the Lord and where is He not?
Why do the Hindu and the Muslim raise the storm?
The Hindus and Muslims have engaged in struggle,
And the two faiths run into opposing camps
Paltoo the slave says, the Lord is in all,
He is not divided at all"[143].

Khaki Sect

Another saint who gave the same message was Malukdas, the

follower of Dadu and the founder of the Khaki sect. He used to say that there is only One God, One Religion and Ram and Rahim are names of the same God.

'Malukdas why art thou in error
Rama and Rahim are names of one"

He condemned the externalia of religions:

"Where is string of beads (mala) and the rosary. (tasbih) Now awake and rely not on them.
Who is infidel (kafir) and who is barbarian (maleccha)
Look upon Sandhaya (Hindu worship) and the prayer (namaz) as one"[144]

Ramsanchi Sect

Ram Chandra was the founder of this order in the 18th century. His followers included both Hindus as well as Muslims.They do not believe in idol-worship and their religious practices are, to an extent, similar to those of Muslims.[145]

The Satnami Sect

Beerbhan, the founder of the Satnami sect was a contemporary of Dadu. Satnamis also call themselves "sadh". They believed in one God. The name given by Beerbhan to God was Satnam that is whose name is truth. They are against caste-system and untouchability. They inter-dine and inter-marry amongst themselves. They are against idol worship and lay stress on meditation, moral character and the equality of all human beings. In the Adi Updesh, the Bible of the Satnamis, are given 12 commandments which are the blending of the best in both Hinduism and Islam.[146]

Pranami Sect

Mihir Chand, better known as Prannath, popularized the cult of Bhakti in the beginning of the 18th century. He founded Pranami Sampradaya sect. Like his predecessors Bhaktas Prannath too, imparted the message of unity, peace, love amity and equality. He tried to reconcile between Hinduism and Islam and bring the followers of the two religions on a common platform.

Prannath had read both Veda and Quran. In his Qulzum Sarup, a work in Gujarati language, he brings together text from both the scriptures and tried to show that they were not incompatible.[147] He propounded his philosophical teachings on the solid foundation of the synthesis of all the religious scriptures. In the following verse, he stressed the unity between Hindus and Muslims by saying that there was only the difference of name and rituals, in fact Khuda and Brahma were the same :

"Nam saro juda dhare, layi sabon judi rasam
Sab me ummat aur duniya, soi Khuda soi Brahm"[148]

In another verse he says:

"Brahman kahe hum uttam, Mussalman kahe hum pak
Dau muthi ek tour ki, ek rah duji khaq" [149]

His disciples used to read jointly, Puran and Quran. According to him, all the religious scriptures revealed the existence of the same Lord. He said:

"Jo kateb so Veda batai / yea mein antar nahi bhai
Yek dhani sahib sab kairi / duji mani citta in fairi
Hindu Turk din dai gaye / tin mil kai dai panth calaye
Senca saneh jagat mei hai / ek arth mil kahat na koi
Ab mein Veda kateb milayun / tin ka arth ek tahraun
Meti virodh jagat jas laun / ek rah pargat kardaun[150]

(Whatever is in the Quran, so is in the Vedas. There is no difference between the two. One supreme God is the Lord of all. Do not be confused by believing them to be different. Hindus and Turks adhere to two religions and they founded two sects. There is a sort of tug of war in the world. No one emphasise on the unity. Thus I seek to remove antagonism and point to the common path).

He condemned both Mulla and Priest for causing divisions' . He said:

"Kahulabe Mohammad ka, Cale na Mohammad sath
Dar jundagi din mein, kahe hum sunnat jammat[151]

(They call themselves the followers of Mohammed but follow him not. They cause disunity in the faith and declare that majority listens to them).

Again he says:

"Jo dukh debe kinka, vo nahi Mussalman
Nabi en Mussalmin ka, nam dharya meharban"[152]

(He who prosecutes others is not Mussalman. The Prophet named Mussalman, the one who bestows kindness)

His mission in his own words was:

"Karna sara ek ras, Hindu Mussalman
Dhoka sab ka bhan ke, sabka kahungi Jnan"[153]

(I would unite all the Hindus and the Muslims. I understand their deceptions I would impart them right knowledge)

Among his numerous disciples was Raja Chhatrasal Bundela. Through his contacts with the saint, the Raja developed a great regard for Islam and Prophet Mohammad in whose praise he recited two couplets every morning after taking bath. According to Murtaza Husain, the Quran and the Puranas were placed on high chairs on opposite sides in the private chamber of the Raja's palace. On each side there sat Muslim Ulema and Hindu priests, who in the presence of the Raja discussed the subject of tauhid or the unity of God. He lived in Panna till the end of his life. On his death Pran Nath was buried and not cremated.[154]

Fearlessly, he preached his philosophy and denounced the orthodoxy of Aurangzeb. When the emperor imposed Jaziya upon Hindus in 1679, Prannath went to Delhi with his Hindu and Muslim disciples and recited his verses echoing the oneness of all the human beings in and around the Jama Masjid. One day, he even intercepted Aurangzeb going on horse-back to Jama Masjid for Namaz and asked him to withdraw the tax but the latter paid no heed with the result he alienated the Hindus and the support of the liberal elements to his rule.[155]

Shivanarayan Cult

Swami Narayan Singh a Rajput of Gazipur district formed this sect in 1734. It had both Hindu and Muslim members and its philosophy contains elements from both Hindu and Muslim traditions. Swami Narayan Singh was inspired by the ideas of Dara Shikoh. The union of all forms of faiths in one universal religion was his dream. Emperor Muhammad Shah was so much influenced by the piety, selfless devotion and the eclectic views of the Swami that he became his disciple after the invasion of Nadir Shah.[156] It is also borne by the following couplets:

"He taught the word to Muhammad Shah
And obtaining this seal propagated the sect"[157]

The seal is still kept in the headquarter of the sect. The sect founded in 1734 in Delhi, was opposed to image worship, use of animal food and intoxicants, and exhorted to follow the path of devotion and self-restraint.[158]

Like the Hindu saints, some Muslim saints too founded their separate sects, some of them still exist in India, Pakistan and Bangladesh.

Khoja Cult

Khoja cult is highly coloured by Hinduism. The founder of this sect was Nuruddin, a Muslim saint generally known by the Hindu name he adopted, Nur Sadguru. He had arrived in India from Persia in the 12th century. He was influenced by Hindu religion and consequently incorporated certain Hindu practices in to his mystic teachings.

Nuruddin in Gujarat had a disciple named Sadruddin who became the head of this sect after his death. He, in accordance with the principle of accommodation, practiced by this sect took a Hindu name and wrote a book entitled Dasavtar, in which Ali was made out to be the incarnation of Vishnu, Brahma to be Mohammed and Adam Shiva.[159] This book has been from the beginning the accepted scripture of the Khoja sect and it is always read by the bed-side of the dying and periodically at many festivals. The Khoja Personal Law also derives largely from Hindu Law. Every Khoja pays one -tenth of his income as a dassondh offering to Aga Khan. Salvation for him lies in recognizing the Imam gaiety, which he has to pass through a cycle of eighty-four births. [160]

A large number of Hindu and Muslim became the follower of this sect. In course of time it spread in other parts of the country and gave rise to many sub-sects

The Shamsis

It is a sub-sect of Khojas and is said to take its name from the great saint of Multan, Pir Shamsuddin Tabrizi. Legend has it that a group of Punjabi Khatris from Behra was going to Hardwar for a dip in the Ganga. On the way they met Sufi Shams-ud-din. When the Sufi came to know that they were pilgrims, he told the Khatris that there was no need to go to Hardwar as he could bring the Ganga there and then. When the Sufi literally made the water of the Ganga flow before them in an instant, the awe-struck Hindus converted to Sufi's faith.[161]

The followers of this sect are called as Shamsis and they regard Aga Khan.as an incarnation of Hindu trinity. They associate Prophet Mohammad with Brahma and revered Bhagwad Gita. They call the corpus of their religious books Atharv-veda and use Hindu caste names like Khanna, Channa, Sapra Baluja, Saluja, Sehgal, Mehndiratta, Bahri, Sachdeva etc.[162] They also observe many Hindu customs like Uthala for departed family members. They have their separate burial ground. The size of this community is dwindling but still they are found both in India and Pakistan.

Members of the Shahadulla, another sub-sect of Khoja, also accept the authority of Atharv-Veda. Pirai another Khoja sub sect localized in Sind is also close to Hinduism in its rituals of life and death.[163]

Ismaili Sect

Ismaili is also a syncretistic sect and has a considerable following. Its followers regard Panjtan (Muhammad Ali, Fatima, Hasan and Husain as divines and Fatima as a Hindu Goddess.) Salat is unknown among them. They cremate their dead like Hindus but they bury their bones. Another Khoja group Guptis, believe Prophet and Ali as an incarnation of the Hindu God Krishna. The Guptis abstain from meat like Hindus and observe neither salat nor fast.[164]

Ali Ilahi

Members of Ali Ilahi sect are found in northern Kashmir and Hyderabad. They regard Ali as the manifestation of God. Ali is identified with the sun. They reject the Quran as partly a forgery. They are vegetarian, do not have mosques and they drink wine. They are monogamous and do not permit divorce.[165]

Mahdawiyya

This sect associated with the name of Wahid Mahmud, appeared in the early 13th century. He claimed himself to be a Mahdi who could lead the people to the right path. He asserted that the religion of Mahmud being obsolete and abrogated must be replaced by a new dispensation. The followers of Wahid are called Mahdawiyya They regard him as their Prophet, venerate the sun and called it their Qiblah; they have their prayer, which they chant with their face turned towards the sun. [166]

Roshaniyya

Mian Bayazid Ansari of Punjab founded it. He claimed to have received divine revelation and proclaimed himself to be a Prophet. He ridiculed Shariat and said that Tarikat was far superior to it. Prayers according to him are necessary but there is no need of turning in a single direction.[167]

Jalaliyan

This sect emerged in the 14th century. Its founder was Sayyid

Jalaluddin Bukhari. Its followers do not observe fast and prayers. They sit before fires but do not keep matted hair. They shaved their body and remained almost naked even in the severest cold and led a wandering life.[168]

The Bohras

The term Bohra is said to be of Gujarati origin. It means trader. The sect emerged and flourished in Gujarat. It is highly influenced by Hinduism. The Bohras keep themselves distinct from other Muslims. They have their own mosques, which they call Jamat- khana and their own exclusive cemeteries. They offer three prayers instead of the usual five and they do not assemble on Friday for Friday prayers Like Hindus, the Bohras give and take loans. Their fiscal year begins on Dipawali. They speak Gujarati language.[169]

Pirzadas

Saint Muhammad Shah Dulla founded this sect in the middle of the 17th century. He wrote a book for his followers in which he quoted selections from both Hindu and Muslim scriptures and set up Vishnu in his tenth or nishkalank (sinless) incarnation as his Supreme Deity.

Besides there emerged new sects like the Din-I-Ilahi founded by Akbar and the Ahmadiya by Mirza Ghulam Ahmad, who claimed himself to be Messiah, an incarnation of Lord Krishna.[170]

Yogi and Qalandariya Cults

Another Hinduized cult that was widespread among Muslims, under various names was the Yogi cult. Particularly there was a class of Muslim Yogis called Rawals who have given its name to Rawalpindi in west Punjab. Lal Shahbaz Qalandar of Sind founded the Qalandariya cult. He was a preacher of love and tolerance. He was called Shahbaz because he was believed to have turned into a falcon to pick up his friend Sheikh Farid Shakar Ganj from the gallows of the fanatics. He was called Lal (red) for the red robe, which he wore all his, life. He was extremely popular both among Hindu and Muslim masses. The Hindus regarded him as the reincarnation of Bharathari, the saintly brother of Vikramditya. This sect was highly influenced by Hinduism. The Qalandars shave their heads and all hair on their face and wander in forests like yogis donning ornaments made of heavy iron-rods.[171]

Madaris

The followers of Saint Sheikh Madar of Makanpur are known as Madaris. The cult founded in the 15th century borrowed many practices from Hinduism. The Madaris neither pray nor fast. They rub ashes on their bodies, roam naked and pass through fire like the Hindus. Even today both Hindus and Muslims in U.P.and Bengal celebrate the festival of Madar Jhanda.[172]

Rishi Order

Sheikh Nuruddin was the founder of this order. It originated in Kashmir in the 15th century. Nuruddin known as Nand Rishi and Shajan preached the gospel of love harmony and spiritual unity He had left home at the age of thirty and passed twelve years in a cave where he subsisted only on the fruits It is there that he realized God.[173] He regarded Lalla an avatar and his guru. He said:

"That Lalla of Padmanpore
She drank Her fill of divine nectar
She was indeed an avatar of ours
O God grant me the same spiritual power.[174]

Like his Guru Lalla, Nur-ud-din also believed that God was everywhere and there was no need to visit any Mosque or temple. He said:

"The universe is the objective manifestation of the essence of Siva
If you realise it through annihilation of self
You will get merged into Him
What will you find after death, if you do not
Recognize Him in this world?
Search Him in yourself and give me keen hearing."[175]

God could be realized only through true devotion and not by reading religious books. Like Sufis and bhaktas Nur-ud-din also condemned the hypocrisy of the priests of both the communities. Once he saw a hypocritical priest at a Mosque twirling a rosary in his hands, who took six platefuls of rice, which were brought to him by six different persons at different times, to each of him he said he had no food at all that day .He then rebuked him thus;

"The rosary is like a snake;
Thou bendest it on seeing the disciples.
Thou hast eaten six platefuls, one like another;
If thou art a priest, then who are robbers?"[176]

He too believed that there was no difference between Hindus

and Muslims. He asked both of them:

"Among the brothers of the same parents
Why do you create a barrier?
Muslims and Hindus are one
When will God be kind to this servant?"[177]

He was a symbol of harmony and strongly believed in the peaceful co-existence of all religions .He advised the Hindus and Muslims as:

"Let Hindus and Muslims (together)
Worship God alone.
We came to this world like partners
We should share our joys
And sorrows together"[178]

Nuruddin had enormous influence over the common masses as well as the rulers of Kashmir. Both revered him and followed the spiritual path shown by him. When he passed away the then king Zain-ul-Abidin, himself was the chief mourner at his funeral among thousands of people. The extent of veneration in which his memory has been cherished may be gauged from the fact that nearly four centuries after his death Atta Mohammad Khan, the Afghan Governor (1808-10) in order to win the sympathy and support of the people of Kashmir, struck coins in the name of Sheikh Nuruddin. No other saint, perhaps in the human history, has ever had coins struck in his honour. Both Hindus and Muslims revered him. His shrine, in Chirar-e-Sharif, is still visited by the devotees belonging to different creeds. [179]

Pirana Sect

A Muslim saint Imam Shah of Piran village of Ahmadabad founded it in the 16th century. His followers who consisted of both Hindus and Muslims regarded him as an incarnation of Indra, while his son, Pir Nur Mohammad was taken for Vishnu's incarnation. The literature of the sect, is the most unusual symbolism of Hinduism and Islam In some works Fatima, the Prophets daughter is equated with Lakshmi.Bibi Ayesha Mohammed's wife corresponds to Savitri while Adam is Mahadeva or Ishvara.Their sacred book is a collection of religious precepts called Shiksha-Patri written by Imam Shah. The followers called themselves Satpanthis or Satpanthi Momin. They keep Ramzan fasts and observe it as a holiday. Besides, they also observe Holi. Diwali, Baleva and Akhtarija and worship Hindu

God Brahma, Vishnu and Shiva.[180] They keep Hindu names, observe all Hindu customs except that their dead are buried with Islamic rites.[181] They don't practice circumcision, and in addition to Nikah ceremony they call a Brahmin and go through a Hindu marriage ceremony They are strict vegetarians and do not eat garlic, onion and asafactide.[182]

The Bauls

Baul sect came in to existence in the early medieval period. Its main preacher was Lalen a Muslim fakir. Members of this sect were known as Bauls. They came from both Hindu and Muslim communities. Their practices and beliefs are drawn partly from the Vaishnava doctrine and partly from the Sufi's teachings. The Bauls follow an obscure and precarious mode of life, living on what people give them in appreciation of their songs. Music is an important part of their religious practice and it is intensely spiritual.[183]

The Kakans

The founder of this sect, Ibrahim Kakan of Kashmir, is said to be the contemporary of Emperor Jahangir. He had a large number of Hindu and Muslim disciples but never induced to change their religion. He never uttered the names of Muslim prophets or Hindu incarnate Gods except Allah and Ram. His followers believed in the unity of Divine Being and followed celibacy as a rule. They used intoxicants like bhang and did not sleep at night.[184]

Satyapir

Founded in Bengal by Sultan Husain Shah. His sect is an amalgamation of Muslim concept of pir and Hindu idea of deity. A wooden plank represented the new divinity of this sect. Both Hindus and Muslims worshipped it. Together they used to make offerings to Satya pir and chant hymns in his praise.[185]

The people of Bengal with great fervor worshipped numerous Pirs. As the verse goes:

"Hindu devta haila Mussalman Pir;
Dui kule seba haila jahir"

(The Gods of Hindus became the Pirs of Mussalmans, manifesting themselves, they receive worship from both sides). The masses solicited the blessings and favours to ward off danger or evil spirits. Khwaja Khizr was worshipped as God of water. Both Hindu and Muslim boatsmen observed this festival in August-September. Fishermen celebrated it by floating lights on the water. The festival was celebrated by Nawab Sirajuddaula also.[186] The name of Pir Badar was invoked by sailors and fishermen before journeying or during storms. Kaloo Rai was worshipped as the patron saint of Tigers. The woodcutters before entering Sunderban worshipped Muhurra Ghazi for safety and protection. Worship of Panch Pirs was also very popular. Maggar Pir was given a Hindu name Lal Jas Raj by Hindus. He was the patron saint of dhobis and bhisties. (Washermen and water-carriers.) Pir Dastgir was worshipped by industrial castes in Punjab. Hussan Teli was the patron saint of the oilmen, while the dyers of Lahore look to Pir Ali Rangrez while Pir Sher Shah of Multan cared for the interest of the prosecuted lovers. Gugga Pir flourished in Rajputana in the 12th century. He had large following in both the communities. His devotees built his shrines even in their houses. The sweeper community of North India revered Lal Beg.[187]

Thus, the philosophy, practices and beliefs of the sects founded by Hindu as well as Muslim saints clearly reflect the influence of the two religions upon each other.. The mixture of two religions in the form of cults was so unique that a Muslim theologist observed "In India more than in any other Muhammadan country, Islam and Kufr had been mixed like Khichri"[188]

The powerful spiritual current encompassed the entire country. Except the orthodox sections of both the communities, common masses were deeply influenced by this new wave. Antagonism or exclusiveness disappeared and a new outlook was ushered in. Respect and reverence for others religions was its essential feature. Gods and Saints of other religions were approached freely by the people for the fulfillment of their desires and easing out of hardships, difficulties and distress. The temple of Gopinath was constructed by Ra'sil of the Shaikhavati Clan in Akbar's service. A childless Rana named Mohal, got a son through the blessings of Shaikh Burhan. The son was called Shaikh and became the patriarch of Shaikhavati Clan.[189] Often Hindus, Muslims and Sikhs joined together to build a Mosque Temple or a Gurudwara with equal devotion. The Hindu shrines of Kangra and Mathura attracted a large number of Muslim pilgrimage.[190] The spirit was not confined only to common masses but even the religious leaders set examples in this direction The Sikh Guru Hargobind built mosques at Hargobidpura, Kartarpur, Amritsar, Bias etc. Mian Mir a Muslim saint laid the foundation of Darbar Sahib at Amritsar.The Muslim

Rebeck players ever since Mardana, an associate and disciple of Guru Nanak continue to attend and play rebeck at the Hari Sankirtan Sammelans in Gurudwaras. The Muslim minstrels became a must in the Gurudwaras including Darbar Sahib.[191] Besides, Shrines and mosques were built closely and some times same object was worshipped by the members of both the communities relating to the particular sign on it as belonging to their respective Gods. There were no fights between the people claiming the particular object or place as the exclusive property of their community instead they shared the same attitude that your God is mine and mine is yours too The Shrine of Shah-e-Hamdan and the temple of Mahakali exist together at Khanqah Mohalla in Srinagar city. The Shrine of Makhdum Saheb and the temple of Goddess Sharika at Hari Parbat are also similarly situated Be it Id or Shivratri, the participation was not only of one or the other community but also of the people of Kashmir as a whole. One Malik of a village in the vicinity of Pahalgam rediscovered the holy cave of Amarnath that was declared lost during the Pathan rule. To this day, the Muslim Malik family receives a share from the offerings made by thousands of Hindus who visit the holy cave annually.[192] At Fatehpura and Waripura, a stone having imprint of a foot was worshipped by the Muslims as Kadam-I-Rasul (the Prophet foot print) and by Hindus as Vishnu pad (Vishnu's foot print.) [193] The foot prints on the Rock Temple at Trichinopoly are worshipped by the Hindus as those of Vibhishana and venerated by Muslims as those of the local Muslim saint Sayyid Babayya Natthar Wali whose dargah is an object of veneration for both the communities. The hills of Palani and Turparankunram are also sacred to both Hindus and Muslims alike. The Nawab of Walajah of Arcot rebuilt and restored worship in the sacred Hindu Shrines of South India, Trichnopoly, Srirangam Tiravani Koil, Samayavaram, Bhikshandar Koil, Truvadi Chidambram and Virdhachalam in South India as they had suffered ruin during the wars with Chanda Sahib and the French. His NaibYusuf khan brought back the Minakshi image from Manamadura and reestablished it in its old place Madura.[194] There are instances when Non Muslims including Brahmins being appointed as muttawali or trustee at Muslim dargahs and tombs at Hyderabad in the South and Dipaliwal near Kalanoor in the North. Najibabadi Pathans built at Hardwar big havelies for accommodating Hindu pilgrims. At Hyderabad (Deccan) a Brahmin family continued to be the muttawali of the dargah of a famous Muslim saint and enjoyed a big Jagir later granted by the Nizam Both the Hindu and Muslim followers of saint Shah Shamsuddin Daryayi appointed his Hindu disciple Deepali as the trustee and keeper of the tomb with unanimous consent.195 In the first half of the 18th century Sitaram Ray captured Fatehabad and Bhasana. He established his headquarter ten miles away from Bhasana and named it Mohammadpur in honour of a saint.[196]

In this harmonious co-existence, it was not uncommon to see a Muslim saint having a Hindu as his chief disciple and Hindu saint's successor a Muslim. One Shah Muntoji Bahmani also known as Murutunjaya (conqueror of death) belonging to a royal family of Bidar received invitiation from a Hindu saint Sahajananda Swami of Kalyani (Bijapur) and afterward became a devotee of Vithal of Pandharpur. Sheikh Muhammad another saint of the same period was initiated into the Bhakti cult, by a Hindu Guru and though he accepted Hindu gods he did not give up his Muslim faith. A happy blending of Islam and Hinduism is found in the famous Maha-arti (grand prayer) composed by him in which more than hundred saints both Hindus and Muslims, for whom he had high regards, have been skillfully knitted together. Ramdas a saint contemporary of Shivaji was full of praise for Sheikh Mohammad whom he immortalized in a prayer composed by him in his honour. He writes; "This body which is a borrowed thing from the five elements is essentially due to your grace and I would sacrifice it for your sake. I do not know what is "bhava"(emotion) or "Bhakti"(devotion) but only this that we have been reared by the saints. Ramdas is, in fact, the dust of the feet of the great saints like you"[197]

Chand Bhonsle, a Hindu saint was initiated by Sufi Raje Mohammad, the father of Sheikh Mohammad.[198] Bawa Fattu, a Muslim saint of Kangra district, received the gift of prophecy by the blessing of Sodhi Guru Gulab Singh. Baba Shahana, a Hindu saint of Jang district was the disciple of a Muslim faqir. Rishi Pir of Kashmir had two favourite Muslim disciples Nanak Shah Azari and Aita Shah Malang.[1999]

Thus, interaction between Hinduism and Islam gave rise to liberal religious-social movement all over the country. It weakened rigidity, exclusiveness and hold of the orthodoxy and inaugurated an epoch based on mutual love, understanding and trust. Sufis, the Bhaktas and the other Hindu and Muslim Saints, contributed greatly in shaping new India by inculcating the spirit of liberalism in every aspect of the social life. They not only revealed the different ways of realizing god, Who was both Ram and Rahim, but also emphasized that service to the needy and the oppressed was the true devotion and an easy way of acquiring salvation. The numerous cults formed by the saints cultivated a new kind of social fraternity. The members of a cult, irrespective of their caste creed, region, religion or social status, formed one large family headed by the saint. Except, for the orthodox section of both the communities, so far as the masses were concerned, these saints became fountains of inspiration and their pure lives and deeds strike the chord of devotional feelings and noble sentiments. Their counsels to the rulers also helped in the establishment of liberal state and bridged the gulf between the rulers and the ruled. Their appeals for harmony and unity does not seem to have gone unheeded as we find a new spiritual and social upsurge taking place, democratic and revolutionary in nature. People selected the religion of their choice, converted to new creeds freely, formed new spiritual Orders and framed new philosophies. Mixing of the two communities on the spiritual platform also brought them closer in other aspects of life and worked in a big way in evolving a common Indian identity overriding all divisions.

REFERENCES

1. T.W. Arnold, *Preaching of Islam,* Renaissance, New Delhi, 1984, p. 265.

2. Sisir Kumar Mitra, *India's Cultural Empire and Her Future,* Aurobindo Library, Madras, 1947, p. 69
Also see Yusuf Hussain, *Glimpses of Medieval Indian Culture,* Asia Bombay, 1957, p. 12.

3. Tarachand, *Influences of Islam on Indian Culture,* Indian Press, Allahabad, 1936, p. 34.

4. *Ibid,* p. 35.

5. *Ibid.*

6. *The Delhi Sultanate,* ed. by R.C. Majumdar, Bhartiya Vidya Bhavan, Bombay 1967, p. 416-18.

7. Tarachand, p. 42-45.

8. *Ibid,* p. 83.

9. Khushwant Singh, *A History of the Sikhs,* Vol. I New Jersey, Princeton, 1963, p. 27.

10. *Ibid.*

11. B.N. Luniya, *Life and Culture in Medieval India,* Komal Prakashsn, Indore 1977, p. 343.

12. Vivek Bhattacharya, *Famous Indian Sages-Their Immortal Message*, Sagar, New Delhi, 1982, p. 334.

13. Khushwant Singh, My *Bleeding Punjab*, UBS, N. Delhi, 1992, p. 16.

14. S.A.A. Rizvi, *Muslim Revivalist Movements in Northern India*, Balkirshna Book, Agra, 1965, p. 17.

15. Yusuf Hussain, p. 33.

16. Bankey Bihari, *Sufis, Mystics and Yogis of India*, Bhartiya Vidya Bhavan, Bombay, 1962, p. 100.

17. T.L. Vaswani, *The Spirit and Struggle of Islam*, Ganesh and Com. Madras, 1921, p. 5.

18. M.A. Macauliffe, *The Sikh Religion*, S. Chand, New Delhi 1983. Vol-III and IV, p. 41.

19. *Khuda Baksh Library journal*, No. 44, 1987, p. 72.

20. Iqbal, Vol. 13. No. I, July 1964, p. 62.

21. *Cultural Heritage of India*, ed. by Haridas, Vol-IV Ram Kishan Mission, Calcutta 1956, p. 392.

22. V. Raghavan, *The Great Integrators*, Publication Division, Govt. of India, N. Delhi, 1964, p. 73.

23. Bulla aaslik hoin yoin Rabb-da, mulmat hoi lakh, I Log Kofir Kafir aakhde to aho aho aakh.

24. Bankey Bihari p. 140.

25. Yusuf Hussain, p. 32 Also see Mirza Wahiduddin, The *Holy Biography of Hazarat Khwaja Moin-ud-Din Chishti*, Rajasthan, 1960, p. 60.

26. Vivek Bhattacharya, p. 319.

27. Zuhurul Hassan *The life and Teachings of Khwaja Moinuddin Chishti*, Asma, Ajmer, 1959 p. 87, 90.

28. Vivek, p. 397.

29. Yusuf Husain, p. 33.

30. Vivek, p. 399.

31. Uday Shankar Srivastva, *Madhyayugeen Hindi ke Itr Musalman Kavi*, Jawahar Pustkalya, Mathura p.174 Mangta hoon yeh Khwaja Qutb tum ji ki murdain Sabhi bhar karna I Dhyooin tumhain, tum se saun paoin lag rahoon tumhare charna II.

32. *Great Men ard Women of India*, Publication Division Govt. of India, New Delhi,1973. p. 30.

33. *Ibid.*

34. Rizvi, p. 25, Yusuf Hussain, p. 33, 37.

35. *Studies in the Cultural Development of India*, ed by N.R. Ray and P.N. Chakravarty, Punthi Pustak, Calcutta 1991, p. 240.

36. Hazrat Nizamuddin Chishti Jari-Jari Baksh Pir, Joi-Joi dheyave tai phal pave mere man ki murad bhar dje Amir. Ram Chandra Shukla, *Hindi Sahitya ka Itihas*, Nagri Pracharni, Kashi 1997, p. 31.

37. Vivek, p. 417-18.
38. *The Cultural Heritage of India*, Vol. IV, p. 389.
39. *Visva-Bharati Quarterly*, May 1940, p. 75.
40. Bankey Bihari, p. 112.
41. *Visva-Bharati*, Aug-Oct 1948, p. 107.
42. *Ibid.*, Feb-April, 1947, p. 323.
43. Waldermar Hansen, *The Peacock Throne*, Holt Rineheart and Winston, New York, 1972 p. 400.
44. Visva-Bharati, Feb-April, 1947, p. 322.
45. *Ibid*, p. 315.
46. K.R. Malkani, *The Sind Story*, *Allied*, New Delhi 1984, p. 64.
47. *The Cultural Heritage of India*, p. 388.
48. *Ibid.*, Also see, Sisir Kumar, *India Vision and Fulfilment*, Bombay, 1982 p. 88.
49. Malkani, p.165-66. Also see Motilal Jotwani *Sufis of Sind*, Publication Division Govt. of India, New Delhi-1986, p. 113.
50. Malkani, p. 165.
51. *Khuda Baksh Library Journal*, No. 44, 1987, p. 69.
52. Motilal Jotwani, p. 136.
53. *The Cultural Heritage of India*, p. 388.
54. Malkani, p. 167.
55. Jotwani, p .146.
56. *Ibid.*
57. Malkani, p. 167.
58. Jotwani, p. 146.
59. Malkani, p. 167.
60. Vivek, p. 480.
61. Ian Austin, *City of Legends*, Viking, Calcutta, 1992, p. 3.
62. Parmanand Panchal, *Hindi Ke Muslim Sahityakar* Bharat-Bharati Prakashan, 1971 p. 47.
63. Yusuf Hussain, p. 39.
64. *Khuda Baksh Library Journal*, No. 44, p. 69.
65. Vivek, p. 183.
66. Iqbal, Vol. 13, No.1. 1964, p. 67.
67. Ishrat Haque, *Glimpses of Mughal Society and Culture*, Concept, New Delhi, 1992, p. 92.
68. G.N. Sharma, *Social Life in Medieval Rajasthan*, Lakshmi Prakashan, Agra, 1968, p. 221.
69. Syed Mahmud, *India of Yesterday*, Indo Middle East Cultural Studies, Hyderabad, 1957, p. 39.
70. Erskine, Esq, *History of India*, Longman, Brown, Green and Longmans, London, 1854, p. 172.
71. J.M. Shelat, *Akbar*, Bhartiya Vidya Bhavan Bombay, Ist edition 1959, Reprint, 1964, p. 189.

72. Satish Chandra, *Mughals Religious Policies*, Vikas, 1993, New Delhi p. 207.

73. Ian Austin, p. 113.

74. K.S. Lal *Twilight of the Sultanate*, Asia, New Delhi, 1963. p. 264.

75. Thomas Keightley, *History of India*, Whittaker, London, 1847, p. 17.

76. Fathullah Mujtabai, *Aspects of Hindu-Muslim Cultural Relation*, N.B.B, New Delhi 1978, p. 100.

77. S.M. Ikram, *Muslim Civilization in India*, Columbia University Press, New York. 1964, p. 185.

78. Satish Chandra, p. 208.

79. *The Indian Antiquary*, July 1931, p. 124.

80. *Ruka 'at-i-Alamgiri*, trs. Jamshid H. Bilimoria, Idara-i-Adbiyat-i-Delhi, 1972, p. 28.

81. Syed, p. 131.

82. *The Cultural Heritage of India*, p. 357.

83. K.S. Lal, p. 292.

84. S.R. Sharna, *India As I See Her*, Lakshmi Narayan Aggarwal, Agra 1956, p. 185.

85. Tarachand, p. 224.

86. *An Outline of Indian Cultural History*, ed. Abdul Latif, Hyderabad, 1958, p. 219.

87. *Ibid*

88. *Khuda Baksh Library*, Journal No. 44, 1987, p. 74.

89. K.S. Lal, p. 307 to 314.

90. Rai Sahib, Dinesh Chandra, *Chaitanya and His Companions*, University of Calcutta Press, 1917, p.16. Also see. *Indian History A Review*, by Baij Nath Puri, Bhartiya Vidya Bhavan, Bombay, 1960, p. 86.

91. V. Raghavan, New Delhi, 1964, p. 69.

92. S.R. Sharma, *India As I see Her*, p. 185.

93. Macauliffe, Vol. VI. p. 102.

94. Iqbal, Vol. 13, No- I, July 1964, p. 49.

95. Radhakamal Mukerjee, *The Cultural Art of India*, p. 262.

96. Tarachand, p. 147.

97. G.H. Wescot, *Kabir and Kabirpanthis*, Sushil Gupta, Calcutta, 1907, p. 12.

98. Ibid., p. 25-26.

99. S.R. Sharma, p. 181.

100. *An Outline of Indian Cultural History*, ed by Abdul Latif, p. 207. Also see K.M. Panikkar, *A Survey of Indian History*, p. 167.

101. *Visva-Bharati Quarterly*, No. 50 Jan 1951, p. 212.

102. *The Delhi Sultanate*, ed by R.C. Majumder, p. 563-64.

103. Westcot, p. 35.

104. *Indian Inheritance*, Vol. I ed by K.M. Munshi, Bhartiya Vidya Bhavan, 1965, p. 199.

105. *Ibid,* p. 43.

106. S.R. Sharma, p. 166.

107. Westcot, p. 14.

108. Tarachand, p.166, Also see N.D., Ahuja, *The Great Guru Nanak,* Kirti, New Delhi 1969, p. 167.

109. G.S. Chhabra, *Advanced Study in History of the Punjab* Vol. I Shararjit, Jullundur, 1960. p

110. Tarachand, p. 176.

111. G.S. Chhabra, p. 57.

112. Yusuf Hussain, p. 27.

113. Gurbachan Singh Talib, *Guru Nanak His Personality* and *Vision,* Gurdas Kapur, New Delhi 1969, p. 63.

114. S.R. Sharma, p. 167.

115. T.L. Vaswani, *In the Sikh Sanctuary,* Ganesh and Comp. Madras, 1922, p. 86.

116. *Ibid.*

117. Macauliffe, Vol. I, p. 38.

118. Teja Singh *Asa di Var,* p.102-104 (Punjabi).

119. Gurbachan Singh, p. 63.

120. Kartar Singh M.A. *Life of Guru Nanak,* Jaidev Singh, Amritsar 1973, p. 111.

121. *Ibid.*

122. *Visva-Bharati,* Jan 1928, p. 372-74.

123. W.G. Orr, *A Sixteenth Century Indian Mystic,* Luttuworth. Press, London, 1947, p. 62.

124. V. Raghavan, p. 70.

125. Tarachand, p. 185.

126. *Visva-Bharati Quarterly,* Jan 1928, p. 375.

127. W.G. Orr, p. 37.

128. *Visva- Bharati Querterly,* Jan 1928, p. 375.

129. W.G. Orr, p. 43.

130. It is interesting to know the application of Lal Ded. She was a yogini and owing to yogic exercises, it is said, her abdoman had projected and enlarged so much that it anwered the purpose of loincloth. At this stage she tore away her garments and peregrinated nakedly. Hence Lal Ded.

131. Mohd. Ishaq Khan, *Kashmir's Transition to Islam,* Manohar, Delhi, 1994, p. 75.

132. *Great Men and Women of India,* p. 42.

133. Tarachand, p. 219.

134. *The History* and *Culture of the Indian People* , ed, R.C. Majumdar, Bhartiya Viday Bhavan, Bombay 1977, p. 722.

135. Iqbal, No. III, Jan 1960, p. 65.

136. *Ibid,* p.64. Also see, Pt Sunderlal, *How India lost Her Freedom,* Popular Prakashan, Bombay 1970, p. IV.

137. Murry T. Titus *Islam in India* and *Pakistan*, YMCA, Calcutta 1957, p. 82, Sisir Kumar, p. 87 and Cyril Modak, *India's Destiny*, Kitab Mahal, Allahabad, 1944, p. 14.

138. Muhammad Yasin, *A Social History of Islamic India*, Upper India, Lucknow, 1958, p. 92.

139. *Ibid.*

140. *The Cultural Heritage of India*, p. 388.

141. *Ibid*, p. 381, Also see Tarachand, p. 196.

142. M.L. Bhagi, *Medieval India: Culture* and *Thought*, Indian, Ambala 1985, p. 192.

143. V. Raghavan, p. 72.

144. Tarachand, p. 190.

145. *The History and Culture of the Indian people*, p. 716.

146. Sunderlal, p. IXXIV

147. Tarachand, p. 198.

148. P.S. Mukharya, *Sant Prannath and the Parnami Sect* in, *Medieval Bhakti Movement in India*, ed by N.N. Bhattacharya, M.M. Publisher, New Delhi, 1989, p. 123.

149. *Ibid.*

150. Bhagwan Das Gupta, *Pranami Sampradaya of Bundelkhand* p. 130.

151. *Ibid*, p. 132.

152. *Ibid*, p. 133.

153. *Ibid*, p. 131.

154. Bhagwan Swaroop Gupta, *Maharaja Chhatrasal Bundela*, Agra, 1950, p. 104-11.

155. K.R. Malkani, *The Sind Story*, p. 49.

156. Zahiruddin Malik, *The Reign of Muhammad Shah*, Asia, Aligarh, 1977, p. 349.

157. Tarachand, p. 200.

158. *The History* and *Culture of the Indian People*, p. 718.

159. Arnold, *Preaching of Islam*, p. 275.

160. Aziz Ahmad, *An Intellectual History of Islam in India*, Edinburgh, 1969, p. 24.

161. Murry T. Titus, *Islam in India and Pakistan*, p.182, Also see, B.N. Luniya, *Evolution of Indian Culture*, p. 439-40.

162. *Hindustan Times*, May 10, 2001, p. 2.

163. Sisir Kumar p. 87, Also see Aziz Ahmad, p. 25.

164. Aziz Ahmed, p. 26.

165. *Ibid.*

166. Iqbal Vol. 13, No. I, 1964, p. 53.

167. *Ibid.*

168. Yasin, *A Social History of Islamic India*, p. 81.

169. Murry T. Titus, p. 103-104.

170. *Ibid.*

171. Malkani, p. 36-Also see Rizvi, p. 31.

172. *Journal of Indian History*, Part I, April 1936, p. 481.

173. R.K. Parmu, *A History of Muslim Rule, in Kashmir*, PPH. Delhi, 1969, p. 110.

174. Jayalal Kaul, *Lal Ded*, Sahitya Akademi, New Delhi 1973, p. 88. Also see S.M. Iqbal, *The Culture of Kashmir*, Marwah, New Delhi 1978, p. 119-20.

175. Ishaq Khan, *Kashmir's Transition to Islam*, p. 103.

176. *Indian Antiquary*, February, 1930, p. 24.

177. Ishaq Khan, p. 103.

178. *Ibid.*

179. R.K. Parmu, p.108. Also sec Vivek, p. 517.

180. M.R. Majumdar, *Cultural History of Gujarat*, Popular Prakashan, Bombay, 1965, p. 254. Also see *Islam in the Sub-continent*, by Annie Marrie Schimmel, p. 73-74 and Luniya, p. 439.

181. Sisir Kumar, p. 88.

182. M.R. Majumdar, p. 254.

183. Ananda Sarkar Ray, *An Outline of Indian Culture*, New Delhi, 1978, p. 63.

184. Yasin, p. 85.

185. *Journal of the Bihar Research Society* (sp. issue) 1968. p. 189.

186. *Ibid* p. 480.

187. Murry, p.145-46.

188. *Journal of Indian History*. April 1976, p. 474.

189. M.L. Bhagi, p. 285.

190. S.M. Ikram, p. 223.

191. Macauliffe, p. 33, N. D. Ahuja, p. 168.

192. *Khuda Baksh Library Journal* p. 67.

193. S.M. Iqbal, *The Culture of Kashmir*, Marwah 1978, New Delhi 1978, p. 116.

194. Raghvendra Rao *Indo-Muslim Culture*, Vichara Sahitya, Banglore. p. 63.

195. N.D. Ahuja., p. 8. Also see Rajendra Prasad, *India Divided*, Hind Kitab, Bombay 1946, p. 34.

196. *History of Bangladesh* ed. Sirajul Islam, Asiatic Society, Bangladesh, 1992, p. 56.

197. *Proceedings of Indian History Congress*, 1970, Vol. I, p. 238-39.

198. *Ibid.*

199. The Indian Antiquary, July 1931, p. 126.

2

Little Known Dimensions of Muslim Rule

Muslim rule in India began with the advent of the Delhi Sultanate in the beginning of the 13th century. Muslim rulers were aliens and belonged to different religion. After conquering the land, their main aim was to maintain and consolidate their rule. This political compulsion forced them to be tolerant and to refrain from antagonizing the Indian masses by interfering with their socio-religious matters. With the passage of time, they cut off their foreign roots and made India their homeland. For the continuity and stability of their rule, it became imperative for them to win over the natives and to wipe out any notion that they were aliens. They refused to pay any heed to the orthodox ulema, who expected them to act as protector and promoter of Muslim Faith. Instead, they sought the guidance, support and blessings of the native saints and tried to identify themselves with the people of the land. In running the affairs of the state the Sultans were motivated by political interest and the principle of religious tolerance.

However, before the establishment of the Sultanate, Sind had been subjugated by Mohammad bin Qasim in 712 A.D The invasion of Sind by Muhammad bin Qasim was not motivated by any religious consideration. The cause of Arab invasion was that Raja Dhar of Sind had looted Arab's ships anchored at Vibal now known as Karachi, Qasim the commander of the Arab forces, then attacked and conquered Sind. During his rule which lasted for a brief period, Qasim practised toleration towards the religions of this land and thus won the hearts of the people of Sind. When he attacked Multan, he saw there a famous shrine revered highly by the Hindus of the land. Qasim did not pull it down. On the other hand, with the permission of the priest, he paid a formal visit to it.[1]

One day the Brahmin pujaris (priests) of Sind collectively approached Qasim and appealed to him saying:

"Our temples need repairs. The merchants, who were hitherto offering sacrifices and giving presents to us, have ceased to do so on account of their fear of you. The presents offered were only source of income with which we used to support our families. You have been kind enough to help all others except us. You returned the property of the merchants, improved their trade and provided source of income to all. But you did not pay any heed to our needs. Now we want you to persuade the Hindus to renew their sacrifices and their presents to temples and offer worship to their idols once again."[2]

Qasim wrote about this appeal of the pujaris to governor Hajaj and on receiving his reply announced that all the temples all over the Sind would be repaired at the expense of the government. He also ordered that three percent of the revenue derived by the government would be allocated for the support of the Brahmins, as was being done during the regime of the Rajas and that out of that amount, aid be given to the Brahmins according to their normal needs, and that rest of the amount be kept in reserve to meet any extraordinary expenses which they might incur in future, and that its amount should be maintained separately, and that the people should be allowed to construct their temples and their idols in whatever manner they liked and worship their Gods in whatever way they pleased. Qasim then called the head of the Brahmins and presented to him valuable garments and conferred on him the title of Rana.[3] He also banned killing of cows in Sind and Multan. His conciliatory attitude and policies won him place in the hearts of Sindhi people. The people of Sind were not hostile towards the Arabs. Sindhi troops were there in the Arab armies.[4] The Arabs ruled in Sind for nearly two hundred years. All religious customs and ceremonies of the Hindus continued to be performed throughout the Arab rule.[5]

Sultan Iltutmish, who is regarded as the first ruler of the Delhi Sultanate, gave it an independent status by severing all relations with Ghazni and Ghaur. He shifted his capital from Lahore to Delhi and ruled as he pleased, ignoring the dictates of the ulema.[6] When approached by some ulema with the request that Hindus should be forced to accept Islam Iltutmish refused to do so. He never implemented ulema's schemes in the political field. His daughter Raziya abolished the Jaziyah, or the poll tax on the non-Muslims despite stiff opposition from the orthodox. She argued and explained eloquently to them the history of the tax as: "it was imposed in the early period of Islam on non-believers because most of the wars then fought on the grounds of our particular faith, and such person as did not subscribe to that faith could not be expected to fight. The believers on the other hand, were obliged to do military service" Balban who was one of her courtiers pointed out that, that was the origin of this tax; but since then its connotation had changed considerably and the Ulema upheld it. Raziya retorted "oh don't talk to me about the Ulema. There are no doubt, some notable exceptions; but many of them are more interested in politics than in religion. That has been our bane." During her reign, orthodox did not have any say in the state matters.[7] Sultan Balban also gave precedence to the affairs of the state over religion. Ziauddin Barani, an orthodox Muslim historian of the medieval period writes:

"In the matter of punishment and exercise of royal authority he (Balban) acted without fear of God and whatever he regarded to be in the interest of government, irrespective of whether it was in accord with Sharia or not, he carried it into action."[8]

Sultan Jalaluddin declined to change his liberal polices towards his non-Muslim subjects under the pressure of ulema. During his reign the Hindus enjoyed complete religious freedom. They freely performed their religious rites and publicly practised idolatry and played music even under the walls of his palace along the banks of Yamuna.[9]

Sultan Alauddin had his own theory of Government, which he observed throughout his rule. Barani writes:

"When Alauddin became king, he came to the conclusion that the policy and government are one thing and the rules and the decrees of the Sharia another. Royal command belong to the king and Sharia`s decrees to the ulema. Sultanate is not bound by the Sharia."[10]

When Alauddin was told by Qazi Mughisuddin that most of his administrative practices were against Sharia, the Sultan was enraged. He showed no disposition to mend his ways maintaining that whatever he did was done for the benefit of his subjects.[11] He did not hesitate to declare publicly "Though I come of a Muslim stock but I know not what Islam is?"[12] Despite the ulema`s displeasure new public temples were built and old temples continually repaired during his reign.[13]

Jain sources enable us to know that Alauddin held religious discourses with Acharya Mahasena who was brought from Karnataka for the purpose. It is also reported that the Digambara Jain Purna Chandra of Delhi and Swetambara ascetic Ramchandra Suri were in favour with the Sultan.[14] Because of his catholicity and impartiality Alauddin was showered with praises and tributes by his non-Muslims subjects. In the Palam inscription, dated in 1280-81, the king of Joginipura (Alauddin) is compared in the goodness of his administration with Vishnu who has retired from the care of the world (entrusting it to the king) and gone to sleep in the ocean of milk"[15]

The Jain monks were invited to the royal court and Jain laity occupied special positions in the state services. Samar Singh Jain was made commissioner by Qutbuddin Mubarak Shah. Sultan Ghiyasuddin Tughlaq regarded him as his own son and sent him to Telingana where he built many temples.[16]

Like his father Muhammad bin Tughlaq had great respect for Jain monks. When saint Jinaprabha visited his court at Delhi in A D 1328, Tughlaq issued farman with royal seal for the construction of a new rest house for the monks. A procession started in his honour at his residence to the accompaniment of varied music and dances of young women and the saint was seated on the elephant surrounded by Maliks.[17]

The Sultan guided by Jinaprabha Suri, visited the Satrunjaya temples at Palatina as well as the idol houses of Girnar. In the Satrunjaya temples he performed same acts of devotion appropriate to a leader of Jain Sangha.[18]

He granted protection of Swetambara Jains at the time of rebellions throughout the empire and also gave lavish grants for the maintenance of the Jain institutions. For all these favours granted to them and the respect shown to their religion, the Jains used to hold Muhammad bin Tughlaq in great esteem and entitled the treatise Satrunjaya-Tirtha as Rajaprasada and Jain monastery at Tajuddin Sarai as Sultan Sarai. [19]

It is also said that the Sultan knew Sanskrit and Prakrit. He used to have religious discourses with Yogis and Monks. He respected all the religions. An inscription of that period states about the construction of a cow temple (gow-math) and a step well together with some gardening done under his personal supervision.[20] At Madhaya Pradesh, a Sanskrit inscription dated A.D 1384 Vikrama year, euologising Muhammad bin Tughlaq states:

"There is a famous king of Muhammad Shah, crest-jewel of all rulers of the earth who by his personnel bravery has crushed the enemies, and is the powerful Saka Lord"[21].

The Sultan had the courage to rise above the rank of bigotry of his age and without succumbing to a blind superstitious reverence for everything that passed in the name of religion, allowed himself to be guided by a rational spirit. His regime was rested on the principle of religious tolerance. During an armed conflict between Gurshap (Sultan's nephew) and Muhammad bin Tughlaq some unruly elements in the royal army damaged the temple at Madhukashwar at Kalyan and the Siva-linga was broken. The trustee of the temple waited on Ahmad bin Aiyaz, governor of Kalyan and requested him to reinstate the deity and arrange for the resumption of the ceremonial worship of Siva-linga. Ahmad bin Aiyaz granted the request and issued an order which runs as follows: "Since worship in the temple is the religious duty of the petitioners, they should follow it."[22]

The order was carried out and the installation of the deity took place amidst formal chanting of mantras. Ibn Batutta noticed that in the province of Thatta (Sind) Multan and specially at Banaras, the Brahmin used to teach the tenets of their religion in their established schools and admirers and students both Hindus and Muslims flocked to them from great distance."[23] Islami one of the contemporary orthodox Muslim historians wrote: "He (Sultan) uprooted the Muslims from Hindustan and installed the Hindus."Islami wrote further:"Hinduism has become dominant all over except in few places. The country has been seized completely by the Hindus. The Muhammadans have taken shelter in enclosures". [24]

The Sultan hated the orthodox and kept them at distance. He regarded narrow minded ulama as degenerate bigots steeped in ignorance and vanity. He never consulted them in state matters.[25] Besides, not showing any reverence for them, he discarded the time honoured sanctity, privileges and freedom the ulema and Sayyids enjoyed.[26] The ulama denounced him and condemned his activities and urged a general revolt against the Sultan. They roused some chiefs of the army and governors to defy the Sultan. They characterized him as Zalim, Kafir, Yazid and enemy of Islam.[27] The ulema carried a secret intrigue to dispose Tughlaq and install his cousin Firoz. After Tughlaq`s death, the ulema succeeded in placing Firoz on the throne. In order to have their supremacy in the affairs of the state, they obtained from Firoz, a promise that "he would rule according to the tenets of justice of law." Firoz Shah was thus obliged to ulema for the throne. Consequently in his reign, the influence and interference of ulema was evident. In compliance with the dictates of ulema, all the non-Sharia things such as pictures and statues of living things and golden and silver utensils were removed from the royal court. The Sultan was asked to use utensils made of stone and clay. On the advice of ulema the Sultan imposed Jaziya on the Brahmins also. The Sultan was also pressed by the ulema to restrict the activities and increasing influence of the liberal minded Sufi saints.[28]

However, Firoz's orthodox posture was merely for demonstration, as he did not allow the ulema to have an upper hand in the governance of the state. During his rule, which lasted for almost four decades, his subjects enjoyed freedom in their religious and social affairs. New temples were erected and old ones renovated. A fragmentary inscription found in the Purana Qila of Delhi written in Persian and Sanskrit, records the endowment of 12 bighas of land to a temple built and dedicated to Lord Krishna during Firoz`s rule.[29] It is also said that during his reign some Hindi verses were ceremoniously recited from the pulpit in the Mosque.[30]

Though all the Sultans used to have a group of theologians and often consulted them but the entire history of the Sultanate shows that the Sultans followed them only when it suited them. Even Sikandar Lodi, who is characterized as an orthodox sultan who maintained a select group of 17 theologians who were in constant personal attendance never allowed them to eat in his presence though they were served with food along with the sultan. They squatted on the floor while the Sultan sat on the coach and had to wait in silence and in hunger till the Sultan had finished. Even then they were not allowed to dine in the royal apartment but had to carry the plates home like ordinary servants. In fact Sikandar was neither fanatical nor strictly orthodox but was quite prepared to make pretence of one or the other in order to realize his ambitions and to further his themes of conquest and consolidation. He never took a risk of consulting the ulema without being assured of their dittoing his point of view.

Ironically, the orthodox Muslims had high praises for him. According to Niamatullah, an historian, Sikandar levelled all the temples at Narwar, in Gwalior territory to the ground, but Abul Fazl, writing about eighty years after Sikandar reign, noted the existence of old temples in the very place. It is apparent that it was a wishful thinking of the orthodox historian and not a fact. An account incorporated in the Waqiat-I-Mushtaqi makes it clear that the sultan did not allow defacement of the images on the walls in such a well-known centre of Hindu influence as Udayagiri, in Chanderi. He did not let his public policy be swayed by religious prejudice and narrowness as clearly illustrated in the tolerance accorded to Kabir and the Mahdawi leader Sayyid Muhammad Jaunpuri Besides his orthodoxy and devotion to Islam did not prevent him from shaving the beard, enjoying the music and wine.[31]

During the Lodi period, the tendency to have religious discourses with the Hindu Yogis developed further. Some of the Muslim nobles are said to have changed their faith under their influence. Among them were Ahmad khan, son of Mubark Khan Lodi, the governor of Lakhnoti and Nasir Khan, Muslim controller of Kalpi who renounced Islam and adopted Hinduism.[32]

Thus, the rulers were Muslims but the state was not theocratic. It was not ruled according to the Shariat but with the clear-cut motive of retaining power and expanding the empire. Most of the Sultans sought the support of the ulema by giving them honours, favours and deference but did not allow them to interfere with the statecraft. Ironically, the ulema had high praises for those Sultans and held them as Ghazi. During Khusrau Khan (a Hindu convert to Islam) reign, mosques were defiled, and copies of the scriptures of Islam were desecrated. When Ghiyasuddin Tughlaq threatened him, he not only paid his army several years of salary in advance but also sent large gifts to the ulema to obtain their blessings and support. Of these only three refused to take any thing from him.[33] In fact all through this period most of the ulemas acted according to Abdal-Muttalib`s theory "Take care of your camel; God will take care of His House." That is why Amir Khusrau considered them "a gang of hypocrites, conceited and detestably selfish."[34]

The early Sultans did not hesitate to adopt Hindu symbols on their coins, though it was a violation of the popular sentiment among their co-religionists. They stamped on their coins such Hindu symbols as lotus, trident, swastika, the letter sree and portrait of

Goddess Lakshmi. On the coins of Sultan Mahmud of Ghazni is found the portraits of the Hindu bull, Siva`s emblem; and Kalima is in Sanskrit. Tankas were issued with humped bull or Rajput horseman and the sovereign's name in Sanskrit till 1280. Sultana Raziya`s coin bears the portrait of the Rajput horseman with Nagari script around as "Sri-Hamirah". Even Balban used Nagari script on his coins. Mohammad bin Tughlaq struck gold coins in imitation to the Hindu kings of Kanouj with the portrait of Goddess Lakshmi on the obverse.[35]

In smaller Muslim states which had made themselves independent of the Sultanate like Bengal and the Bahmani kingdom of Deccan or which did not fall under the sway of Delhi, i.e., Kashmir, a much more equitable policy had been followed by the rulers which endeared them to the masses.

Sharqi ruler, Ibrahim Shah was liberal in outlook. When he conquered Tirhut and gave it to Kirti Singh, he allowed Hindu customs to be followed in matters of coronation ceremony. The Sankh tremple was allowed to be played at the auspicious hour. His outlook accounted for the popularity of the Sharqui kingdom in eastern India.[36]

In the Deccan the religious liberalism was more profound than in the north. Alauddin Hasan (1347-58), the founder of the Bahmani kingdom, was a servant of a Hindu astrologer named Gangu Bahman. Once Hasan, while tilling the field chanced to discover a copper pot full of gold coins, which he carried to his master. Being impressed by Hasan`s honesty, he introduced him to the king who appointed him to command of [100] horses. Later Hasan became the sultan of Daulatabad. After being crowned Hasan called Gangu to his court, appointed him incharge of the finance department and called himself Gangu Bahmani and his regime as Bahmani kingdom.[37]

Shahabuddin Ahmad I (1422-36) was a disciple of a Sufi saint Gesuderaz. He believed in universal brotherhood and had high regard for Hindu Saints.He was loved and respected by both communities. He was called 'Hazrat Ahmad Shah Wali' by the Muslims and 'Allama Prabhu' by the Hindus. Even today on his death anniversary hordes of Hindu and Muslim men and women assemble at his grave and beg him to intercede with the Almighty on their behalf. Everyday, during the Urs, the Jangamor, the religious leader of the Lingayats, enters the Sepulcher in the garb of a Muslim

Darvesh, accompanied by a group of musicians and makes offerings of flowers which shows what strong influence the sovereign had on his people during his life time.[38]

Shahabuddin`s son and successor, Alauddin AhmadII (1436-1458) is praised by the writer of Guru-caritra as a raja who is a devotee of the Brahmans and gracious to his subjects without distinction of caste or creed He used to have discussions with the Pundits on religion and sought their counsel. Saint Narasimha Saraswati comforted him in his last illness.[39]

Similarly Adil Shahis of Bijapur (1490-1686) and the Nizamshahis of Ahmad Nagar (1490-1637) held liberal attitudes and adopted liberal policies. Ali Adil Shah (1558-1580) took delight in being called Adil Shah Sufi; held discussions with Brahmans and did not allow the ulema to interfere with the state policies. They tried to dissuade the king from praising the gods the Hindus as it was unbecoming for a Muslim. They pointed out: "The Brahmans who find God in cow, fire, sun, water etc, and regard what is intangible are ignorant people and therefore the Muslims who worship them go to hell." The king however did not appreciate this attitude of the orthodox and justified the Hindu practices and pointed out the futility in condemning other religions with a view to establishing one's own creed.[40]

Ibrahim Adil Shah II had two pandit advisors named Anter and Lakhu. He worshipped Hindu Goddess Sarswati. Signs of his reverence to this deity spilled over into the revenue bureaucracy as many of his official government documents, written in the Perso-Marathi language began with an invocation to her 'aj puja shrine Saraswati.' He used to join the Hindu musicians in their worship at the Saraswati temple in Bijapur It is also said that he had an image of Saraswati installed in the royal palace for his personal worship.[41]

In 1618-19 he granted some land endowments for the upkeep of a Hindu Temple at Chinchwad near Poona.[42] He also declared Thursday as holiday in honour of a Hindu god Dattacharya.[43] His Hindu subjects, out of affection, called him Jagat Guru (the Preceptor of the world).

Not only the kings but their nobles too shared the same spirit towards Hinduism and the Hindu institutions. General Ranadullah Khan of Bijapur's letter to first Guru (the spiritual head) of the Sringeri Math clearly makes it evident. He wrote:

"Salutations (Salam) of Ranadullah Khan. The blessings you

sent we reaa and listened to with great respect and regard and were pleased herewith. On further questioning your Yellappa, we understand your ideas fully. As your Yellappa represented that your Matha possesses Manya (rent-free) lands in Siva Maga (Shimoga) sime and you want takiti letters (letters of direction or command) from us to the effect that the villages should be compelled to be made over to your Math, we have got the necessary tikiti voles written and dispatched with letters of instruction. This may satisfy you and you may arrange to dispatch letters every now and then as to how for you require help from us and convey your blessings". [44]

Ibrahim Qutub Shah (1550-80) the ruler of Golkunda was called Malikbhram which associate his name with Rama.[45]

In Bengal, Hussain Shah was a liberal ruler. He gave equal respect and honour to all the religions and himself instituted the common worship of a new God, Satyapir. During his reign Bhakti movement led by Chaitanya flourished and even two of his ministers got converted to Vaishnavism. At Narayanpur, temples of Kali were erected by one Mirza Hosen Ali.[46] Mahmud Begarha became the sultan of Gujarat in 1459. He was benevolent and tolerant. A poem written by a poet Udayaraja called Mahmudacarita depicts the character of the king as:

"In battle Mahmud is equal to Bhima, in beneficence he surpasses Karna, in support he is like Narayana, in mercy he resembles Rama, in wisdom he is better than Brihaspati and in beauty he excels Mana matha."[47]

Sultan Muzaffar Shah II who ruled Gujarat in the 16th century revered Goddess Saraswati and respected the Brahmins.[48]

In Kashmir the kings followed the path shown by the Sufi- saints. The Muslim kings performed the Homa ceremony at the time of coronation, a tika (Hindu-mark) was applied on their forehead and offerings of gold and silver were made. The kings also performed Yagna (a religious Hindu ceremony) to avert the famine. Jonaraja writes that Shihabuddin, Sultan of Kashmir possessed of a spirit of religious tolerance. Once when the treasury was empty, his ministerUdayasri suggested the easy expedient way of melting the metal images of God and converting them into coins. Thereupon the king admonished him in the following words:

"Some have obtained renown by setting up images of God, others by worshipping them; some by duly maintaining them; and I shall be

Eternally disgraced by demolishing them, King Shihab-ud-din, it will be said, plundered the images of God; and this bad renown will torment men in future"[49]

Shihabuddin continued to scribe the figure of the Goddess Lakshmi on his gold coins, a fact, which indicates the extent to which religious liberalism existed. After Shihabuddin's death, his brother Qutbuddin became the Sultan. He, too, like his brother was liberal in religious matters. In Alaudin.Pur, for example, there was a temple, which was a temple, which was visited every morning by the Sultan and his Muslim subjects. To overt famine Qutbuddin once performed the Yagna and distributed large gifts to Brahmins and in contravention of Islamic teachings, he had two wives who were sisters. In Kashmir, religious tolerance was at its zenith during the reign of Zainul Abidin. He issued a decree that in his dominions there should be no discrimination between one and another on the basis of religion.[50] He persuaded all those new Muslims who had embraced Islam recently under compulsion to renounce it and to return to their former religion.[51] The Sultan on the advice of Sriyabhatta, reduced Jaziya to the nominal. That he did not entirely abolish the Jaziya was due to his respect for the opinion and sentiments of the Ulema. In actual practice, however, it was as good as abolished, for it was never collected. He abolished banned cow-slaughter, revived Hindu pilgrimage and constructed buildings for the accommodation of pilgrims.[52] He repaired old temples and built new ones. He frequently visited the famous Hindu shrines of Amarnath and Sharda Devi temples and had built there rest-houses to provide comfort to the pilgrims.[53] He used to perform Havans, studied Nilamatapurana, Vasishta, Gita Gobind and practised Yoga.[54] He restored grant of stipends to learned Brahmans and took an agreement from them that they would not act in contravention to what was written in their books.[55] Zain knew many languages including Sanskrit Tibetan, Persian and Kashmiri. He held the Sufis, Brahmins and Pandits in great respect and granted them lands. Pandits read out from various Shashtras while Srivara used to recite to him the Vashishtha, Brahmadarsana of Valmiki and Samhita along with their explanations and annotations.[56]

According to Jonaraja (Jonaraja died in the 35th year of the reign of Zain-ul-Abidin and his work was continued by his pupil Sivara), the Sultan daily fed fishes in some springs at Paryagas and forbade catching of birds and fishes in certain lakes and springs.[57]

He also invited the Hindus to study Persian. The first to study this language were the Kashmiri Sapru pundits who because of their intimacy to Sultan, were called the Sultan Pandits.[58] Zain was called Bud Shah (the great ruler) by all the Kashmiris and Bat Shah on account of his patronage of the Bats or the Pandits.[59]

Sher Shah, though a devout Muslim showed respect to Hindu saints and did not discriminate among his subjects on the basis of religion. So much so that he was described as "externally Muslim but Hindu internally."[60]

Delhi Sultanate had given complete religious freedom to the Hindus, recognised their personal law and maintained the pre-eminence of the Brahmins. Barani, laments the fact that the Sultans were not performing their religious duties and were tolerant. He wrote:

"...in the cities of Mussalmans the customs of infidelity are adhered to with great insistence than before. Openly and without fear, the infidels continue the teachings of their religion. They also adorn their idols and celebrate their festivals with the beat of drums and dhols and with singing and dancing."[61]

All this belies the view presented by the writers like Murry T. Titus that "during the first period, covering eight centuries, there seems to have existed in the minds of invaders, their resident Viceroys and the independent kings the hope that they would be able as thoroughly to Islamize the country..."[62] In Titus view the whole object of the sultans" was the religious one of either converting the infidels or of sending them to hell with sword.[63]

Infact the Sultans never intended to spread Islam by sword besides they did not pay any heed to the counsels of the ulama if it did not promote their political interests. Instead, in order to win over the hearts of the people, they followed the traditions of the land while making state policies and were not guided by the Shariat. This attitude initiated the process of liberalism of the Muslim rulers and laid the foundation of religious tolerance. With the passage of time, their initial policy of toleration had changed to respect for all religions, which became the cardinal principle of the state policy during the Mughal rule.

Mughal Rulers

The Mughal emperors except Aurangzeb believed in harmonious co-existence. They did not mix religion with politics and theirs was a liberal state. Religious liberty during their rule was not confined to believing in one's own religion but ushered a new atmosphere in which new religions like Sikhism and many syncretic cults emerged and freely flourished.

Babar, the founder of the Mughal empire in India, after the victory over Ibrahim, halted on the Jamuna bank opposite Delhi, in order to pay respect to the tombs of the Sufi saints.[64] During the invasion of Syedpur, the inhabitants were made prisoners on the order of Babur. Among them were Baba Nanak and Mardana. Hearing Baba Nanak`s hymns and Mardana`s spiritual music on the rebeck, Babar approached Nanak and asked for forgiveness. Nanak rebuked him to his face and said:

"Babur rules over Thurasen
Babur terrifies Hindustan"[65]

On Nanak`s advice Babar released not only all the prisoners but also ordered that all the prisoners should be clothed with robes of honour.[66] It is also said that Baba Nanak went to Babar again for getting the release of prisoners of other villages. He stayed with him for three days. Babar released all the prisoners and said to the Guru "Now, O Holy man of God, do pray for me that my empire in India may last from generation to generation" The Guru blessed him and said:

"If thou desirest to establish an empire in India, be one of the people of India. Make this country thy home. Treat thy Hindu and Muhammadan subjects alike. Let thy rule be a rule of justice and kindness. Deal mercifully with the vanquished and oppress not the non-combatants. Give up wine, gambling and other ignoble habits of today and worship God in spirit and truth"[67]

Babar followed Nanak`s advice throughout his life. In his short reign orthodoxy and fanaticism had no place. Babar gave the same advice to his son and successor Humayun. He instructed him to be just and kind towards his subjects and to respect all religions. In his secret Will Babar advised his son as:

"O my son! the empire of Hindustan consists of various religions, domination and sovereignty whereof has been bestowed on you by the grace of Almighty.It is incumbent that religious bigotry should be wiped off the tablet of the heart and justice meted out to each religion according to its tenets. Specially abstain from sacrifice of cows, as this would tend to win the hearts of the people of Hindustan. And the populace of the country would be adherent to royal favours. The temples and places of worship of whatever religion under the royal authority may not be desecrated…."[68]

Babar`s counsel was followed by Humayun. When he was fleeing from Hindustan after his defeat, he went to Guru Angad, the spiritual successor of Baba Nanak, at Lahore to seek his blessings and guidance. The Guru blessed him and said to him:

"Hadst thou not put thy hand on the hilt of thy sword, thou shouldst at once have obtained thy kingdom. Thou shalt now proceed for a time being to thine own country Persia, and when thou returnest thou shall recover thy possession"[69]

The emperor acted accordingly. Having obtained a reinforcement of cavalry from the king of Persia, he returned to India and after a pitched battle recovered his empire and captured Delhi. After his success, he felt grateful to the Guru. By this time Guru Angad was no more and Guru Amar Das reigned in his place.[70]

Emperor Akbar like his grandfather and father respected all the religions and religious saints. He visited the saints to get their blessings and guidance. In his reign complete religious freedom prevailed. Sikhism flourished and Guru Granth Sahib, the Holy book of Sikhs was compiled. The Sikh Gurus, too prayed for the prosperity and stability of his empire Guru Amar Das (1479-1574A.D) advised Emperor Akbar that he should establish a common and conciliating rule in India with the active assistance of Hindu Rajas and nobles to maintain a balance against Afghans from whom the Mughals had wrested the empire of Hindustan in 1526A.D.[71]

The Guru had also prayed for the success of Akbar in his expedition on Chittor and Akbar was successful. During one of his periodical visits to Lahore Akbar made a detour to Goindwal and paid a state visit to the Guru. The emperor out of respect for the Guru, waited on the bare ground as he approached his residence. He was told that he could not have an interview with the Guru until he had taken Langar (food) which consisted of coarse unseasoned rice. He asked for some and partook of it as if it were ambrosia. On seeing the Guru, Akbar bowed and touched his feet.[72] Having seen the large number of people being fed from the Guru's free kitchen, Akbar requested the Guru to accept his services and offerings. When the Guru declined, Akbar assigned the revenue of several villages to Bibi Bhani, the Guru's daughter. On Guru's request Akbar remitted the whole land tax of Lahore for the year with the remark that "Gooroo was the friend of the poor" [73]

The land on which, the city of Amritsar developed was given by Akbar to the fourth Guru Ramdas. The ground bestowed being of circular form was named Chukkur Ramdas. In this enclosure the Guru built Amritsar. Mian Mir laid the first foundation brick of the temple Sri Darbar Sahib at Amritsar.[74]

Akbar was blessed by fifth Guru Arjun Dev. (1563-1606) The emperor called himself the slave of the Guru and sought his instructions for happiness and peace for the soul. The Guru said:

"The welfare and happiness of the monarch depend upon cherishing their subjects and doing justice. The monarchs whose subjects are happy shall himself be happy in this life and in the next obtain praise, glory and honour"[75]

Akbar followed the advice and won a place in Indian history, which no other monarch has ever occupied. He was the most popular, highly respected and deeply loved by his people. Guru's activities and increasing influence aroused the wrath of the Brahmins and they complaint to the Emperor that the Guru was against Hinduism. Akbar however did not find any hostility against Hinduism. He said:

"To repeat or not to repeat the Gayatri is at his own discretion. It certainly doth not concern me to cause the

Gayatri to be repeated or twilight devotions performed...There is no difference between God and His darwesh."[76]

Then the emperor like a head of the family took aside the Guru's representative and told him to request the Guru, who before his conversion to Sikhism, used to make a yearly pilgrimage to the Ganges, to make one pilgrimage more in order to divert the wrath of the Brahmins.[77]

When Guru Arjun compiled Guru Granth Sahib, some Qazis and Pandits made a complaint to Akbar that in the Holy Book the Prophets and the Hindu gods were spoken of with contempt. Upon this Akbar invited the Guru to clarify about the charges made. The Guru sent his representatives Bhai Budha and Bhai Gurdas with the Holy Book. The emperor himself heard Guru's own compositions and the hymns and teachings of Guru Granth Sahib. He then gave his decision:

"Excepting love and devotion to God. I so far find neither praise nor blame of anyone in the Granth Sahib. It is a volume worthy of reverence"[78]

He also made an offering to the Holy Book of 51 gold mohars

(English Guinea) and dresses of honour to both Bhai Budha and Gurdas. He sent one dress for guru Arjun along with his salutations. At the guru's request, he also remitted the annual revenue of the district to ameliorate the condition of the peasants who had been hard hit by the failure of the monsoon.[79]

Not only the emperor but his ministers and officials too paid reverence to the Guru when the Guru visited Lahore. A large number of people, along with the local Sufi saints and officials assembled for his blessings and instructions. The Viceroy of Lahore too paid a visit to the Guru and ordered for the excavation of a Bawli in Guru's name at his own expense. Wazir Khan, the emperor's assistant prme-minister was also a disciple of the Guru and always espoused his cause.[80] Emperor's patronage and admiration gave momentum to Nanak's movement. Many Muslims adopted Sikhism during Akbar`s reign.[81]

Even emperor Jahangir, as prince Salim is said to have himself made a grant of land in Kartarpur to Guru Arjun Dev in admiration and veneration. He handed over Chandu Shah (Guru's enemy) to Guru Hargobind, son and successor of Guru Arjun Dev. The Guru was held in high esteem by the emperor and even used to be invited by the ladies of the royal family for consultation.[82] Jahangir also visited Guru Hargobind at Amritsar, on way to Kashmir. He felt extremely happy to see the Guru`s magnificent Darbar Sahib and presented cash and kind worth thousand of rupees to him. He also made an offer to the Guru to bear all the expenses for the completion of the building of Akal-Takht, which the Guru politely declined. Empress Nurjahan and her co-queens also visited the temple and also went to meet the Guru's mother who gave them instructions and blessed them.[83] Jahangir also took him to Kashmir for the sake of his holy company. Jahangir was struck with the beauty of a rosary the Guru carried. He asked for one of its beads. He would add it to his own rosary and preserve it in memory of the Guru.[84]

The reverence for the Sikh Gurus by the Mughal emperors reflects in a letter written by Shahjahan to Guru Har Rai. Aurangzeb had administered tiger's whiskers in a dainty dish to prince Dara Shikoh who became dangerously ill in consequence. Emperor Shahjahan wrote to Guru Har Rai who had the medicine for the disease:

"Thy predecessor, the Holy Baba Nanak granted sovereignty to the Emperor Babar, the founder of my dynasty; Guru Angad was exceedingly well-disposed to his son, the Emperor Humayun and

Guru Amardas removed many difficulties from my grandfather Akbar`s path. I regret the same friendly relations did not subsist between Hargobind and myself and that misunderstandings were caused by the interference of strangers. For this I was not to blame. My son Dara Shikoh is now very ill. His remedy is in thy hand. If thou give me the myrobalan and the clove which are in they store-house and add to them thy prayers thou wilt confer an abiding favour on me."[85]

The Guru gave the medicine, which cured Dara.[86] Prince and the heir apparent, Dara paid frequent visits to Guru Har Rai and also sought his help against Aurangzeb. For this Dara met the Guru on the right bank of the Bias. Guru instructed him as: "Go to Lahore, fortify thy position, fight when necessary and obtain victory. God assists those who assist themselves." Before departing to Lahore Dara requested the Guru to impede as much as possible the progress of pursuing army sent by Auragzeb.[87] The Guru provided a force of armed retainers to make good his escape and thus saved his life. On the conclusion of hostilities, Aurangzeb summoned Guru Har Rai to explain his conduct. The Guru sent his son, Ram Rai, to represent him. Ram Rai succeeded in winning the confidence of the emperor. Aurangzeb gave him land in Dehradun, where two gurudwaras were built.[88]

Emperor Bahadur Shah, Aurangzeb`s son and successor had high regards for Guru Gobind Singh. In the war of succession between Bahadur Shah and his brothers, Guru Gobind Singh sent his army to fight for Bahadur Shah, which helped him to win. After the success the two became good friends. They met at Humayun tomb, Delhi and discussed their future plans and also witnessed an elephant and bullfight, organized for their entertainment. Later a Gurdwara Damdama Sahib was constructed at that spot.[89] The emperor sent trays of rarities and fruits to Anandpur to the Guru. And the Guru was the only one who was allowed to enter the fort of Bahadur Shah wearing arms. This makes explicit how much trust Bahadur Shah had on the Guru.[90]

When an Afghan wounded the Guru the emperor sent his own physician to treat the Guru. After Guru's death, Bahadur Shah refused to confiscate his property of considerable value as per rule. The emperor with the remark that he was not in want of the goods of a Darwesh, ordered the whole to be relinquished to the heirs.[91] Emperor Muhammad Shah granted the village of Mustipur Taradih to mahant Lal Gir of Bodh Gaya. The income from the zamindari area amounted to several lakh rupees. The Natha jogis of Jakhbar received revenue grants during the reign of Muhammad Shah. Besides all the grants made to the priests and faqirs during the previous regimes continued. When Raja Jai Singh Sawai submitted a petition to the imperial court that at Barielly, the officers confiscated the goods of some bairagis and mahants after their death, Shah Alam issued an order for the restoration of the deceased's properties to their lawful heirs. It was stated in the order: "The present auspicious reign is the fountain and source of peace and tranquility to all creatures of God. These faqirs are the holy recluses who are revered by the Hindus and the Muslims alike; and they form the army of dua-goyan."[92]

This spirit of religious liberalism was not confined to Mughals only. It in fact was the norm of the day.

The Nizam of Hyderabad made an endowment for the upkeep of Guru Gobind Singh's mausoleum at Nander by the grant of five villages in addition to the salary of the granthi.[93] A well-known Gurdwara Akal Bhoonga was built there. When the Gurudwara used the drums and bugles, the Muslim objected to music before the Mosque, which stood next door. But the rulers did not shift the Gurdwara as demanded instead converted the Mosque into one "for women only." No women however went to offer Namaz. It remained closed.[94]

Once Nawab of Hyderabad sent a grand canopy as one of the gifts to Maharaja Ranjit Singh, who found it too good for his royal use and gave it to the Harmandir Sahib to provide a cover for the sacred Granth Sahib.[95] The Nizam of Hyderabad also established a department of Sikhs (Mahikma-I- Sikhan) and sent two costly Chandanis with pearls and gems with rupees one lakh each for Nander and Darbar Sahib Amritsar. He fixed a jagir worth thousands of rupees for free Langer at Nander. He also wanted to build a Gurudwara there with gold bricks and pearls as mud and cement in the memory of Guru Gobind Singh.[96]

Thus, during the age when fanaticism and bigotry were rampant in other parts of the world, in India, religious liberalism was the guiding principle of the state. Equal respect and attention and no discrimination and prosecution on the basis of religion by the rulers ensured the development of all religions including Hinduism

Hinduism

In the quest of realizing the Almighty, not only the masses but the rulers also sought the guidance from the saints belonging to different religions. Akbar used to hold discussions with saints in order to ascertain the religious truth. His letter written to Philip XI of Spain speaks of his religious quest and liberal outlook towards all religions:

"As most men are fettered by the bonds of tradition, and by imitating the ways followed by their fathers ancestors, relatives and acquaintances, everyone continues, without investigating the arguments and reasons to follow the religion in which he was born and educated, thus excluding himself from the possibility of ascertaining the truth, which is the noblest aim of the Human intellect. Therefore, we associate at convenient reasons with learned men of all reasons and thus drive profit from their exquisite discourses and exalted aspirations"[97]

Akbar acquired the knowledge of Hinduism through Puzukhotam and Debi. He listened to Vedas and respected the Hindu saints. Dadu was one of them. It is said that he wished to attend Dadu`s Brahm Society and accept its teachings. In 1586 Akbar met Dadu and talked to him for forty days. Akbar was deeply impressed by his devotion and even took his women-folk to receive the saints blessings.[98] Akbar along with Tansen visited Mirabai.He paid homage to her and she accepted from him a necklace as an offering to be made at the lotus feet of her Lord Krishna.[99] The emperor also went to see Saint Surdas along with Tansen. It is said that Akbar's relations with saint Jadrup initiated him in to the doctrines of Vaishnavism. Akbar held the saint in a high esteem and whenever he passed by Ujjain, he paid a visit to Jadrup in his cave. He used to have religious discourses with the saint who satisfied his spiritual quest.[100]

The emperor conferred the title of 'Goswami'upon Vithaleshvara, who had impressed him with his learning and piety. In 1576-77 he visited the saint for religious discourses and gave him a gift of lands of Gokul. A Farman was issued which stipulated these lands free from any taxes. Hamida Bano Akbar`s mother too issued Farmans in favour of the saint.[101] At Gokul, Vithaleshvara allowed Akbar the darshan of his beloved Shri Nathji.[102] Akbar`s liberal approach in the matters of religion was appreciated and acclaimed by saint Tulsidas also.[103] Akbar advised Todarmal to be liberal in religious beliefs rather than follow the orthodox path blindly, when the latter lost his idol, without whose worship he did not take even a morsel.[104]

Jahangir wrote about Akbar`s religious liberalism in his Tazuk as:

"But in his character one prominent feature was that every religion he seems to have entered, through life, in to terms of unreserved concord and with the virtuous and enlightened of every class, of every sect and profession of faith, he did not scruple to associate, as opportunities occurred".[105]

All religions flourished during his reign as he being the sovereign paid respect to all alike. He gave generous endowment to temples and himself raised a temple in Kashmir. Abul Fazal wrote the following inscription for it:

"O" God in every temple I see people that seek Thee, and in every language I hear spoken people praise Thee, Polytheism and Islam feel after Thee, Each religion says, Thou art one without equal.[106] It was also stated" This temple was erected for the purpose of binding together the hearts of the Unitarians of Hindustan and especially those of His worshippers who lived in the province of Kashmir.

By the order of the Lord of throne and the crown,
The lamp of creation, Shah Akbar.
He who from insincere motives destroy this temple
Should first destroy his own place of worship;
For if we follow the dictation of the heart,
We must bear up with all men, but if we look
To the external we find everything proper to be destroyed.[107]

On the order of the emperor a small temple was built within the fort of Fatehpur Sikri.[108]

As was the emperor so were his ministers. Abul Fazal too had a high opinion of Hinduism and held the Kashmiri Brahmins in high esteem. He even rationalised and justified idol worship.[109]

Thus the gods of other religions were no stranger and were equally respected and revered by the believers of other religions. Akbar like a Hindu devotee, presented a golden umbrella to the shrine of the fire goddess of Jwalamukhi in the modern district of Kangra in Punjab.[110] Akbar visited and spent sometime in Gorkhatri, a shrine of Jogis in Peshawar.[111]He worshipped the Sun and had collected 1001 Sanskrit names of the Sun and read them daily. He prostrated every morning in the worship of the Sun. He regarded fire as manifestation of God, and 'a ray of His rays'[112]. He had ordered that a fire-flame should be burning at a specified place in the royal fort for all twenty-four hours. The practice of everybody present standing up in reverence when the lamps were lit in the evening became a ceremonial in his Court.[113] He sent a copy of the Mahabharta and a list of the names of God to his son Murad to help him in his prayers.[114] Abul Fazal writes in Ain-i-Akbari that on Emperor's command the epics of other religions were read to him.[115]

Akbar also issued two gold and one silver coins, known as Sia-Ram coins (one gold coin is kept in British Museum and another in France .The silver coin is kept in Kala Bhavan at Kashi. One side of the coin mentions the year and the other side has the pictures of Sita and Ramchandra.)[116] His reverence for Hindu gods won him the highest regard from the Brahmins who regarded him as Ram-Krishna's incarnation.[117]

Akbar wanted all faiths to flower and their followers to live in peace and with equal dignity. The following verses make explicit his religious approach:

"I hate the rancor of their caste and creed,
I let them worship, as they will, I reap,
No revenue from the field of unbelief
I call from every faith and race, the best.
And bravest soul for counselor and friend"[118]

Akbar in a letter to Shah of Persia opined:

"The various religious communities are divine treasures entrusted to us by God. We must love them as such. It should be our firm faith that every religion is blessed by Him and our earliest endeavour to enjoy the bliss of the ever- green garden of the universal toleration. The eternal king shower his favours on all men without distinction. Kings who are shadows of God should never give up this principle."[119]

In a letter, written to his son Murad Akbar emphasized his secular outlook: "don't be offended by diversity of religion. Struggle hard to sit in the shade of peace with all."[120] He instructed both Murad and Daniel his sons when put in charge of a suba"Let not difference of religion interfere with the policy."[121]

Like Zainul Abidin, Akbar also promulgated a decree, which declared that no person was to be interfered with on account of his religion. A strict action was taken against those who tried to impose their religious convictions upon others. Under one of his regulations Hindus who had become Muslims under pressure were allowed to return to the faith of their forefathers.[122] His ministers were vigilant to ensure that the state should secular and stood for justice. When a Mughal official converted a Hindu temple into a Muslim school, he was severely punished by Todarmal.[123]

The Hindus were made to feel that the emperor considered himself as much their protector as of any one else. In deference to the Hindus sentiments, he prohibited the slaughter of the cow. It was a crime punished by amputation.[124] He prohibited the eating of beef and himself abstained from beef, garlic and onions. In 1563 he abolished the tax on Hindu pilgrims at Mathura and other Holy places and in 1564 Jaziya was done away with throughout his dominions.[125]

In such a cordial environment diversity in spiritual matters led to the development of all faiths much to the annoyance of orthodox who were denied any special privileges and interference in the running of the state administration. A Sharif of Amul, who was expelled on account of his religious views from every Muslim country found safe asylum in India where he was allowed to preach his own philosophical view-point. He wrote:

"Hindustan is a wide country where there is an open field for all and no one interferes with another's business so that everyone can live just as he pleases."[126]

Disgruntled Mullas made desperate attempts to dislodge the secular sovereign. He was condemned and characterized as 'Devil'. A mullah of Jaunpur urged a general revolt against Akbar. The orthodox also made contacts with Akbar's brother Mirza Hakim, the ruler of Kabul and invited him to Hindustan in order to raise him to the throne. Though failed in their attempt, they never forgave him and went to the extent of denying him a burial according to Muslim rites.[127]

Jahangir, the son and successor of Akbar followed the path shown by his father. He respected Hinduism, held religious discourses with the Hindu saints, sought their guidance and visited the Hindu shrines.

Jahangir was deeply influenced by saint Jadrup whom he met with his father who took the prince to the saint for his blessings. When Jahangir became the emperor he visited the saint many a times and revered him like a true devotee. In his Tazuk (memoirs)

Jahangir writes:

"On Saturday, for the second time, my desire for the company of Jadrup increased. After performing the mid-day devotions I ran and enjoyed his society in the retirement of his cell. I heard many sublime words of religious duties and knowledge of divine things. Without exaggeration, he sets forth clearly the doctrines of Sufism and one can find delight in his society. He is sixty years of age. He was twenty-two when forsaking all external attachments, he placed the foot of determination on the high road of asceticism and for thirty eight years he had lived in the garment of nakedness... God Almighty had granted him unusual grace, a lofty understanding, an exalted nature and keen intellectual powers etc...On Wednesday I again went and bade him god-bye. Undoubtedly parting from him weighed upon my mind which desires the truth".[128]

Such was the influence of Jadrup on Jahangir that the latter not only released prince Khusrau from prison upon his intercession but often changed laws in the state to make them conform to Hindu standards. In the Tazuk-i-Jahangiri; the emperor himself speaks of how at the suggestion of Jadrup he had been tempted to change the laws even of his revered father, Akbar and how accordingly he had ordered that thenceforth the weighing of seer would be thirty- six dams, in accordance with what is laid down in the Hindu text, setting aside the old decree of Akbar that the seer should be thirty dams which had prevailed then. The Muslim nobles were not slow in following the footsteps of their masters. Many Muslim nobles visited the saint and sought his blessings. Abdur Rahim Khan-I-Khanan used to offer Sijda to Jadrup. The author of Dabistan-I-Mazhib himself met the saint and learnt from him the mantar Suraj (dua'ai Aaftab, worship of sun).[129]

The British Ambassador Sir Thomas Roe, records another instance of Jahangir's devotion to Hindu saints. He writes;

"This miserable wretch, clothed in rags, crowned with feathers, covered with ashes, His Majesty talked with, for about an hour with such familiarity and show of kindness that it must needs argue a humility not easily found among kings. The beggar sat where his son (Jahangir) dare not do...and after many strange humiliations and charities, raising the old wretch not being nimble, he took him up in his arms, which no cleanly body durst have touched, embracing him; and three times lying his hands on his heart, calling him father, he left him and all of us and me in admiration of such virtue in a heathen prince".[130]

He revered saint Surdas and Tulsidas and is said to have visited Swami Tulsidas to get his blessings. He got his picture made for himself and also offered some lands which the saint declined.[131] Both the saints wrote their immortal works during his reign. Had the state been theocratic or hostile to other religions these works could not have been written.

Like his father, Jahangir too used to offer salutations to sun as it rose in sight. He instructed a commission of religious persons to arrange for him a collection of the simple names of God. He was furnished with a list of 522 exactly double the number of those contained in Akbar`s rosary. The names were arranged under twenty numerical letters that Jahangir inscribed in his mantle.[132]

Jahangir continued Akbar`s practice of inviting Hindu scholars and divines to the court and held discussions with them. He was very keen to meet the Jogis and visited for the purpose the Gorkhkhatri near Peshawar which was an important centre of the jogis.[133] The emperor visited the temple of Goddess Durga at Kangra. When he visited Jwalamukhi temple, he gave order that the adjoining buildings should also be repaired and added to the temple.[134] He visited several other important Hindu religious centres and gives descriptions of the temple of Brindaban, Hardwar and the lofty temples of Kashmir. His description of Hardwar that was visited according to Roe by over half a million of pilgrims every year is worth mentioning. He writes;

"Hardwar is one of the most famous places of worship of Hindus and many Brahmans and recluses have chosen a corner of retirement in this place and worship God according to the rule of their religion. I gave alms in cash and goods to each of them according to their requirement".[135]

At Kangra, he visited the famous Bhawani Temple located inside the fort (Punjab). In his Memoirs, he writes that not only the Hindus, crowds on crowds of the Muslims, traversing long distance used to bring offerings and prayed goddess Bhawani. Magnificent temples were made during his reign at Brindaban, Banaras and Mathura and were visited by a large number of Muslim pilgrims besides Hindus. The emperor gave rich grants to the temples and the Pundits. He issued a Farman and provided land in Mauza Pushkar to Hindu religious leaders who were responsible for looking after the ceremonies of the Hindu Pilgrims.[136]

Jahangir maintained the secular approach of the state. Sir Thomas Roe wrote in 1616 concerning what he had witnessed of Jahangir's administration as follows:

"Tamerlain`s offspring brought in the knowledge of Mohammad but imposed it on none. By the law of conquest, leaving consciences at liberty."[137]

Akbar`s policies continued during Jahangir's reign. Once he was advised to impose Jaziya, he got furious He was not content simply to repudiate the suggestion and rebuke the rash and selfish proposer of it, but punished by cutting his head for having "had the temerity to seek his own profit at the expense of his Sovereign's reputation, the welfare of the community and good ordering of the state."[138] Besides, he maintained previous orders of not slaughtering animals twice a week, on Sunday and Thursday. This was strictly enforced. He used to visit the city in order to discover how far his orders were being obeyed. Once he discovered meat being sold on one of his visits. The Kotwal, the officer responsible for seeing that the royal orders were observed, was called for and flogged. So strict, however, was Jahangir in enforcing his injunctions that in the in the fourth year the Id fell on a Thursday, the sacrificial slaughter of animal was postponed to the following Friday.[139]

Jahangir's son and successor Shah Jahan and Prince Dara, Shah Jahan's son had liberal outlook in religious matters. Shah Jahan honoured Pandit Jagannath with the title Panditraja. The emperor reserved the right of giving final decision in religious matters and was daily blessed by Pandit Jagannath with address as "Dillishwara -ba Jagdishwara" (The Lord of Delhi is the Lord of Universe) Manrique states that in Orissa Peacocks, regarded as sacred animals were not allowed to be killed during Shahjahan`s reign. Dara was a disciple of Baba Lal and patronized a number of Banaras Brahmins. Goswami Narsimah Sarswati and pundit Jagannath enjoyed his special favour.[140] The great dream of Dara's life, which was shattered by his untimely death., was the brotherhood of all faiths and unity of mankind. For long years he studied Sanskrit and along with her sister Jahanara studied Hindu epics and Vedas with great avidity. At his command fifty of Vedas were translated into Persian.[141] He presented a stone railing to the temple of Kesho Rai at Mathura. He gave full liberty to Jai Singh, Raja of Jaipur to appoint the presiding Priest at the temple of Brindaban built by Man Singh.[142]

Dara's study of Hinduism and Islam had convinced him that

there was no difference between the two. In his Tariqat-al-Haqiqat Dara wrote:

"Thou art in the Kaaba as well as in the Somnath Temple;
In the convent as well as in the tavern
Thou art at the same time the light and the Moth;
The wine and the cup, the sage and the fool;
The friend and the stranger
Thou art thyself the rose and the amorous nightingale
Thou art thyself the moth around the light of thine own beauty."[143]

Besides Dara wrote an interesting introduction to the Persian translation of a compendium of the Joga Vishshta Ramayana made under his supervision with the title Tarjuma-Joga Vashishta in 1656 A.D it runs:

"When I had gone with the Persian translation of this book which is attributed to Sheikh Sufi, I saw in a dream two dignified figures of calm appearance, one of them standing on a higher level than the other. I was drawn involuntarily to their presence...and Vashishta with great affection and graciousness placed his hand on my back and said: 'Rama here is an earnest seeker of knowledge and a comrade(brother) of yours in true Search of the Reality; embrace him. Ramchandra held me in his embrace with great warmth and love. Then Vashishta gave to Ramchandra some sweets, which I ate out of his hand. Having seen this in dream my desire to have this translated became greater than ever; and one man among my servants was appointed to translate this work. This translation was completed under the supervision of the Pandits of Hindustan."[144]

Dara's approach towards Hinduism like his great grandfather Akbar was that of a seeker of truth, in whose heart was burning passion for knowledge. In this quest for unity of God, he came to know that Hindu Monotheists had given a clear exposition of the same, and so turning towards Hinduism he observed;

"Therefore I considered on what account is Hindustan conspicuous for monotheism, is there so much discourse on Divine Unity and wherefore in the exterior and interior practices of this most ancient sect of Hind, is their no disavowal of the Divine unity and no apostasy against the Unitarians."[145]

Dara wrote in his work Risala-i-Haqnuma: "ba-zer-i-but imanist pinhan" i.,e. Faith lies hidden beneath the idol.[146] He translated the Upanishads because he regarded them as Divine Secrets and

"Without doubt or suspicion, the first of all the heavenly books, in point of time, the source of the fountain of the Reality and an ocean of Monotheism, in conformity with the Holy Koran and even a commentary thereon."[147]

Because of his liberal views, the forces of conservatism and reaction termed him as an apostate and a heretic. The author of Alamgir Nama charged Dara with the zeal of an orthodox Muslam:

"Dara Shikoh in his later years did not restrict himself to the free thinking and heretical notions which he had adopted under the name of Tasawwaf (Sufism) but showed an inclination for the religion and institution of the Hindus. He was constantly in the society of Brahmans, yogis and sanyasis...He considered their books which they call Bed (Vedas) as being the word of God and revealed from the heaven, and he called them ancient and excellent books, in the translation of which he was much employed. Instead of the sacred name of Allah, he adopted the Hindu name Prabhu (Lord)... and he had this name engraved in Hindi letters upon his ring...Through these perverted opinions, he had given up fasting and other religious obligations imposed by the law and... it became manifest that if Dara Shikoh obtained the throne, and established his power, the foundations of Faith would be in danger and the precept of Islam would be changed for the rant of Infidelity (Hinduism) and Judaism".[148]

Dara's Majma-ul-Baharin (meeting of the two oceans) in which he made a comparative study of fundamentals of Islam and Hinduism, again annoyed the fundamentalists. However Dara convinced of his viewpoint never cared of their opposition. He and his wife like Akbar and Jahangir made their obeisance to the sun every morning and when the lamps were lightened in the evening, every member of their household stood up in reverence to the Goddess of Fire.[149]

Even orthodox emperor Aurangzeb, who is known for demolition of temples held Hindu saints in respect and conferred jagirs on the temples and the pundits, maths and yogis. While camping at the fort of Mandsaur, on his way to Deccan. About three hundred years have passed since the death of Aurangzeb, yet up to this day the priests of many Hindu temples in India have in their possession copies of royal farmans according to which jagirs were bestowed upon those temples under orders of Aurangzeb. The Hindu Priest of the temple of Someshwarnath in Arail, near Allahabad and of the Jangamwari Shiva Temple in Banaras still have copies of Aurangzeb`s Farman in their possession.[150] In 1659 to 1685 he issued Farmans in favour of Jangum Badali Shiva temple and great temples of Mahakateshwara Ujjain, Balaji temple Chitrakut, Umanand temple Gauhati and the Jain temple of Shtrunjal and Abu. He gave land endowments to Hindu temples at Maheshwar Nath, Benars, Mahshpur Multan and to the maths in the state of Marwar, in Rajasthan.[151] It is also said that Aurangzeb issued an order by which a jagir of ten villages in the Devsar Pargana (Kashmir) was given as present to Rishi Pir. He also conferred upon him the title of Padshah-i-har-do-jahan.[152] Besides he continued all through fifty years of his reign strict enforcement of the prohibition against cow-slaughter throughout his empire.[153]

Capt.Alexander Hamilton, in describing the conditions in Bengal, during the reign of Aurangzeb wrote:

"There are above one hundred different sects...but they never have any hot disputes about their doctrine or way of worship. Everyone is free to serve and worship God in his own way and prosecutions for religion's sake are not known among them".[154]

Emperor Bahadur Shah, son of Aurangzeb made a grant in favour of Swami Paramhansa of the Sharda Math in the sacred place of Kanchi, embodying in it an annual grant of 115 varhas meant for the worship and daily offerings to the God Candramaulisva and for feeding the brahmins.[155] Sultan Mohammad Murad Bakhsh made a grant that a four seers of ghee be given annually from the stores of Ujjain so that the temple of Mahakal may be illuminated every night.[156] The Nawabs of Awadh offered grants to Vaishnava priests and Gosains of Mathura and Ayodhya. Asafuddualah patronised saint Jagjivandas, founder of Satnami sect.[157]

Jainism and Zorastrianism

Besides, Sikhism, Hinduism, Jainism, Zorastrianism too developed and got favours from the Mughal rulers. Jain Gurus were held in high esteem and Jain institutions were given liberal grants. Vijayasena Suri, Bhanuchandra Upadhayaya made a profound impression upon Akbar and influenced his mode of life. In obedience to their teachings, Akbar almost wholly abstained from eating flesh, renounced his beloved sport of hunting, prohibited slaughter of animals, earmarked days on which consumption of meat in any form was totally prohibited and ordered the release of the caged birds.[158]

Akbar conferred the title of Jagadguru on Harivijay Suri. The Adisvara temple on the sacred hill of Satrunjaya near Palitana in Kathiawar combines the praise of this teacher with that of his patron Akbar.[159] Akbar issued Farmans to the Governors, Jagirdars and other officials of the subas of Agra, Lahore, Multan, Malwa, Gujarat, and Bengal, granting the request of Harivijya Suri, the Acharya of the Jain Swetambara sect to hand over the control of the Kothis, temples, places of pilgrimage of the Jain Swetambara community throughout the empire. In the order it was also prohibited to kill the animals near these territories.[160]

Emperor Jahangir had many Jain Monks in his court. One of them Siddhi Chandra was honoured by him with the title of Nadir-i-Seamen and Khushfahm. During his reign many Jain images were consecrated and in the inscriptions of some of them the name of Padshah Jahangir were also engraved. In the middle of [1618], the emperor in accordance with the tenets of Jainism took a vow of not injuring any living creature.[161] Shah Jahan and Dara Shikoh also respected Jain Monks and their religious institutions.

Zorastrianism too had an impact on the life and thinking of the Mughal rulers. Its influence reflected in the reverence of fire by Akbar. He adopted the Persian names for the months and days and celebrated the fourteen Persian festivals. He wore under his clothes the sacred shirt and the girdle of the Parsees.[162] He bestowed on the Parsee priest Dastur Maharaj ji Rana of Gujarat two hundred bighas of land as a free grant in perpetuity and in 1595 added further grant of a hundred bighas of land to his son Kaikubad.[163] Mughal rulers, except Aurangzeb followed Akbar`s catholicity. Orthodox Aurangzeb even discontinued the royal celebrations of Nauroz festival of the Parsees.

Christianity

Christianity was also given equal respect. The Mughals from Akbar to Dara Shikoh were cordial towards Christian fathers. Akbar received the Gospel with reverence and sometimes took off his turban to show respect to the Christian's sacred book and relics. Akbar used to visit the Chapel and prostrated before the pictures of Jesus and Mary.[164]

Akbar took many Europeans in his service. Among them there being many Catholics, they petitioned the king to permit their religious priests to settle in Agra for the fact that without priests they could not exist. Akbar sent envoys to the city of Goa to obtain priests, whereupon the Jesuit fathers came. For them he ordered the construction of a Church in Agra. He entertained Jesuit Fathers at his court and also built a church in the palace and there he often attended Christian worship.[165] He gave the Fathers permission to baptize all those who wished to become Christians, to open a school to teach Portuguese and to build a Church at Lahore, Cambay and Agra.[166] In 1599 Lahore Chapel was completed to which Akbar sent costly gold and silk clothes for its adornment. He also sent from his own collection a picture of Mary for the chapel. When the Church at Lahore was consecrated, the Mohammedan Viceroy of Lahore honoured the ceremony by his presence. Great crowds of the city thronged the Chapel. Akbar went so far as to adopt the son of a Christian, Yaqub of Aleppo, who was also known as Mirza Iskandar, but did not convert him.[167] The liberality of the rulers reflected when the Fathers were allowed even to criticise Islam freely. A man who attempted to destroy the Church was imprisoned and was released only when the Fathers interceded for him Besides, the Fathers were empowered to give refuge to those who had offended against the law as the church had been declared a sanctuary by a royal decree.[168]

Akbar's broader outlook led him to entrust the education of his son Murad to the care of Fathers. He charged Abul Fazal to translate the Gospel and to distribute among the ulema. He often subscribed his letters with the sign of cross and as a symbol of appreciation of Christianity, he wore round his neck a cross and a locket containing the portraits of Jesus and Mary.[169]

Jahangir too had great regards for the Jesuit and bestowed several gifts upon them and their Churches. He also provided them large sum to erect their religious places. In a Farman Jahangir granted to Christians six Bighas of land situated in Mauza Agra.He also gave them a house and a church in Lahore. Officers were further ordered not to molest them for any tax and no obstruction should be caused during offering of their prayers.[170] Fathers were allowed to take out a procession through the town of a dead body of a Portuguese who had died at Fatehpur Sikri with Crucifixes and lighted tapers and to bury him with all publicity. He also permitted them to build a hospital and to establish a medical mission.[171]

The emperor also wore round his neck a locket-containing portrait of the Savior and the Virgin, marked his letters with the

Christian symbols and even permitted the Fathers to convert the people if they liked. At Agra twenty baptisms took place in 1606. Church processions with full catholic processions with catholic ceremonial were allowed to parade the streets and cash allowances were paid from the treasury for church expenses and the support of the converts.[172] But the most sensational of the conversions was the public baptism of Daniyal`s sons and a grandson of the emperor in 1610.

"The Princes clothed in Portuguese costume and wearing crosses of gold round their necks, proceeded on elephants from the palace to the church through the streets packed with eager spectators. At the church the princes were received with every sign of rejoicing and the bell was rung with such violence that it broke".[173]

They were baptized and given new names of a European complexion. However, after some time, they gave up their new faith and returned to Islam Terry commented on Jahangir`s religious state policy as; "All religions are to be tolerated and their priest held in high esteem."[174]

Dara had a secular approach in religious matters. Bernier wrote about Dara`s viewpoint regarding other religions as:

"Born a Mohammedan, he continued in the exercise of that religion; but although thus publicly professing his adherence to the faith, Dara was in the private a Gentile with a Gentile and a Christian with a Christian".[175]

A Dutch traveller, named Stavorinus, who visited India during the years from 1765 to 1776 wrote:

"These three distinct nations, the moors (Muslims), the gentoos (Hindus) and the Parsees whose religion is very different, yet exercised great toleration and indulgence in this respect towards one another. No one is molested on account of his religion, they may be seen together in and near the river, offering up their prayers, each to that being whom he adores, without any marks of derision or contempt being shown to anyone..."[176]

The non- sectarian and `peace with all` approach on the part of the rulers was not only confined to north. It was a principle followed by the rulers all over the country. The Mahanbhan Math of Otur (Poona) which was established by Chaitanya received land grant from the Nizamshahi rulers and confirmed by the subsequent rulers. It was for a short period confiscated but Chand Bibi renewed it in 1599 with this note that the officers should respect all such grants to

Hindus and Brahmins.[177]

The rulers of Hyderabad respected Hinduism, the Hindu saints and their institutions The Nizam made a grant to the Temple of Sitaram in the town of Hyderabad.[178] One of the inscriptions of Nizam Ali Khan, dated 1781 A.D. states that on a representation made by the agent of the Matha of Sringeri, on the strength of a former sanad issued to the swami of Sringeri, an order was issued under the Nizam seal to all the officers concerned, intimating that all the privileges accorded to Sacchidananda Bharti (1770-1814) of paying contributions on the marriages and other occasions should be continued, that the property of the disciples who died without heirs should vest in the Matha and that the swami had full powers to order inquiries in to the conduct of his disciples and to punish the delinquents. Later, in 1813 A.D. Chandulal, a prime-minister of Nizam addressed a letter to swami Narsimah Bharti expressing his pleasure at the swami's proposed visit to Hyderabad and submitting an order from the government of the Nizam to the effect that no one should disobey the authority of the swami in the matter of religion.[179]

In Mysore Haider Ali and his son Tipu Sultan were the patron of the Hindu saints.Col.Wilks described Haider as "half a Hindu" because he had ordered "the Jebbum to be performed in the Hindoo temples"[180] The Sultan used to seek the blessings of both Hindu and Muslim saints before embarking on any military campaign"[181] The letters of the Sultans makes evident the nature and depth of their respectful attitude towards the Hindu Shrine of Sringeri. Three such records in this temple of Sringeri belong to the reign of Haider Ali One such letter says:

"You are a great and holy personage. It is but natural for every one to cherish a desire to pay respect to you. As Saheb Raghunath Rao desires me to send you to him so that he may pay his homage to you, I request that you will accordingly undertake the journey and pay him a visit. For your journey I have sent by Ramaji one elephant, three horses, one palanquin and five camels; gold cloth for the Goddess; five pieces of silk cloth for the standard (nisari) a pair of shawl for your use and ten and a half thousand Rupees for expenses. Two pairs of cloth have also been sent."[182]

This letter ends by saying that it is from Nizam Haider Ali Khan Bahadur and is also decorated with a gold illumination. Another letter addressed to Abhinava Narsimha Bharti, acknowledges the swamis benedictory letter (asirvada pattrika) and presents, gives him his assurance of the continuance of inams and other grants to the Matha.[183]

Another letter relating to the days of Haider is stated to have been written in 1780 A.D. is addressed by him to all his officers concerned, directing them to see that that no obstruction is put in the way and the representatives of the Sringeri Matha in collecting the usual contribution and dues.[184] Sri Ranganathan temple was venerated by Hyder as well as his son Tipu. The explosion of a neighbouring magazine blew off once the temple tower. Hyder immediately ordered that the gopuram should be repaired at once by his own soldiers.[185]

Tipu Sultan was no less a devotee of the Sringeri math He sought the help of its Guru like a real Hindu when he was hemmed in with danger and often prayed for his blessings. Several of Tipu's letters (These letters were originally noticed in the Mysore Archaeological Report in 1937 are in Kannad and bear the 'Sun' seal of Tipu along with his signature in Persian) refer to an attack on his kingdom by three of his enemies, evidently the Nizam, the Maratha and the English, who so often harassed him He requested the Swamiji to bring about the destruction of these foes by means of religious ceremonies such as the Sata Chandi Japa and the Sahasra Chandi japa.[186] All the expenses for the performance of these ceremonies were given by Tipu. In one such letters Tipu requested the Swami to feed one thousand of Brahmins every day and to perform the ceremony according to the prescribed rites, making money gifts to the Brahmins engaged. When the ceremony was performed he sent Mohammad Raza, to see that no disturbance was caused by mischievous people during the ceremony. Later Tipu sent orders to Nagar to forward a palanquin for the Goddess Sarda and another for Swamiji's personal use.[187]

Tipu's reverence for the Swami becomes evident by the following letter dated 1793 A.D:

You are a jagadguru. You are always performing penance in order that the whole world may prosper and that the people may be happy. Please pray to God for the increase of our prosperity. In whatever country holy personages like yourself may reside, that country will flourish with good showers and crops"[188]

Moreover, Tipu did not confine his patronage only to Sringeri temple; he extended it to other temples of the kingdom as well. From the inscriptions on four silver cups, a silver plate and a silver spittoon belonging to the Lakhmikanta temple in the village of Kalale, it appears that the vessels were presents from Tipu. At Melukota, the Narayanaswami temple possesses some jewel and gold and silver vessels with inscriptions telling that Tipu presented them. He also gave to this temple twelve elephants and a kettledrum jewelled cup set with five kinds of precious stones at the bottom in the Srikentheswara temple at Nanjangud was a present from Tipu Sultan Padshah. There is a proverb in Kanakala of South Canara district "Tippu Sultan Ale Ruppe"in referring to the silver jewels that Tippu Sultan presented to Veer Hanuman Temple of Kanakala.

More than hundred and fifty six temples received lands and grants annually from Tipu.[189] In one instance he even ordered the construction of a temple. When Haider had invaded the Carnatic in 1780, he had laid the foundation of a Gaps Temple in Canjeevaram, but he could not complete it. When Tipu visited the town during the third Anglo-Mysore war, he made a grant of 10,000 Huns towards the construction of the temple and during his stay there he participated in the celebrations of the chariot festival and bore the cost of the fireworks on the occasion.[190] Out of the total sum 2,33,959 pagodas spent annually on religious places by Tipu, the Hindu temples received-1,93,959 pagodas, Mutts of Brahmins-20,000 pagodas and the mosques and dargahs-20,000 pagodas. These figures were given by his wazir Poorbiah who had betrayed Tipu and had gone over to the British. This belies the view that Tipu was anti Hinduism.[191] The Narsimha and the Gangadharesvara the two big temples are inside the fort and near his palace. He, as was customary with the rulers of Mysore, daily visited the temple of Lord Ranganatha located inside the fort of Seringapatnam before taking his breakfast.[192]

The last Mughal emperor Bahadur Shah used to visit the Hindu temples with a hallowed mark on his forehead and was welcomed by the Hindu priests who took him for a Brahmin. Bahadur Shah himself says:

"Butkhanon mein jab gaya main khenchkar qashqa Zafar
Bol utha woh But Brahman ye nahin to kaun hai.[193]

(When after applying tika I went to the Idol houses O Zafar the Idol bust said, if he is not a Brahmin who else can it be?)

Again he says:

"Qashqa mathe pe hai Zunnar gale mein hai Zafar
Bangaye ishq mein us But ke Brahman suchmuch"[194]

(With formal sandal mark on his forehead, Zafar wears round his neck the Brahmanic thread. Verily Bahadur Shah Zafar has become a Brahman out of his love for the Idol).

Thus the Muslim rulers though devoted to their own religion, had deep respect for all the religions of the land. They revered not only Allah but also Rama Krishna Nanak and Christ They prayed not only in Mosques but also visited Temples and Gurudwaras and sought the blessings of all the gods and goddesses The observance of counsels of saints belonging to different religions liberalized the outlook of rulers. The inter-religious marriages too contributed the spirit of assimilation and harmony and did much to soften the acrimonious differences between the two communities and intensified the process of liberalization of the Muslim rulers.

The Mughals were not the pioneers of this policy. The practice had begun as early as the Arab conquest of the Sind. According to Chach-Nama Muhammad bin Qasim had married a Hindu woman named Ladi.[195] Allauddin married Kamla Devi of Gujarat and princess Jhitai, daughter of Ram Deo of Deogger. Prince Khizar Khan was publicly married to Dawal Rani a Rajput Princess in [1315] (When sultan Kafur blinded Khizar, Dawal Rani nursed him with devotion. Later Sultan Kafur was assassinated and Mubarak Shah ascended the throne in Delhi. He asked for Dawal's hand and on refusal he killed Khizar khan)[196] Amir Khusrau's mother was a Rawal Rajput lady. Sultan Tughlaq's brother Rajab was married to Bibi Naila the daughter of Rana Mall Bhatti of Abhor. She was held in high esteem and her son Firoz became the king inspite of other claimant of the throne.[197] Sultan Firoz Shah was married to a Hindu Gujar girl.[198] Sultan Bahlul Lodi had married a Hindu wife and nominated her son Sikandar as successor to the throne to the exclusion of his sons and grandson of purer Afghan lineage.[199] Daughter of Rana Udai Singh of Mewar, was married to Ghias Shah. Bhawani Das, a relative of Rana Rai Mal gave her daughter's hand to Abdul Muzaffar Nasiruddin Shah in 1504. She was given the title of Rani of Chittori. Sultan Kutbuddin of Gujarat was married to Rani Rup Manjari. His successor Sultan Mahmud Bigarha was also married to a Hindu. Sultan Muzaffar Shah II too married three Rajput princesses, Rajbai, the daughter of Rana Mahipat, Laxmibai, daughter of Gohal Rajput and Bibi Rani. The last one had control of the palace and the army in her own hand. Seven thousand servants were in her service and she was counselor of great influence in the affairs of the kingdom.[200] In

Bengal, Sultan Shamsuddin Nika married a Hindu widow Fulmati who exercised great influence in state matters. Hussain Shah's two daughters were married to the sons of the highly respectable Brahmin Raja of Sakotia.[201]

In Deccan the Bahmani Sultan Firoz married the daughter of Devaraya, king of Vijayanagar in 1407. It was an arranged marriage and the Sultan along with his Barat went to Vijaynagar where the marriage took place with great pomp and show. The Sultan stayed at Raya's palace for three days and returned with his Hindu bride and a rich dowry.[202] The Sultan, Ibrahim Qutub Shah married a Hindu lady named Bhagirati. Sultan Mohammad Quli was born from her. Prince Mohammed Quli too was married to his beloved a Hindu girl called Bhagmati. It was an arrange marriage and it is also said that she was not converted after the marriage. The prince not only made her queen but also erected a modest temple for her alongside his own small mosque in the palace garden. He built a splendid new city a few years later and named it Bhagnagar.[203] Ahmad Shah Wali, the ninth Bahmani ruler wedded with the daughter of the Sonkhed.[204]

Yusuf Adil Shah, the first king of Bijapur married the sister of Mukand Rao, a Brahmin and she became his chief queen.[205] In Rajputana, Muhammad Shah of Gujarat married the daughter of the Raja of Idar in 1485. Rao Maldeo had married one of his daughters Bai Kanka to Sultan Mahmud of Gujarat and another Lal Bai to the Sur ruler, Haji Khan Pathan.[206]

In Kashmir Sultan Shihabuddin married Lakshmi and Shoba.[207] He founded a town named after his wife Lakshmi.[208] Sultan Qutbuddin was married to Sura Rani, a Hindu. Their eldest son Sikandar, who ascended the throne after his father, marrried Mira, the daughter of the Raja of Ohind. Sultan Zain-ul-Abidin married a Hindu girl Sunder Devi, daughter of Sunder Sena Raja of Rajauri. She was called with affection Sundermaji.[209] A daughter of Raja Manakdeo of Jammu was married to Raja Jasrath, the Muslim Gokhar chief.[210] On the other side, the Hindu was far too ridden with caste inhibitions to receive a Muslim lady in the inner most sanctum of his palace yet such instances were not unknown.

In Punjab Maharaja Ranjit Singh had two Muslim wives Gul Bahar and Moran. He had arranged marriages with both of them and consulted them in state matters. Gulbahar often went out riding on the same elephant with the Maharaja. She built a mosque also.

(The British Govt. paid her pension of rupees12000 per year until her death in 1863) Moran was Ranjit`s favourite wife. She did not wear veil and used to appear unveiled in public with Ranjit Singh. She was the only one in whose name Ranjit Singh issued a coin Moran Shahi. The coin bore a figure of a peacock in keeping with the queen's name. There is a Mosque named after her near the Moti Chowk in Lahore. A village in the district of Amritsar also bears her name.[211] The love affair of Peshwa Baji Rao with a Muslim girl Mastani is well known He married her despite the stiff opposition of his first wife and sons. Mastani accompanied the Peshwa even in the battlefield. She also bore him a son named Shamsher Bahadur. Baji Rao named a part of his palace, after Mastani. The Mastani Gate of the Shaniwar palace at Poona even today reminds the love of Peshwa for Mastani. She lived in the palace despite the displeasure of the Peshwa's family. When Baji was away, his family forcibly removed Mastani and kept her in confinement. When Shahu (Baji was Shahu's Chief-minister for twenty years) came to know about the plight of Mastani he asked Baji Rao's family to release her and to restore her to the Peshwa. Inspite of the royal wishes, Mastani was not released. It is said that Baji Rao could not bear her separation. He fell ill and died at the age of forty. When Mastani heard about Baji Rao's death she too died.[212] In 1787 when Mahadji Sindhia suffered reverses, reinforcements were dispatched from the south under the command of the Ali Bahadur as representative of the Peshwa's house.[213]

Emperor Akbar married Jodhabai, a Rajput Princess who exercised a great influence upon him. Akbar's marriages with the Hindu princesses were not forced upon Rajputs. These were the willing alliances as matrimonial alliance was not treated as a test of loyalty and submission. In the words of Prof. Satish Chandra "... no matrimonial alliances were entered in to with the Hadas earlier when Rao Surjan surrendered, nor with the rulers of Sisodia, Banswara etc. when they submitted to Akbar."[214] Akbar's son Salim (Jahangir) was married with Manbai, daughter of Bhagwant. She was given the title of Shah Begum. Khusrau was born from her. Jahangir`s another son Khurram (Shahjahan) was born of Jagat Gosain. Daniyal was married to the daughter of Rai Mal son of Rao Maldeo. Shahjahan was married to Bai Lilawati, a grand daughter of Raja Gaj Singh.[215] Aurangzeb also had two Hindu wives. Nawab Bai was the daughter of the Rajput Raja of Rajouri in Kashmir state.

Another Hindu wife was Udaipuri, mother of his favourite son Kambkash.[216] Though orthodox yet he continued the Mughal tradition of seeking Hindu brides for his sons Prince Azam and Muazzam were married to Hindu Princesses. Sulaiman Shikoh, eldest son of Dara Shikoh was married to the daughter of Amar Singh. Emperor Farukh Siyar had a Hindu wife named Inder Kunwar.[217] Emperor Muhammad Shah was married to Udham Bai. Mother of the last emperor Bahadur Shah Zafar was also a Hindu named Lal Bai.

The inter-religious marriages worked on a big way in the process of indianizing the Muslim rulers, secularizing the Indian State and harmonizing the Indian society. Ghiyasuddin Tughlaq, Sultan Firoz Shah, Sikandar Lodi, Mohammad Quli of Golkonda, Muzzafar Shah, Sultan Sikandar and Sultan Ali Shah of Kashmir, Emperor Jahangir, Shahjahan, Ahmad Shah and Bahadur Shah Zafar were born of Hindu mothers. They thus were as much Muslim as Hindu. Both mother and father shaped their ideas, ideals and outlook. They not only respected but also adopted the traditions, customs and ways of life of both the communities despite the ire of the orthodox of both the religions.

Emperor Akbar was born at Amarkot in Sind in a palace of a Hindu Raja, Rana Virsal Prasad. It was at the breast of Bibi Rupa that Akbar tasted Hindu milk. He married Jodhabai, a Rajput Princess without making her accept Islam.[218] Jodhabai had a little temple in the palace. Hom were prepared daily at Fatehpur and worship of Hindu deities was also observed.[219] Akbar used to drink only Ganges water and regarded his motherland Hindustan sacred to him. He ordered that the people should be buried with their heads towards the east and their feet towards the West. He even commenced to sleep in this position.[220] The soil where they were born was holy for them and they wanted to be buried here. Nadira, Akbar`s great grand daughter and wife of unfortunate Dara, died at Malik Jivan`s territory where Dara had taken shelter. Nadira before her death made a request to give her burial on the soil of Hindustan.[221] The last Mughal emperor Bahadur Shah Zafar died in exile at Rangoon crying for a small piece of land in his motherland for his dead body. The following couplet speaks of his yearning;

"Kitna hai badnasib Zafar dafan ke liye
Do gaz zamin bhee na mili kuae yar mein

Living together for centuries had made all the inhabitants of this land as one people. Customs and traditions of one community were adopted by the other and with passage of time it became difficult to mark a dividing line between the two communities. Akbar used to mark his forehead like a Hindu and had jeweled strings tied on his wrist by Brahmins by way of blessings. He also shaved the hair of the crown of his head and let the hair at the sides grow.[222]

The Hindu customs and conventions influenced the Muslim kings Ibn Batuta witnessed the ancient Hindu custom of carrying away the bride by real or pretended capture. (Rakshasa form of marriage) during the marriage of Sultan Muhammad Tughlaq's sister with Bedouin Sayyid.[223] Akbar followed many Hindu customs and ceremonies both in his private and public life. He did not circumcise his son Jahangir. His wife Jodhabai stuck steadfast to some orthodox practices of her birth by retaining the Ganges water, sacrificial fire, Tulsi plant and a Brahmin cook. Besides, he performed Jahangir`s wedding with a Rajput Princess in a Hindu fashion. The Barat of Jahangir consisted of Akbar and the principal men of the kingdom who paid a visit to the residence of Amber with whose daughter Man Bai, Jahangir was going to be married. There the marriage was solemnized with great splendor. The ceremonies observed were both Hindu and Muslim. Akbar personally participated in the marriage ceremonies. First of all Nikah took place in the presence of a Qazi and a sum of rupees two crores of tankas was fixed as marriage settlement for the bride (mehr). After this customary Hindu ceremonies of walking around the fire (fere) were observed. The couple went round the fire to the chanting of Vedic Mantra by Pandits, Bhagwant Das gave a rich dowry to the couple. The bridegroom Jahangir and Akbar both lent their shoulders to the palanquin in which the bride was to be conducted from her father's place.[224] Akbar like a Hindu scattered jewels and coined money over the bride and the bridegroom from the Raja's residence to his own place of encampment.[225] On the occasion the Raja gave expression to the feeling of elation and pride as:

"Our daughter is the maid servant of your palace and we are your slaves"

To this Akbar promptly replied: "your daughter is the Queen of our Palace and you are the Sardars"[226]

Prince Azam, son of Aurangzeb was married to the daughter of Kirat Singh, son of Raja Jai Singh. The princess was not converted to Islam.The Raja gave a rich dowry to the couple in the Hindu fashion.[227] Emperor Farukh Siyar was married to the daughter of Ajit Singh. On this occasion both Hindu and Muslim ceremonies were observed.[228]

Ibn Battuta, Mohammad-bin-Tughlaq's contemporary writes that the Sultan like a Hindu used to kiss his mother's feet in public.[229] Sultan Firoz performed tonsure like a Hindu during the period of mourning on the death of his son Fateh Khan.[230] On his mother's death and that of his chief nurse, Jiji Anaga, Akbar shaved his head, beard and moustaches. He cast off his turban and donned the garb of woe.[231] He participated in the traditional Yagya ceremonies to bring solace to the soul of the deceased. Following him his ministers Faizi and Abul Fazal also shaved their head on the death of their father. Aziz Koka did the same to mourn his mother's death.[232] Emperor Jahangir celebrated his father's shradha in the mausoleum at Sikandra.[233] When Balmati, Khurram`s mother died, Jahangir, attended no public entertainment and subsisted on simple vegetarian food for twenty-one days.[234]

Hindu teachers were engaged by the rulers to teach the young princes about Hindu mythology and philosophy. All the Mughal emperors including Aurangzeb observed Hindu ceremony of Tula Dan (weighing himself against different commodities and giving them away to ward off evil.)[235] The rulers also followed the custom of making the Tika sign on the forehead of their Hindu Rajas when they ascended the throne. [236]

Native names were adopted by the Muslim rulers as early as the establishment of the Sultanate.Balban`s nephew and other nobles had Hindu nicknames like Chajju and Kachchan. Mohammad bin Tughlaq named his temporary capital on the Ganga as Swargdwari.[237]

However with Akbar Indian names of places and different products became a common practice. He changed the names of the following garments:

Jama (coat) was named by Akbar as Sarabgati, i.e., covering the whole body

Izar (drawers) Yariparidhan (the companion of coat)

Nintanah (a jacket) Tanzeb;

Fautah-Patgat

Burqa (a veil) Chtragupita

Kulah (a cap) Sis Sobha

Muibaf (a hair ribbon) Kesghan

Pajjar (shoes) Charandharan.

Akbar invented a gun and named it Sangram. Besides, he named his Shawl as Param Naram; and a tank in his courtyard as Anup Talao.[238] The names of his two favourite elephants were Gujmukta and Gajraj. After the war of Haldi Ghati an elephant of Maharana Pratap Ramprasad was presented to Akbar who named him Pirprasad. His son was born in the hills of Fatehpur Akbar used to call Murad Pahary, or the Mountain born. Akbar's daughter was bestowed the name of Meethi (sweet) and another one as Lala Begum.[239] Akbar named Abul Fazal's son as Pashotam.[240] Names of Jahangir`s elephants were Giranbar and the Indra Gaj (the elephant of Indra) Khusrau`s elephant was Apurva Aurangzeb changed the title of the imperial slaves from Ghulam to Chela. [241]

When prince Azam requested his father Aurangzeb to suggest names for the unknown variety of Mangoes, the latter named them as 'Sudha-Ras' and Rasana- Vilas two Sanskrit names.[242]

All the Mughal rulers consulted Hindu astrologers before embarking on any campaign or taking any action. Humayun, on the advice of a sadhu, had evaded to see his new born son for thirty days. As an enthusiastic adept of astrology, Humayun fitted up seven houses of audience named after the seven planets. He himself wore clothes of the colour of the planet of the day and he recommended the same practice to his entourage.[243] Humayun would invariably lead with the right foot and if any one entered his residence with the left foot he would require him to go back and return in the correct fashion.[244] Akbar also wore different suits of clothes of different colours, each of which was worn on a particular day of the week in honour of the seven colours of the planets.[245] Gobind Ray was an astrologer of Akbar and Jagannath was that of Shah Jahan. Hindu Pundits prepared the horoscopes for Akbar, Salim, Murad and Daniyal. Jotik Roy, the court astrologer of Jahangir was once weighed against gold and silver for reward.[246] Aurangzeb sat on the throne on the day suggested (21st July1658) as auspicious by his astrologers[247] In Golkonda, Sultan Mohammad Qutub Shah was blessed by a son in the year 1614. Before the event the Court astrologers had predicted that the child's birth would not be auspicious for the Sultan. They stated that the Sultan should not see his heir before the boy's twelfth birthday. So Abdullah, as the boy was named was raised in a private quarters away from the royal palaces. In 1626 the boy was taken to the palace and introduced to his father. Strangely shortly after the first meeting between father and son, the father died.[248]

Emperor Muhammad Shah got built the Delhi Jantar Mantar in 1710. The observatory was used for naked eye sighting, continuously monitoring the position of the sun, moon and planet in relation to background stars in the belt of the Zodiac.[249]

Tipu Sultan had a firm faith in astrology. He himself wrote a book on astrology, named Zabarzad He used to consult astrologers daily about his stars. He daily shaved his beard and acted as advised by his astrologers. He daily fed the Brahmins and sought their blessings. He used to make offering to the seven stars of seven different kinds of grain, of an iron-pan full of seasame oil, of a blue cap and coat and the black sheep and some money. All these articles were distributed among the Brahmins and the poor.[250]

Various Hindu and Muslim festivals were celebrated by the rulers with great enthusiasm and impartial splendor. Sultan Zain-ul-abidin, the ruler of Kashmir, used to participate in the feast and festivals of his non-Muslim subjects. When the Monks of Shri, Jain monastery celebrated the worship of the vessels, the Sultan took part in it and fed the monks. Similarly every year on the day of Nagayatra and Ganachakra, he fed the devotees for five days and presented them with quilts money and other things.[251] The Rajatarangani (The saga of the kings of Kashmir) gives a detailed account of how the king took part in the annual Nagayatra festival when he would don the robes of a mendicant and perform the journey in the company of other pilgrims.[252] He used to see the display of lamps on both sides of the river on the occasion of the worship held to celebrate the birth of Jhelum. Seated in a boat on the river, the Sultan spent the whole night listening to songs and witnessing worship performed by the citizens.[253] Many Hindu festivals were officially recognized by the Mughals like Diwali, Shivratri, Dussehra, Baisakhi and Ramnavami. Akbar included the festivals of different communities within the list of the holidays of the Empire. Special ceremonies were connected with each of them and the state treasury made grants specified for the purpose. They sent soldiers to accompany Tazias at the Muharram and to follow the immersion of Hindu Idols.[254] Kotwals were instructed to the method of observance of these festivals.[255] On Dussehra, the imperial horses and elephants were arrayed in a decorated canopy and paraded for inspection. On the occasion of Sankrati festival of Hindus, Emperor Jahangir used to give alms of one thousand tolas of gold and silver and several thousand of rupees. At the time of Diwali, a puja Darbar was held and two decorated cows with garlands of cowries placed round their necks used to be brought in to the royal garden by the Brahmins. The Brahmins blessed the emperor and the latter used to give Brahmins valuable presents.[256] All the Mughal emperors including Aurangzeb observed the custom of giving banquet on the occasion of Dussehra. Aurangzeb used to distribute robes of honour among his Hindu nobles on that day. [257] Emperor Jahandar Shah always witnessed the burning of the effigy of Rawana.[258] Diwali was celebrated with gaiety. Lamps were lighted and palace decorated. Abul Fazal writes about the celebration of Diwali by Akbar when the emperor was in Kashmir in 1592. He writes:

"The Diwali festival was celebrated, and by order, the boats, the river banks and the roofs (houses) were adorned with lamps presented a splendid appearance".[259]

Gambling was also allowed in the palace. Goverdhan Puja followed Diwali. It was observed as Cows' day when cattle were washed, ornamented, fed and worshipped. Akbar also took part in the celebrations and several adorned cows were brought before him. Shivratri was observed and both Akbar and Jahangir used to meet and eat with the principal jogis on the night of the festival.[260] Nor were Id and Shab-e-Barat neglected On the Rakshabandhan day, the Hindu nobles fastened strings (auspicious thread) on the emperor's wrist.[261] Mughals played Holi and allowed their Hindu wives to perform Havan puja and to visit their holy places to offer prayers. Even during the reign of Aurangzeb, the festival of Holi was celebrated with great enthusiasm. Muslim nobles too joined freely with their Hindu brothers in this festival. Bhimsen, the Hindu biographer of Aurangzeb reign states that on the "festival of Holi, Bahadur Khan (Khan Jahan Bahadur Kotlashah) everyday went to the house of Raja Subban Singh, Rai Singh Rathore, Rai Anup Singh and Mokham Singh Chandrawat and watched the celebrations; and Mir Ahsan and Mir Muhsin, sons of Khan were more forward than Rajput themselves"[262] Members of Aurangzeb's family used to participate in the Holi celebrations with great fervor despite the displeasure of the Aurangzeb who wrote sarcastically to his son Azim Shah who on the occasion of Holi, had dressed like a Hindu "A saffron colour helmet on the head, a red garment on thy shoulder, thy venerable age verging on forty-six years hurrah on thy beard and moustache"[263] In Bengal the Muslim Nawabs like Murshid Quli khan, Alivardi, Sirajuddaula and Mir Jafar, too celebrated Holi and other Hindu festivals with great enthusiasm.[264] Shahamat Jung and Swlat Jung, the nephews of Alivardi once celebrated the festival of Holi for seven days in the garden of Motijhil where coloured water and heaps of Abir (red powder) and saffron had been prepared for the festivities.[265] The Nawabs of Oudh adopted such Hindu symbols as fish, sun and cow on their standards. They regularly observed different festivals and feast of Vasant Panchami along with their Hindu subjects.[266] No less enthusiasm was displayed in the southern states. Dussehra was celebrated with great pomp and show in Mysore. Both Haider and Tipu participated in the festival and blessed their subject. Tipu not only attended the Chariot festival of certain Hindu gods at Kanchi, but he himself walked in the festive procession. He used to ignite the fire-works to heighten the festive spirit of the occasion.[267]

This proximity was reflected in the social relations also A Hindu did not mind greeting his Muslim friend with Salam and the Muslim with Ram-Ram. Raja Ram Singh, as a token of respect, touched the feet of the older Shaista Khan who embraced the Raja and kissed his head. The sons of the Nawab in turn touched the feet of the Raja and accompanied him for a considerable distance.[268] The Muslim rulers shared the happiness and the sufferings of their Hindu relatives like their own kith and kin. Raja Bir Singh Baghela had friendly relations with Babar. He had joined Babar against Rana Sanga at the battle of Kanwaha. His successor, Raja Birbhanudeva offered asylum to emperor Humayun during his precipitate flight after the battle at Chausa. Humayun regarded the Raja as his brother. According to Sanskrit Kavya, emperor Humayun, delighted at the news of the birth of a grandson to Birbhanudeva, sent many valuable gifts as a token of friendship, and wrote to him saying, "This grandson is as good as my own, for there is hardly any difference between one's own grandson and that of his brother"[269] When Bahadur Shah invaded Chittorgarh, Rani Karnawati, the youngest wife of the deceased Sangram Simha sent a Rakhi (bracelet) to Humayun calling for his aid. Humayun was so pleased with the trust, engaged as he was in the conquest in Bengal, he responded to the call of chivalry. He went and expelled the foe from the Chittorgarh and restored Rajput supremacy. He became the Rakhi-band Bhai (brother) of the Rani.This Rakhi was preserved with care by Humayun`s successors.

Nurjahan used to show it to the members of the royal family with respect and honour.[270] In Deccan, Ali Adil Shah had very intimate relations with Raja Ram, the ruler of Vijaynagar. When the son of Ram Raj died, Ali Adil Shah went to Ram Raj with just a few attendants to condole with Ram Raj. The Queen of Ram Raj adopted Ali Adil Shah as her son and her daughter accepted him as her brother.[271]

Mir Gholam Hussein Khan mentions an episode in Siyar-ul-Mutakherin which shows how intimate relations existed between the two communities. When General Serbuland Khan, defeated Raja Abi Singh Rathore in Gujarat, the latter had to make a retreat. However there were no ill-feelings when the battle was over. Serbuland Khan, "in the evening of the day of the battle, put on a white dress, without his armour and rolling a white turban round his head, he with no other relative than a few chopdars or mace bearers and a private servant advanced to visit the Hindu prince. Abi Singh though at first extremely surprised, thought himself highly honoured by such concession. He rose at his approach, advanced to the door of his tent to meet him and after the usual embrace, he took the veteran by his hand, made him sit on his own masnad and showed him every mark of respect. Serbelend Khan, after some conversation, turned towards the Hindu prince and spoke to him in these words: 'Young man' said he, 'you will be surprised when I inform you that there ought to subsist much friendship between us, for there was a time when your father and I exchanged turbans as brothers and therefore look upon you as my nephew. The trifling contest that has passed between us was to defend my honour and to maintain my character as a soldier; but there must not be the least enmity between you and me in future; nor did I see why, being an hereditary friend of your family, I should abstain from paying you this visit. The Imperial service is the point in question-it is on that very service I came into this country; but this being now committed to it, and I wish you may bring the government into proper order. I have no further business here. I came only to request you a travelling equipage and some money to defray my expense to the capital' Abi Singh was moved by this gesture. The two exchanged turbans and embraced each other".[272]

Religion did not stand as a barrier between the Muslim rulers and their Hindu relatives. Akbar displayed complete confidence in the Rajputs. His relation with them was based on trust, respect and affection. He appointed Jodhabai's brother Bhagwant Singh and nephew Man Singh in high posts. He assigned his son Daniyal who was born in 1570 to the care of Bhara Mal`s wife (Jodha Bai`s mother) at Amber. In 1572 when Akbar embarked upon the Gujarat campaign, Bhara Mal was sent to the capital Agra to take charge of it, on account of a possible threat from the side of Ibrahim Hussain Mirza.[273] Rai Singh of Bikaner was given the charge of Jodhpur and Sirohi so as to stem any possible inroads towards the capital by the Mirzas. In the battle of Samel, Bhupat, brother of Raja Bhagwant Singh was killed in the engagement Akbar took an unusual step of sending Jodhabai to Amber for mourning. Later Akbar himself speared to death the captive Shah Madad, foster brother of Hussain Mirza who had been responsible for the death of Bhupat. As a mark of trust, the arch rebel Muhammad Hussain Mirza was after his capture, handed over to Rai Singh for custody. Mirza Kaiqobad, son of Mirza Hakim, Akbar's half brother was handed over to Jagannath for Punishment.[274] Prince Salim was directed to pay a visit of condolence on the death of Raja Bhagwant Singh who died in 1589.[275] When Abhay Singh, the eldest son of Ajit Singh succeeded his father, emperor Muhammad Shah personally paid a visit to his residence and honoured him with a rob of honour and also bestowed on him, the province of Nagaur in jagir.[276] Jahangir had intimate relations with Rai Singh. So great was Jahangir's concern for Rai that on one occasion, prince Dalpat Singh rebelled against his father, Rai Singh. Jahangir of his own accord and without any request for help on the part of Rai Singh deputed two seniors Mansabdar to bring about an amicable settlement between father and son. When Khusrau rebelled against Jahangir, his father, and suddenly left for Agra, the emperor went in pursuit of his son. So great was his trust in Rai Singh that in full confidence he left Rai in charge of Agra, the capital. Later when Jahangir desired to call the empress and other ladies of the harem, to his camp at Lahore, Rai was placed in the important and responsible charge of the travelling of the harem.[277] Later Jahangir kept Khusrau his rebel son in the custody of Rai.

Shah Jahan who was more a Hindu than a Muslim, (his father was Jahangir born of a Hindu mother and Shahjahan's mother was Jagat Gosain daughter of Moti Raja.) trusted the Rajputs. When he fell ill and feared a coup by his ambitious sons, he showed more confidence in the Rajputs than in any one else Manucci who was in Dara`s service, states:

"He ordered the gates of the fortress to be closed leaving only two wickets open placing no reliance on the Mohammedan commanders. He ordered Jaswant Singh to post himself at one gate with his men and the other he made over to Raja Ram Sing. These officers guarded the fortress on all sides with thirty thousand soldiers, all of them Rajputs".[278]

Prince Dara had very warm relations with Rajputs and his son prince Sulaiman Shikoh was married to Jai Singh's daughter. He used to call Jai Singh as Dada Bhai.[279] In 1681 Aurangzeb's son Azam invaded Bijapur. He left his wife Jahanez Banu, daughter of late Dara, with a strong Rajput guard under Anurudh Singh Hada and advanced further in to the enemy camp. One of the Maratha division then attacked the begum's camp. Jahanez Banu quitted her covered chair and getting upon a war-elephant, she pushed forward the enemy. She threw her veil and started shooting arrows incessantly and encouraged both officers and men to repulse the enemy.[280] On the way calling Anurudh Singh she said "Sharm-e-Chaghtaia-ba Rajputa ek-ast."(To the Rajputs the honour of Chagtai dynasty is equal to their own.) Then a great battle was fought. Many Rajputs were killed and the battle was won. Jahanez Banu comforted the wounded Anurudh Singh and gave him her own necklace of pearls of forty thousands and placed round his neck by her own hands.[281] In May 1754, during Marathas attack Malika-e-Zamani Udhambai, mother of emperor Ahmad Shah escaped for safety along with other royal ladies in a carriage. The Maratha soldiers captured the carriage and looted the jewellry and other belongings of the women. The women were kept as captives in the Maratha camp. Later in the day Malika-e-Zamani, who was also a captive in the Maratha camp, summoned Malhar Rao to her presence and rebuked him. He slapped his own face in the Queen's presence and pleaded his innocence saying that it was the work of plundering Pindaris attached to the army. Malhar Rao then caught hold of a few culprits and cut off their heads in her presence. He then collected all the ladies and their goods together and sent them two lacs for their expenses.[282] When Imad-ul- Mulk, wazir of the emperor, invaded the Jat territories and reached Mathura, Malhar Rao sent a message to Imad-ul-Mulk saying that "It (Mathura) enjoys a religious sanctity and is a place of pilgrimage of the Hindus, therefore he should stop his soldiers from maltreating the inhabitants" Imad-ul-Mulk immediately issued strict orders in this regard and respecting Malhar Rao's religious sentiments, paid some cash to the Brahmins and Bairagis. Malhar's son Khande Rao was killed during Maratha siege of Kumbher, Imad-ul-mulk, came to condole him remarking, "Henceforth look upon me as your son in the place of Khando"[283] Madhoji Sindhia was badly wounded in the third battle of Panipat. He lay in a ditch until evening, when a Muslim water-carrier, named Rana Khan driving his bullock cart home, caught sight of the Maratha Chief. "Help me O brother", the wounded Sindhia cried. Rana Khan lifted him on his bullock and took him to a place of safety. Sindhia later called Rana Khan as his brother and made him a commander in his army.[284]

Emperor Shah Alam, after defeat in the war at Buxar and the consequent grant of Diwani rights of Bengal, Bihar and Orissa to the victorious East India Company, had to live as a refugee for twelve years in Allahabad. The capital was in the hands of Rohilla deputies of Ahmad Shah Abdali. Shah Alam was able to occupy his throne only with the help of Marathas. Marathas by then had become very powerful and could themselves capture the throne but they did not go beyond the act of restoration of the empire to the Mughal emperor. Previously Alamgeer too was replaced on the throne with the Maratha's help Madhoji Sindhia himself escorted emperor Shah Alam to the capital. On his way from Agra to Delhi in 1784, the emperor gave expression to his state of dependence on Sindhia as:

"Mulk-o-mal sab kho kar pade tumhare bus"

(Having lost my kingdom and wealth I am in your hands).[285]

When Ghulam Qadir Rohilla blinded the emperor, the latter among others appealed to Madhoji Sindhia to avenge his insult as:

"Redress my wrongs and kingly rights restore;
Thee too O Sindhia, Illustrious chief;
Who once didst promise to offer relief,
Thee I invoke, exert thy generous aid,
And ye, O faithful pillars of my state
By friendship bound and by my power elate"[286]

Sindhia collected his reinforcements and sent under his commander-in-chief Rane Khan to capture Ghulam Qadir. Rane Khan caught the culprit and sent him to his master who cut off the head of Qadir from his body and sent it to Shah Alam. The emperor was deeply moved. Once again the faithful Maratha had enthroned him. He called Sindhia his son and decorated him with the title of "Exalted and Illustrious Centre of Affairs".[287]

Shah Alam made a Hindu woman, who had throughout the

night guarded the body of his assassinated father, emperor Alamgir, his sister. He invited her in open Darbar and called her his sister and rewarded her. Afterwards, every year, the woman would visit the Court on the days of Salunon and Bhayya Duj and would tie a silken Rakhi of real pearls. After Shah Alam's death, his descendants Akbar Shah and Bahadur Shah Zafar maintained brotherly relations with the woman's family, accepted Rakhi and offered rich presents.[288] The famous Maratha statesman Nana Fadnavis used to call Haider Ali his 'right arm' and the two were as close to each other as real brothers.[289]

Thus all sorts of barriers between the two communities broke up. The Muslims had become the sons of the soil and regarded their motherland sacred and their religion as one of other religions of the land. Neither Babur nor any of his successors recognized the Caliphate.[290] But this does not mean that they were not believers. They were devout Muslims and followed the practices of Islam. Yet their religion did not stand in the way of promotion of other religions. Fanaticism or sectarianism found no place in their public or private life and the state ensured equality and freedom, which promoted feelings of fraternity. People lived the way they wanted to live. Peace prevailed, prosperity showered and unity in diversity flourished. Harmony was thus a rule than an exception.

It were the British, the Hindu as well as Muslim fundamentalists, combined together, tore this harmonious fabric by distorting history, by describing the medieval age as the dark age and by presenting the Muslim rulers as fanatic, bigots and anti-Hindu. One Aurangzeb was imposed on the entire medieval period and the rest of the rulers were completely ignored. This misrepresentation sustained the British rule for almost two centuries but also put the communalists in the forefront, provided them credibility and later led to the division of our country.

REFERENCES

1. Syed Mahmud, *India of Yesterday*, Indo Middle East Cultural Studies, Hyderabad, 1957, p. 21.

2. *Ibid*, p. 23

3. *Ibid*, p. 24-25. Also see Elliot and Dowson, *History of India as told by its own Historians*. Vol. I, first edition, London 867, Low Price, Reprint 1990, p. 184.

4. S.M. Ikram, *Muslim Civilization in India*, Columbia, University Press,

New York, 1964, p. 17-18.

5. *Ibid.*, p. 34.

6. R.P. Tripathi, Some *Aspects of Muslim Administration*, Allahabad, 1936, p. 29.

7. Rafiq Zakaria, *Raziya: Queen of India*, Popular Prakashan, Bombay, 1966, p. 69.

8. *Khuda Baksh Library Journal* No. 44, 1987, p. 16.

9. Mahdi Husain, *Tughalq Dynasty*, London University, London, 1935, p. x

10. *The History* [and] *Culture of the Indian People.* ed by R.C. Majumdar, Vol. VI, Bharatiya Vidya Bhavan, Bombay 1967, p. 25.

11. Sidney J. Owen, *From Mahmud Ghazni to the Disintegration of the Mughal Empire*, Kanishka,Delhi, 1987, p. 81.

12. *Khuda Baksh Library Journal*, 1987, No. 44 p. 16.

13. *Ibid.*

14. B.N. Luniya, *Evolution of Indian Culture*, Laxmi Narayan Aggarwal, Agra, 1955, p. 429.

15. A.B.M. Habibullah, *The Foundations of the Muslim Rule in India*, Central Book, Allahabad, 1945, (Reprint) 1971, p. 331.

16. Mahdi Husain, *Tughlaq Dynasty*, p. 2.

17. *Delhi Sultanate*, ed. by R.C. Majumdar, Bhartiya Vidya Bhavan, Bombay 1967, p. 86.

18. Mahdi Husain, Tughlaq Dynasty, p. 321.

19. *Proceedings Indian History Congress*, 1941, p. 215, 302.

20. Mahdi Husain, p. 333.

21. N.R. Ray and P.N. Chakravarty, *Studies in Cultural Development of India*, Punthi Pustak, Calcutta, 1991, p. 246.

22. *Ibid.*

23. Yasin, *A Social History of Islamic India*, The Upper India, Lucknow 1956, p. 89.

24. N.R. Ray and P.N. Chakravarty, p. 308.

25. A.B. Pandey, *Early Medieval India*, Central Book, Depot, Allahabad, 1960, p. 190.

26. *Iqbal*, January 1965, Vol. 13. No. 3. p. 45.

27. Mahdi Husain, p. 308.

28. *Iqbal*, Jan 1965, p. 49. Also see K.S. Lal, *Legacy of the Muslim Rule in India*, Aditya Prakashan, New Delhi, 1992. p. 221.

29. Habibullah, p. 324.

30. Mahdi Husain, p. 510-11.

31. *Niamatullah's History of Afghans*, trs. by Nirodbhusan Roy, Shantiniketan,1938, Bengal, p. xix.

32. *Ibid.*, p. xxii, Also see Iqbal, July1964, Vol. 13, No-I, p. 44.

33. S.M. Ikram, p. 88.

34. *Iqbal*, Jan-1965, p. 52.

35. V. Raghvendra Rao, *Indo-Muslim Culture*, Vichara, Sahitya,

Bengalore, p. 65.

36. *Proceedings Indian History Congress*, 1956, p. 258.

37. Fathullah Mujtabai, *Aspects of Hindu Muslim Cultural Relations*, M.B.B. Delhi, 1978, p. 135.

38. Yazdani, *Bidar-Its History* and *Monuments*, Oxford University Press, London, 1947, p. 34, 56.

39. Fathullah, p. 135.

40. *Proceedings of the Indian History Congress*, 1970. Vol. I, p. 234.

41. Richard Maxwell Eaton, *Sufis of Bijapur*, Princeton University Press, New Jersey, 1978, p. 100.

42. *Ibid.*

43. *Proceedings* of *Indian History Congress*, 1970, Vol. I p. 234.

44. *The New Review*, Vol. VI. 1937, p. 566.

45. Fathullah, p. 137.

46. Sisir Kumar, *India Vision and Fulfilment*, Bombay, 1982, p. 89.

47. *Comprehensive History of India*, ed by Mohd. Habib, P.P.H. New Delhi1970, p. 867.

48. *Ibid.*, p. 889.

49. Mohibbul Hasan, *Kashmir Under the Sultans*, Iran Society, Calcutta, 1959, p. 52-56.

50. *An Outline of the Cultural History of India*, ed. by Abdul Latif, Hyderabad, 1958, p. 184.

51. Mohibbul Hasan, p. 86.

52. *Ibid*, p. 87.

53. *Ibid.*

54. R.K. Parmu, *A History of Muslim Rule in Kashmir*, P.P.H. Delhi, 1969, p. 112.

55. *The Delhi Sultanate*, p. 382.

56. Mohibbul Hasan, p. 81, 91.

57. Parmu, p. 145.

58. *An Outline of the Cultural History of India*, p. 184.

59. Mohibbul Hasan, p. 71.

60. S.R. Sharma, *Mughal Empire in India*, Lakshmi Agra, 1974, p. 86.

61. Ziyauddin Barani, *Fatwa-i-Jahandari*, Publised by Department of History, Muslim University, Aligarh in, *Medieval India Quarterly*, July-Oct. 1957, p. 5.

62. Murry T. Titus, *Islam in India* and *Pakistan*, YMCA, Calcutta, 1957, p. 16.

63. *Ibid.*

64. Alexander Dow, *History of Hindustan*, Vol. I, Today and Tommorrow, New Delhi 1973, p. 120.

65. T.L.Vaswani, *In the Sikh Sanctuary*, Ganesh, Madras, 1922, p. 22.

66. Max Arthur Macauliffe, *The Sikh Religion*, S. Chand andCompany New Delhi 1983. Vol.I. II, p. 121.

67. Kartar Singh , M.A. *Life of Guru Nanak*, Jaidev Singh, Amritsar, 1973, p. 220, 230.

68. Murry T. Titus, p. 163.

69. Macauliffe, Vol. I-II, p. 19, 20.

70. *Ibid*.

71. *Problem of Communalism in India*, ed, by Ravindra Kumar, Mittal, New Delhi 1990, p. 22.

72. G.S. Chhabra, *Advance Study in the History of Punjab*, Vol. I, Sharanjit, Jullandhur, 1960, p. 132.

73. W.L. M 'Gregor, *The History of the Sikhs*, James Madden London 1846, p. 52.

74. *Ibid*. p. 53.

75. Macauliffe, Vo. l.III-IV, p. 83-84.

76. *Ibid*., Vol. I-II. p. 108.

77. *Ibid*.

78. *Ibid*.

79. *Ibid*, p. 82, 83. Also see Khushwant Singh, p. 58.

80. *Ibid*, Vol. III-IV, p. 17-27.

81. Tripathi, p. 352.

82. Hem Chandra Rai, *Romance of the Fort of Gwalior*, Marathi, Press, 1931, p. 440.

83. Macauliffe, p. 33.

84. *Ibid*, p. 28.

85. *Ibid*, p. 279.

86. *Ibid*.

87. Anil Chandra, *Medieval Studies*, Mukheriee and comp, Calcutta, 1958, p. 122 Also see W.L. M. 'Gregor, p. 58.

88. *Problem of Communalism in India*, p. 23, Khushwant Singh, p.69.

89. Mehr Singh, *Sikh Shrines in India*, Publication Division of Govt. of India, New Delhi, 1975, p. 24.

90. *Sikhan Di Raj Di Vikhia*, trs. Henry Court, Sushil Gupta, Calcutta, 1959, p. 52.

91. William Irvine, *Later Mughals*, Orient Book, 1976, New Delhi p. 90.

92. Zahiruddin Malik, *The Reign of Muhammad* Shah, Asia Aligarh 1977, p. 354.

93. G.M.D. Sufi, *Kashmir*, p. 704.

94. K.R. Malkani, *The Sind Story*, Allied, New Delhi 1989, p. 152.

95. R.L. Ahuja, *Maharaja Ranjit Singh-A Man of Destiny, Punjab,* Writers Co-operative Society, Delhi, 1983, p. 59.

96. N.D. Ahuja, p. 21.

97. *Ain-i-Akbari*, Abul Fazl Allami, trs. by Blochmann, Asiatic Society Calcutta 1873, p. 180. Also see Indian Antiquary, 1887,

p. 135, 136.

98. *Visva Bharati Quarterly*, Jan 1928, p. 379.

99. M.L. Bhagi, *Medieval India: Culture* and *Thought,* Indian Ambala, 1985, p. 183.

100. *The Aryan Path*, June 1931, p. 350.

101. J.M. Shelat, *Akbar*, Bhartiya Vidya Bhawan, Bombay 1964, p. 219.

102. *Ibid.* Also see *Cultural History of Gujarat*, by M.R. Majumdar, p. 214.

103. Tulsidas, *Dohavali*, Doha No. 5.

104. See for detail *Muntakhab-ul-Tawarikh* II by Abdul Qadir, p. 365.

105. *Memoirs of Jahanguier*, trs.Major David Price, Rare Book, Delhi 1904, p. 84.

106. Yusuf Husain, *Glimpses of Indian Culture*, p. 47.

107. *Ibid.*, Also see *Ain-i-Akbari*, p. IV.

108. *Ibid.*

109. Azra Alvi, *Socio-Religious Outlook of Abul Fazl*. p. 36.

110. *Indian Historical Quarterly*, 1937, Vol. XIII, p. 312.

111. *Akbar Nama of Abul Fazl*, trs. by Henry Bevcidge Vol. III, Calcutta 1930, p. 528.

112. *Ain-i-Akbari*, p. 200.

113. *Ibid.* p. 184.

114. *Ibid.* p. 105. Also see Shelat, p. 264.

115. *Ibid.*, p. 106.

116. Bhagwati Prasad Singh, *Rambhakti Kala aur Sahitya*, Hindi Pustak Agency, Calcutta,1974, p. 83. Also see *Hindustan Times*, July 1987.

117. *Ain-i-Akbari*, p. 202.

118. *A Sidelight on Akbar's Genius* in *The Muslim University Journal*, Vol. III, 1936, p. 230.

119. Abid Hussain, *National Culture of India*, Asia, New Delhi 1956, p. 101.

120. Muni Lal, *Akbar*, p. 273.

121. *Modern Review*, April 1969, p. 266.

122. *Ain-i-Akbari*, p. 207.

123. *The India Historical Quarterly*, 1937, Vol. XIII, p. 304.

124. *Ibid.* 1936, p. 37.

125. *Ain-i-Akbari*, p. 183.

126. A.L. Srivastva, *Akbar the Great*, p. 249.

127. Pradwin, *The Builders of Mughal Empire*, p. 156.

128. *Tuzuk-i-Jahangiri*, trs. by Alexander Rogers and ed by Beveridge, Royal Asiatic Society, London, 1914, p. 52.

129. *Ibid.*

130. *The Embassy of Sir Thomas Roe to India 1615-19* ed. by Sir Willaim Foster, Oxford University Press, London 1926, p. 328.

131. Goswami Tulsidas and Budmala, p. 102.

132. *Memoirs of Jahangueir*, p. 3.

133. *Ibid.*

134. Beni Prasad, *History of Jahangir*, The Indian Press, 1922, p. 407. Also see *Tuzuk*, p. 847.

135. *Proceedings* of *The Indian History Congress*, 1984, p. 448.

136. *Tuzuk*, p. 847.

137. *A General Collection of the Best* and *Most interesting Voyages*, ed. by, John Pinkerton, London 1811, Vol. VIII, p. 460.

138. Sindey J. Owen, *The Fall of the Mughal Empire* p. 8.

139. *Indian Culture*, 1937, p. 317.

140. *The Aryan Path*, Jan 1947, p. 22 Also see. M.L. Roy Choudhry, *The State and Religion in Mughal India*, p. 111, 216.

141. *Ibid*, p. 21.

142. *India Historical Quarterly*, 1936, p. 30.

143. K.R. Qanungo, *Historical Essays*, Shivlal Aggarwal, Agra, 1968 p. 204.

144. *Ibid*. p. 204.

145. *The Visva Bharati Quarterly*, 1939, p. 281.

146. Qanungo, *Dara Shikoh*, VoL. I. p. 401.

147. *The Visva Bharati Quarterly*, p. 282, 83.

148. *Ibid*. p. 286.

149. Muni Lal, *Shah Jahan*, Vikas, 1986, Delhi p. 289.

150. Pt. Sunderlal, *How India lost Her Freedom*, Popular Prakashan, Bombay 1970, p. ci.

151. *Khuda Baksh Library Journal*, No. 44. p. 40. Also see N.D. Ahuja, p. 41.

152. *Indian Antiquary*, May 1931, p. cxii.

153. Sunderlal, p. cxii.

154. *A General Collection of the Best* and *Most Interesting Voyages*, p. 321.

155. *The New Review*, 1937, p. 565.

156. Rajendra Prasad, *India Divided*, Hind Kitab, Bombay 1946, p. 35.

157. Ishrat Haque, *Glimpses of Mughal Society* and *Culture*, Concept, New Delhi, 1992, p. 92.

158. *The Aryan Path*, 1931, p. 351.

159. *The New Review*, 1937, p. 564.

160. *Bias in Indian Historiography*, ed by Devahati, OK Publication, New Delhi, 1980, p. 369.

161. M.L. Roy Choudhry, p. 205.

162. *Ain-i-Akbari*, p. 195.

163. A.L. Srivastva, *Akbar the Great*, p. 239.

164. *Ibid*. p. 255-256.

165. S.M. Burke, *Akbar the Greatest Mogul*, Manohar, Delhi, 1989, p. 119.

166. *Ibid*. p. 119.
167. M.L. Roy Choudhry. *The State* and *Religion in Mughal India* , p. 293.
168. S.M. Burke, p. 120.
169. *Ain-i-Akbari*, p. 182.
170. *Bias in Indian Historiography*, p. 369.
171. S.R. Sharma, *Mughal Empire in India*. p. 220.
172. *Ibid*.
173. *Ibid*.
174. *Ibid*.
175. Francois Bernier, *Trevels in The Mughal Empire*, S. Chand, Delhi 1968, p. 6.
176. Ishrat Haque, p. 107.
177. Mohibbul, p. 52, 82.
178. Rajenders Prasad, p. 34.
179. *The New Review*, Vol. VI 1939, p. 566.
180. Surendra Nath Sen, *Studies in the Indian History*, University of Calcutta, 1930, p. 166.
181. *Great Men and Women of India*, Publication Division of Govt. of India, New Delhi-1973, p. 67.
182. *The New Review*, p. 567, 68.
183. *Ibid*.
184. *Ibid*.
185. V. Raghvendera Rao, *Indo-Muslim Culture*, p. 59.
186. *New Review*, p. 570.
187. *Ibid*.
188. *Ibid*., p. 573.
189. *Proceedings* of *The Indian History Congress*, 1944, p. 416.
190. Mohibbul Hasan, p. 360-61.
191. Syed, p. 172.
192. *Khuda Baksh Library Journal*, No. 44, 1987, p. 33.
193. Mahdi Husain, *Bahadur Shah*, M.N. Publication New Delhi 1986, p. 37.
194. *Ibid*.
195. Mahdi Husain, *Tughlaq Dynasty*, p. 18.
196. Mohd. Wahid Mirza, *The Life* and *Works of Amir Khusrau*, Baptist Mission Press, Calcutta, 1935, p. 180.
197. W.H. Moreland and Atul Chandra. *A Short History of India*, Longman London, 1936, p. 171.
198. Mahdi Hussain, *Tughlaq Dynasty*, p. 408.
199. Alexander Dow, *History of India*, Vol. IV, p. 139.
200. *Comprehensive History of India*, ed by Mohd. Habib, P.P.H. New Delhi 1970. p.888. Also see Sir Edward Clive Bayley, *Local Mohammedan Dynasties-Gujarat*, W.H. London, 1846, p. 154.
201. Sisir Kumar, *India Vision* and *Fulfillment*, p. 89.

202. Haroon Khan Sherwani, *The Bahmanis of Decean*, Manohar, New Delhi 1985, p. 101.

203. Ian Austin, *City of Legends*, Viking, Calcutta 1992, p. xix.

204. Sisir, p. 89.

205. *Khuda Baksh Library Journal*, No. 44, 1987 p. 17.

206. Satish Chandra, *Mughals Religious Policies*, Vikas, New Delhi 1993, p. 17

207. Mohibbul, p. 52.

208. *The Delhi Sultanate*, p. 378.

209. Mohibbul. p. 52.

210. *Ibid.*

211. Faqir Syed Waheedudddin, *Real Ranjit Singh*, Oriental, New Delhi, 1976, p. 172.

212. C.K. Srinivasan, *Baji Rao I- The Great Peshwa*, Asia Bombay 1961, p. 125, 28.

213. *Khuda Baksh Library Journal*, No. 44, p. 18.

214. Satish Chandra, p. 23.

215. *Ibid.*, p. 75.

216. Manucci, *Storia Do Mogor* trs. by William Irvine, John Murry, London 1908, p. 271.

217. Muni Lal, *Shah Jahan*, p.278, Also see Irvine, *Later Mughals* p. 400.

218. Muni Lal, *Akbar*, p. 10.

219. *Ain-i-Akbari*, Vol. I. p. 184.

220. *Ibid*, p. 51, 52, 206.

221. Tripathi, *Rise* and *Fall of the Mughal Empire*, p. 498.

223. Muhammad Yasin, *A Social History of Muslim India*, p. 66.

224. Syed. p. 120.

225. A.L. Srivastva, *Akbar*, New Delhi 1962, p. 328-29.

226. *Visva Bharati*, Nov. to Jan. 1951 p. 212. Also see Yusuf Hussain, p. 112.

227. Satish Chandra, p. 75.

228. Irvine, p. 305.

229. *Tughlaq Dynasty*, p. 510.

230. *Ibid.* p. 510-11.

231. Muni Lal, *Akbar*, p. 224.

232. C.M. Aggarwal, *Akbar and His Hindu Officers*, ABS Jullundur, 1986, p. 5.

233. Azizur Rahman Mallick, *British Policy* and *the Muslims in Bengal*, Asiatic Society, Dacca, 1961, p. 4.

234. Muni Lal, *Shah Jahan*, p. 32.

235. *India Historical Quarterly*, 1936, p. 24 Also see *Ain-i-Akbari*, p. 267.

236. *Ibid.*

237. Irfan Habib, *Barani's Theory of the History of the Sultanate, in Indian Historical Review* Vol. VII, No. 12, 1980- 81. Delhi 112.
238. *Ain-i-Akbari*, p. 90.
239. Memoirs of Jahangeuir, p. 807.
240. Rahul Saskrityana, *Akbar*, Kitab Mahal, Allahabad, 1957, p. 96.
241. H.A. *Rose, Religious Life of the Indian People*. p. 503.
242. *Ruka' at-i-Alamgiri*, trs. by Jamshid H. Bilimoria, Idara-i- Adbiyat, Delhi 1972, p. 12.
243. Pradwin, p. 84-85.
244. S.M. Burke, *Akbar the Greatest Mughal* p. 27.
245. *Ain-i-Akbari*, p. 183.
246. *Tuzuk-i-Jahangiri* Vol. II, p. 160.
247. *Maasir-i-Alamgiri* of Saqi Must' Ad Khan trs. by Jadunath Sarkar, Royal Asiatic Society, Calcutta, 1947, p. 4.
248. Ian Austin, p. 50.
249. K.S. Lal, *The legacy of the Muslim Rule in India*, Aditya Prakashan, New Delhi 1992, p. 29.
250. Mohibbul Hasan, *History of Tipu Sultan*, The World Press, Calcutta, 1957, p. 378.
251. *Ibid*. p. 88.
252. *Khuda Baksh Library Journal*, No. 44, 1987, p. 65.
253. Mohibbul Hasan, p. 88.
254. Jadunath Sarkar, *Aurangzeb*, Vol .I V, p. 406.
255. *Tuzuk-i-Jahangiri*, p. 52.
256. Syed, p.109.
257. Muhammad Qammaruddin, *Society* and *Culture in Medieval India*, Delhi 1985, p. 12.
258. Zahiruddin Malik, *The Reign of Mohammad Shah*, p. 352.
259. A.L. Srivastva, p. 394.
260. *Ain-i-Akbari*, p. 201, 216.
261. *Ibid*, p. 184.
262. Yasin, p. 50.
263. *Ibid*. p. 91.
264. Siraj-ul-Islam, *History of Bangladesh*, Asiatic Society of Bangladesh, Dacca 1992, p. 49.
265. Azizur Rahman, p. 4.
266. V. Raghavendra, p. 84.
267. V.D. Savarkar, *Six Golorious Epoches of Indian History*, Published by V.D. Savarkar, Bombay 1971, p. 228.
268. *Islamic Culture*, April 1934, p. 71.
269. Niamatullah's, *History of the Afghans*, p. 198.
270. *Dawn*, June 1901, Calcutta, No. II, p. 324.
271. Syed, p.142.
272. Gholam Hussein Khan, *The Seir Mutaqherin*, Calcutta 1789, Reprint: Oriental, Lahore 1975, p. 233.

273. Satish Chandra, p. 22- 23.

274. *Ibid.* p. 24, 25.

275. A.L. Srivastva, *Akbar the Great*, p. 385.

276. Pt. Bisheshwar Nath, *Glories of Mewar*, Jodhpur, Archeological, Deptt. 1943, p. 39.

277. Alakh Dhari, *Raja Rai Singh*, Published by Alakh Dhari, Bikaner, 1935, p. 131, 32.

278. Manucci, p. 241.

279. Satish Chandra, p. 189.

280. Gholam, Hussein, p. 176.

281. Sir Jadunath Sarkar, *Studies in the Aurangzeb Reign*, M.C. Sarkar and Sons, Calcutta 1933, p. 65.

282. G.S. Sardesai, *The New History of Marathas*, Phoenic, Bomaby 1948, p. 379.

283. Sir Jadunath Sarkar, *The Fall of the Mughal Empire*, Vol. I, p. 326 Also see Muhammad Umar, *Islam in Northern India During Eighteenth Century*, Manohar 1993, p. 403.

284. Bhabani Bhattacharya, *Glimpses of Indian History*, Sterling, New Delhi 1996, p.179.

285. Ishrat Haque, p. 50, Also see Hari Om Gupta, *History of Punjab*, Minerva Book, Lahore 1944, p. 252.

286. W. Franklin, *The History of the Reign of Shah Alam*, p. 257, 258.

287. Hari Om Gupta, *We Are One*, Haryana Publication Division, 1973, p. 57, Also see Bhabani, p. 189.

288. Hari Om Gupta, p. 45.

289. *Ibid.*

290. S.M. Burke *Akbar, The Greatest Mughal*, p. 8.

3

Political Animosities

From the very inception of Muslim rule in India till the end of the Mughal Empire, there were frequent conflicts and wars between the rulers either for the expansion or for the protection and preservation of their respective state boundaries. Hindu rulers fought with Hindu rulers and the Muslim with the Muslim kings but unfortunately the wars between the rulers belonging to different religions were given communal colours by the communalists of both the communities. These were projected as wars either for imposition or for the protection of the Faith. The real mundane motives were relegated to the background and religious reasons were highlighted so as to divide the people on communal lines and to use their support in the name of Jihad or Dharma.

The invasion of Sind by Mohammed bin Qasim was not a Jihad against Hinduism as projected by Muslim fundamentalists. Commercial and not the religious considerations led Qasim to capture the region. He had no hatred for Hindus and had no zeal to spread Islam, as after the invasion of Sind, the administration was left entirely in the hands of the natives. Permission was given to the Hindus to worship their gods. Nobody was forbidden or prevented from following his own religion.[1] When the city of Alrur, besieged for several months, finally surrendered on the condition that Qasim should spare the lives and not touch the temples, he conceded, saying: "The laid temples shall be unto us like the churches of the Christians, the Synagogues of the Jews and the temples of Magians"[2] "Build temples, traffic with the Mohammedan, live without fear and strive to better yourselves in every way" was the law in Mohammad bin Qasim's days.[3]

Qasim looted and burnt many temples not because of his

fanaticism but because they were the repositories of wealth. His raids meant more of a personal profit and gaining military glory than a gain to Islam. "The very fact that he employed a large body of Hindu troops in his army vitiates much of the force in the argument that his raids were in any way a part of the Holy war"[4] After defeating Rai Dahir, Qasim appointed Sisakar, the minister of Dahir, his wazir in the southern Sind. Kaska a learned man and philosopher of Hind was made wazir and counsellor in all affairs in northern India. Kaska took precedence in the army before all the nobles and commanders. He collected the revenue of the country and the treasure was kept under his seal. He assisted Qasim in all his undertakings and was called by the title of Mubark Mushir (prosperous counsellor)[5] Besides these two, there were many other Hindu officers, holding high positions in the army as well as in the administrative system; and it is interesting to note that none of them was forced to change his faith.[6] His religious persecutions were directed mainly against Muslim heretics who threatened to disturb the authority and peace of his Empire.[7] Thus Qasim was not a champion of Islam and his invasion of Sind was not motivated by religious zeal. In fact, religious hatred did not exist. Baladhuri, historian of the 10th century, writes that when the local Hindu Chiefs of Sindan in Sind rose against the Muslim ruler of the city and destroyed his power, they did no harm to the Muslim population, did not destroy the mosques and left the community free to perform their daily worship.[8]

Like Qasim, Mahmud of Ghazni too, was neither a fanatic nor a missionary. His raids were motivated by his greed for gold. He fought with Hindus and Muslims alike for the extension of his empire.[9] He attacked shrines, razed temples to the ground and broke idols to pieces not because it was meritorious from the religious point of view but because they were fortified places, containing treasure of India's fabulous wealth. Dr. Ishwara Topa argues "It may also be observed that the temples of India which Mahmud raided were storehouses of enormous and untold wealth and some of these were political centres. The temples, in fact, were broken during the campaigns for reasons other than religious but in times of peace Mahmud never demolished a single temple"[10] Mahmud used to wander over Gujarat, Punjab and Kannauj but he never destroyed any temple there. In Multan, Sultan Abul Fatah, who belonged to the Kharanti tribe, had snatched the state from the Ummiyah family and had not only closed the Jamia Masjid of Multan built by them but destroyed the temple which was close by and constructed a new mosque in its place. When Mahmud captured Multan from Abul Fatah, he closed the newly constructed mosque, for the main reason that the place on which the mosque stood had been illegally occupied. He reopened for prayers the Jamia Mosque which had been closed by Abul Fatah and rebuilt the temple which had been destroyed and opened it for-worship therein.[11] This shows that he had no hatred for any religion.

When Mahmud entered the Somnath temple. It is said that Mahmud broke the idol with his own hands and took away with him all the jewels that came out of the hallow stomach of the idol but according to W.W. Hunter no such jewel was ever found on the idol. The idol had no shape: it was a mass of stone in the shape of a lingam. He writes, "The idol of Somnath was merely one of the twelve famous lingas or phallic emblem erected in various parts of India. But Mahmud having taken the name of 'Idol-Smasher', the modern Persian historians gradually converted the plunder of Somnath into a legend of his pious zeal". He writes further "The growth of this myth can be clearly traced but it is still repeated by uncritical historian. The Linga or solid stone fetish of Somnath had no stomach, and could contain no jewels".[12] He immediately took possession of temple's wealth but he was not a religious fanatic, as he never forced the people whom he looted to accept the creed, which they did not believe. "Mahmud" writes S.M. Jaffar in his book Medieval India under Muslim Kings "was more of a conqueror than a fanatical propagandist or a pious missionary. To say that he invaded India time and again for the spread of his religion is historically wrong and psychologically untrue. In the first place, there is no scrap of evidence in the contemporary chronicles to show that he ever won converts, whether by force or by peaceful means"[13] Ironically, to the Muslim communalists Mahmud was a Ghazi, a champion of faith who tried to wipe out infidelity.

The attacks on the temples were not out of hatred but for acquiring the huge wealth concealed therein. In the words of Sidney Owen "...Temple forts provided the best means of preserving their (Raja's) riches from greedy hands...Naturally, these temple fortress at Kangra, Somnath and elsewhere became sure magnates to draw the attacks of the invading forces as they richly rewarded them. The early Muslim practice of dividing all the spoils of war between the soldiers and keeping only one fifth of the booty for the commander, may probably have further encouraged the soldiers to follow leaders who could easily promise them for rewards".[14]

Mahmud not only harassed the Hindu Rajas but also the Muslim kings. He attacked them with equal ferocity. During his first attack on Lahore, there were many Muslims who fought against him on behalf of its Hindu Raja. He twice waged hostilities against Multan whose ruler was a Daud Muslim and killed many local Muslims. The drama of plunder and bloodshed was enacted in Iran and Transoxiana also whose sovereigns were Muslims.[15]

Mahmud took away gold but never forced his Hindu soldiers to join his creed. His Hindu soldiers were free to blow their conchs and bow before idols even in Imperial Ghazni.[16] His religious policy was based on toleration. Elphinstone tells us that "It is no where asserted that he ever put a Hindu to death except in battle or in the storm of a fort"[17] Mahmud was an intimate friend of Raja of Kannauj. He attacked the Raja of Kalinger, simply to avenge the wrong done to his friend, the Raja of Kannauj. When he reached Kalinger, its Raja expressed his regret for the wrong he had done to the Raja of Kannauj. Mahmud returned without launching any attack.[18]

Under him Hindus enjoyed perfect religious freedom. They were entrusted with highly responsible posts and religion was not a condition of their service. He kept three Hindu divisions in his army. At least three Hindu generals, Sunder, Nath and Tilak rose to positions of high eminence and status in Ghaznavid army. Many of his lieutenants and even his governor in Lahore were Hindus.[19] Raja Tilak served Mahmud first as his Mir Munshi and then as the commander of his forces. Mahmud's son Masud employed Servand Rao in his fight with his brother. Sultan Masud discarded Ghazni and set up his capital in India. He brought back with him not only all the wealth that Mahmud had taken but also what had been collected from Iran, Khurasan, Kabul and Baluchistan. Masud died in India and all his wealth thus passed back to India. Tilak was general of his troops. He was the formost nobleman among the nobility of Ghazni and held the title of Amir-ul-umara or the Amir of Amirs or the prime nobleman.[20] Kettledrums were beaten in his quarters according to the customs of Hindu chiefs and banners gilded tops were granted. He had an army under his command, the tent and umbrella of Ghaznavid and sat in the charmed circle of the Sultan's confidential officers. Tilak suppressed the rebellion of Ahmad Nialtigin, governor of the Indian province. Again he raised

Hindu troops to fight against the Saljuk Turks, while his successor deputed the kotwal of Ghazni to recall Bijai Rai, a Hindu general to Ghazni from where he had fled on account of some political dissenssions.[21]

Thus neither Mahmud nor his successor were fanatic or anti-Hindu or Hinduism. They were greedy plunderers who for the lust of money and power, looted and oppressed all irrespective of their race or religion. They destroyed the temples and not the mosques, not because they hated those places but because they knew that the temples were the repositories of vast wealth in cash, jewelry and golden images. On the other hand, the architecture of mosque being such, there is hardly any place for the storage of wealth. Exasperated Hindus too did not spare temples when required. Harsha, who ruled in Kashmir in the eleventh century A.D. himself appointed special officers to destroy the metal idols of the temples so as to acquire the wealth for the treasury. A large number of Jain temples at Dabhoi and Cambay near Ahilwara in Gujarat were plundered by the Parmara king Subhatavarman of Malwa between 1193 and 1210 A.D.[22]

After the Ghaznavis, came the Ghoris. Their first exploit was the destruction of the city of Ghazni that Mahmud had converted into one of the most beautiful cities in the world. Mohammad Shahabuddin Ghori next turned his attention towards India. It was Raja Jaichand Rathore, the ruler of Kannauj who invited the Sultan of Afghanistan to India to settle his score with Prithviraj, the ruler of Ajmer and Delhi. He attacked the Ghaznavid ruler of Lahore in alliance with the Hindu Raja of Jammu. Both sacked and plundered the temples, but only those of their enemies and during the operation of wars.[23]

The victories of Shahbuddin Ghori are described as a victory of Islam by the Persian chronicles but the facts are otherwise. C.V. Vaidya writes:

"It cannot be alleged that the religious fervour actuating Shahbuddin and his Mohammadans was stronger than actuating the Rajputs. Although Mohammadan historians describe the former as making a religious war, Shahbuddin was fighting for the conquest of the territory and not for extending religion. Indeed we find that conversion of the people to Mohammadanism was not his motive. It was conquering northern India."[24]

For retaining power, the Sultans crushed their opponents

whether they were Hindus or Muslims. Muhammad Ghori killed his foe Prithviraj but appointed his son as the Governor of Ajmer.[25] Sultan Qutbuddin and Iltutmish were never motivated by religious factors. They ruled over their Hindu subjects without imposing their religion upon them or interfering in their religious matters. Jalaluddin suppressed Siddi Mulla's rebellion who wanted to assume both spiritual as well as political leadrship.[26] Sultan Alauddin was also not a fanatic. He had appointed many Hindus to important posts. The Chancellor of his Exchequer was also a Hindu.[27] When Ram Deo of Deogir was defeated and brought before the Sultan, the latter treated Ram Deo with great honour and presented him with a green canopy along with the title of Rai Rayan. He was further given a lac of tankas and sent back with honour to Deogir with his family and followers and Deogir was reconfirmed upon him.[28] Sultan Ghiasuddin Tughlaq sent Raja Rameshwar to rule over Mithila. Religion did not matter in the relationship between Hindu and Muslim rulers.[29]

In 1327, the second year of Mohammad bin Tughlaq's reign, the sultan's cousin Bahauddin Gurshap rose in revolt and the rebellion spread throughout the Deccan before it was crushed. Gurshap then took refuge with the Raja of Kampila who assured him full support. He said:

"You have done well to come to me and I am prepared to sacrifice my own life and whatever I possess in order to save you and protect you; no harm whatever will be done to you as long as there remains the last drop of blood in my body; I swear by the Gods-Khurshid, Zunar, Lat and Manat".[30]

The Raja beat the first attack made by the Mohammad bin Tughlaq's troops but on the arrival of reinforcements, the fall of the palace was certain. The Raja, no longer able to protect his Muslim guest, sent him to Vira Ballala III Hoysala for sanctuary and then, after the women had all perished in the rite of johar, led out his fighting men to meet a Rajput death. The Raja sacrificed his own life and of his kith and kin to save his friend. However Vira Ballala betrayed the trust and handed over Gurshap to the Sultan who later killed him.[31] In South India, many rebellions broke out during the reign of Mohammad bin Tughlaq. Even the Muslim officers revolted against him, so much so that the Hindu and Muslims in the Deccan unitedly entered into an alliance against the king. These rebels appointed a common leader named Zafar Khan, who at one time had been a slave of a Brahmin and with whose help he had risen in life.[32] The Brahmin predicted to him a brilliant career, stipulating to be his minister when he should be the king of Deccan. The prophecy came to pass and Zafar kept his word with the Brahmin.The title by which he mounted the throne was Alauddin Hasan Gungu Bahmani.[33]

Mohammad bin Tughlaq employed Hindus to the high posts and trusted them. He appointed a Hindu Sai Rai as his wazir. Dhara Dhar was appointed naib-wazir of Deogir and head of the Diwan-i-Uslub. Another Hindu Ratan was honoured with the title of Azim-us-Sind (Raja of Sind). [34] He also made him the governor of Sind and granted him the Iqta of Sinistan and its dependencies. Further he conferred upon him Muratib, an honour which was usually conferred on Amirs, namely the trumpets and distinctive marks. These caused a rebellion under the leadership of two officials of the Sultan who detested the predominance of a Hindu over them. The royal army crushed their rebellion and executed their leaders.[35]

Sultan Firoz Tughlaq imposed Jaziya upon Brahmins but did not force them to pay when the wealthier citizens of Delhi agreed to pay on their behalf. This suggests that it was only money that matter and not those who paid. He trusted the Hindus so much that even his personal bodyguards consisted of Rajputs headed by Bhiru Bhatti.[36] Firoz saw the pillars of Ashoka at Meerut and Topra, and was "so fascinated by them, that he had them transported to Delhi, difficult as this was one of them was placed in a commanding position on the roof of his citadel. He was curious to know what the inscription said, but no one could read it, the script having changed since the time of Ashoka. He was told that it was a magical charm and that it was associated with religious rituals. If objects of infidel worship had indeed been so abhorrent to Firoz, he would have had the pillars destroyed; instead they were placed in the position of prominence".[37]

Sultan Bahlol Lodi because of his policies and attitude was called Kafir by Muslim theologians.[38] Sultan Sikandar's policy was guided by his political ambition rather than by religious bigotry though he made it a point to display his devotion to his faith. "He was a very shrewd despot. He wanted no opposition to his will within his own camp. He knew that his Hindu origin might make him unacceptable to Muslims in general and Afghans in particular. He must have therefore, been anxious to carry favour with Muslims by making a display of his devotion to Islam and contempt of Hinduism"[39] Sikandar ruled for twenty-eight years. Rai Ugra Sen, Kachwaha, Vinayak Dev, Raja of Dholpur, Balbhadar Rai, Man Singh, Raja of Gwalior commanded great respect in Sikandar's Court. Hindu nobles like Kapurchand of Gwalior and Ugra Sen Kachwaha acted respectively as emissaries on behalf of Sikandar to Sultan Khilji and to Bihjat Khan, governor of Chanderi.[40]

Both Hindus and Muslims fought together shoulder to shoulder against invaders no matter whether they were Hindus or Muslims. When Timur invaded India he met resistance everywhere. He fought a battle with Mahmud Tughlaq of Delhi in 1398 and defeated him. When Timur was moving towards Delhi, the inhabitants of Fathabad and Rajabpur, who were mixed people- Hindus as well as Muslims- fled on hearing of Timur's approach Muslim jats of Tohana met with a worst fate, for Timur did not spare them and killed two thousand Muslims, denounced them as demons and made prisoners both Hindus and Muslims.[41]When Timur arrived at Meerut, its governor Malik Ilyas Afghan, undaunted by the fate of Delhi, decided to defend their charge. He along with Ahmad Thaneswari and a Hindu chieftain Rai Sagi resisted the invader. They gave a determined fight, burnt their women folk in the fire of Johar and did not surrender till end. Timur called Ilyas and other Muslims, who fought against him, infidel, though they belonged to the same religion. Pingle Kennedy has rightly pointed out:

"It is noticeable in men of Timur's type that their holy war does not confine to infidels alone. If true Mussalman opposes him so much the worse for them. They have ceased to be Mussalmans and have become of the tribe of kafirs".[42]

Thus Timur's invasion of Hindustan cannot be called jihad, as his battles were mostly fought against the Mussalmans. The Muslims of India did not support him and sided with their Hindu brethren. Timur had no thoughts to bestow on idol breaking. In the whole of his one-year war, there is not a single instance of temple demolition or desecration. Tughlaq dynasty was however extinguished.[43]

Imposition of Jaziya is a black spot in the history of the early medieval period but it was a military and not a religious tax as priests preachers and religious preceptors were exempted from it. It was also not imposed upon those non-Muslims who rendered military service in the army. Hindus in the army of Mahmud Ghazna were not required to pay Jaziya. Besides women, children old and insane were exempted from jaziya.[44] If the Hindus paid Jaziya, the Muslims had to pay Zakat. Besides the Hindu rulers also levied Poll- tax upon the Muslims. Chandradeva Gahadavada seized Kannauj by the end of the 11th century. He levied a poll tax on the Muslims, which was known as Turushka danda. His successors continued the tax over Muslims till its final annexation by Iltumish.[45]

The Muslim rulers did not have the zeal to undertake a program of conversion as they were not Ghazis.Their Hindu subjects-rajas ranas and rajput nobles, known for their loyalty were not forced to convert to Islam In the words of W.H. Moreland "Forcible conversions was not entirely unknown but it was relatively unimportant" and "most of the conversions which occurred were independent of official pressure"[46] Many of the forcible conversions were the outcome of momentary fury and not hatred. Not only the Muslims, the Hindu rulers also did not hesitate to resort to conversion to express their ferocity. After the Muslims conquered Sind, Appa Raval of Mewar attacked not only Sind, he married a Muslim princess and converted her to Hinduism. Raimal, king of Marwad, captured 600 Muslim women and after converting them to Hinduism, married them publicly to several noblemen of his court. Puran Mal, the Governor of the fort of Rai Sen in Sher Shah reign is, reported to have converted many Muslims to Hinduism.The Hindu Rajas also married the daughters of the defeated Muslim kings. Raval Cheehak of Jaisalmer married the daughter of Sultan Haibatkhan, and named her Soma Devi. When Kanwar Jagmal, the eldest son of Rao Malinath Rathod of Marwad defeated the Sultan of Gujarat and annexed it to his domain, he married publicly daughter of the Sultan called Gindoli.[47]

Though the Delhi Sultanate had established, the power of the Hindu Rajas had remained undiminished during more than three centuries of Muslim rule in India. Cordial relations existed between the Hindu and Muslims during the Sultanate period. Common interest decided the alliances and not religious considerations In Malwa, Basant Rai was the wazir of Abdul Muzaffar Nasir Shah while his successor Mahmud Khalji II leaned heavily for some times on Raichand Parabia to whom he gave the title of Medini Rai.[48] However differences occurred between the two and ultimately led to war. Medini Rao sought and got the assistance of Rana Sanga. In the war the Sultan was defeated, wounded and taken prisoner. However bitterness evaporated after the war. "His enemy Rana Sanga of Cheitur" says Ferishta, "caused him to be brought in to his own tent, dressed his wounds, attended him in person, and showed him every mark of attention; and after his recovery, furnished him with an escort of one thousand Rajput horse, who conducted him back to Mandu where he resumed the reign of his government"[49] According to Ferishta, the relations between the two communities were so cordial that Sultan Mahmud II Khalji requested the assistance of Hindu rulers to put down the turbulence of his Muslim nobility.[50] Sultan Ibrahim invaded Gwalior, defeated its ruler Vikramaditya, but treated him with generosity. He assigned him the fief of Shamsabad. This touched the heart of Vikramaditya so much that he remained firmly attached to the Lodi Monarch and died fighting in his cause in 1526.[51] Thus religion did not stand as barrier in the relations between the rulers belonging to different communities. The rulers were loved or hated by their subjects not because of their religion but because of their activities and attitudes. Raja Man Singh, the ruler of Gwalior, was extremely popular with his entire subject because of his liberal views. So much so that according to Niamatullah, he was "taken to be a Muslim by the Muslims and a Hindu by Hindus"[52] The chronicler also states that it was because of his popularity and friendship with the Muslims that no Muslim ruler could gain ascendancy over him.[53]

Rulers whether Hindu or Muslim never hesitated to take the support of the outsiders for political gains in their country. Rana Sanga was the head of the Rajput Principality of Chittor. He had defeated Sultan Mahmud Khalji, the king of Malwa. He had engaged in hostilities with Sultan Ibrahim of Delhi and twice had met the Sultan himself in the pitched battles.[54] He invited Babar to contain the rising power of Ibrahim Lodi. "Sanga allied himself with Babar against Ibrahim Lodi and agreed to attack Delhi from the South and the West whilst Babar attacked from the north. This, he believed would enable him to take the capital and having done so he would dispense with Babar and inherit the Sultanate. Trouble from Gujarat, however prevented Sanga from keeping his part of the agreement and the battle of Panipat ended in victory for Babar. What was worse for Sanga, was the realization that Babar intended to stay in India and rule from Delhi. The alliance broke on this..."[55] Immediately after the battle of Panipat, he made efforts to gather together a coalition which would help him either to compel Babar to leave India or to confine him to Punjab. Then he sought the support of the Muslim kings of India against Babar. Ahmad Yadgar, in his Tarikh-i-Saltan-Afghana writes: "Rana Sanga who was at that time a powerful chief, sent a message to Hasan Khan saying "the Mughals have entered Hindostan, have slain Sultan Ibrahim and taken possession of the country; it is evident that they will likewise send an army against both of us; if you will side with me, we will be alive and not suffer them to take possession."[56] The struggle was not between Hindus and Muslims, though Babar denounced those Afghan Chiefs who joined Sanga as Kafirs and Mulhids.[57] Even Babar, before the battle of Panipat, was assisted by Yogis of Balaknath and in the post Panipat period, a large number of Hindu Zamindars, Rajas and local Chiefs assisted him in his campaigns.[58] The very author of his elevation was Rangaildas who taught him how to conquer and how to govern.[59] On the other hand, Sultan Mahmud Lodi, brother of Ibrahim Lodi was proclaimed by Rana Sanga as the rightful successor to the throne of Ibrahim after the battle of Panipat. Rana Sanga was assisted also by Sultan Mahmud and Nusrat Shah, son of Hussain Shah the ruler of Bengal, against Babar. Hasan Khan Mewati was killed in the war.[60]

Soon after Rana Sanga died in 1527, apparently poisoned by his Sardars who had no desire to renew the conflict with Babar. On his death, Babar paid a tribute of respect to the Rana by saying that "the high eminence, he then held he had attained but recently by his valour and sword"[61] Ironically, Rani Karmeti (Karmavati), a widow of Rana sent a message to Babar on behalf of her son, Vikramjit to whom the Rana had assigned Ranthambhor. The Rani offered to accept Babar's suzerainty in return for his help in ousting Vikramjit's elder brother, Ratansi (Ratan Singh) from Chittor. She also offered to present to him the jeweled crown and belt captured from Mahmud Khalji by Sanga in 1518, these having become a bone of contention between Ratan Singh and Vikramjit Singh.[62]

During his reign, Babar never involved himself with trifling religious matters. Nor did he ever show fanaticism by forcibly converting the Hindus to his faith or by persecuting the Hindus or prohibiting the religious assemblies and movements of the Hindu saints or the Hindu pilgrims from one region to another. In Punjab, over which he had firm control, he allowed Guru Nanak to carry on his mission without interruption.[63] "Except in the case of Jain idols in the Varwa valley, Babar never gave orders for the destruction of the temples of other places. As regards the Varwa valley, he himself has mentioned in his Memoirs that "the naked idols are its defect, I for my part ordered them to be destroyed"[64]

He had no hatred for other religions and did not destroy religious places. In the words of Radhey Shyam:

"It may be observed that it would be quite injudicious to hold in any way Babar responsible for the destruction of the famous Janamsthan temple. Destruction of temples was neither in consequence with his policy, nor his attitude, especially at a time when he needed the support of the non-Muslim population."[65]

If Babar could record the destruction of Jain Temple in his Memoir, he would also have mentioned the destruction of Ram Temple and the construction of the Babri Mosque. Not only Babar, his descendants also make no mention of the destruction of the temple. There is no record of the incident in Abul Fazal's Ain-I-Akbari, Akbarnama or Mulla Abdul Qadir Badayuni's Muntakhab-ul-Tawarikh or Emperor Jahangir's Memoir. Besides, Saint Tulsidas and Surdas have not referred it in their immortal works like Ramcharitamanas and Sursagar. Besides no historian, even during the reign of Aurangzeb has recorded it. Babar's Will to his son also speaks that he was not a fanatic.

"Had he been fanatic, the temples of Mathura and other places would have been reduced to the ground and Mathura would have not been allowed to grow as the centre of neo-Vaishnavites, nor could there been cordial relation between him and the Hindu chief. Vir Bhanudya Kavyam speaks of the friendly relations between Babar and Raja Bir Singh Deo, the Baghela ruler of Arail. Babar was a true Sunni of the Hanifi school, but he did not allow religion to override politics"[66]

Babar's son and successor Humayun too was free from sectarian feelings. His treatment with the widowed and orphaned family of the martyr Vikramaditya of Gwalior is praiseworthy inspite of the fact that the late Hindu Chief had fallen fighting against Babar and Humayun. He saved the honour of Hindu ladies by personal intervention. The family in gratitude gave the Kohinoor Diamond to Humayun, which ultimately passed in to the hands of the British and now decorates the crown of the British queen.[67]

When Sher Shah defeated Humayun and made his exist difficult by blocking all routes of his escape, Raja Prabhan, a Rajput Chief, volunteered with his followers to check the advances of the enemy forces, so as to allow His Majesty to escape. Humayun accepted the offer and reached Agra safely.[68]

Humayun and Rana Virsal Prasad joined together for punitive action first against Shah Hussain who had murdered Rana's father and then against Sher Shah Sur whom they considered to be the arch-usurper and a common foe. On the other hand Sher Shah too had the support of Hindus. So much so that his army was manned by the Hindus to a considerable extent; his great general was Vikram, a Hindu.[69] One of his best known general was Brahmjit Gaur, whom he sent in pursuit of Humayun. His army included a contingent of Rajputs. Raja Ram Singh of Gwalior is said to have been in his service. Todarmal too was originally in his service.[70]

It was in the Rana Virsal's palace at Amarkot that Akbar was born. A tribal Hindu Chief gave a gift of a dagger with a gold handle studded with diamonds to Humayun at the christening ceremony of Akbar saying that:

"This is a family heirloom of great antiquity. While entrusting it to your charge, O'Prince of Princes, I pray that the Lord may give the strength not only to safeguard the honour of the house of Babar Padshah but also to protect the interests of all those who may happen to come under your sway. Our astrologers predict for you, O' luster of the eye of Humayun, a long and prosperous reign equal in glamour to the majestic authority of the Alexander and Asoka. Keep this dagger in safe custody; its sheen will protect you and your family from the evil eye and its sharp edge will serve as a shield against the wicked designs of your enemies".[71]

Akbar is well known for his secularism both in his private and public life He appointed Hindus in high posts and trusted them completely Raja Man Singh, Todarmal Birbal and Tansen are well known. Man Singh, whom he called Farzand,(son) played a major role in extending the boundaries of his empire. Raja Todarmal was the revenue Minister. On many occasions, the emperor sent him to command the troops in the field. He enjoyed the trust of his master He was sent to suppress the revolt of Ali Kuli Khan as Akbar was suspicious that the Muslim generals might act in collusion with Ali Kuli Khan.[72] Tansen and Birbal, two other jewel of his court kept him happy and entertained him with their unique talent in music and wit.

Akbar treated Muslim rulers differently from Hindus; on conquest, a Muslim was usually displaced and his territories taken under direct administration, but a Hindu who accepted the situation was assured of an honorable position within the empire and accordingly retained practically complete authority within his dominions.[73]

Akbar's fight with Rana Pratap was "not a Hindu Mohammedan question, nor a conflict between Hinduism and Islam. It was simply a conflict between the Mughal Empire and the state of Marwar. Had it been otherwise, Rana Pratap would not have placed one of his divisions under Hakim Khan Sur, nor Akbar his whole army under Man Singh...If Marwar were ruled over by Mohammadan Prince, Akbar would have dealt with him in the same manner. There is not a shred of evidence that Akbar was actuated by any other but purely political motives".[74] The Haldighati war was an assertion of local independence The princes of Marwar, Amber, Bikaner and Bundi took part with Akbar against Rana Pratap.[75] The hatred of Rana Pratap for Akbar "was excited not by the latter's religion but by his usurpation. He refused to give his daughter to the emperor not because he really considered it a misalliance but because he wanted to work himself and his people up in to conviction of the vileness of the enemy-thereby forging a sword, keen and invincible, for self protection and the maintenance of the integrity of his dominion".[76]

Rana Pratap's fight with Akbar had nothing against Islam or the Muslim community. His own brothers (Jaimal and Shakti Singh) were in Akbar's military service and many a time fought against him. On some occasions the two brothers were facing each other in the battlefield. Even his son Rana, Umrao Singh was in Akbar's court.[77] When Pratap's eldest son, Kanwar Amar Singh, captured Rahim Khan-i-Khanan's family and brought it to Pratap, he received the ladies with courtesy and admonished his son for laying his hand on women and thereby denouncing the Rajput's tradition of chivalry. He immediately made arrangement for sending them back to Rahim, who was the Governor of Ajmer.[78] When Rahim came to know this his heart was touched. Poet as he was, he at once exclaimed:

"Bhram rahsi dhra, khis jase khursan,
Amar bisambhar uprain, rakhio nahchyo ran.[79]

(All is unstable in this world, land and wealth will disappear, but the virtue of a great name lives forever. Pratap abandoned wealth and land, but never bowed his head alone, of all the princes of Hind, he preserved his honour)

Rahim never forgot the kindness and when after a resistance of twenty-four years, the Rana was on the point of negotiating with

Akbar, the proposal for submission, the Khan-i-Khanan sent a letter urging him to keep faith in God and continue the fight.[80]

Not only Rahim but Akbar, too was touched by Pratap's chivalry. He immediately ordered a cease-fire and issued a proclamation that in future no harm should come to Rajput women at the hands of an imperial soldier. Pratap's attitude struck a sympathetic chord in his heart; his respect for Pratap increased and he decided to let the valiant Rana live in peace. Thus came to an end a decade of costly campaign in Marwar.[81]

Not only Rahim, Todarmal also had cordial relations with Pratap and the two visited each other inspite of their belonging to different camps.[82]

Akbar's eventual co-existence with Rana Pratap was in fact an admission that in Rana, he found a foe worthy of respect and admiration. "It was not a momentary emotional upsurge that brought tears to Akbar's eyes when he learned of the death of Pratap in 1597; rather it was a soulful homage of the great monarch to another"[83]

When the news of Pratap's death reached to Akbar, a famous poet Rai Dursa of Rajasthan was in attendance at the court and he at once expressed his feelings in the following verses:

"As laingo andag padh laingo abnami I
Go ada gabdaye, jiko bahto dhur bami II
Navrojo na gayo, nego atsan navalli I
Na go jhrokhan heth, jeth duniaya dhalli II
Gahlol Rana-jit gayo, dasn mund rasna dasi I
Nisas mook bhariya nayan, to mrit shah Pratpasi" II

(O Pratap, you kept your horses unbranded, your head unbowed, your fame untarnished. You were strong enough to carry on your work against heavy odds. You never participated in the Nauroz festival, nor did you mount guard on the imperial presence down the jharokha darshan. You attained a very high place in this world. On hearing of your death, O Pratap Akbar's eyes were dimmed and his tongue stuck in his throat, for you had really won after all.)

Durse recited the verses in the presence of the emperor. This appreciation of his foe did not annoy Akbar instead he appreciated and rewarded the poet.[84] Besides he also built a statue to the memory of Rana Pratap.[85]

There were conflicts and conciliation between the Muslim and Hindu rulers purely on political grounds. Ferocity or hatred remained only confined to the battlefield and once the war was over, cordiality appeared. Emperor Jahangir's son Khurram (Shah Jahan) fought and won a war with Amar Singh, son of Rana Pratap but when the battle was over bitterness vanished. A treaty was signed between the Rana and Khurram to end hostilities. Rana presented a precious ruby, which had belonged to the house of Sisodias for eight hundred years, as a goodwill gesture. Khurram embraced him and said:

"I respect and admire your sentiment. But please remember that I am not here to deprive you of the heirloom of your illustrious family. May I implore you to accept this precious stone back from me as a pledge of your lasting friendship. The Mughals respect the heroism and valour of your tribe. The past is past and past forever. We look forward to the future with faith and confidence"[86]

After the conclusion of the treaty, Rana Amar Singh, Prince Karan Singh and Khurram sat and ate together at the same dastarkhan. Amar Singh sent his son Prince Karan Singh to meet Jahangir at his Court. When the prince arrived "he was graciously received. Jahangir called him within the railing and embraced him. This was a rare honour of the Mughal Court... He was given a Mansab of 5,000 Jats and 5,000 swars." After the conclusion of treaty, which also contained some of the conditions which were unprecedented, the emperor issued a Farman impressing it with the mark of his own palm. (This Farman was wrapped in a piece of Dacca muslin and bore the impression of the King's hand in saffron colour. It is still preserved among the Archives of the Udaipur Darbar) As per the terms of the treaty all the territory taken from Mewar during the reign of Akbar and Jahangir, including the fort of Chittor was returned to the Rana. Besides a substantial Jagir was granted to the Prince.[87] The Rana was not required to attend the Court in person and no tribute was imposed. In the words of Tod "seldom has subjugated loyalty met with such consideration" and "to win his heart" the emperor bestowed on the prince Karan Singh every day the richest presents of all sorts so that by the time of his departure after a stay of nearly four months, his presents amounted to the value of more than 200000 rupees, besides numerous elephants, horses and other things presented by Khurram, Nurjahan and other ladies of the harem.[88] About two years later, two marble equestrian statues of Rana Amar Singh and Prince Karan were placed at Agra in the garden just below the Jhrokha. Thus Jahangir treated the brave descendants of Mewar with chivalry and offered them a generous treatment which was in contrast "with the vulgarity of their co-religionists, the Marathas".[89]

Jahangir gave high posts to the talented and loyal persons and did not discriminate against them on the basis of religion. Mohan Das acted as Jahangir's diwan in the third year of his reign. Departments were often placed under the charge of Hindus; e.g., the Diwan-i-Tah and Diwan-i-Buyatal (department of escheated property) under Mukand Das. The post of provincial Diwan was held by Beni Prasad in Behar; Rai Dayanant Rai in Deccan and Rai Shobha Chand in Lahore. Jaswant Singh and Jai Singh were the chief Amirs of the state and also served as Provincial Governors.[90] He conferred the title of Raja on Ramdas, who was the guard of Akbar's treasury and had refused to hand over its key to Man Singh, who supported Khusrau against Prince Salim on the throne. Jahangir also rewarded Ramdas with a flag, a drum, an elephant, a horse and the fort of Ranthambhor as his jagir.[91] During his reign, the fortress of Gwalior, the great state prison was commanded by Ani Rai Singhdalan.[92] Rana Singh was appointed as the superintendent of Akbar's tomb.[93] The son of Rai Rayan Raja Bikramjit was made the master of his ordnance or the Superintendent of his department of artillery. This department was always ready for service with sixty thousand camel-mounted guns, each supplied with the ten seirs of powder and twenty shots; and 20,000 other pieces with every requisite equipment. Rai Rayan had for some time held the appointment of Diwan under Akbar. He was immensely rewarded by Akbar and had no equal in wealth even among the Hindus. He possessed ten crores of Ashrafis.[94]

Political animosities led to oppression, torture and execution. Religion was later used to justify or denounce such actions. The rulers irrespective of their religion behaved in a similar manner when their power was challenged. Jahangir got his son Khusrau jailed and blinded when the latter made an unsuccessful attempt to dislodge him from the throne.[95] Jahangir was not hostile either to Guru Arjun or to his faith. In fact he had great admiration and veneration for the Guru though many of the Muslims under the influence of the Guru had renounced Islam and had adopted Sikhism. When he came to know that the Guru had blessed and helped his rebel son Khusrau, he addressed the Guru: "Thou art a saint, a great teacher and holy man; thou lookest on all, rich and poor, alike. It was therefore not proper for thee to give money to my enemy Khusrau"[96]

He asked the Guru to pay rupees two lakhs but the Guru refused to pay the money. Thereupon the Guru was imprisoned. Chandu, to whom the Guru was entrusted, tortured the Guru in prison. It was not a Muslim Sikh question as Mian Mir made appeals to the emperor for his release and the punishment to his torturers. Chandu and other enemies of the Guru kept him for three hours seated in caldron heated by a blazing fire. But he did not submit to Chandu's condition namely to allow his son Hargobind to marry Chandu's daughter.[97]

Jahangir did not spare Hasan Beg and Abdul Rahim supporters of Khusrau. Even an exalted Muslim Sheikh Jalal Thaneswari who enjoyed the dignity and reputation of a religious luminary was not spared for his reported blessing to the Prince. Sheikh Ahmad Sirhindi and Ibrahim Baba were also imprisoned by Jahangir.[98] Thus political reasons led Jahangir to punish all those who stood on the side of his rebel son, no matter to which community they belonged. Had Jahangir's persecution of the Guru been directed by religious motives, he would have persecuted the Sikhs as well. Neither Sikh traditions nor Muslim fanaticism tell us anything of any further persecution of the Sikhs.[99] The persecution of the Guru was primarily due to political reasons as neither any other Sikh was molested nor any interdict was laid on the Sikh faith. Jahangir also imprisoned Guru Hargobind, but again he was not dictated by religious reason. Macauliffe writes that it was again Chandu who largely bribed Jahangir's astrologer who advised Jahangir who was indisposed at that time to send Hargobind in to the fort of Gwalior to do penance there and pray for his good health to ward of evil influence. Again Wazir Khan spoke in the Guru's favour. When Jahangir came to know about the real character of Chandu, he felt sorry. He not only released the Guru but on latter's request released all the Rajas detained in the fort.[100] The Guru was called Bandi Chhor or the liberator of the prisoners. There is still a platform in existence inside the fort, which is named the platform of Pir Bandi Chhor, over which a Mohammedan lights the lamp in the memory of the departed Guru.[101] He also handed over Chandu to the Guru who was latter mercilessly killed by the Guru's followers. He told the Guru that Chandu had exceeded the orders, he had received on the subject of Guru Arjun's treatment.[102] Both the Guru and Jahangir became good friends. According to the author of Dabistan II "Hargobind was always attached to the stirrup of the victorious Jahangir..."[103]

That Jahangir was not fanatic and was not hostile to Sikhism becomes evident from the fact that during his reign conversions of Muslims to Sikhism were taking place and it was in the knowledge of the emperor but he did not oppose voluntary conversions. Once a Qazi's unmarried daughter escaped to the Guru, with the help of Mian Mir. The Guru converted her to Sikhism and gave her the name Kaulan. Qazi, father of Kaulan reported the matter to Jahangir and begged for justice. The emperor passed the following order:

"Art thou not ashamed of thyself. It became thee not to have acted as thou has't done. It is not proper for thee to quarrel with priests. Though oughtest rather to do them reverence. In open court, thou hast rent the veil of thy modesty and rendered thyself despised of all men. Thy daughter was obliged to leave her home"[104]

The Guru caused a tank to be excavated in her name. The tank is still famous as Kaulsar (Kaulan's tank) in the city of Amritsar. The conversion of Kaulan by the Guru and no action against him also make it clear that Guru Arjun's execution was not guided by religious but by political reasons.

Guru Hargobind also had no feeling of revenge towards the emperor and respected Islam. Once while hunting, the Guru is said to have saved Jahangir's life. He also had a large number of Muslim soldiers including Pathan mercenaries and the Mughal deserters. The special type of Dhad singing on the martial tunes was started by the Guru. The special Dhadis or the bards such as Abdul and Natha Mal were appointed to sing heroic stories set to the martial tunes. Besides the Guru had a band of devoted Muslims in his entourage and many Muslims as personal friends.[105] That Sikhism spread rapidly during Jahangir's reign speaks of religious tolerance and harmony.

Political reasons led Jahangir to take actions against the Jains also. Jain Guru Man Singh had predicted after the succession of Jahangir that his reign would not last for more than two years. This encouraged some big Jain officials and chiefs to revolt and join Khusrau in his rebellion. Rai Singh of Bikaner actually revolted and gave much trouble to Jahangir. This led Jahangir to turn the Jains out of his kingdom for some time.[106]

After Jahangir' death Shah Jahan became emperor. Like his father and grandfather, he followed a liberal policy in state matters. The Rajput Sardars had a great influence in his Court and the emperor not only appointed Hindus in high posts but also fully trusted them.

We learn from the Padshah Nama that there were 110 Hindus among Shah Jahan's 580 commanders of 500 horses and upwards.[107] Once Mohabbat Khan, a close relative and top-ranking noble of Shah Jahan insulted Raja Amar Singh Rathore who beheaded Mohabbat Khan in the very presence of the emperor.[108]

Shah Jahan treated all the religions alike and did not allow anyone to insult or hurt other's religious feeling. He restored a temple to the Jains, which was converted in to mosque by Aurangzeb near Ahmedabad. Shah Jahan got the minarets demolished and the temple restored.[109] However, his successor Aurangzeb's orthodoxy did an irreparable damage to the heritage of harmony.

Aurangzeb

Aurangzeb's fanaticism and orthodoxy was the outcome of his lust for the throne. Dara Shikoh being the eldest son was the heir apparent. Because of his non-sectarian views, Dara was quite popular with the Hindus and the non-orthodox section of the Muslim community. Aurangzeb, in order to get the support of the orthodox who were unhappy with Dara's approach, became the champion of orthodoxy. He could visualise that his own leaning towards orthodoxy if ventilated through his action would at once divert the attention of the orthodox section towards him. Once convinced Aurangzeb steadily went on taking steps to highlight his stand and even to display his personal orthodoxy that stood in marked contrast with Dara.

The victory of orthodoxy not only led to the execution of Dara as a person but of liberalism as a state policy. The pliant theologians in the emperor's pay signed a decree that "Dara deserved death on the ground of infidelity and deviation from Islamic orthodoxy". The execution of Dara was an outcome of the political ambition of Aurangzeb who could never feel himself safe so long Dara lived but the official chargesheet framed against Dara was based on religion.[110]

Though Dara was liberal and was related to Hindu nobles, yet all the three important rulers of Rajputana, Raja Jaswant Singh, Raja Jai Singh and Rana Raj Singh were on the side of Aurangzeb. Dara's touching appeals to them and reference to help rendered by him when they needed, fell on deaf ears.[111] Rajputs, except Hadas did not support Dara. The task of capturing Dara dead or alive was assigned to Raja Jai Singh and Jaswant Singh. Dara was betrayed by Jiwan who was indebted to Dara, both for his fortune and life. He would have been trampled under the feet of an elephant, by the order of Shah Jahan for an offence; if Dara had not solicited his pardon.[112]

Aurangzeb not only executed Dara but also those who expressed his sympathy for Dara. When the people came to know about the fate of the unfortunate Dara, they lamented and cursed Aurangzeb. On the order of Aurangzeb, an inquiry was made and some of Dara's slave boys and guards were caught. Aurangzeb did not order to put them to death. He once again used the muftis and the ecclesiastical doctors from whom he asked what the law decreed against such seditious people? The doctors gave the judgement, the emperor desired. They gave the following verdict:

"That as a commission of a little evil for the attachment of a mighty good was lawful in some cases and expedient in others, there might be no harm in putting to death people convicted of having opposed the Caliph's intention or resisted his commands"

After this sentence "those unfortunate people" writes Seid Gholam Hossein Khan in 'The Seir Mutaqherin' "who so far from having acted by premeditated malice, had only given way to the violence of their feelings were all seized and executed with all the forms of law".[113]

Aurangzeb did not spare even his father Shah Jahan who was deeply attached to Dara. After the merciless execution of Dara, his head was cut off from the body and sent to Shah Jahan as a present who refused to see it. His headless body was paraded to terrorise the people, through the streets and lane and then buried without the customary washing and dressing, in the tomb of Humayun.[114]

Roshanara, the sister of Dara, who stood on the side of Aurangzeb, held a gala feast to celebrate the execution of Dara and distributed a million copper coins to make known her joy at the grim event.[115] That festivity was inspired and financed by Aurangzeb himself.[116]

After removing Dara from his way, Aurangzeb turned his evil eye upon Dara's son Sulaiman Shikoh who had been given shelter by Raja Prithwi Singh. He appointed Jai Singh to use his influence and diplomacy upon Prithwi Singh, who was unwilling to deliver Sulaiman to Aurangzeb. Jai Singh prevailed upon the Raja. Prince Sulaiman was handed over to Aurangzeb, who put the prince to death, by slow-poisoning.[117]

Aurangzeb even tried to wipe out the memory of Dara from the public mind. He ordered for the removal of the stone railing in the temple of Keshav Rai at Mathura, which had been presented by Dara, on the plea that in 'the Muslim faith it is a sin to look at temple and this Dara had restored a railing in a temple.' Removal of the railing served a double purpose; while it assumed the shape of an act of piety of the emperor, it also removed a relic, which was associated with the name of Dara and was keeping his memory fresh. So much so that when he went to the mausoleum of Humayun to offer prayers for the repose of his son Sultan Muhammad's soul, he saw a white bier cloth upon a tomb, he asked who was buried there. On hearing that it was Dara's grave he ordered the cloth to be taken away and imposed the penalty of death on anyone who should pray there. Even Dara's famous palace at Lahore was demolished and a mosque was erected.[118]

In order to justify his inhuman acts and to present himself as a pious person he took the refuge of religion. Sir Jadunath Sarkar writes:

"Aurangzeb no doubt had an orthodox bent of mind but when he found himself put in a situation where justification of his action was necessary to recover public respect which had suffered due to his action against his father, he posed as the champion of orthodox, as the reluctant and compelled instrument of the Divine Will in a mission of much needed religious reform. Hence, he displayed extreme zeal in restoring the ordinance of pure Islam and removing heretical innovations, so that people might forget his past conduct as a son and as a brother, till at last his court historian could write of him 'Hisi imperial robe of state of thinly veiled the dervish's frock that he wore underneath it".[119]

Aurangzeb did not stop pouring venom against Dara even after his execution. He used to condemn Dara as a heretic, an idol-worshipper and his court historians characterized Dara Shikoh as 'Be Shikoh' the undignified.[120]

In a Machiavellian way, Aurangzeb eliminated one after another, all the claimants to the throne. When he rebelled against Shah Jahan, he wrote a letter to his brother Shuja explaining about Dara and Murad's evil designs. About himself, Aurangzeb stated that "not even in remote imaginations and will, the desire of kingship crossed my mind".[121] In a secret letter to Murad, Auranzeb asked him to take over the reigns of the empire. He wrote: "I want to see you on the throne. I don't like the crows. After your succession to the throne I will turn mendicant and go to Mecca for pilgrimage".[122] Thus

Aurangzeb, represented himself as a humble but a pious Muslim whose only desire was to squelch Dara's apostasy. He even started addressing Murad "His Majesty" while Murad deferred to Aurangzeb as "His Holiness".[123] Aurangzeb flattered Murad as most worthy of rule and secretly denounced Shuja as a heretical Shia or Rafizi and Dara as Mulhid (non-believer).[124]

Putting one against the other and presenting himself as the well wisher of both his brothers Aurangzeb succeeded in fulfilling his ambition. He successfully created suspicion between his own son Muhammad, who had married Shuja's daughter, and Shuja. Muhammad who sided his father-in-law against Aurangzeb fell in the trap and was arrested and sent to Gwalior fort where he died after seven years. Shuja having fled to Arakan was betrayed by the Raja and he with all his family perished. When this news reached Aurangzeb, he ordered grand funeral obsequies and gave alms, principally to those learned in the faith, praying them to supplicate God for that Prince dying in the realm of Arakan, within a heathen and idolatrous land. Similar obsequies were ordered to be performed in all the principal cities of the empire. He made these demonstrations of piety, not for his love to the deceased prince but to make known to all the people that Shah Shuja was dead. Thus they would, he hoped, accept him (Aurangzeb) as absolute Lord of the Mughal Empire.[125]

After Shuja was the turn of Murad. Aurangzeb under the veil of piety and of an austere virtue knew how to conceal all the vices of a boundless covetousness and an insatiable ambition. Seid Gholam writes:

"Moradbaqsh, who had been so instrumental in that victory, the only return he made him, was endeavouring by every means in his power to circumvent that unsuspecting youth. The unsuspecting youth upon his invitation, had set from Gujarat his Government at the head of his troops and had rendered him considerable services in the battle against Maharadha Djesvent Rat-hor and then in that which ruined Dara-Shecoh in the plains of Udjein, in both of which he fought like a common trooper and received several wounds that had set his military character in the strongest light. But all these merits did not avail. The artful Aurangzeb kept this simple youngman in good humour. By ordering his officers to present him with their nazurs for his victory and by making him believe that their master's whole ambition being to spend his days in the two Holy Cities, he would of course leave the empire to his disposal. The young Prince, who had a deal of frankness in his temper, and no less simplicity in his turn of mind, yielded so much belief to his protestations, that he used to frequent his artful brother without the least suspicion. To no purpose did several of his faithful servants advice him to be more cautious and to beware of his brother; for all answer they received a reprimand; nor could he bring to believe that so many promises and so many protestations, with such an appearance of humility and abstinence, would end in artifice and perfidy".[126]

When Murad and Aurangzeb were encamped outside Mathura, the latter proposed that as had been agreed between them, Murad's accession should be formally celebrated. The day of coronation of Murad was fixed for the 15th of June 1656. The tents were set up in front of the Mosque of Mathura. It was there that Murad was to receive the turban and the imperial sabre, from the hand of the Qazi. The evening that was to precede the ceremony Aurangzeb invited Murad to his tent for the purpose of consulting with the astrologers whether the day fixed for the coronation would be a fortunate one.

Murad's faithful officers and advisors warned him against it. "I will go to fetch the crown", replied Murad. "It is from his hands I shall receive it" Ignoring the advice, Murad went to Aurangzeb. "Cunning Aurangzeb caused his brother to be seated in the place of honour. He chased away himself the flies that molested him; with a piece of linen he wiped off perspiration which ran down his face. During the conversation, which was long, he repeatedly called Morad, his master, his lord and his sovereign. A bath of rose water was prepared for him and a grand repast was afterward served up".[127]

Murad was made to drink to celebrate the occasion. Aurangzeb, who hastily withdrew pretending sudden illness, bribed a slave girl to remove Murad's sword immediately. Thereafter, Aurangzeb's guards fell upon the unarmed prince. He was shackled with chains and his property confiscated.[128] Murad's son was also captured and both father and son were placed in a covered howda on an elephant and sent off at speed during the night to Delhi, escorted by [4000] cavalry. In the morning Aurangzeb's agents saluted him as the emperor and Murad's officers were invited to enter the usurper's service with a promise of double pay, which after some hesitation, in their desperate circumstances, they did.[129]

On arriving at Delhi, the unfortunate prince was publicly paraded as a prisoner, previous to his being consigned to a fort.

Manucci who was an eyewitness to this scene wrote:

"It was very pitiful to see poor Murad Baksh, make this miserable entry in to Delhi visible to all, his face dejected, wearing a blue turban, ill put on; behind him an executioner with a naked sword in his hands, ready upon any attempt at rescue to cut off his head".[130]

Murad was confined to Gwalior fort. Where on hearing that " he had found friends in the palace and had attempted to effect his escape, he without the scruple, resolved to put him to death. For this purpose he had made choice of one of his dependants, whom he engaged to revenge thereby the death of his own father, who had been put to death by Muradbaqsh, on suspicion that he intended to join Dara Shecoh, against whom he was then marching from Gujarat; he even proposed that murder to him as a religious duty to which he was obliged by the Tallion law".[131]

Aurangzeb believed in the maxim "Kingship knows no kinship'. He did not spare even his sons and daughter. Muhammad Sultan, who defected to his uncle Shuja during the war of succession was imprisoned wherein he died in 1676. Prince Muazzam was jailed for seven years on the suspicion of being in league with the ruler of Golkonda. When Akbar revolted against Aurangzeb, his property was confiscated and his wife and two sons were imprisoned. Akbar fled to Persia where he died in 1704.[132] Zebunissa was imprisoned on the charge of being in league with Akbar. Her pension was stopped. Her property confiscated and she was lodged in Salimgarh at Delhi where she died in 1702. Ironically the same emperor richly rewarded his own sister Roshanara for aligning with him against Dara.[133]

In order to prevent future Dharmat among his sons, he in his Will divided his kingdom among his three surviving sons and appointed Muazzam as his successor. But his Will was not carried out either by Azam or by Kambaksh because they successively declared war against their eldest brother Muazzam for the throne and in turn lost their lives in the field".[134]

After committing all brutalities against his brothers, sons and even his father whom he kept under detention so long he was alive, he again put on the mask of a pious Muslim. He commenced abstaining from jewels or any rich stuff, rejected any other colour than the white in his own apparel and he forbade any of his Grandees to be admitted in his presence, that should wear either rich stuffs, jewels or gaudy colour so that simplicity became now the etiquette of the court. He posed himself as puritan, a devout and a defender of Faith. Once he passed near the mausoleum of Jahangir, his grandfather, but declined to pray at it, saying that it was the burial-place of an infidel. On the contrary, he issued orders to remove the precious stones and jewels from it.[135]

Perhaps his guilt prevented him from visiting his father. He did not come to meet him for eight years but he wrote him letters justifying his action and characterizing his war against Dara as Jihad. He wrote:

"But owing to your Majesty's illness the prince (Dara), usurping all authority and bent upon propagating the religion of Hindus and idolaters and suppressing the faith of the Prophet, had brought about chaos and anarchy throughout the empire... Consequently I started from Burhanpur, lest I should be held responsible in the next world for not providing a remedy for disorder".

Aurangzeb boasted that he was crowned by God "If God had not approved of my enterprise, how could I have gained victories which are only the gift of God" Shah Jahan wrote back to him as:

"...a man who rebelled against his father, treated his brothers cruelly and drank so much blood, not sparing his own sons, would never be able to do useful works for others".[136]

Seeing himself unmasked Aurangzeb stopped writing to him. He came to Agra after two weeks of Shah Jahan's death. He banned the traditional scattering of gold and silver coins from over the body of a ruler. "A state prisoner cannot be permitted to be honourd that way" ran the decree. Jahanara sent two thousand gold coins to be given to the poor; but the guard seized the whole, saying that the prisoners could not give away anything.[137] No descendant of Shah Jahan, no grand amir, bore his bier. Aurangzeb did not attend his funeral.

He did not forgive even those who dared to say the truth and did not toe the line of his paid theologians. He executed a Sufi saint Sarmad, who said on his face that he was irreligious, inhuman and power hungry. But as usual, he again summoned the council of Ulemas which passed an order for the execution of the saint of insanity.' Aurangzeb saved himself from the charge of execution. The charge levelled against the saint was that he recited only the first part of the Kalima and denied the physical ascension of the holy Prophet. The fact is that Aurangzeb was afraid of Sarmad's influence over the masses of Delhi and he feared lest he bring a revolution against him.[138] Sarmad was executed publicly as a warning to any one who dared to go against him. A platform had been erected, for the execution outside the main gate of Delhi's Jama-Masjid. Sarmad was not the only one, twelve other holy men in Delhi, who had prophesied to Dara that he would be emperor of the whole Mughal Empire were imprisoned by Aurangzeb. Another Saint Mulla Shah, who lived in quiet hermitage in Kashmir, had initiated Dara and Jahanara in to Qadiriya order, had to face the wrath of Aurangzeb. Though his head was spared yet he had to pass last years of his life in great distress and fear.[139]

On the occasion of his second coronation, the Chief Qazi of the Empire had given the opinion that it was not valid to read Khutba in Aurangzeb's name since his father was alive. Aurangzeb was greatly perturbed till Qazi Abdul Wahab came to his rescue by arguing that since Shah Jahan had become too feeble to exercise his functions, there was no legal objection to Khutba being read in Aurangzeb's name. As a reward, Qazi Abdul Wahab was appointed the Chief Qazi.[140]

Khafi Khan, the historian, who had been for a length of years in Court and was a friend of the emperor and had had been an eyewitness to all the transactions, accuses Aurangzeb of invading Hyderabad. He asserts that the Alamgir found his conscience guilty at the time of attack on Hyderabad, so he wanted the Sheikh-ul-Islam to give his expedition religious sanction but the Qazi Sheikh-ul-Islam refused to give a Fatwa that the war against Bijapur and Golkonda was a Jihad. He was dismissed and forced to proceed on Haj. Qazi Abdullah was also punished for suggesting peace with Golkonda.[141] He stated that as the Kings and soldiers of both the kingdoms were Muslims and that the massacre of the masses on both sides was repugnant to the spirit of Islam, the attack on these kingdom by Aurangzeb was unjustified. This verdict infuriated Aurangzeb. In the words of Seid Gholam "This insinuation was very ill received; little more and the Cazy would have been undone forever. Some of the Princes of the blood, with many of the principal favourite, interposed their good offices to prevent the Judge's punition, and the Judge's extreme liberty was forgiven him; but he was forbidden the court as well as the Imperial presence, and he remained disgraced for the long time"[142]

Failing to secure the sanction of the religion, he resorted to other means. He sent Mirza Muhammad as an envoy to Abul Hasan, giving him secret instructions to misbehave with the King, so that the latter might be compelled to give an exhibition of such a gesture as are likely to give him (Alamgir) excuse for the declaration of war against him.[143] Thus he always tried to use the religious garb for his political designs and when he failed, resorted to treachery.

One Qazi Mir openly castigated Aurangzeb saying "Your Majesty must repent and ask God's pardon for having given the true faith to the flames and not following its commands. Nay, for acting contrary to it, seizing your father, slaying your brethren, usurping the dominions of others and unjustly ruining many princes and vassals."Aurangzeb got him killed in 1690.[144]

The destructive religious zeal of Aurangzeb was not applauded by all sections of the Muslim society. Even the Shah of Persia accused him of unmanliness. In a letter to Aurangzeb, he wrote: "You style yourselves a world conqueror while you have only conquered your father (and murdered) your brothers... you have failed in every undertaking requiring manliness".[145]

The Khalifa at Mecca, was also critical of Aurangzeb's religious policy. According to J.T. Wheeler the religious policy followed in India by Aurangzeb was considered anti-Islamic by the Khalifa, who on this ground refused to receive an ambassador from the emperor. Shah Abbas of Iran too, did not approve Aurangzeb's fanaticism in the name of religion. He wrote him to 'Struck coin upon a round of cheese: Aurangzeb, brother-slayer, father-seizer'[146] Aurangzeb thus used religion and religious leaders for his irreligious actions. He posed himself to be a pious Muslim but discarded the religious dictums if these did not suit his designs. The Ulema's verdict was taken for public consumption but he did not allow them a share in shaping state policies. In a reply to a petition requesting the dismissal of non-Muslims from the posts, Aurangzeb pointed out: "religion has no concern with secular business and in matters of this kind, bigotry should find no place" and after quoting the Quranic text "To you your religion and to me my religion" stated that if the Petitioners requests were to be acceded to "We shall have to destroy all the Rajas and their subjects".[147]

Though Aurangzeb is known for his anti-Hindu stance yet it is also a fact that he not only won the war of succession but also maintained his rule with the cooperation of the Hindus. He firmly maintained the policy of allying with the Rajputs and other non-Muslim elements of Indian society. He granted Jai Singh and Jaswant

Singh a higher position in Imperial affairs and in the Imperial hierarchy than had been accorded to any Hindu since the days of Man Singh.The number of Hindus in the nobility did not decline but actually increased after 1679. [148] He trusted only Hindu guards and richly rewarded all those whether Hindus or Muslims, who were loyal to him. His private secretary was a Hindu, named Wali Ram. Aurangzeb was fond of him and the latter hold that office for twenty long years. Raghunath, a Hindu was his deputy minister (he died in 1663) Aurangzeb conferred upon him the title of Raja.[149] He used to address Jaswant Singh as Rajaji. He asked his son Azam to favour and praise Pahar Singh a Hindu officer by assigning him the independent governorship of a province.[150] Dalpat Rao Bundella was a Hindu chief and general of Auranzeb's army. His father Subhkaran also had served Aurangzeb as general. Bhim Singh of Mewar was given the title of Raja and his command was raised to 5000. In 1682, the emperor gave the title of Raja to Udwat Singh son of Maha Singh Bahaduriya.[151]Even in his private life he had cordial relations with the Hindus.[152] Prince Azam was married to the daughter of Kirat Singh, son of Mirza Raja Jai Singh. The princess was not converted to Islam and the Raja gave a rich dowry in the Hindu fashion at the time of her marriage.[153]

To placate the Muslims, Aurangzeb instead of the solar year, which had been in use in India from the time of Akbar, directed the Mohammedan lunar year to be employed because the former, in his opinion, was the invention of idolaters. He also issued a Farman to the effect that the corrupt Hindu Diwans and Collectors of revenue should be dismissed and Muslims appointed instead. This Farman was however modified by another which required the appointment of one Hindu and another Muslim in all departments, both Civil and Military so as to check each other.[154] Hindu representation in administration increased during his reign. During Akbar's time out of total 247 Mansabdars, there were 32 Hindus. But in Aurangzeb's time out of the total 539 there were 104 Hindus.[155]

Economic and political necessities led Aurangzeb to impose Jaziya upon the Hindus. It was not the true faith and his deference to the suggestion of theologians, as the reason for the reimposition of Jaziya. Aurangzeb himself was well versed in the Sharia. It took twenty-two years from his accession to the throne to arrive at the orthodox position regarding Jaziya. Besides Jaziya was not imposed upon the servants of the state on the order of Aurangeb. They were exempted from it.[156]

When Aurangzeb reviewed his finances in the thirteenth year of his reign, he found the expenses had exceeded income during the preceding twelve years. Consequently a number of economic reforms were effected, including the retrenchment of many items in the expenditure of the Royal budget. The continuous wars in the Deccan too had badly strained the Royal treasury.[157]

Another factor for the reimposition of Jaziya was the growing unemployment among the clerical elements. So rampant was the unemployment that even the descendants of Shaikh Moinuddin Chishti, the patron saint of the Mughals, were living in poverty and want. By earmarking the proceeds of Jaziya for distribution in charity among the learned, the fakirs, the theologians etc. and further by providing that the new department of jaziya, with its own treasury and set of Amins, should be staffed predominantly by these sections, Aurangzeb offered a huge bribe to the orthodox clerical elements. Through clerical influence Aurangzeb hoped to rally all sections of Muslims behind him.[158] Besides, it was an outcome of a deepening political crisis. By the time Aurangzeb had ascended the throne, the political and religious conditions in India had gone under a great change, the Sikhs in Punjab, the Bundelas in Central India and the Marathas in Deccan were busy acquiring political power under the guise of service to their respective faith. Aurangzeb, in order to have the support of his community presented himself as the protector not only of the faith but also of their economic interests.

However, all were not happy with the imposition of Jaziya. A powerful section of the Muslim nobility including his own sister Jahanara and his son Akbar opposed its revival. She visited her brother and begged him to reconsider an act of such devastating regression. She argued that 'India represented an ocean sustaining the ship of the Mughal royal family; what emperor could tax the ship on which he sail?' Predicting widespread rebellion, she ended by trying to throw herself at Aurangzeb's feet. But Aurangzeb remained unmoved, he invoked justification of Mohammad and the Quran.[159]

His son Akbar who had escaped to Persia wrote a letter to Aurangzeb criticising the decision of Jaziya as:

"Your Majesty puts your trust in hypocrites wearing huge turbans and accepted as theologians because they carry a Quran under the arm and hold a chaplet in their hand. Yet are these men nothing but snares of hell, with their hypocritical exterior of piety. They gave false counsel and by their appearance misled the world. From this class of riffraff your Majesty has selected your councillors and courtiers. These are your guardian angels... men who are dealers in adulterated wares".[160]

Aurangzeb never forgave him. He was not shocked to hear the news of Akbar's death instead observed "The great disturber of Hindustan has subsided".[161]

He was not anti Hindu or Hinduism but against all those whether Hindus or Muslims who dared to oppose his directives. An incident proves the real character of the emperor. Once Aurangzeb came to know about Rishi Pir of Kashmir who was called Padshah (king) by the people and had also engraved Padshah-I-Jahan on his seal. He became incensed and deputed an orderly to Kashmir to seize and conduct Rishi Pir to his presence at Delhi. However some of his ministers assured Aurangzeb that it was a false report and the Rishi being a man to whom worldly power was repugnant. Then Aurangzeb issued a second order countermanding the first and commanding that Rishi Pir should be called by the title of Padshah-i-har-du-Jahan (king of both the worlds, i.e., this world and the next).[162]

Actually he did not stop co-operating with Hindu princes and he did not spread his faith with the sword. He discontinued the practice of Jharokha darshan introduced by Akbar not because he considered it to be a Hindu practice but because it was inconvenient and dangerous. In those days if the emperor did not appear at the fixed hours 'stories of his death got about'.[163] As Shah Jahan failed to appear at Jharokha, rumours of his death, precipitated the war of succession. Aurangzeb did not want to take any risk.

Though, he banned the construction of new temples but at the same time he also prohibited the destruction of the ancient ones. At the same time he also prohibited the Mughal officials in Banaras from interfering with or disturbing the Brahmans or any other Hindus who visited the temples.[164] Besides all his regulations cannot be considered to be anti-Hindu in tone because many of the ordinances affected Muslims as well. He banned the celebrations of Muharram. The prohibition against music, for example, also applied to religious hymns sung on the anniversary of the birth of the Prophet. On Thursday night's lamps used to be lighted on the tombs of the saints. Aurangzeb discontinued it. Nauroz festival too was banned.[165]

There are instances that proved beyond doubt that Aurangzeb demolished some temples. But it seems that reasons for their destruction were other than religious. Rani Hadi, widow of Jaswant Singh, in order to get tika for her son secretly made an astounding offer that the Rathors would themselves destroy all the temples in Marwar if the tika was given to a son of Jaswant Singh. Aurangzeb rejected it.[166] This makes it clear that he had no hatred for Hindu temples. In fact he made grants of land to many temples all over the country. He did order the demolition of Vishwanath temple at Varanasi but the reason that was given out for the demolition of the temple may give benefit of circumstances to Aurangzeb. The story regarding the demolition of Vishwanath temple is that while Aurangzeb was passing near Varanasi on his way to Bengal, the Hindu Rajas in his retinue requested that if the halt was made for a day, their Ranis may go to Varanasi, have a dip in the Ganges and pay homage to Lord Vishwanath. Aurangzeb readily agreed. Army pickets were posted on the five miles route to Varanasi. The Ranis made journey on the Palkis. They took their dip in the Ganges and went to the Vishwanath temple to pay their homage. After offering Puja all the Ranis returned except one, the Maharani of Kutch. A thorough search was made of the temple precincts but the Rani was to be found nowhere. When Aurangzeb came to know of it, he was very much enraged. He sent his officers to search for the Rani. Ultimately they found that the statue of Ganesh, which was fixed in the wall, was a moveable one. When the statue was moved, they saw a flight of stairs that led to the basement. To their horror, they found the missing Rani dishonoured and crying, deprived of all her ornaments. The basement was just beneath Lord Vishwanath's seat. The Rajas expressed their vociferous protests. As the crime was heinous, the Rajas demanded exemplary action. Aurangzeb ordered that as the sacred precincts have been desecrated, Lord Vishwanath may be moved to some other place, the temple be razed to the ground and the Mahant be arrested and punished.[167]

There are instances when the Hindu rulers also destroyed mosques. Kumar Bhim Singh made a powerful diversion by the invasion of Gujarat. He captured Idar, raided some towns and destroyed [300] mosques. Dayal Shah, the finance minister, headed a flying force, which ravaged Malwa. "For once" writes Tod, "they avenged themselves in the imitation of the tyrant, even on the religion of their enemies; the qazis were bound and shaved and the Koran thrown in to the well"[168]

If Aurangzeb destroyed the temple he also destroyed Jama Masjid of Golkonda. A puritan can never think of the destruction of his religious place but as said Aurangzeb used religion for his selfish interests in this case the purpose was to get the money hidden underneath the Mosque. "The ruler of Golkonda, the famous Tanashah, after collecting revenues of the state, did not pay his due to Delhi. In few years, they were accumulated into crores. Tanashah buried the Khazana and erected a Jama Masjid over it. When Aurangzeb came to know of it, he ordered the demolition of the mosque. The burried Khazana was seized and utilised for the benefit of the people".[169] This shows that Aurangzeb did not make any distinction between a temple and a mosque, in the matter of judicial findings. He had no hatred for Hinduism or Hindu saints and did not justify the unjustified claims of the Muslim theologians against the Hindus. Munshi Sujan Rai of Batala, the famous historian of the time of Aurangzeb, mentions in the Khulastul-Twarikh, a village Dipavali where the tomb of Shah Shamsuddin Daryayi is situated. He writes:

"Both Hindus and Muslims have a great faith in Shah Shamsuddin. But a Hindu name Deepali has proved superior to both Hindus and Muslims in his faith. After Shah Daryayi's death Deepali was appointed the first trustee and keeper of the tomb with unanimous consent of both Hindus and Muslims although he was not Muslim by religion.... Some years ago the Mussalmans tried to get the Hindu keeper dismissed, so much so that the religious reasons were urged for this. But the Alamgiri Hakumat did not allow this agitation to succeed".[170]

This version of the Munshi Sujan Rai places Aurangzeb in to different picture. Dow in his History of Hindustan, points out that Aurangzeb did not prosecute the adherents of other persuasions in the matter of religion. Elphinstone states that "not a single Hindu suffered death, imprisonment or loss of property for his religion or indeed, that any individual was ever questioned for the open exercise of the worship of his father".[171] Norris, a British ambassador to India during 1699-1702, writes that there were no communal feelings or tension between the different religious bodies during Aurangzeb's reign.[172] Besides not a single temple was demolished in Deccan where he spent the last twenty seven years of his reign. Thus, he used religion and religious leaders for his political ambitions that remained supermost in his life. His son Akbar too followed his father's tactics. When the prince rebelled against his father, he got a fatwa from some Mullas that Aurangzeb was irreligious.[173]

Shivaji

The religious plea taken by Aurangzeb also provided a similar slogan to such Hindu Chiefs who were not serving under the Mughal Emperor. Shivaji, on the death of his father, assumed the title of Rajah and began to coin money-the mark of independent soverignty.[174] Shivaji could appeal to the Hindu sentiment and posed their champion and protector. The coronation of Shivaji characterized by observing the orthodox Hindu rites performed by Brahmins was a parallel declaration as that of Aurangzeb. The Brahmins were like the Ulamas, richly rewarded of course with in the means of Shivaji. "The titles which Shivaji assumed, viz., Kshatriya-Kulavatasa, Sinhasanadhishwara Chhatrapati, his avowed profession of the protection of the cows and Brahmins as his goal, the significant motto on his seal so thoughtfully composed, his deliberate adoption of Sanskrit synonyms for Persian court terms, his acceptance of Marathi as the Court language and his translation into practice of the old Shastric injunctions about the ministers and their duties as also his avowed acceptance of the system of four castes in which he claimed for himself the position of Kshatriya, all these clearly point to a pan Hindu ideal".[175]

The ideal he put before his people was a Hindu Swarajya, a Maharashtra Padshahi but above all a Dharam Rajya. He consciously emphasized the religious aspect of his military ventures and claimed to fight for Hindus against Muslim rule.[176] In the name of Bhawani, Shivaji summoned princes and peasants, the proud Hindu Chiefs and the toiling farmers to fight against Mughals. In the words of Kedarnath "The name of Bhawani was not invoked from any firm and deep rooted belief in the deity, but with the object of serving his own selfish purposes. He knew the discontent that prevailed, the firm hold of the religion had on Hindu mind.... and shrewd man of the world that he was, he made religion serve as lever for his own selfish ends"[177]

He wrote a note of protest to Aurangzeb when the latter imposed Jaziya, knowing fully well that protest from him was meaningless for Aurangzeb. But by this protest he appealed to the Hindu sentiments and posed before them as a champion of their cause.

Besides, "Defence of the Brahmin and the cow as used by Shivaji, were of the same nature-talisman for the safeguarding of the Hindu ascendancy. Shivaji's flag was the ochre robe of the ascetic, symbolic of renunciation. What can apparently be more absurd than this unfurling the banner of renunciation for the purpose of acquisition?"[178]

For his political goals, he followed Kautilya's policy of Sam, Dam, and Dand Bhed. He treacherously killed Afzal Khan and Raja of Javali. Shivaji's men demanded a private interview with the Raja of Javali. They were sent to seek matrimonial alliance of Raja's daughter with Shivaji. But when Raja granted them interview, they stabbed him to death. The sons of the Raja were captured, given a bath and sumptuous meal and then beheaded at Nimgaza to the south of Poona.[179]

Whenever the emperor or the other Mohammadan kings were at war with Shivaji, he took to differentiate between his various opponents. He tried to be friendly with Jaswant Singh and openly won over Jai Singh. He wrote to Jai Singh:

"O Great Kshtriya, you have been using your strength to increase the power of Dynasty of Babar. You are shedding the blood of Hindus, in order to make the red-faced Muslims victorious. Do you not realize that you are thereby blackening your reputation before the world? If you have come to conquer me, I am ready to lay down my head in your path; but since you have come as the Deputy of the emperor, I am utterly at loss to decide how I should behave towards you. If you fight on behalf of the Hindu religion, I am ready to join and help you. You are brave and valiant, it behoves you as a powerful Hindu Prince, to take the lead against the emperor. Let us go and conquer Delhi itself".[180]

However, Jai Singh did not shift his loyalty. Some years of inconclusive fighting followed, but in 1664 Aurangzeb sent Raja Jai Singh to bring matter to a decision and the Raja succeeded so well that the next year Shivaji submitted and became a vassal of the empire.[181]

Shivaji like other rulers of the day raised money for financing his campaigns. C.V. Vaidya writes that Shivaji constantly plundered and continuously harassed the people under Delhi and Bijapur. Indeed every year Shivaji had a plundering expedition in these territories and his large army was maintained by plunder.[182] In [1664], Shivaji's fleet succeeded in making considerable captures. "Amongst others, they took some Mughal ships bound for Mecca and exacted heavy ransom from all the rich pilgrims proceeding to the shrine of their Prophet".[183]

The fights between Shivaji and the Muslim rulers were not fights between Hinduism and Islam as projected by both the Hindu and Muslim communalists. Hindus and Muslims were on both the sides. There was no hatred or enmity on the ground of religion. Shivaji respected Islam and used to make offerings to the shrines of Muslim saints. Mosques were maintained by state allowances.[184] His Maratha soldiers had strict orders not to molest any women or rob any Muslim saint's tomb or hermitage. Copies of the Quran which were seized in the course of his campaigns, were ordered to be carefully preserved and then handed over respectfully to some Mohammadans.[185]

Shivaji had a large number of Muslims in his own service. Had he been anti-Islam or anti-Muslim neither would he have employed Muslims nor Muslims would have served him faithfully. Shivaji's secretary was a Muslim named Qazi Haider. He had a many Muslims in his army both soldiers as well as officers. Some of them held very important positions. General Siddi Hullal and Nur Khan were his trusted military officers. In his navy, there were three Muslims admirals-Siddi Sambal, Siddi Misri and Daulat Khan.[186]

Shivaji was against the bigotry of Aurangzeb and not his religion. Malkani writes:

"Shivaji rose against the bigotry of Aurangzeb but he never offended Muslim religious susceptibilities. He killed Afzal Khan for political reasons but he built him an impressive tomb on the spot for the courteous reasons. He never desecrated a Mosque. And although he married as many as seven times mostly for political reasons, he was too conscientious to accept the captive daughter of the Subedar of Kalyan".[187]

He treated her as his sister and sent back to her relatives with presents.[188]

Shivaji's letter written to Aurangzeb speaks of Shivaji's respect for Islam. He stated: "May it please Your Majesty!

"If you believe in the true Divine Book and word of God, you will find therein that God is styled Rubb-ul-alamin (the Lord of all men), not Rubb-ul-Mussalmin (the Lord of Muslims alone). Verily Islam and Hinduism may be terms of contrast; but they are diverse pigments used by the Divine Painter for blending the colours and filling in the outlines of His picture of the entire human family. If it be a Mosque, the call to prayer is sounded in remembrance of Him. If it be a temple, the bell is rung in yearning for Him alone. To show bigotry towards any man's creed or religious practices is to alter the words of the Holy Book. To draw new lines on a picture is tantamount to finding fault with the Painter"[189]

Shivaji's family members served the Muslim kings with devotion. His grandfather Maloji had joined the service of the king of Ahmednagar.[190] His father Shahji worked under Nizam, Shah Jahan and Adilshah and rose to be the most important general of Bijapur. He served the Sultan with the same devotion as Raja Man Singh did for Akbar. Shahji crushed all the remaining Hindu Polygar chiefs in Deccan and Karnataka. The Sultan honoured him by appointing him the governor of Karnataka.[191]

When Shivaji took possession of the Jagir of Poona and made himself the master of the northern Concan, the king of Bijapur immediately threw Shahji in to prison as a hostage for his son. Shivaji then immediately entered the service of Shah Jahan and through his help, Shahji was rescued and set at liberty.[192] Even Vyaonkji his (Shivaji's) half brother was officer in Adilshahi service He fought against Shivaji during the latter's alliance with the Mughals. In 1655 when Aurangzeb was sent to the Deccan, and was acting against the king of Golconda Shivaji was so audacious as to plunder the Mughal provinces; but when he saw the Prince more successful than he had anticipated, he sued for pardon and was forgiven.[193] Aurangzeb later sought Shivaji's co-operation for gaining the throne of Delhi for himself. He wrote him a letter, sent presents, together with a golden tablet, by which he granted to him the collection of a fourth part of the revenue of some provinces of the Dakhin Province, then held by himself.[194] When Aurangzeb became Emperor Shivaji wrote to Maharaja Jaswant Singh "I am sending my son Sambha, so that he may be honoured with a mansab and a job in some contingents of Royal army"[195] In 1686 Achalji, son in law of Shivaji, received the rank of 5000/2000. Achalji also received a banner, a jeweled Punchchi and an elephant on the day of interview.[196]

Religious animosities did not exist as the rulers belonging to different religions freely took each other's help in crisis. Shivaji exchanged letters with prince Muazzam, Murad and others and there is not the least expression of hostility or bitterness.[197]

After the treaty of Purandar, Shivaji assisted the Mughals in the invasion of Bijapur.[198] When Aurangzeb sent a letter to Muazzam to capture Shivaji and to send him to Delhi, the latter sent a secret runner to warn Shivaji not to accept any Mughal invitation. At the same time he advised the Commander of the Maratha cavalry at his court to leave quietly at night.[199] When Shivaji was a captive of Aurangzeb at Agra, his life was saved by a Muslim Faras (bed-servant) named Madari Mehtor.[200]

The enmity between Aurangzeb and Shivaji was political and both fought as political rulers and not as the representatives of their religion or community. When the news of Shivaji's death reached Aurangzeb, he paid his tribute as:

"He was a great captain and the only one who had the magnanimity to a kingdom. My armies have been employed against him for nineteen years and nevertheless, his state has been always increasing".[201]

Hindu or Muslim, the rulers grabbed powers by all means. After Shivaji's death, his second son Raja Ram, who was only ten years of age, was crowned at Raigarh by his mother Soray Bai in April [1680]. Sambhaji, confined then in the fort of Panhala, decided to seize the throne. He put the commandant of the fort to death and escaped. He went to Raigarh and with the help of Hambir Rao Mohite, the commander chief, set aside Raja Ram, threw him and his mother into prison and declared himself as king.[202]

Akbar, Aurangzeb's son, joined hands with Sambhaji, Durga Das and Ajit Singh against his own father and proclaimed himself emperor in 1681. In return of his support, Durga Das succeeded in getting the rebel Akbar to recognise Ajit Singh as the legitimate heir of Jaswant Singh, the title of Maharaja and the mansab as commander of 7000 troops that accompanied the recognition. Durga Das also held in custody the son and daughter of Prince Akbar. Later he was able to bargain with Aurangzeb who pardoned him and gave a suitable jagir in exchange for the return of Akbar's children who after defeat had fled to Persia.[203]

If Prince Akbar defected to Marathas against his father Aurangzeb, Sambhaji too defected to Mughals and fought against his own father, Shivaji. Sambhaji, who had been imprisoned by Shivaji escaped along with his wife Yesu Bai and joined the Mughals. Along with Sambhaji, the Mughals invaded Bijapur. The Regent of Bijapur, Sidi Masud appealed to Shivaji for help, the latter responded and attacked the Mughals who by that time had laid the seize of

Bijapur.[204]

Durga Das and Ajit Singh had fought against Aurangzeb for twenty years but ended their rebellion when Aurangzeb gave them appointments in imperial service. Their "rebellion was not a general uprising by the people of Marwar against Mughal authority nor a concerted effort by the Rathore clan to resist Mughal imperialism; it was merely a contest between competing factions of the Rathore clan for the control of the officers of Marwar".[205]

Thus, factors other than religious determined the course of history. It is said that 'some of the leading Brahmans disgusted with Sambhaji's conduct (he was considered unworthy and autocratic) conceived the design of destroying him. They informed some imperial officers and got troops placed in ambush. Then luring Sambhaji in to the diversion of hunting caused him to be led into the trap where the Mughal enveloped him.[206] As usual Aurangzeb, who never forgave his opponents, himself did not order any punishment for Sambha and referred the matter to the 'Masters of the Holy Law and Faith' who in turn, decreed Sambhaji's execution.[207]

Aurangzeb, however made it clear that his enmity was towards Sambhaji, as an individual and not towards the descendants of Shivaji. Thus following the execution of Sambhaji, the lives of his family members were spared. They were lodged in the Gulabar, next to the emperor. Annual pensions were fixed for all of them according to their position. Shahu, the nine year old son of Sambhaji, was given the mansab of seven hazari, the title of Raja and a rob, a jeweled dagger, arsi, horses, elephant, kettledrums and standard. Madan Singh, Adhu Singh his younger brothers were given mansabs and gifts and were allowed to live with their mother and grandmother. Imperial clerks were appointed to the establishment of each, to manage their household"[208] This was in sharp contrast to the attitude adopted towards the deposed rulers of Bijapur and Golkonda who were sent to the prison fortress to spend their last days.[209]

Aurangzeb did not force any one for conversion. Shahu was the son of his enemy and lived with him, was not converted and so were the other members of family. He was looked after by Aurangzeb's daughter as her son. A sirkar was established for him in which were appointed one Diwan and one Bakshi. His tents always stood beside the imperial one.[210]

According to the strict tenet of Hinduism, a Hindu prisoner does not take meals in prison. Shahu took therefore, only fruits and sweet meats. When this was reported to Alamgir, he sent Hamid-ud-Din Khan with the message that he was not in prison but in his own house and he must therefore take meals without harboring any dishonour.[211] When news of Raja Ram's death reached the Mughal camp, Shahu fell ill. His mother Yesubai and Begum, Aurangzeb's daughter, were worried. Even Aurangzeb felt uneasy, when he heard of the serious illness of Shahu. He paid a visit to Shahu and sat by his bedside for a long time, trying to console the prince and assuring him that he would be restored to his Raj.[212]

When Shahu attained his eighteenth year, the Begum talked to Aurangzeb about Shahu's marriage. Jayotaji, Keskar and Moropant were deputed to find out befitting brides of Hindu family for Shahu. The brides selected were Ambikabai, daughter of Rustomrao jadhav and Savitribai, daughter of Sindhias of Kanheirkhed. Shahu's marriage was celebrated with due pump and show by Aurangzeb. Money was spent lavishly and the ceremony performed was worthy of the "Kings of the Marathas".[213]

After the marriage Aurangzeb called Shahu with wives to his presence and gave his blessings. Shahu received sanads for the five parganas from Aurangzeb who also conferred one gold tilted sword-the Bhawani sword of Shivaji and the sword of Afzal Khan on the newly married prince.[214]

This was another face of Aurangzeb. Likewise, he got two of his daughters married to sons of Dara and Murad. His enmity was thus political and had nothing to do with religion. Had he been fanatic, as projected by the communalists, he would have converted Shahu and had not arranged his marriage with Hindu girls in accordance with the Hindu traditions.

The guilt of using religion for political purposes perhaps troubled his inner being. On the threshold of his death, Aurangzeb cried in a letter to his son Kam Baksh as "I have sinned terribly and I do not know what punishment awaits me".[215] After Aurangzeb's death, Bahadur Shah (Muazzam) restored Shahu his kingdom of Satara. At the time of Shahu's departure, the Begum wept, as she could not bear separation from Shahu who was to her like her own son.[216] Shahu too did not forget the kindness and affection of the emperor and the Begum. He expressed his gratitude by visiting the spot where Aurangzeb had died and distributed gifts. He also visited the tomb of Aurangzeb at Khuldabad and paid his homage.[217] Shahu regarded himself a faithful vassal of the Mughal Empire and did not attack Delhi even when he was politically superior to the Mughal emperor.

Guru Gobind

Aurangzeb's regime put a permanent scar on Sikh Muslim relationship. His policies towards the Sikhs rendered him hateful to the Sikh community for all times to come. However Aurangzeb was not against the Sikh faith and did not prosecute the Sikhs on that ground. When Dara was defeated, Guru Har Rai had to surrender his son as a hostage, for helping Dara. The youth was treated with distinction.[218] In the disputes for succession between the two sons of the late Guru Har Rai, i.e., Ram Rai and Guru Harkishan, Aurangzeb, to whom the matter was referred, declared the right of Guru Harkishan to be indisputable and accordingly recognized him as head of the Sikhs.[219] Guru Teg Bahadur travelled to different parts of the country and propagated the Sikh faith during Aurangzeb's rule. When he arrived in the vicinity of Delhi and was in the Mughal Court of Delhi, Ram Rai who had gained the confidence of Aurangzeb and was in the Mughal Court had him arrested as an imposter and a disturber of peace. After investigation the charge was dropped and the emperor allowed the Guru to proceed.[220]

Aurangzeb was not against the Sikh faith but had a grouse against the Sikh Gurus because they had interfered in politics. Aurangzeb eliminated all those who stood in the way of his political ambition. He made religion a veil to cover his political tyranny. "The real motive of the cruelty to Teg Bahadur was" in the words of Browne, "most probably, resentment for having allowed his followers to call him The True King; and his having used a military title, which was not granted by Royal Patent, agreeably to the customs of that government, of all which he was exceedingly jealous".[221] Thus the martyrdom of the Guru should be attributed to the policies of Aurangzeb and not to any other cause.

It was the British historians who gave a religious twist to the non-religious issues. They presented the political fights as fights between the religions of the rival parties. By putting one community against the other on religious ground, they presented themselves as the saviour of the religion of the non-ruling classes. From Macauliffe's writings, one could easily carry an impression that Islam, Hinduism and Sikhism were antagonistic to one another and the British rule stopped injustice being inflicted on the basis of religion. Dorothy

Field, another English historian, states that the British rule in India was divinely ordained as both the Hindus and Sikhs were being persecuted by Aurangzeb. The British appeared as their saviour by destroying the Mughal rule.[222]

Macauliffe, in order to place the British in a positive frame, writes that the fall of the Mughal rule and the establishment of the British power in India was prophetic. He points out that the Guru in the prison had made a prophecy in this context. The Guru told Aurangzeb:

"I was looking in the direction of the Europeans, who are coming from beyond the seas to tear down thy pardas and destroy the empire".[223]

The fact is that the Guru was against the policies of the emperor and was not against Islam or the Muslims. He had not only a large number of Muslim followers but also had Muslim friends. While going to Delhi to meet Aurangzeb, the Guru visited his intimate Muslim friend Saif-ud-din who lived in Saifabad in Patiala State. The Guru lived with him during rainy days Influenced by the Guru, Saif-ud-din became a Sikh.[224] When the order of the Guru's execution came, even the Muslim Governor of the jail began to weep. Aurangzeb is stated to have felt remorse and to have repented when he came to know about the actual execution of Guru Teg Bahadur. His mind is said to have been agitated like leaves moved by the wind and he reflected:

"As the Guru by his death hath fixed a stain on me, so I think that my own life will now be my guest for only a few days".[225]

In his general distress at what had happened, he was not able to take his dinner and retired hungry. He was unable to sleep the remainder of the night and endeavoured to lull his conscience by repetition of the creed and the prayers of his religion.[226]

Likewise the fight between Guru Gobind Singh has been projected as a fight between Sikhism and Islam. Irvine states that "his (Gobind) own precept prohibited all friendship with Mohammedan" and that he was inspired with the mission of destroying the Mughal Empire. Dorothy goes further and adds new dimension by emphasizing that Sikhism being a superior religion should keep its distinctiveness from Hinduism as well:

"...they (Sikhs) show a tendency to reabsorb in to Hinduism. They employ Brahmin priests at marriages, deaths and at all important domestic events. In reality the pure teachings of Nanak discredits the formalities of Hindu religion and therefore in so far as Sikhs submit to these they are falling back from the highest teachings of the Granth. Pure Sikhism is far above dependence on Hindu ritual and is capable of distinct position as a world religion..."[227]

According to Dorothy the Guru then declared:

"When the Sikhs become selfish and tangled in worldly affairs, corrupt and forgetful of their religion; when they relapse in to Hinduism, than the English shall rule and their glory increase".[228]

Dorothy also states that the Guru had prophesized the fall of the Mughal Empire:

"In the sambat year (A.D. 1843) the Turks who survive shall lose their empire. A Christian army shall come from Calcutta. The Sikhs who are at variance with one another will join them".[229]

Macauliffe, writing on Sikh Religion, too keeps in mind the English interest and states without mentioning the source, that when it was represented to Guru Gobind Singh that a Mohammadan army would eventually come to overpower the Sikhs, he replied:

"What God willeth, will take place, when the army of the Mohammadan comesth, my Sikhs shall strike steel on steel. The Khalsa will then awake and know the play of battle. Amid the clash of arms the Khalsa shall be partners in present and future bliss tranquillity, meditation and divine knowledge. Then shall the English come and join the Khalsa, rule as well in the East as in the West. The holy Baba Nanak will bestow all wealth on them. The English shall possess great power and by force of arms take possession of many principalities. The combined armies of the English and the Sikhs shall be very powerful, as long as they rule with united councils. The empire of the British shall vastly increase and they shall in every way obtain prosperity. Wherever they take their armies they shall conquer and bestow thrones on their vassals. Then in every house shall be wealth, in every house religion, in every house learning and in every house happiness".[230]

Three conclusions emerge from the views of English historians, first that there was religious enmity and hatred of Sikh Gurus towards Islam and the Mughal empire and secondly; it is the Sikh Gurus who had prophesied of the coming English rule and thus provided the English rule a divine sanction; and thirdly that the Sikhs had to be loyal towards the British as has been directed by their ninth and tenth Gurus.

The views of English historians make it clear that their purpose in distorting Indian history was to get the support of the opponent of the Mughals by giving religious colours to the political differences and fights and presenting the British as just and saviour of the oppressed.

The fact is that both the Gurus had no enmity or hatred either towards Islam or the Muslims besides they did not seek the destruction of the Mughal Empire. Guru Gobind Singh wrote in Bachitra Natak:

"The successors of both Baba Nanak and Babar were created by God Himself. Recognize the former as a spiritual and the latter as a temporal king. Babar's successors shall seize and plunder those who deliver not the Guru's money"[231]

Instead of aiming at the destruction of the Mughal Empire the Guru recognizes in it a creation of God, legitimizes it by calling upon his followers to acknowledge the temporal authority of Babar's successors, and even invokes its assistance for the punishment of those 'who deliver not the Guru's money.'

The Guru's fight was with the Emperor and not Islam as, in his views God was one and there was no difference between mosque and temple. He preached:

"Karta (creator) and Karim (beneficent) are the same;
Razak (provider) and Rahim (merciful) are the same;
Let no man even by mistake suppose there is difference;
The temple and the mosque are the same;
The Hindus worship and the Muslim-prayers are the same.[232]

The Guru never led any offensive expedition against the Mughal emperor Aurangzeb or his provincial deputies.[233] He had many Muslim followers and friends and many had accepted Sikh faith under his influence. Many Muslims called him Hind ka Pir. He got shelter with the families and even the harem of Muslims. One such friend was Nihang Khan Kotla, of Kotla Nihang, near Ropar where Gurudwara Bhatta Sahib is situated.[234] One of his closest associate was a Muslim fakir. Ibrahim who got converted to Sikhism and was renamed Ajmer Singh.[235] Among the numerous admirers of the Guru were two Muslim nobles, Rahim Baksh and Karim Baksh. They were so much impressed by the piety that they made to him an offering of two gardens and some land. (This property now belongs to the Sikh temple at Patna) The Guru was also had intimate with two famous divines, Pir Bhikan Shah of Ghuram and Pir Arif Din of Kabul.[236]

The nucleus of the Guru's private army consisted of five hundred Pathan mercenaries. Many Muslims had aligned with Guru Gobind Singh against the imperial armies. Time and again, his Muslim friends saved his life. At Duraha, a Syyid of Balwara told a lie to save him from his pursuers. At Anandpur Saheb, when the Mughal army led by Dilawar Khan's son reached the bank of river, an attendant named Alam awakened the Guru. The Guru immediately raised the sound of alarm and won the battle.[237] Pir Buddhu Shah sacrificed four of his sons and a number of disciples in the battle of Bhagini, fighting on the Guru's side. At Machiwara, where the Imperial troops again closed on him, the two Pathan brothers Nabi Khan and Ghani Khan carried Guru Gobind on their shoulder in a curtained palanquin and passed the Mughal santries, with explanation that they were carrying their Pir. When the Mughal Commander got suspicious, he summoned Qazi Pir Mohammad from the village to know the identity of the occupant of the Palanquin. The Qazi had taught the Guru Persian and Arabic at Anandpur. He admonished the soldiers for having obstructed the holy pir and asked the officer to let him pass without any interference.[238] The Guru escaped safely to Behlolpur and stayed with his Muslim friend. The Guru ate food with him and at his suggestion, disguised himself. He put on a blue dress and made himself like a Haji (Muslim Darvish) and speedily reached Bhatinda.[239] Henceforward the Guru retained the garb of a Darvish in memory of his friend and his escape and he made it the distinctive dress of his followers' also.[240]

Aurangzeb took action against the Guru in response to the call of the Hindu Rajas for aid and action against the Guru. It is said that after the creation of Khalsa, the Hindu Hill Chiefs got angry with the Guru. The abolition of the caste system and opposition of idolatry was too much for them. They wanted to restrict the rising influence of the Guru. The joint forces of the Hindu Rajas and Aurangzeb proceeded against Guru Gobind and seized him at Anandpur. The Guru, however, managed to escape. The allied forces continued to harass his retreat. Two of the Guru's sons, who fell in an encounter at Chamkaur, were Guru's elder son Ajit Singh and Jujhar Singh. The Guru had entrusted his mother, wife and two younger sons to a Brahmin servant named Gangu, who betrayed them and handed them over to Wazir Khan, the Governor of Sirhind. In the beginning, despite his enmity with the Guru, Wazir Khan treated the children with kindness. It was Suchanand, Dewan to Wazir Khan, who had some enmity with the Guru, suggested Wazir Khan to finish the children. Nawab Sher Khan of Malerkotla earnestly pleaded to Wazir khan to spare the children. Initially Wazir Khan was unwilling to destroy the innocent children and hesitated for long. Suchanand pressed the Governor and is reported to have said: "To kill a cobra (Guru Gobind) and to spare its progeny is not the act of wise men. The offspring of a wolf is always a wolf".[241]

Wazir Khan called upon two Pathan youth whose father had been killed in a battle by the arrows of the Guru and wished to hand the two boys over to them for vengeance they liked to wreck on them. But the Pathan youths declined to do any injury to the children saying "No sir, we will fight the enemy in the battlefield; but not like cowards slay these two innocents".[242] Wazir khan then got the two minor sons of the Guru mercilessly bricked alive.

Thus Hill Rajas, Gangu Brahman and Suchanand Khatri are not less responsible for the loss of four sons of the Guru. Despite all this the Guru had no enmity with either Muslims or Hindus. His enmity was with Aurangzeb as a person and not as a Muslim. He wrote a letter, Zafarnama, in the form of a long Persian poem, which contained bitter complaints against the Mughal emperor, but its appeal, was in the name of humanity and Islam. Aurangzeb was neither annoyed nor angry with the content instead readily expressed his willingness to meet the Guru. Murray T Titus writes: "Inspite of its scathing tone, the letter Guru Gobind had sent to Aurangzeb by Daya Singh was not taken amiss. The ill and aged emperor was moved to read it. He dictated from his sick bed a letter to Munim Khan, his wazir, asking him to show friendliness to Gobind and invite him. The Wazir was also instructed to pay the Guru, out of his property as much cash, as he desired for his travelling expense and provide him with a guide. But before the letter could reach, Aurangzeb died."[243]

After the death of Aurangzeb, a war of succession broke out. Bahadur Shah had shown consideration to guru Gobind in his troubles with the hill chiefs. Bahadur Shah, at that time as Prince Muazzam, had reduced the hill chiefs to subservience. He gave secret instruction to general Mirza beg, not to bother the Guru. Gobind was left unmolested for twelve years and was thus able to reorganise his community. The Guru felt it was his turn to help the prince and he sent a detachment of Sikh soldiers who fought for Bahadur shah in the battle of Jajau. This belies J.N Sarkar's view that Guru had begun a policy of open hostility to Islam and Mughals.[244]

The Guru was honoured by Bahadur Shah when the latter became the emperor. There was no animosity between the Sikhs and the Muslim emperor. Bhai Nand Lal, a disciple of the Guru, was secretary to Bahadur Shah.[245] When the Guru was injured by the two pathans, Bahadur Shah sent his own physicians to attend the Guru.[246] Cordial relations and mutual understanding existed between Muslims and Sikhs even in the 18th and 19th century. When the bloodiest battle was fought between the Sikh Misaldars and Ahmad Shah Abdali's soldiers, only a few miles away from Malerkotla, the Muslim town of Malerkotla was deliberately not destroyed by the Sikhs, nor even in 1947, as mark of Sikh gratitude to the Muslim Nawab.[247]

Later Mughals

Political ambitions and not the religion determined the actions and policies of all the rulers whether Muslims or Hindus or Sikhs.To win over the support of the Hindus, Farrukh Siyar, who sat on the throne in 1712, was married to the daughter of Ajit Singh, who after the death of Aurangzeb had posed himself as the saviour of Hindu religion. Ajit Singh forbade the call of prayers from the Alamgiri Mosque and destroyed all the mosques in his dominion Jodhpur. He ejected the imperial officers from Jodhpur and took possession of Ajmer. Same Ajit Singh, for political advantages gave the hand of his daughter to Farrukh Siyar and also sent his son Abhay Singh to the imperial Court. Farrukh on the other hand sought Ajit Singh's help to counter the influential Sayyid brothers, who wanted to remove him from the throne. Despite of his relationship with Farrukh, Ajit Singh, secretly joined hands with Sayyid brothers. Consequently Farrukh Siyar was dethroned and brutally murdered. The Sayyid paid Ajit Singh for his loyalty. They appointed Ajit Singh the Governor of Ahmedabad. His daughter, widow of Farrukh Siyar was sent back to Ajit Singh along with one crore property despite the ruling of the qazi against it. (Ajit Singh was murdered by his own son Bakht Singh. Ajit Singh's body was cremated on 7th June 1724 and 84 wives and concubines immolated themselves on his funeral pyre).[248]

After Farrukh, Mohammad Shah became the Emperor. He could get rid of a rebellious and dictatorial wazir like Safdarjung only by invoking the aid of Rajput Madho Singh, the Raja of Jaipur. The grateful emperor placed on the Raja's head his own jewelled turban and loaded his followers with gifts and what was more welcome to Madho Singh, the fort of Ranthambhore was returned to Rajputs.[249]

In 1730 emperor Mohammad Shah appointed Abhay Singh, the governor of Gujarat and bestowed on him a robe of honour as well as the province of Ajmer. When Ahmad Shah Durrani invaded Punjab, the emperor called Abhay Singh for his aid. Abhay Singh sent his younger brother Bakht Singh who helped Prince Ahmad Shah in defeating the Afghans at the battle of Sirhind and in retaining Lahore.[250] Religion was used for gaining support of the masses against the enemy if he belonged to the other religion. By appealing to the religious feelings Bajirao easily entered Malwa and made his hold upon that province for good. He united the local Hindu chieftains as well as the neighboring Rajputs of Jaipur and Mewar with the Marathas in an alliance against the Mughals, depicting the latter's as the oppressor of their religion. This point comes out very clearly in Sawai Jai Singh's letter to Nandlal Mandaloi (the choudhry of Indore) after the latter had treacherously caused an immense slaughter of his master's (Emperor's) troops by his collusion with the Marathas (Oct 1731):

"A thousand praises to you, because you in sole reliance upon my word and with a view to benefit your Dharma have destroyed the Muslims in Malwa and firmly established Dharma there. You have fulfilled my heart's wishes".[251]

However when alliances and terms seemed beneficial, religion was kept aside. Nizam-ul-Mulk, who had, as a wazir opposed the policy of appeasement of the Marathas, himself accepted Bajirao's demand of chauth and sardeshmukhi in 1734, in order to have his hold in Deccan. Bajirao not only assured the Nizam of Maratha's cooperation but also accepted a mansab of 7000.[252] Many Maratha Chiefs joined the service of Nizam-ul-Mulk when dispute between Raja Shahu and his cousin Sambhaji arose for succession. These Maratha defectors induced Nizam-ul-Mulk to champion the cause of Sambhaji and install him on the throne of Shivaji.[253] However, forgetting all the infightings and differences, the Marathas joined the Mughals against Nadir Shah who attacked India in 1738. Bajirao professed his loyalty to the emperor and pledged to serve under him. The Peshwa mentioned this in a letter written to his general Pilaji jaden:

"I shall march to northern India by regular stages. The Persian sovereign Tahmasp Quli has come to conquer the world. To help Muhammad Shah I am sending the Malwa force under Malhar Rao Holkar Ranaji Sindhia and (Udaiji) Puar. It is a glory to this monarchy (i.e., the Maratha state) to help the emperor of Dehli at such a time".[254]

Mohammad Shah and the Peshwa were on such friendly terms that the emperor asked the Peshwa to march to the rescue of Aliwardi Khan and also made a grant of chauth from Bengal in favour of him along with many royal presents. "The Peshwa felt highly gratified at the rare honour conferred on him by the emperor".[255]

As soon as Nadir, the Persian died, Ahmad Shah Abdali, the Afghan arrived on the scene. Momin Khan of Kasur and Lakhpat Rai of Lahore, along with their Zamindars paid tribute to Abdali who later appointed them Governor of these areas.[256] On the other hand, Ahmad Shah, the emperor and his wazir in Delhi signed a Mughal Maratha treaty in 1752 duly attested by all the Hindu deities to face Abdali jointly. The Peshwa was given the responsibility of guarding the Mughal northwestern frontiers from the perpetual danger of an Afghan invasion in lieu of an imperial recognition of the claim of chauth on all most all the provinces of the empire.[257] Hindu, Muslim and Sikh formed a united front and fought together and frustrated the nefarious designs of Abdali in 1758. After the successful operation and the retreat of Abdali, Adina Beg erected in the Shalimar garden, at the cost of one crore of rupee, a magnificent platform, on which Raghunath Rao, the Maratha general and brother of Peshwa was seated and given a public reception. The fountains of the garden were made to play with rose water and the whole city was illuminated.[258]

Abdali attacked India again in 1761.The general who fought most furiously against him was Ibrahim Khan Gardi, a Muslim. Ibrahim Khan Gardi was in the service of the Peshwas of Poona. He commanded trained battalions of infantrymen in the Maratha army. Besides, he was also in charge of the Maratha Park of artillery. In 1760, he fought on the side of the Marathas against the Nizam of Hyderabad and defeated him. In the battle of Panipat he fought against Abdali on the side of Marathas. Abdali tried his level best to seduce Ibrahim in the name of Islam and also being an Afghan brother, to desert Marathas and to join him in the holy war against them, but Ibrahim rejected all such advances and remained loyal to his chief Sadasivrao Bhau. In this battle Ibrahim's son and son-in-law lost their lives. He himself was badly wounded and captured.

When Abdali asked him why he fought against his co-religionists Gardi replied that he had to remain true to salt eaten by him. Abdali grew furious and mercilessly killed Ibrahim who was his co-religionist and Afghan brother.[259]

During the expedition in 1762 Abdali also decided to recover Kashmir from Sukhjivan Mal, his nominee, who had thrown off his allegiance and had submitted to the Mughal emperor. In this attempt Abdali was supported by Ranjit Dev of Jammu.Abdali also purchased the loyalty of Bakht Mal, the commander-in- chief of Sukhjivan Mal and easily captured and killed Sukhjivan Mal. Thus both, the Hindu Raja and the Hindu Commander-in chief betrayed Hindu ruler against a Muslim invader.[260]

Religion was used only for political expediencies and when the ambition was achieved, the rulers completely changed their colours like chameleon. After Zakariya Khan's death, his eldest son Yahiya Khan was appointed Viceroy of Lahore. However, the second son of Zakariya Khan, named Shahnawaz sought the post for himself and tried to displace his brother, but failed. Desperate Shahnawaz then opened communication with Ahmad Shah Abdali. He sent his envoy to Ahmad Shah with the message, "Crown to Ahmad Shah and Wazirship to Shahnawaz". He also got himself converted to Shia religion and in his official seal replaced the names of the Mughal

Emperors by the twelve imams with a view to win the favour of the Persian soldiery of Ahmad Shah. In Delhi, the Wazir when came to know about this, wrote a conciliatory letter and allotted Shahnawaz five provinces. Shahnawaz agreed and prepared to oppose the invader, whom a little while before he had invited.[261]

Shah Zaman, the grandson of Abdali attacked India in the last decade of the eighteenth century. He was helped by Sahib Singh of Patiala, Nizamuddin Khan and Sansar Chand of Kangra, the two powerful chiefs of the region. When he proceeded towards Delhi, the people who suffered most at the hands of the invader were the Punjabi Muslims, who believing that the Afghans would not touch their co-religionists, did not leave along with Hindus and Sikhs, and had remained in their homes.[262]

In Delhi Gholam Qadir descerated a place of his own religion. He fleeced the Qadam-I- Sharif shrine at Delhi (The shrine preserved the holy footprint of the Prophet) and took away all its gold and silver articles donated to it by the devout Muslims.

Qadir also blinded and imprisoned Emperor Shah Alam. It was

Sindhia who got Qadir killed and rescued the helpless emperor and for this Timur honoured him. Sadullah Khan, an ambassador of Timur Shah, visited Delhi and then went to Mahadji Sindhia. Timur had sent a Khillat to Mahadji for punishing Ghulam Qadir. Sindhia honoured Sadullah Khan by bestowing upon him rupee 12,000, some jewels and a rob of honour of five pieces and gave rich presents including elephants for Timur Shah.[263] On the other hand Jassa Singh Ramgarhia of Lahore gave shelter to Ghulam Qadir's mother and younger son and also granted her the revenue of five villages amounting to rupees seven thousand a year.[264] Thus all the rulers as well as invaders were guided not by religious but by other considerations in their campaigns and the maintenance of their rule.

Political rivalries and wars continued but communal bitterness or hatred did not exist. No attempt was made by any power to replace Shah Alam who himself, despite his disability and helpless position remained very particular about his status as the nominal sovereign of India. Notwithstanding the decayed condition of Delhi many independent states repeatedly applied to be received as subjects and tributaries and sought confirmation of all titles and posts from the emperor. As late as 1789, a Mughal Prince Mirza Ali Bakht Bahadur Muhammad Zahiruddin Azfari escaped from the palace and wrote a diary of his travels, which shows that throughout his wanderings he was treated with respect and honour due to a Mughal Prince. The rulers of Jaipur, Awadh and Carnatic considered it their honour to accord him such a treatment. The Raja of Jaipur, Swai Pratap Singh, presented a nazar to the prince and even refused to sit in his presence.[265]

Maharaja Ranjit Singh

For three years after the departure of the Afghans, three Sikh chieftains misruled Lahore. Tired of them, the Muslim, Hindu and Sikh citizens of Lahore sent a joint deputation to Ranjit Singh and invited him to take over the city, promising him all help.[266]

After assuming power, Ranjit Singh ruled as a secular ruler and respected all the religions equally. His first public act as the ruler of Punjab was to pay homage at the Badshahi Mosque and then at the Mosque of Wazir Khan, which was one of the most frequented in the city. Ranjit Singh was deeply religious as a person but he was against mixing religion with politics. Sectarian ideas had no place in his thinking. He abolished the rule of Akal Takht so far as political matters were concerned and associated Hindus and Muslims as well in the governance of the state. Fakir Nur-ud-Din was the Home minister and his personal physicians, Mian Gaus, the commandant of his artillery and Imam Baksh, the head of the Lahore police. Qazi Nizamuddin was nominated the religious head of the Muslims, Hakim Nuruddin was put in charge of the Public Health, Azizuddin became the advisor and later the minister of Foreign Affairs.[267] The Maharaja raised infantry battalions of Punjabi Mussalmans. Muslim gunners manned his batteries. Ghaus Elahi Baksh rose to the highest rank in this branch of service.[268] He even entrusted the charge and defence of some important forts like Gobindgarh to Muslim officers.[269]

The maharaja fully trusted his Muslim officers and these men helped him to establish his kingdom on a firm footing and were with him till last. Azizuddin was sent as an envoy for negotiated settlement, to Dost Mohammad when the latter advanced towards Peshawar with the intention of recovering the city from Ranjit Singh. Dost Mohammad tried to win over Azizuddin but when failed called Azizuddin Kafir and infidel. Azizuddin replied to him that it was his "duty as a good Muslim to be true to my salt and to defend my country against aggression."[270] When after a stroke Ranjit Singh lost his power of speech and could communicate by means of sign only, Azizuddin was one of the two courtiers, who could understand and interpret the sign of language. Azizuddin used to remain near Ranjit Singh through out the day.[271]

In dealing with fallen enemies, the Maharaja like Akbar, showed his secularism and unprecedented generosity. When in 1809 he conquered Kasur from Nawab Qutbuddin, he gave him the jagir of Mamdot, which brought revenue of 190,000 rupees a year. In 1818, he conquered the province of Multan, but granted a big jagir to the Nawab's sons. In 1834 when Peshawar was made a part of the Punjab, he gave to Sultan Mohammad Khan the fertile track of Hasht Nagar.[272]

In Bengal, the Muslim Nawabs trusted the Hindus and placed them in important positions. Murshid Quli Khan, Nawab of Bengal Suba had appointed Bhupat Ray, a Brahmin, his dewan and chief advisor. Raswant Ray got the post of Munshi, Kinkar Sen became the Peshkar of the dewan and Alamchand held the post of dewan of Orissa. Lahori Mal and Dilpat Singh Hazari became chief of the army. Mritunjay and Raghunandan were entrusted the responsibility of revenue collection. Raghunandan was appointed Daroga of the mint as well.[273] During Nawab Sirajuddaula's reign, Hindus had immense influence in the administration of the Bengal suba. Nawab Sirajuddaula appointed Mohan Lal, a Kashmiri, his personal Dewan and conferred upon him the title of Maharaja. Janaki Ray was appointed dewan-i- khalsa and was honoured with the title of Ray-Raiyan. Ras Bihari was appointed an army-chief and faujdar. Manikchand and Nand Kumar were faujdar at Calcutta and Hugli respectively.[274] The selfish interest of Mir Jafar, Jagat Seth and Aminchand not only brought the downfall of the Nawab but their treachery enslaved the country to the English for two hundred years.

The Nawab was a patriot. He was a thorn in the eyes of the English officials, as he wanted to restrict the Company's increasing interference in the state matters. The Company's officials, like Lord Macauly, observed "...The odious vices of Siraj-ud-Dowlah, the wrongs which the English had suffered at his hands, the danger to which our trade must have been exposed had he continued to reign, appears to us fully to justify the resolution of desposing him."[275]

Mir Jafar, who commanded a large part of the Nawab's army, withdrew at the decisive moment in accordance with his secret deal with Clive. Mohan Lal, Nawab's general officer remained loyal and sacrificed his life for his master. When Siraj fled from the capital Mohan Lal was captured and handed over to Rai Durlabh who seized his vast wealth and put him to death.[276] The English won the battle of Plassey with only twenty-two casualties on their side and five hundred wounded and killed on Siraj's side. The Nawab was captured and sliced to bits, his mangled body crushed under the feet of an elephant and displayed through the Bazaar of Murshidabad.[277]

The Company rewarded Jafar for his treachery by making him the Nawab of Bengal. Clive, a school dropout youth, an employee of the Company, moved in to the palace surrounded by beautiful gardens. The treasury of Bengal was emptied and the Company became the real ruler. When the Nawab tried to resist the company, he too was removed and was replaced by Mir Qasim, a puppet of Clive. Omichand, who was also a party in the conspiracy against Siraj, also met the same fate. Clive refused to pay him. "The unhappy wretch fell back in a swoon in to the arms of his attendants, by whom he was conveyed to his palanquin, and thence to his house, where he remained for some hours in a state of stupor. A few days after he waited on Clive, who advised him to undertake a pilgrimage. He did as directed, returned insane, and died within the space of a year and half."[278] Jafar was deported to Calcutta where he was kept under detention and was given a pittance of rupees 2000 for his personal expenses. Clive, the epitome of treachery and fraud, became the richest man. In his home country, he was honoured with a Peerage and a statue in England.[279]

To gain the throne Mir Qasim had sided with the English but to retain the throne he sought the help of Emperor Shah Alam. The combined armies of Mir Qasim and the emperor fought at Buxar in 1764 but were defeated. Clive obtained from Shah Alam the Diwani of Bengal, Bihar and Orrisa.

Dividing one against the other and using all means was the policy of the Company from which it never deviated throughout its rule in our country. From trade, it diverted to capture the political power of the entire country. In Oudh, it tried first to purchase the loyalty of Jhao Lal, the favourite minister of Nawab Shujauddaula and later of his son Asafuddaula, but when failed, it forced the Nawab to dismiss Jhao Lal. The Company then placed their own agent Tafazzul Hussain as the Nawab's Chief Minister.[280]

The same drama was enacted in Mysore with Tipu Sultan. The Sultan was liberal in outlook and was popular with his subjects. It was not easy to dislodge him, as his army was loyal towards him. He was tolerant and not bigoted as projected by the British historians and the Hindu as well as Muslim communalists His enemies were not only Marathas and the English but also the Nizam. Though a devout Muslim Tipu respected other religions and accorded the religious institutions equal favours. He was shocked to know the desecration of Sringeri Matha by some Marathas. Several of Tipu's letters refer to great loss sustained by the Sringeri Matha in consequence of a raid by the Marathas under Parasuram Bahu during which not only was the Matha wealth looted; nearly six Lac rupees but they pulled down the sacred image of Sarda from her pedestal; killed and wounded men, Brahmans and other people and carried off everything found in the Matha.[281]

Tipu Sultan himself wrote a letter to the swami of the Matha, who had left Sringeri after the raid and was living with four of his disciples at Karkala:

"We are pushing the hostile armies that have marched against our country and are harassing our subjects. You are a holy person and an ascetic... We request you to pray to God along with other Brahmans of the Matha, that all our enemies may suffer defeat and take to flight and all the people of our country live happily, and send us your blessings."[282]

The swami therefore informed Tipu that without the government's assistance, in the shape of money and other things, it was not possible to reconsecrate the desecrated image of the Goddess. To this Tipu replied:

"People who have sinned against such a holy place are sure to suffer the consequences of their misdeeds at no distant date in this Kali age, in accordance with the verse 'Hasadhih kriyate karma rudadbhir anubhuyate-people do evil deeds smiling, but will suffer the consequences weeping'. Treachery to Guru will undoubtedly result in the destruction of the line of descent. An order is enclosed to the Asaf of Nagar directing him to give on behalf of the government 200 Rahati worth of grain for the consecration of the Goddess Sarda and to supply other articles, if desired for money. Having thus consecrated the Goddess Sarda and fed the Brahmans, please pray for the increase of our prosperity and the destruction of our enemies".[283]

The language and the sentiments of this letter make it crystal clear that Tipu was neither a fanatic nor an intolerant bigot whereas the head of the Maratha state was a Brahman, the commander of the invading army was a Brahman, the Maratha displayed the ochre-coloured banner, the symbol of renunciation, desecrated the temple and displaced the image of Sarda. On the 24th May 1791, Trimbak Rao sent from the Maratha camp the following account of this deplorable incident to Bala Saheb of Miraj:

"The army crossed the Tunga but the Lamans and the Pendharis had previously proceeded towards Shivmoghe. They went to the Swami's village of Sringeri and plundered it. They robbed the Swami of all his belongings, including the Danda and Kamandalu (ascetic's staff and water jug) Even women were molested and some of them sacrificed their lives, the images belonging to the Swami, consisting of those of Gods were plundered. The lamans brought away all the elephants and horses. The swami fasted for five days and died" (in consequence).[284]

The swami fasted in order to bring his grievances to the notice of Maratha authorities and afterwards repeatedly wrote to the Peshwa for the restoration of the property but the culprits were never brought to book. Tipu on the other hand helped the Hindu saint to reinstall the image of the Goddess Sarda.[285]

When Tipu conquered Malabar and was near Agruiwar, some of his soldiers had set on fire a portion of a famous temple of Agruiwar. The pujari had already shifted the idol of Vishnu to Travancore in order to save it from dishonouring. The officers of the army having come to know of this, came at once to the temple and put the fire out and sent the pujari of the temple to report the matter to the Sultan who had camped few miles away of this temple. The Sultan immediately marched to Agruiwar and noticed things himself. He severely punished the sepoys concerned and made immediate arrangements to repair the temple and ordered that the revenue from the place, instead of being remitted to the state treasury, should be paid direct to the pujari of the temple. He was rather angry at the pujari (priest) for having shifted the idol to Travancore and asked them to go and fetch back the idol and restore it to the temple.[286]

If Tipu crushed the Hindu Coorgs and Nairs, he did not spare Muslim Mophlas. His conversion of some Coorgs and Nairs were not motivated by religious zeal but by political reasons. Forcible conversion used to be the harsh punishment in those days. The Coorgs and Nairs, despite warning by Tipu, time and again rose against him. He punished them by converting them to Islam. [287]

It was not only the Marathas but also the Nizam who fought against Tipu.[288] Both for their self-interest supported the English against Tipu. Religious considerations never matter in these wars. When Tipu was defeated in the third Mysore war by Cornwallis and had to give as hostage his two minor sons, both Hindu and Muslim rulers including Shah Alam II sent congratulatory messages to Cornwallis. The important rulers among others, who greeted the English, were Asafuddaulah of Oudh, Nawab of Murshidabad, Rampur, Ram Raja of Travancore, Rani of Burdwan, Raja Ram Ishar, Raja of Jaipur, Raja of Tunnohil etc.[289]

Tipu was a thorn in the eyes of the English. He refused to be their tributary like many other Indian Rajas. He, like his father, had understood that English rather than any native power was the enemy, and he never leagued himself with her against his neighbours. "Had the Maratha chieftains, sinking their internal differences, possessed his singleness of purpose and all consuming hate, the final advance of British supremacy might have been long delayed".[290] Tipu was brave and fearless. The Tiger was his emblem. It was present on his flag, on his swords, dagger handles and on much of his ornaments. The uniforms of his soldiers were made of tiger-stripe cloth. His throne that he never ascended was also decorated with eight tiger heads. An English priest has written that British mothers used to mention Tipu's'name to silence their children. It was not possible to defeat Tipu in the battlefield as he was loved by his people, had their support and an unflinching loyalty of his army. The English then hatched a conspiracy to get rid off Tipu as they had successfully done in Bengal. They purchased the loyalty of his most important officers like Mir Sadiq, the huzur Diwan, Purnaiya, the head of the Mir Miran department, and Qamar-ud-din, an important advisor to Tipu and Mir Nadim, commandant of the Fort. Tipu died fighting for his country. When his body was found, an English soldier made an attempt to detach his sword-belt, then the Sultan with all his remaining strength made an attack and wounded him on the knee. The English hatred for this patriot can be seen when they called him a 'monster in the human shape'. None of Tipu's sons was placed on the throne, instead a five years old son of the ancient Raja was made the king.[291] As the price of betrayal, the English generously rewarded the Mysore officers.

Despite the hard efforts made on the part of the English to divide the people on communal lines, the trust and, mutual understanding between the two communities continued. Emperor Akbar II sent Raja Ram Mohan Roy to represent his case regarding pension to the British Queen. When Nana Saheb became the Maharaja of Bittur, after the death of Baji Rao in 1851, he sent Azimullah to London to plead his case and secure for him the pension paid to Balaji Baji Rao.[292] Emperor Bahadur Shah had his trusted lieutenant in Sobharam, the chief advisor of Nana Saheb was Azimullah, a Muslim. The most loyal adherents of the Rani Jhansi, who manned her guns, were Muslims. In Oudh, Begum Hazrat Mahal enjoyed full support of the Hindu nobility. The Hindu nobility led by Jay Lal placed the Begums's ten years old son Birjis on the throne against the displeasure of the Company.[293]

In the lust of expanding their empire, the English forced the Rajas one after another to submit to their terms. Those who did not accept their dictates faced hardships, humiliations and were ultimately dislodged no matter whether they were Hindus or Muslims. On refusing to sign a treaty on February 4,1856, Nawab Wajid Ali Shah of Oudh, was deposed and taken to Calcutta where he was imprisoned.[294] The English tried to create wedge between different communities on the basis of religion but they themselves were not the friend of any religion or community. They exploited all for their selfish interests. Ultimately, this gave rise to a national revolt against them. People belonging to different religions and regions united together to oust the English from the country. The leaders of the revolt selected Bahadur Shah Zafar as their commander who made appeals to both the Hindus and Muslims to drive away the English. The emperor wrote personal letters to the Rajas of Jodhpur, Bikaner Alwar and others to join in the effort of liberating the motherland from the English. He wrote:

To drive away the Firangis from India by any means and at any cost is my only desire. I want to see the whole of India free and independent. If you Rajas draw your sword to drive away the enemy and then form a confederacy and government I would gladly entrust the sovereignty to you and will thus be free from responsibility."[295]

Bahadur Shah issued printed Farmans asking the Hindus to take an oath on the sacred Ganges, Tulsi and Saligram and Muslims by Quran to drive away the Firangis. Nana Saheb declared himself as subedar of the emperor. He along with his Bhagwa jhanda (saffron flag), unfurled the crescent flag. His coins were struck in the name of the emperor and all orders were issued in his name. He along with his principal advisor, Azimullah, toured different parts of the country rousing the patriotic sentiments of the people against the common enemy, the English. He proclaimed:

"The English who are Kafirs came to this country under pretence of carrying on trade. Afterwards investigating sedition among our Surinjamadars and practising treachery they seized all the Hindus and Mohammadan kingdoms, imprisoning some of the descendants of the former kings and driving others to beggary, they themselves enjoy the country"[296]

Nana Saheb also proclaimed that he was commissioned by God to throw the Kafirs, i.e., English out of this country. He said:

"Tyranny, wickedness and injustice having been practised by the Kafir English on the faithful and the sin-fearing. I have been commissioned by God to punish the kafirs by annihilating them to re-establish the Hindu and Muslim kingdoms as formerly and to protect our country."[297]

Awadh under the leadership of Begum Hazarat Mahal, who was about twenty five to twenty six years old, joined the nationalist forces. She also organized groups of women in well-trained bands of freedom fighters under her direct supervision. Both Hindu and

Muslim masses stood on the side of the Begum. She herself appeared in the battlefield on February 25, mounted on an elephant and herself fought the battle of Ballie Guard with extraordinary courage. The British sent several messages to the Queen to come to their side promising to her many inducements, including even the return of the kingdom to Wazid Ali Shah but the Queen declined their offer and asked them to quit the country.[298]

Rani Laxmi Bai had 1500 trusted Muslim officers who always accompanied her in the battlefield. Ghulam Mohammad Ghaus khan and Khudabaksh, her two faithful warriors sacrificed their lives to protect the Rani who immortalized herself by making the supreme sacrifice for her country. (There is a Mazar of Ghaus Khan inside the fort of Jhansi even today).[299]

The unity of the people frightened the English Holloway who participated in the war of 1857 observed "For both these representatives of the religious bodies perfectly agreed whilst prosecuting the scheme for overthrowing our dominion in the East" Keith Young recorded with dismay that instead of fighting among themselves the Hindus and Muslims have all joined together to make a vigorous attack".[300] Another official of the company of the official admitted in despair "In this instance we cannot pay off them against the Hindus".[301] However, confident of the victory, a firangi mocked at Bahadur Shah Zafar who had taken up his sword at the old age to defend his motherland and satircally said:

"Dumdame mein dum nahi ab kheir mango jan ki:
Ay Zafar bus ho chuki shamsheer Hindustan ki.

To this Bahadur Shah shot back:

"Hindiyon mein boo rahegi jab talak iman ki,
Takhte London par chalegi teg Hindustan ki.[302]

After the suppression of the revolt, the English established the rule of their Queen in India and deposed the Indian Emperor to Rangoon where he died lamenting for being away from his homeland.

Thus harmony existed till the end of Mughal Empire. The wars fought between the Hindu, Muslim and Sikhs were not religious wars. Besides the armies of the rulers consisted of soldiers belonging to different religions. The destruction of the religious places or the forcible conversion were few and were out of greed or momentary fury and not out of hatred. Masses were not divided on communal lines and religion did not affect their loyalty towards their ruler.

Feelings of brotherhood, oneness and affinity continued. It were the British who gave a communal colour to all the rifts, conflicts and wars that occurred in medieval India. During their rule in the country, they communalised the entire environment by their continuos propaganda and policies. The result was that they maintained their rule in our country and exploited all its resources for the progress of their own country and for the expansion of their empire. Till today, after independence and division, India, Pakistan and Bangla Desh look at them and seek their support for the solution of their internal problems and external disputes. It is a tragedy of the sub-continent.

REFERENCES

1. Sisir Kumar Mitra, *India's Culture Empire and Her Future,* Arobindo Library, Madras 1947, p. 68.

2. *Ibid.*

3. *Ibid.*

4. B.G. Gokhale, *The Making of the Indian Nation,* Asia, Delhi 1958, p. 41.

5. Mohammad Habib, *Collected Works,* Vol. II, PPH, Aligarh University, 1981, p. 20.

6. Fathullah Mujtabai, *Hindu Muslim Cultural Relations,* N.B.B. Delhi 1978, p. 131.

7. Tarachand, *A Short History of Indian People,* Macmillan, Allahabad 1940, p. 131.

8. *Ibid.*

9. S.M. Ikram, *Muslim Civilization in India,* Columbia University Press, New York, 1964, p. 17.

10. Habib, p 103.

11. Syed Mahmud, *India of Yesterday,* Indo-Middle East Cultural Studies, Hyderabad, 1957, p. 39.

12. W.W. Hunter, *The Indian Empire,* Smith and Elder, London, 1892, p. 327.

13. S.M. Jaffar, *Medieval India Under Muslim Kings,* Idara-i- Adbiyat, Delhi Reprint 1972, p. 97.

14. Sidney J. Owen, *From Mahmud Ghazni to the Disintegration of Mughal Empire,* Kanishka, Delhi 1987, p. 17.

15. Herman Kulke and Dietmar Rothermund, *A History of India,* Manohar New Delhi, 1987, p. 165.

16. Habib, p. 103.

17. Ibid, p. 78.

18. Syed Mahmud, p. 39. Also see Hunter, *Brief History of the Indian People,* Morrison and Gibb. Edinburgh, 1881, p. 105.

19. Habib, p. 101.

20. Syed, p. 39.
21. Habib, p. 86.
22. ABM. Habibullah, *The Foundations of Muslim Rule in India*, Central Book, Allahabad 1945, p. 321.
23. Hunter, *Brief History of the Indian People*, p. 105, Syed, p. 44.
24. C.V. Vaidya, *Medieval Hindu India* Vol. II, Poona, 1926, p. 361.
25. S.M. Ikram, p. 39.
26. *Proceedings of Indian History Congress*, 1953, p. 226.
27. Baij Nath Puri, *Indian History-A Review*, Bhartiya Vidya Bhavan, Bombay 1960, p. 80.
28. Habib, p. 256.
29. Tarachand *A Short History of Indian People*, p. 211.
30. *Futuhu's Salatin or Shah Namah-i-Hind of Islami*, ed by Agha Mahdi Husain, Vol. III Asia, Aligarh 1977, p. 655.
31. *Ibid.*
32. Thomas Keightlely, *History of India*, Whittaker and Company London 1847, p. 16.
33. *Ibid.*
34. Agha Mahdi Husain, *Rise and Fall of Muhammad Bin Tughlaq*, Orient, London 1938, (Rept 1972 Idara-i-Adbiyat, Delhi) p. 12.
35. Muhammad Qamaruddin, *Society* and *Culture in Medieval India*, Delhi 1985, p. 246.
36. A.B. Pandey *Society and Government in Medieval India*, Central Book, Allahabad, 1965, p. 52.
37. Romilla Thapar, *A History of India*, Vol. I Penguin Books, Delhi 1966 p. 232.
38. Niamatullah's *History of Afghans*, trs. by Nirodhbhusan Roy, Shanti Niketan, Bengal, 1938, p. 65.
39. Pandey, p. 52.
40. Niamatullah's *History of Afghans*, p. xxxiii.
41. Agha Mahdi Husain, *Tughlaq Dynasty*, London University, London, 1935, p. 463.
42. K.S. Lal, *Twilight of the Sultanate*, Asia House Delhi, 1963, p. 33.
43. Agha Mahdi Hussain, *Tughlaq Dynasty*, p. 463.
44. Sisir, p. 80.
45. Tarachand, *A Short History of India*, p. 133.
46. W.H. Moreland and Atul Chandra, *A Short History of India*, Longman, London 1936, p. 190-91.
47. M.R. Majumdar, *Cultural History of Gujarat*, Popular Prakshan Bombay, 1965, p. 128. Also see V.D. Savarkar *Six Glorious Epoches of Indian History*, Published by V.D. Savarkar, Bombay 1971, p. 199.
48. William Ersqine Esq. *History of India*, Longman, Brown and others, London 1854, p. 480.
49. *Ibid.*

50. *Ibid,* Also see K.M. Panikkar, *A Survey of Indian History*. The National Information, Bombay 1997, p. 52-53.

51. A.B. Pandey, *The First Afghan Empire in India*, Bookland, Calcutta, 1956, p. 178.

52. Niamatullah's *History of Afghan*, p. xxiii.

53. *Ibid.*

54. S.R. Sharma, *Mughal Empire in India*, Lakshmi, Agra, 1974 p. 22.

55. Ersqine, p. 461.

56. S.R. Sharma, p. 22.

57. Satish Chandra, *Mughals Religious Policies*, Vikas New Delhi, 1993, p. 8.

58. Radhey Shyam, *Babar*, Janaki Prakashan, Allahabad, 1978, p. 450.

59. *History of the Mughal Dynasty in India Founded on the Memories of Manucci*, J.M. Richardson, 1826, p. 56.

60. *Ibid*, p. 463.

61. Ersqine, p. 461. Also see Satish Chandra, p. 10.

62. Satish Chandra, p. 10.

63. Radhey Shyam, *Babar*, p. 449.

64. *Ibid*, p. 452.

65. *Ibid*, p.458. It is said that Rana Sanga demolished the Mosque of Idr and built a temple on its ruin. See Niamatuallah's *History of Afghans*, p. 30.

66. *Ibid*, p. 460.

67. Ersqine, p. 438.

68. Thomas Kieghtley, *History of India*, p. 37.

69.S.M. Ikram. *Muslim Civilization in India*, 140.

70. *Ibid.*, p. 140.

71. Muni Lal, *Akbar*, Vikas, New Delhi 1980. p. 8.

72. Stanley Lane Poole, *Medieval India Under Mohammadan Rule*, London 1912, p. 187.

73. Moreland, *A short History of India*, p. 216.

74. R.P. Tripathi, *Rise and Fall of Mughal Empire*, Central Book Depot. Allahabad, 1963, p. 223.

75. S.R. Sharma, *Mughal Empire in India*, p. 135.

76. *The Hindustan Review* and *Kayastha Samachar*, p. 193.

77. R.P. Tripathi, p. 219, Lala Lajpat Rai, *Shivaji the Great Patriot*, Metropolition, Delhi 1980, Reprint p. 22, Muni Lal, p. 205.

78. Muni Lal, p. 26.

79. S.R. Sharma, *Maharana Pratap*, V.V.R. Institute Hoshiarpur, 1954, p. 109, 114.

80. Saryu Prasad Aggarwal, *Akbari Darbar ke Hindi Kavi*, Lucknow University, Lucknow, 1943, p. 140.

81. Muni Lal, p. 210.

82. Abdul Qadir Badayuni, Muntakhab-ul-Tawarikh, trs. by Kumud Ranjan Das, Sarswati Library, Calcutta, 1970, p. 46.

83. Muni Lal, p. 211.

84. S.R. Sharma, *Maharana Pratap*, p. 124-25.

85. T.L. Vaswani, *The Spirit* and *Struggles of Islam*, Ganesh and comp. Madras 1921, p. 11.

86. Muni Lal, Shah Jahan, Vikas New Delhi 1981, p. 40.

87. Tripathi, p. 377.

88. P. Saran, *Provincial Governments of the Mughals*, Kitabistan, Allahabad, 1941, p. 136-37.

89. N. Manucci, *Storia Do Mogor*, Vol. I, trs. by William Irvine John Murry London 1908, p. 207.

90. *Proceedings of Indian History Congress* 1953, p. 258.

91. *Ibid*, p. 256.

92. Beni Prasad, *History of Jahangir*, The Indian Press, Allahabad, 1962, p. 104.

93. *Memoirs of Jahangeir*, trs. by Major David Price, Rare Book, Delhi 1904 p. 52.

94. *Ibid*, p. 47, 48.

95. *Ibid*, p. 216.

96. Manucci, Vol. I p. 359.

97. *Ibid*.

98. *Ibid*. Also see *Proceedings of Indian History Congress* 1984, p. 448.

99. Manucci, Vol. II, p. 120, 129.

100. Max Arthur Macauliffe, *The Sikh Religion*, S. Chand and Comp, New Delhi 1983, Vol. III-IV, p. 26, 29.

101. Hem Chandra Rai, *Romance of the Fort of Gwalior*, Marathi Press Delhi 1931, p. 47.

102. Macauliffe, p. 29.

103. Khushwant Singh, *A History of the Sikhs*, New Jersey Princeton, 1963, p. 64.

104. Macauliffe, p. 32, 33.

105. G.S. Chhabra, *Advanced Study in History of the Punjab* Vol. I. Sharanjit, Jullundar, 1960, p. 200, 213.

106. Manucci, p. 248.

107. B.N. Luniya *Evolution of Indian Culture*, Laxmi Narayan Aggarwal, Agra 1955, p. 177.

108. Manucci, Vol. I, p. 208.

109. Panna Lal Dhar *India* and *Her Domestic Problem*, Punthi Pustak, Calcutta 1995, p. 6.

110. U.N. Day, *Some Aspects of Medieval Indian History*, Kumar Bros, New Delhi 1971, p. 216.

111. Manucci, p. 305.

112. *Ibid*, p. 360 Also see Saqi Mustad Khan, *Masir-i- Alamgiri*, trs. by Jadunath Sarkar, Asiatic Society, Calcutta 1947, p. 288.

113. Seid Gholam Hussein Khan, *The Seir Mutaqherin* Vol. IV, p. 134.

114. Manucci, p. 120, 193.

115. *Ibid*, Vol .II p. 221.

116. *Ibid*.

117. *Ibid*., Vol. I, p. 378.

118. *Ibid*, p. 195, 120.

119. Jadunath Sarkar, *History of Aurangzib*, Vol. III, Published by M.C. Sarkar, Calcutta 1916, p. 165.

120. Waldermar Hansen, *Peacock Throne*, Holt, Rineheart and Winston, New York, 1972 p. 422.

121. *Futuhat-i-Alamgiri*, Ishwar Das Nagar, trs. by T. Ahmed Idara-i-Adabiyat-i- Delhi. 1978, p. 57.

122. *Ruka 'at-i- Alamgiri* trs. by Jamshid H. Bilimoria, Idara-i- Adbiyat-i- Delhi, 1972, p. 69.

123. Manucci, Vol. I, p. 253.

124. *Ibid*, Vol. III, p. 14.

125. Manucci, Vol. I, p. 377.

126. Seid Gholam Hussein, *Seir* p. 126.

127. *Ibid*. p. 125.

128. Manucci, Vol. IV, p. 113.

129. *Ibid*, Vol. I. p. 306.

130. *Ibid*.

131. Seid Gholam Hussein, *Seir* p. 129.

132. William Irvine, *Later Mughals*, ed by Jadunath Sarkar, Orient Books 1971, p. 409.

133. *Maasir-i- Alamgiri*, p. 139.

134. *Ruka 'at -i- Alamgiri*, p. 74.

135. Seid Gholam Hussein, *Seir* p. 139, Manucci, p. 121.

136. Manucci, Vol. II, p. 20.

137. *Ibid*.

138. *Visva Bharati Quarterly*, Feb-April 1947, p. 327.

139. *Ibid*., May 1940, p. 77.

140. Manucci, p. 275, 76.

141. Seid Gholam Hussein, *Seir*, p. 165.

142. *Ibid*.

143. Maulana Shibli Nomani, *Alamagir*, trs. by S. Abdur Rahman, Idara-i-Adabiyat, Delhi 1981, p. 6.

144. Manucci, Vol. I, p. 119

145. *Ibid*, p. 131.

146. *Ibid*, p. 131.

147. Z. Faruki, *Aurangzib and His Times*, Idara-i-Adbbiyat-i-Delhi 1972, p. 120.

148. Satish Chandra, p.179, 181.

149. *Ruka 'at -i- Alamgiri*, p. 60. Also see V. Raghvendra Rao, *Indo-Muslim Culture*, Vichara Sahitya, Benglore, p. 41

150. Ruka 'at-i-Alamgiri, p. 24.

151. *Ibid.*

152. *Ibid*, p. 74.

153. Satish Chandra p. 75.

154. Thomas Keightley, *History of India*, p. 39.

155. C.K. Kareem, *What Happened in Indian History*, Collin, Cochin1971, p. 134.

156. *Futuhat-i- Alamgir*, p.117.

157. Satish Chandra p. 172.

158. *Ibid* p. 181.

159. Manucci, p. 275.

160. *Ibid*, 173.

161. *Maasir-i-Alamgir*, trs. by Jadunath Sarkar, p. 288.

162. *Indian Antiquary*, March 1911, p. 69.

163. Pringle Kennedy, *A History of the Great Mughals*, Thacker, Calcutta, 1905, p. 89.

164. Robert C. Hallissey, *The Rajput Rebellion Againt Aurangzeb*, University of Missouri Press, London 1977, p. 85.

165. Manucci, Vol. I, p. 267.

166. Satish Chandra, p. 89.

167. DR. Pattabhi, Sitaramayya, *Feathers and Stone*, Cited from *Khuda Bakhsh Library Journal*, 44, 1987 p. 44.

168. Cited from Faruki, p. 229.

169. *Khuda Bakhsh Library Journal* 44. 1987, p. 44, 45.

170. Rajendra Prasad, *India Divided*, Hind Kitab. Bombay 1946, p. 34.

171. Elphinstone, *History of India*, Murry J. London, 1857, p. 672.

172. *The Norris Embassy to Aurargzeb*, by Hari Das Mukhopadhyay, Calcutta, 1959, p.165.

173. Jadunath Sarkar, *Aurangzeb*, Vol. IV, p. 406.

174. Thomas Keightley, p. 37.

175. Richard Temple, *Shivaji and the Rise of Marattas*, Sashi Gupta, Calcutta. p. 94.

176. Herman Kulke and Dietmar Rothermund, p. 207.

177. Kedarnath, *Shivaji Festival*, *in The Hindustan Review* and *The Kayastha Samachar*, July 1902, p. 39.

178. *Ibid*. p. 193.

179. Faruki, p. 352.

180. Richard Temple, p. 95.

181. W.H. Moreland and Atul Chandra, p. 256.

182. C.V. Vaidya, *Shivaji the Founder of Maratha Swaraj*, Published by C.V. Vaidya, Poona 1931, p. 319.

183. Baba Saheb Deshpande, *Shivaji the Great from Agra*, Rao Saheb, S.K. Deshpande, Poona 1929, p. 14.

184. Surendra Nath Sen, *Foreign Biographies of Shivaji,* Vol. II, The Book Comp., Calcutta, 1927, p. 18.

185. Jadunath Sarkar, *House of Shivaji*, S.N. Sarkar, Calcutta 1940, p. 81.

186. S.V. Venkateswara, *Indian Culture Through Ages*, Longman Green and comp London 1932, p. 233.

187. Panna Lal Dhar, *India* and *her Domestic Problems*, p. 61.

188. C.V. Vaidya, *Shivaji the Founder of Maratha* Swaraj p. 326.

189. S.R. Sharma, *Our Heritage*, Hind Kitab Bombay 1947, p. 139.

190. David Kincaied, *The Founder of Maratha Empire*, Discovery, New Delhi Rept 1984, p. 27.

191. Lala Lajpat Rai, *Shivaji the Great Patriot*, p. 52.

192. Thomas Keightley, p. 37.

193. *Ibid.*

194. Manucci, Vol. I, p. 247.

195. Shibli Nomani, *Alamgir*, p. 19.

196. Satish Chandra, p. 200.

197. Jadunath Sarkar, *House of Shivaji* p. 81.

198. *Faruki*, p. 358.

199. David Kincaied, p. 249.

200. Richard Temple, p. 99.

201. Dennis Kincaied, *The Grand Rebel*, Collins, London 1937. p. 324.

202. Ishwari Prasad, *India in the Eighteenth Century*, Chugh, Allahabad, 1973, p. 1, 2.

203. Robert C. Hallissey, *The Rajput Rebellion Against Aurangzeb*, p. 70-81.

204. A.L. Srivastva, *The Mughal Empire*, Shiv Lal Aggarwal and Comp, Agra 1964, p. 403.

205. Robert C. Hallissey, p. 82.

206. S.R. Sharma, *The Founding of Maratha Freedom*, Orient Longman, New Delhi 1964 p. 265.

207. *Ibid.*

208. Saqi Must 'ad Khan, *Maasir-i-Alamgir*, p. 200.

209. Shibli Nomani, *Alamgir*, p. 23. Satish Chandra, p. 201.

210. *Ibid*, p. 23.

211. *Ibid*, p. 23, 24.

212. Mukund Womanrou Burway, *Life and Times of Shivaji* 11-*Chhatrapati Shahu*, 1680-1749, M. W. Burway, Bombay 1932, p. 41.

213. *Ibid*, p. 41-42.

214. *Ibid.*

215. *Ruka 'at -i- Alamgir*, p. 73.

216. Burway, p. 46.

217. Irvine, *Later Mughals*, p. 162.

218. J.D. Cunningham, *History of the Sikhs*, Sanyal and Comp, Calcutta 1908, p. 78.

219. *Ibid.*

220. Khushwant Singh, *A History of the Sikhs*, Vol. I, Princeton University Press, New Jersey 1963, p. 71,

221. Browne, *The History of Sikhs* in *Indian Studies Past and Present*, vol-II. 1960-61, Calcutta 1960, p. 563.

222. Dorothy Field, *The Religion of the Sikhs*, John Murry, London 1914, p. 22-23.

223. Macauliffe, Vol. I, p. 381.

224. *Ibid*, p. 373.

225. *Ibid*, p. 388- 89.

226. *Ibid*, p. 389.

227. Dorothy, p. 34.

228. *Ibid*, p. 29.

229. *Ibid.*

230. Macauliffe. Vol. I, p. xviii.

231. *Ibid.* Vol. 5, p. 305.

232. *Ibid*, p. 275.

233. Browne, p. 564.

234. N.D. Ahuja, *The Great Guru Nanak*. p. 19.

235. Murry T. Titus, *Islam in India* and *Pakistan*, YMCA Calcutta, 1957, p. 144.

236. Harbans Singh, *Guru Gobind Singh*, G.G. Foundation, Chandigarh 1966, p. 16.

237. *The Indian Historical Quarterly*, 1926 Vol. IX, p. 839.

238. The Sikh Review, Jan 1987, Vol. XXXV, No. 397, p. 6.

239. Cunningham, p. 101.

240. Faruki, p. 256.

241. Browne, p. 567.

242. Prof. Puran Singh, *The Ten Masters*, Chief Khalsa Diwan Amritsar, 1973 p.110.

243. Murry T. Titus, p. 151.

244. Jadunath Sarkar, *History of Aurangzeb*, Vol. III, p.359. Also see Khushwant Singh, p. 94.

245. Puran Singh, p. 91.

246. *Journal of Indian History*, Part I-II, 1941, Vol. XX, p. 132.

247. N.D. Ahuja, p. 20-21.

248. Ajit Singh was murdered by his son Bakht Singh. Ajit Singh's body was cremated on 7th June 1724. Eghty four wives and concubines sacrificed themselves on the funeral pyre.

249. A.L. Srivastva, *The First Two Nawabs of Awadh*, Shiv Lal Aggarwal, Agra 1933, p. 233. Also see S.R. Sharma, *Mughal Empire in India*, p. 454.

250. Pt. Bisheshwar Nath, *Glories of Mewar*, Archaeological Deptt., Jodhpur 1943, p. xiii.

251. Jadunath Sarkar, *Nadir Shah in India*, Naya Prakash, Calcutta, 1973, p. 4.

252. Zahiruddin Malik, *The Reign of Mohammad Shah*, Asia, Aligarh 1977, p. 107.

253. *Ibid*,

254. Irvine, p. 336.

255. Zahiruddin, p. 270.

256. R.L. Ahuja, *Maharaja Ranjit Singh-A Man of Destiny*, Punjab Writers Co-operetive Society, Delhi,1983, p. 10-11.

257. *Ibid*.

258. Hari Om Gupta, *Later Mughal History* of the Punjab - 1707-1793, Minerva Book, Lahore 1944, p. 94.

259. Hari om Gupta, *We are one*, Director Public Relation, Haryana, 1973, p. 59-60, *Hindustan Review, Kayastha Samachar*, 1904, p. 277.

260. Hari Om Gupta, *Later Mughal History* of the Punjab p. 194.

261. *Ibid*. p. 69.

262.Personal enmity too led to massacre of the innocent masses belonging to a particular community. Jaspat Rai, brother of Lakhpat Rai, a Dewan of the Lahore government, was murdered while harassing the Sikhs at Eminabad. when Lakhpat Rai came to know about this, he ordered the general massacre of the Sikhs in 1746. It is called by Sikhs as chhota Ghalughara, or the smaller holocaust. It took about 40,000 Sikhs lives according to an estimate. Backed by the Nawab of Lahore Yahya Khan, Lakhpat Rai inficted all sorts of atrocities upon the Sikhs. The Dewan forbade the Sikhs from reading their scriptures, prohibited the use of the word Gur for sugar candy as it sounded like Guru and also of the word Granth which was to be replaced by Pothi. He also ordered the destruction of all Sikh books Granths and Pothies.

263. Hari Om Gupta *Later Mughal History of the Punjab*, p. 254. Also see Mohammad Umar, *Islam in Narthern India*, p. 320

264. Hari Om Gupta, *We are one*, p. 58.

265. Ishrat Haque, *Glimpes of Mughal Society* and *Culture*, p. 14. Also see A.L.H. Polier, *Shah Alam* and *His Court*, p. 41-42.

266. Faqir Syed Waheeduddin, *The Real Ranjit Singh*, Oriental, New Delhi, 1976. p. 65.

267. Teja Singh M.A., *Essays in Sikhism*, Sikh University Press, Lahore 1944 p. 102, Also sec Faqir, p. 9.

268. Khushwant Singh, p. 205.

269. N.D. Ahuja, *The Great Guru Nanak*, p. 21.

270. Faqir Waheeduddin, p. 41.

271. *Ibid*, p. 42.

272. Teja Singh, p. 43.

273. *Ibid*, p. 49.

274. *History of Bangladesh*, ed. Siraj-ul-Islam, Vol. III Asiatic Society, Bangladesh, 1992, p. 50.

275. E.H. Nolan *Illustrated History of the British Empire in India* and *the East*, James and Virtue, London, (year not mentioned) p. 252.

276. Upendra Nath Ball, *Modern India*, Doaba Publication, London, 1939, p. 438.

277. *Hindustan Review*, July 1946, p. 3.

278. Thomas Keightley, p.17.

279. Pt. Sunderlal, *How India lost Her Freedom*, Popular Prakashan, Bombay, 1970, p. 55—p. 39.

280. Purendu Basu, *Oudh and the East India Company*, Maxwell, Lucknow, 1943, p. 6, 15, 165.

281. Surendra Nath Sen, *Studies in the Indian History*, University of Calcutta, 1930, p. 160.

282. New Review 1937, Vol. VI, p. 571.

283. *Ibid*. p. 572.

284. Surendra Nath, p. 162.

285. *Ibid*., p. 163.

286. Syed Mahmud, *India of Yesterday*, p. 170.

287. Mohibbul Hasan, *History of Tipu Sultan*, The World Press, Calcutta, 1951, p. 328.

288. *Ibid*.

289. *Ibid*.

290. Roberts P.E. *Historical Geography of India*, Printwell Jaipur, 1995, p. 247.

291. Thomas Keightley, p. 138.

292. Pt. Sunderlal, p-cxiv. Also see, *1857-The Dividing line of Indian History*, ed. Sarkar Sen Gupta, Indian Publication, Calcutta 1957, p. 38.

293. *The Journal of Bihar Research Society*, Vol. XXXVI. No. I, March 1960, p. 158.

294. *Ibid*, Special. Issue, 1968, p. 227.

295. Mahdi Husain, *Bahadur Shah II*, M.N. Publishers New Delhi, 1986, p. ixvii.

296. Sashi Bhushan Choudhri, *Theories of the Indian Mutiny*, The World Press, Calcutta, 1965, p. 30.

297. Mahdi Husain, p. ixvii.

298. *The Journal of Bihar Research Society* sp. Issue 1968, p. 235.

299. Sri Niwas Balaji Hardikar, *Rani Laxmi Bai* (Hindi) National Peoples, Delhi 1968, p.164, 65.

300. Mahdi Husain, p.15, Sashi Bhushan, p. 48.

301. 1857-The Dividing Line, p. 137.

302. Uday Shankar Srivastva, *Madhya Yugin Hindi ke Sufi Itr Musalman Kavi*; by Published by- Jawahar Pustkalya, Mathura, year not mentisned p.176.

4

Kings and Their Subjects

Medieval India witnessed kings belonging to different creeds, enjoying love, affection and an unflinching loyalty of their subjects. They completely identified themselves with the interests of their subjects and worked for their well-being. Conflicts and confrontations were here and there, but generally peace prevailed and prosperity ushered in which made India one of the richest countries in the world.

After the initial bloodshed and acquisition of power, the new rulers tried to conciliate the people of the land. To maintain their rule and to run the administration, they needed the support and co-operation of the natives. They could not afford to antagonise the people by being intolerant and oppressive, as they themselves were not only outsiders but also few in numbers. This compulsion made them make such policies as could win them the confidence of the people. The historian Al-Baladuri tells us that seventeen-year old Mohammad bin Qasim, the conqueror of Sind who ruled over the region for a little over three years, was very popular with the Sindhis on account of his liberal attitude and tolerant administration When Qasim informed Hajaj, the Governor of Basra, about his conquest of Sind, the latter issued orders to Qasim as follows:

"Strive for the welfare of the subject people. Give protection to every one who asks you for it. If learned Hindus come to you, give them gifts of costly apparel and accord to them honourable reception. Keep the promises made, lest your broken word and your misbehavior spoilt the name of Islam. Of every one who believes in one God and is loyal to you, protect intact his wealth and his honour in exactly the same manner, as you would do to your own. And fight him who fights you till he submits to you. Spend the entire revenue on the welfare of the land. Remember that the prosperity of the farmers, artisans, merchants and professionals is the prosperity of the country. Show sympathy and kindness to the people. So that they might, in turn, show you respect. Differentiate between the good people and the vicious. If you enter in to treaty relations with any Raja, fulfil scrupulously its conditions" [1]

Qasim faithfully, followed the instructions of his master. He distributed twelve dirham of silver per head among all the merchants, artisans and farmers of the land as compensation for the possible loss of property and tools during the days of conquest. The revenue collecting officers were ordered to collect as much revenue as the people could easily pay. He further instructed them to attach more importance to the welfare of the people than to the collection of revenue.[2] For the efficient administration, and for the convenience of the people he divided the country in to several administrative units and appointed suitable officers for each one of them. During his reign, the Hindus occupied all the high posts and no post was reserved for Muslims only. So much so that Indian soldiers joined his army and fought on his side against the Indian Chiefs.[3]

According to the same writer the Hindu subjects of Sind wept when the latter was called back to Iraq from Sind. They not only lamented his departure but also made and installed a statue of his at Kairaj to keep him in remembrance. They worshipped it for a pretty long time. This indicates the height of Qasim's popularity among the people of Sind.[4]

Even king Mahmud tried to prove himself as a just ruler. In Punjab where he had set up his rule, he did not make discrimination between the Hindus and Muslims. Once a peasant reported to Mahmud that an officer of his army used to enter his house forcibly during the night times and make love to his wife who happened to be very beautiful. On hearing this, Mahmud disguised himself and with a sword by his side came to the house of the peasant in the night and found the army officer asleep. He put out the light and killed the officer. Having put on the light he looked at the dead officer and wept and expressed his gratitude to God, and called for water and drank it. The peasant looked aghast. Looking at the peasant's bewilderment, Mahmud said to him:

"I thought that in my kingdom no one would have had the daring to enter another's house forcibly and hurt the honour of its owner except my own son or nephew. So, I first put out the light, so that the very sight either of my son or my nephew might not prevent me from doing my duty. After I had killed the man, I called for the light, and when I found that the dead man was neither my son nor my nephew, but some one else, I sighed a sigh of relief and wept in gratitude to God that no member of my family had been guilty of such a crime. I had made up my mind not to take water until I killed the criminal. When I came to your house, I was thirsty; and that is why I drank water, only after I had discharged my duty"[5]

There are many stories, not only of his valour and piety, but also of his thrift. One day a poor woman complained that the robbers in a distant desert of Iraq had killed her son. Mahmud said he was sorry, but that it was difficult to prevent such accidents so far from the capital. The old woman rebuked him with the words, "Keep no more territory than you can rightly govern"; and the Sultan forthwith rewarded her, and sent troops to guard all caravans passing that way.[6]

Qutbuddin Aibak, the first Sultan of Delhi, was an efficient general and a generous ruler. Throughout Asia, he was known for generosity and had earned the sobriquet of "Lakh Baksh" (the giver of charity).[7] Aibak's impartiality was extolled in the metaphorical phrase that the "wolf and the sheep drank water out of the same pond." The roads, during his reign were free from robbers and Hindus both high and low were treated with royal benignity. In the words of Elphinstone, Aibak left a "permanent reputation" as a competent and efficient ruler. Briggs, too states that "Aibek's kingdom was governed by best laws"[8] Iltutmish started the practice of hanging a chain of justice outside his palace and of going about incognito in order to see if justice was administered satisfactorily. For prompt action regarding crimes that were usually committed during night hours, he installed two huge images of tigers at the gate of his residence and hung by their necks an iron chain holding a huge bell, so that whoever sought justice in any part of the night might come unhesitatingly and ring the bell to awaken him. He issued orders that any person who suffered a wrong should wear a coloured dress. Whenever he happened to notice any one in coloured clothes, he attended to his complaints personally.[9] The Sultan built a large water-reservoir called Hauz Khas to meet the requirements of the citizens of Delhi. Iltutmish did not consider his sons' worthy to sit on the throne hence, he nominated his daughter Raziya as his successor. She had proved her self as a good administrator when she was entrusted to manage the state affairs in the absence of Iltutmish, when the latter went on military campaigns. Iltutmish was so much impressed by Raziya that her name was included along with that of the king in a series of coins.[10] The Amirs and Maliks however were not happy to have a woman as the Sultan. Raziya made a bold bid for the throne. Clad in red, she appeared before the people gathered for Friday prayers in the principal mosque at Delhi and appealed to them in the name of Iltutmish to give her a chance to show her worth. This gesture got ready response and the people accepted her claim.[11] Nizam-ul-Mulk, who was against placing a woman on the throne said "Women are so gentle and weak; they need to be protected". Raziya reacted sharply, "Protected against whom?"She asked "against your fellow men? You want us to wear veil-purdah-but why should you subject us to such humiliation when the sin does not lie in us but in the eyes of men? Instead of our faces, your eyes and mind should be veiled".[12] In a few months Raziya crushed all her opponents and acquired the submission of Amirs and Maliks She changed her dress, assumed the royal robes, and each day sat in public unveiled, giving audience and administering justice.[13] She was an enlightened ruler, progressive in outlook, dynamic in action, an able warrior and politician. She advocated social and emotional integration of Hindus and Muslims and stood for placing the former into high posts but was opposed by the powerful nobles of her Court. Despite her short span of rule, which lasted for a little less than four years, she opened schools, academies, research centres and public libraries where the books of great philosophers were studied. The Hindu treatises on sciences, Philosophy, Astronomy and Literature were also given special recognition and were included in various courses in schools and colleges.[14] She moved freely, riding on horse or elephant, among the people of Delhi in order to have the first hand knowledge of their grievances. Her non-discriminatory and pro-people approach won her the love of all her subjects. It reflected when in her hour of need her subject especially the Hindu Rajas and the Hindu people rallied round her in their thousands and took up arms to uphold her right to the throne of Delhi after she was dethroned by her courtiers. When she was killed, the people of Delhi deeply mourned the loss of their wise and generous queen.[15] In 1246, Nasir-ud-din, a grandson of Iltutmish, became the Sultan. He was just, efficient and generous. It was his conviction that whosoever, being able-bodied, did not work for his bread, did not deserve any bread at all. He used to support himself by copying books and never took a single pie from the treasury for his personal use. Once a nobleman of the Court purchased a copy of the Quran written by the Sultan for a high price. When Nasir came to know of this, he was much grieved. Thereafter, they were sold at the market price without revealing the identity of the copyist.[16] One day, as he was showing a Koran of his own writing to one of his Omrahs, the latter pointed out a word which he said was wrong, the king assented and drew a circle round the word. When the Omrah was gone, he began to efface the circle. "I knew", said he to one who was present, "that the word was right, but I thought it better to erase it than to hurt the feelings of a poor man by brining him to shame".[17] This prince had no concubines, and had only one wife, whom he made to do all the housewifery herself. One day she complained to him that she had burnt her fingers baking bread, and requested him to get a maid to assist her; but he replied that he was only a trustee for the state and would burden it with no needless expenses. He exhorted her to persevere in her duty and said, "God will reward her".[18] He appointed Ghiasuddin Balban as his minister. At the time of his appointment, he told him: "I am placing my honour in your hands and I am placing faith in you and, therefore, hope that you will not commit any act which you cannot account for satisfactorily before God".[19] He ruled for twenty years and after him his wazir Balban occupied the throne. Like his master Balban was impartial with his subjects. Stanley Lane Poole writes that "in the administration of justice Balban was inflexible, showing no favour to his brothers or children, to his associates or attendants; and if any one of them committed an act of injustice, he never failed to give redress and comfort to the injured person".[20] Once a Governor of Badaun, in a state of intoxication, killed a Hindu servant. When Balban visited Badaun, the widow of the servant complained to the Sultan who immediately ordered that the Governor should suffer the same fate, which his servant had suffered. The Sultan himself flogged him so severely that the Governor died in consequence. The other story is about the Governor of Oudh, whose name was Haibat Khan. He killed a Hindu. His widow approached Balban to seek justice. The Governor was flogged in a regular Darbar in the presence of all his courtiers, and was handed over to the widow to deal with him as she pleased. The friends of the Governor paid the widow rupees 20,000 and she released him. But out of shame, the man never stirred out from his own house until his death. Besides the Sultan also punished the official news writer who had not communicated the incident to the king. The result was that owing to the fear of reports reaching the Sultan "none among the provincial governors or other officers and their relatives and servants dared injure anybody without cause or offence and if by chance any provincial governor or ruler were guilty of cruelty, he would try to propitiate the sufferer in whatever way the latter demanded and would not leave him with a grievance".[21] Jalaluddin Khalji is said to have humanised politics and Indianised the system of government. His genuine piety treated all living beings with kingly impartiality. He refused to award the sentence of death to robbers and rebels as being opposed to Shariat. There is an incident, which shows that he never misused his powers in the capacity of Sultan. This concerns a Hindu Zamindar who injured Jalal-ud-din with his sword when he was a chieftain of Kaithal. When he became Sultan, the same Hindu was caught and brought before him for having committed a crime. The Sultan said, "Release this man at once, lest my memory of the past might arouse in me the spirit of vengeance".[22] He regarded all as the creature of God and hence was against killing anyone. Once, the Sultan left Delhi with his army to subdue the Raja of Malwa, who had revolted against him. He sent word to him to yield; but the Raja would not. He shut himself in the fort. The Sultan then surrounded the fort and issued orders to dynamite its walls from an underground passage. But soon he changed his mind and ordered his troops to march back to Delhi, saying to his officers that it was not possible to capture the fort. Malik Ahmed Habib, his nephew, remonstrated, "What are you doing? I shall capture this fort easily. You need not worry". The Sultan replied sharply, "I too can capture the fort very easily. I have repeatedly told you, I do not like killing God's creation and I cannot bear the wailings of orphans and widows" He then returned to Delhi. [23]

Sultan Alauddin, like Kautilya, believed that the interest of the state was the only norm, which the ruler should adopt. He used to say, "I issue such orders as I conceive to be for the good of the state and for the benefit of the people".[24] A strict system of price control was enforced by Alauddin. He personally fixed the prices of even needles, combs, shoes, pitchers and cups. Prices of necessities were kept low and offenders were punished severely. There was in his time, a special department to control prices. Inspectors used to visit and inspect markets. Every day a schedule of rates for all articles used to be submitted to the King, together with a statement showing how much grain was sold and how much remained in the market every day. The result of this arrangement was that the foodstuffs and other articles of daily use were obtained at a cost within the means of the masses. The Sultan used to give money to widows and children to go and make purchases in the market and himself used to watch the merchants in disguise. Besides strict control was maintained on weights and measures. [25] In his reign "there was not a chance of a single coin being taken dishonestly or as a bribe from any Hindu or Mussalman.[26] The revenue officers checked and controlled that for five hundred or a thousand tankas they were imprisoned and kept in chains for years.[27]

The Sultan was generous and richly rewarded those who were found sincere, honest and hard working. Among his personal bodyguard were two Rajput brothers of the Tanwar clan, named Parmal Dev and Adhar Dev. One night in the depth of winter, rain was falling in torrents, accompanied by a fierce freezing gale. The Sultan happened to come out on the balcony of the palace at the dead of the night. He was surprised to behold only two tall-silhouetted forms doing guard duty in drenching rain outside. They stood at their posts with drawn swords heedless of the raging elements and unaware of the keen pair of the royal eyes, which were admiringly fixed on them from above. Inclement weather had driven the rest of the guards to forsake their post and skulk under cover. The Sultan was unable to distinguish the features of the faithful guards under the balcony and without uttering a word retired. A searching enquiry was, however, made in the morning and it was ascertained, beyond doubt, that the stalwart Tanwar brothers were the only two soldiers who had discharged their duty on that fearful night. Allauddin was exceedingly pleased with them. He summoned the two gallant soldiers in the Court and asked to name their reward. The Rajputs gave expression to their deep gratitude for this royal appreciation of their conduct but begged to be excused from asking for a reward. Allauddin was determined to reward them and insisted that they must ask for one. Parmal Dev, the elder of the two brothers, thereupon begged the emperor to give them Gwalior. The royal promise was readily made good and the necessary Farman was handed over the two Tanwar brothers.[28] It is no wonder that Ibn

Battuta found the memory of the Sultan enshrined in the hearts of his subjects as a paternal ruler. He writes, "Of all the Sultans of Delhi, Alauddin was the best and the people of India eulogised him highly".[29] In an inscription, dated in the reign of Alauddin Khalji at Jodhpur, the Hindu writer pays tribute to King's just and efficient government through whose "God like valour, the earth was rid off all tyranny and impurities".[30]

Mohammad bin Tughlaq was a very popular Sultan and had endeared himself to his subjects because of his non-discriminatory attitude and policies. Hindus were happy in his regime and never rose in revolt against him.[31] Ibn Battuta observes "I did not see any king as just as Mohammad bin Tughlaq. He did not discriminate between poor and rich, low born or high born".[32] Once Muhammad bin Tughlaq referred an appeal of a gatekeeper who was wounded by the Sultan's own brother-in-law, to the Qazi. The Qazi tried the case and pronounced the judgement that was carried out. The Sultan appeared himself in the Qazi's court several times and after the case had been proved against him, insisted on penalty being paid.[33]

Sometimes he himself tried to judge cases in a fair manner. When some Hindus were accused of treachery by a Qazi and were likely to be killed, the Sultan came to their rescue and saved their lives.[34] Once an eminent Hindu filed a suit against the Sultan and had summoned him in the court before the Qazi. The Sultan walked on foot, completely unarmed, to the court, where he saluted and bowed and stood before the Qazi who gave the verdict against the Sultan ordering him to compensate his opponent for the blood of his brother. The Sultan gave compensation to his satisfaction.[35] There is another incident which reveals, the kind of a person, the Sultan was. Once, the son of a Hindu nobleman filed a case against the king stating that the Sultan had beaten him without a cause. The Qazi issued orders to the Sultan to the effect that he should bring the boy round, failing which the boy should be allowed to beat him in exactly the same manner as he had beaten the boy. Despite the efforts of the Sultan, the boy was not prepared for any compromise. Then the Sultan called the boy to a public Darbar and handed him a cane and asked him to beat him in the same manner as he had beaten him. The Sultan made him take an oath not to hesitate in using his cane. The boy therefore gave him twenty beatings with the cane so that Sultan's cap fell down on the ground.[36]

He cared and worked for the well being of his entire subjects.

Once during his time, there occurred a famine in Delhi and several famine-stricken people began to gather in the city. The Sultan came in person to their camp and issued orders to distribute six month's provisions to each villager from the government store. Every village accordingly received the requisite quantity of provisions. He set up 70 hospitals and 1200 physicians for the sick and alms- houses for widows and orphans on the most liberal scale.[37] Sometime, he used to visit hospitals to look after the patients and whenever he came across any patient suffering from a serious illness, he used to discuss with the physicians in charge of the details of the treatment given to the patient. The Sultan also gave impetus for the spread of education in the country; and in the province of Delhi alone there were about one thousand schools.[38] He was the fore-runner of Akbar both in his restriction on sati and his employment of Hindus in high military and civil posts. Ibn Battuta informs us that both Hindus and Muslims lived on good terms. Barani tells us that Hindu nobles rubbed shoulders with the Muslim aristocracy. They possessed horses, lived in splendid houses, dressed magnificently and owned slaves and Mussalman servants were found in their suit. Barani, who himself was a noble in the Sultan's court, states that before the Hindu aristocracy of wealth, the poor Muslims used to come as supplicants and were seen begging at their doors. Even in the Capital City, the Hindus enjoyed the honorifics of Rao, Thakur, Sahu, Mahant and Pandits.[39]

Sultan encouraged the artisans and 'kept the wheel of industry moving" He employed 500 manufacturers of golden tissue who wove the golden brocade. Amir Khusrau refers to fine muslin of Bengal which was so light that a hundred yards of muslin could be rapt round one's head and still one could see the hair. The art of embroidery was highly developed. Gold and silver wires were used and gorgeous robes were made. The weavers were so expert in joining the threads that they could even join the veins. Amir Khusrau also refers to the manufacturing of swords by goldsmiths, which were as thin as the leaf of a willow that trembled without any slap of the wind. A certain bow maker, according to Khusrau, made such an arrow that it could pierce ten layers of heart. Arms were exported to other countries also. Besides, stone-cutting, the art of dyeing, wood carving and paper industry were also highly developed.[40] All this development could not have taken place had there been disharmony and distrust and discrimination in society.

Sultan Firoz Tughlaq, in the words of Stanley Lane Poole "was a father to his people".[41] He was loved but not feared. He "was the first Muslim king of India who believed in the principle that the duties of the Sovereign are not limited only to the protection of the person and property of his subjects but that the state must also adopt measures which contribute to their happiness and general welfare".[42] He took care of the needy and unemployed, refused to dismiss old officials but let their sons act for them.[43] He provided jobs to the weak and indigent and freely fed the blind and the helpless. The captives of war, who were made slaves, were distributed among the karkhanas where they were taught different arts and crafts so that they might start their work as independent artisans.[44] Many articles were manufactured in royal karkhanas. The Sultan himself invented a clock, which helped the people of the city in finding correct time. Old and ancient buildings were repaired and new ones were constructed. During his reign education was encouraged and several schools and colleges were opened where free education was provided to the people. During his reign, thirty six thousand tanka used to be given as scholarships to both Hindu and Muslim students.[45] He set up state hospitals for the sick of all classes The Sultan set aside some rich villages to provide for the expenses of the hospitals, medicines, food of the patients were borne by the state treasury.[46] The Central hospital in Delhi became famous throughout the state. There were separate wards for Hindus and Muslims and the expenditure of this hospital used to come to twenty-six lakhs of tankas every year.[47]

Sultan Firoz Shah abolished judicial mutilation. He also reduced the share of war plunder due to the sovereign from four-fifth to one-fifth, while increasing that of the troops to four-fifth from one. During his reign, state provided pension for all soldiers invalidated by wounds or by age. All public servants convicted of corruption, as well as persons who offered bribe, were severely punished.[48]

He cancelled the bonds of the agricultural loans advanced by Mohammed bin Tughlaq that the peasants were unable to pay. He built a canal that ran for more than [150] miles to irrigate the desert country up to the city and thus greatly increased the economic activities. It was named Hisar-Firoza.[49] He founded the towns of Firozabad, Fatehabad, Hissar, Badayun, Jaunpur and others. Being fond of gardens he planted 1200 of them in the vicinity of Delhi.[50] Besides, he is credited with no less than 845 public works, canals dams, reservoirs, bridges, baths, monasteries and inns for the pilgrims. He built a fort at Sirhind, which he called Firozpur.[51] Prevailing goodwill and lack of ill will led to the development of the country and prosperity of the people. Sultan Firoz had often to borrow money from Hindu Sahukars when he went on campaigns.[52]

Murry T, Titus is incorrect when he states that "the early Muslim conquerors and rulers seldom took a sympathetic interest in their Hindu subjects from a purely humanitarian or cultural point of view. Their whole object, apparently, was the religious one of either converting the infidels, or of sending them to hell with the sword."[53]

In fact during the Sultanate period both Hindus and Muslims closely cooperated and contributed together in taking India ahead of other countries in the world. The "sultan was believed to be the richest person in the country as there was no distinction between his privy purse and the state treasury but none of the Sultans seems to have built up a fund of personal wealth" Their entire revenue was spent on building cities, palaces, dams gardens, etc.[54]

In the kingdom of Kashmir most of the Sultans commanded respect from their entire subjects for their non-discriminatory approach and policies. The Sultans took into service persons known for their ability and integrity. Udayasari and Kota Bhatta were two ministers in whom Sultan Shihabuddin placed great confidence. His military commanders were Malik Chandra, Sura Lolaka and Achal Raina, a descendant of Ramcandra, whom the Sultan gave the village of Chadura as jagir. Sultan Qutbuddin retained Udayasari in his service. He forgave Udayasari even when the latter hetched a conspiracy to displace the Sultan. After him, his son Sikandar ascended the throne; but as he was minor, his mother queen Sura acted as Regent. Her Prime minister was Rai Magre. Like his father, Sikandar also forgave Rai Magre when the latter revolted against the Sultan. Zainul Abidin, who ascended the throne at the age of 19, was universally loved and respected. He was an efficient administrator, an advocate of communal harmony and regarded the welfare of his subject, his uppermost duty. Tilakacharya, a Buddhist was his counsellor. Rupyabhatta and Simha, the two Brahmans were his Court astrologers. Karpurbhatta was his Brahman physicians. Sriyabhatta was the superintendent of the king's curt of justice. He introduced system of price control by which prices of articles were regulated by the government. The government issued notifications in the form of bulletins that were inscribed on copper plates and were fixed at all important centres and in the towns.[55] He also prevented governors from exacting illegal cesses and gave the peasantry much taxation relief. He extended irrigation facilities to the remotest villages, which enormously increased the area of cultivation and promoted the prosperity of the people. The village folk and farmers were protected from the exaction of revenue officers by a law. Zain had forbidden the acceptance of gifts by revenue collecting officers. He also enforced the joint responsibility of villagers for thefts and robberies committed within the borders of the village. Whenever a theft or robbery was committed, the village headman was fined and this system is said to have prevented crime.[56] During his long and peaceful reign, he built floating islands on which crop was sown. He created the charming islands of Sona Lake and Rupa Lake in the Dull lake.[57]

He established non-sectarian residential educational institutions where students were provided with teachers, books, clothing, and food free of charge. The Queen even gave to the Sultan her most valuable necklace for the promotion of learning. He set up a university at Srinagar. He also gave six- Lac rupees for the educational institution at Sialkot.[58]

To bring about increase in the food production, he reduced the state share to one fourth of the total produce in some areas and one seventh in others. He encouraged art and craft. It is said that it was in his times that papermaking, papier-mâché, cocoon rearing, stone cutting and polishing were introduced in the Valley. The Kashmiris were hitherto ignorant of the art of papermaking and bookbinding. He, therefore, sent two persons to Samarqand at government expense to receive training in these arts and in their absence supported their families. On their return to Srinagar, they taught these arts to others. According to Srivara, Zain knew how to make fireworks and he taught this art to others. Before his time the powder used for fireworks was imported from outside.[59]

The Sultan had a high sense of justice. He did not favour the infliction of capital punishment, which he reserved for the serious crimes. For ordinary offences he preferred milder punishment. Thus he decreed that thieves and robbers should not be executed but were to be put in shackles, and then to dig earth or work on public buildings. He himself heard cases and gave decisions on the advice of Qazis and Pandits. He took great pains to find out the truth in all complicated cases and gained repute for his Solomon like dispensation of justice.[60] No who committed a crime was spared however close he was to the throne. One Mir Shah, who was favourite of the Sultan, killed his wife in a fit of rage. The Sultan refused to pardon him and ordered him to be put to death. One Sadullah, a learned man, whom the Sultan respected, killed a Brahman Yogi out of jealousy. Zain consulted the Shaikh-ul-Islam about him and was told that he deserved the punishment of death. However as Sadullah had committed the crime in a state of drunkenness, the Sultan commuted the sentence and instead ordered, him to ride on an ass through the market with his face towards the tail, his beard drenched in urine, his head shaved, his hands tied with the entrails of the deceased and the spectators spitting on him.[61]

Zain's officers were loyal and competent and worked with their Sultan for the extension of the boundaries of the state. Zain extended his sway over the Punjab, from Peshawar to Sarhind, which was regarded as the southeastern frontier of the state.[62] When he died, Srivara, his biographer writes "no one cooked food on the day (he died), no smoke arose from the houses; all were dumb with grief. They lamented and said that the king was the greatest among all the sovereigns".[63]

It is a far cry from Kashmir to Bengal but there too, a similarly popular tolerant ruler arose in Hussain Shah. "His name", writes V.A. Smith, "is still familiar throughout Bengal; and no insurrection or rebellion occurred during his reign of twenty four years. He died at Gaur (Lakhnauti) having enjoyed a peaceful and happy reign, beloved by his subjects and respected by his neighbours".[64] At Jaunpur, Ibrahim (1402-1440) played an important part in the spread of education among the people. He was a great patron of learning, He opened hundreds of schools and colleges. Scholars from different parts of the country flocked to Jaunpur for acquiring higher education.[65]

Bahlol Lodi was a just and virtuous Sultan and treated the Hindu and Muslims nobles and ministers with equal regard. He appointed Pratap Rai as the Governor of Manipuri and Bhongaon and awarded great honours to Narsing Rai. During his reign of thirty nine years, he did not sit on the throne and worked for the welfare of the country.[66] He deemed it a duty to enquire into the circumstances of the needy and never turned away a beggar. He personally listened to the complaints of the people and did not depend on ministers. Sultan Sikandar Lodi, Bahlol's successor was benevolent; and courageous. His equity beheld the weak and the strong with the same eye and always tried to make his subjects happy.[67] He founded schools in Mathura and Marwar, which were opened to all without any discrimination of caste or creed.[68] He engaged many Indians and foreign scholars for writing books on every science.[69] He won proverbial reputation for his impartiality in the administration of justice. He took personal interest in the complicated cases brought before the highest tribunal, received daily report of the progress of the cases and took special care to prevent needless delay in delivering justice. At the headquarter of the capital, he had ordered his vakil to be present in his seat from early morning to the first quarter of the night to receive all complaints.[70] So careful was he on affording justice to every one in need of it, that even when travelling on a horse, if any one should seek justice at his hands, he would at once dismount and listen to the complaint with the utmost attention.[71]

Sher Shah Sur was another king who was deeply loved and respected by his subjects. His real name was Farid. The well being of his subjects was his aim for which he worked relentlessly throughout his life. Though he was a ruler yet he worked like a common man. Once Humayun sent his officer with a proposal to Sher Shah who, by then had become the ruler of Bihar. The officer found Sher Shah digging the land himself. The Sultan continued working while talking to the officer of Humayun.[72] Ferishta tells a story which may be taken to illustrate his ideals."On being told that his beard grew white", Sher Shah replied: "It was true that he obtained the throne in the evening of his life", a circumstance he always regretted as it left him so short a time to be of use to his country and to promote the welfare of his people".[73] He repaired, improved, organized and perfected every single department of the state with admirable skill and expedition. Peace, security and prosperity dwelled in the land and confidence in the intentions and ability of the king followed. He bequeathed to his successors the legacy of a thoroughly well organized administrative structure and traditions of a durable and good government.[74]

People felt safe and secure. "Such was the public security during his reign that the travellers and merchants depositing their property on the road side, lay down to sleep without apprehension of robbery".[75] He arranged conveniences for facilitating commerce. To encourage the trade, he established a network of roads. Of his four great roads one ran from Sonargaon in Bengal through Agra, Delhi and Lahore to the Indus one from Agra to Jodhpur and Chittor and one from Lahore to Multan. On either side were planted fruit trees and besides there were erected 1700 carvan sarais with separate lodgings for Muslims and Hindus and servants were engaged to supply food to those of each religion. Grain and fodder were supplied for horses and cattle. A police official kept peace and prevented crime and two post-horses were stabled in each building for the use of riders conveying the royal mail. Sher Shah also built towns, to develop into important trade centres. One of them was the town of Patna. Built on the ruins of the famous old town Pataliputra.[76] Crime was rigorously suppressed and the headmen of villages were held responsible for the surrender of those who committed crimes in their villages and criminals who took refuge in them. Even the historians of Timurids admit that in the reign of Sher Shah an old woman with a basket of gold could safely sleep in the open plain at night without a guard.[77]

He affected a reformation in the weights and measures of the country. Before his time the use of scales was unknown. All commodities were sold by guess. To help trade and industry and to encourage sales, he reformed coinage. Standard weights were also adopted and uniform signs for all coins issued so that these could be easily accepted without any fear of any discount being charged later on. Gold, silver and copper coins were issued from various mint towns.[78]

The efficiency of government was at its best under Sher Shah. He used to get up at 2 a.m. His maxims were "it behoves the great to be always working" and "a king should not have corrupt vakils or Vazirs".[79] He was like a father figure to his subjects. He once said "If my life last enough, I shall build a fort in every district to be a refuge for the oppressed and a curb to the turbulent and make all earthen rest-houses of bricks for the safety and protection of the highway.[80] "The cultivators are the source of all prosperity" he declared; "I have encouraged them and I shall always watch over their condition that no man may oppress and injure them, for if a ruler cannot protect the humble peasantry from the lawless, it is a tyranny to exact revenue from them".[81] In one of his farmans he said "if scarcity of rains destroy the crops of the year, it is necessary that the poor should be helped with money from the treasury so that as far as the resources of the state permit they might be saved from the whirlpool of destruction".[82] On one occasion he gathered farmers from different parts of the state and addressed them as follows:

"With all my heart, I am your well-wisher. If you find yourself in any difficulty at any time, come and talk to me. I shall at once, remove your difficulties. Remember your distress is my distress."[83]

Under Sher Shah's rule, the soldiers had to watch that no damage was done to fields or crops. The cultivated land was measured every year and the taxes assessed according to the produce. In every district while one official had to effect the collection, another had to see that the cultivators were not oppressed. Two clerks kept record or accounts in Hindi and Persian and to prevent abuses the officials were changed every year or two. He maintained spies everywhere who provided daily reports which were sent to Sher Shah and the punishment was ruthless.[84]

No one slept hungry during his rule as the private kitchen of Sher Shah was very extensive and several thousand people were fed there every day. The daily cost of these meals was 500 gold pieces or ashrafis or rupees 2,23,25,000 per year.[85]

He provided justice to every one and regarded it as the most excellent religious duty. In the exercise of this duty he did not spare even members his family. The following verdict of Sher Shah speaks of his sense of justice;

"One day Sher Shah's eldest son Adil Khan Sur riding on an elephant through a street of Agra, passed a house, the walls round which were in disrepair, observed the wife of the inhabitant, a shopkeeper undressed and bathing herself, struck with her beauty, he fixed his eyes, threw a bira-pan (betel leaf) and passed on. The woman considering that by this freedom, he had treated her as a wanton and feeling her honour wounded, resolved not to survive the affront. Her husband when informed of the incident had great difficulty in preventing her intention. He went straight to the Levee of Sher Shah and among other suitors, proffered his complaint. The king having investigated the circumstances, pronounced the judgement ordering the law of retaliation to be enforced; and that the shopkeeper mounted on the elephant, should in his turn, throw a bira-pan to the Prince's wife when undressed and preparing for the bath. Great influence was exerted on the king, but in vain. Such he said was the law of the religion and in administering justice, he knew no difference between prince and peasant; and that it should not be said that a man because his son could injure a subject whom he was bound to protect. The complainant, in delight withdrew his complaint, saying that now he had gained his right, his character was restored and he was satisfied; and at his entreaty the matter was ended".[86]

Sher Shah treated all women including of his enemies with respect. When Humayun was forced to quit Delhi and Sher Shah became the master of the palace, the queen of Humayun became, with the rest of her women, the captive of the conqueror. "Although she (Humayun's wife) was possessed of a beauty which might have captivated his fortunate rival Sher Shah" writes Father Francois Catrou "Who was truly a great Prince and more a man of honour, treated the queen with distinction and respect. He did more so as soon as he knew that she was with child, he released her from captivity and sent her to her husband in Persia. Humayun was persuaded by relatives and friends that an enemy, who had dethroned him, would not scruple to assail the honor of his wife. The princess repulsed by her husband made Sher Shah acquainted with the bad treatment she suffered. 'I am' she wrote to him 'an unfortunate princess, of whose entire innocence you are not ignorant; it is incumbent upon you to bear testimony to my purity'. Sher Shah touched by the affliction of the queen wrote to Humayun in her favour; rendered testimony to her virtue and swore upon the Quran that he never had the fidelity of the princess suffer the slightest taint. Upon receiving such unequivocal evidence of her virtue Humayun recalled her to his palace".[87]

He did not discriminate between his subjects on the basis of religion. Hindus of his kingdom loved Sher Shah. His treasury was guarded by Hemchandra (Hemu), who later served his son Islam Shah with the same devotion. [88]

Sher Shah's rule lasted for five years. He was burnt while he was preparing for the assault on a fortress, that a rocket with gunpowder thrown against the wall rebounded and burst when falling on an ammunition dump. The whole dump flew up and the Shah together with his nobles was dreadfully burnt and lost his life.[89] However, his work for the welfare of his subjects immortalised his name. Even his enemies admired him. He has been characterized as "one of the ablest man of the age" and a man of "extraordinary intellect".[90] In the words of H.G.Keene, "...the acts of Sher Shah are attested by his enemies, writing when he was dead and when his dynasty had passed away for ever." Keene remarks further "No government, not even the British, has shown so much wisdom as this Pathan".[91]

Babar, the founder of the Mughal empire in India, from the very beginning of his rule treated Indians as his subjects and not as his prey and severely punished marauders among his own soldiers.[92] He was brave and possessed the courage to swim against the current. While addressing the general assembly, he had called his Amirs and officers, when he was in adverse circumstances, said that it was better to die with honour, than to live with infamy:

"Give me but one fame, and if I die I am contended,
If fame be mine, let Death claim my body"[93]

He was kind and humane. In the words of Erskine, "No part of his character is more admirable than his uniform humanity and kindness of disposition. If in the course of his Memoirs, some cruel execution appear, they belonged to the age, not to the man. The historians of his reign remark that, whenever any, either of his nobles or brothers revolted, or entered into cabals against him, no sooner did they acknowledge their offence and return to their duty then... contrary to the custom of the princes of Persia, Arabia, or India, he not only forgave them, but never retained towards them any feeling of resentment." [94] He not only assigned Ibrahim's mother an estate for her maintenance but when she tried to take his life by administering poison in his food, even then Babar refrained from taking her life.[95] "Wisdom and justice accompanied him throughout his career"[96] Babar enacted laws with the guidance of Rangiuldas. Everyday in a saloon, he used to give audience to his subjects, listened to their complaints and punished the guilty.[97] The good of the people always guided his policies. As a result fortune which abandoned him in Tartary favoured him always in India. Manucci writes "A government in which the authority of the prince was so absolute and so well maintained, without nevertheless violating the ancient rights of the primitive inhabitants acquired Babur the love and veneration of the people. The submission to his rule was universal and his state in a short time became very flourishing".[98] Babar's generosity earned him the title of Kalandar and endeared him to his subjects.

Humayun, Babar's son and successor followed his father's footsteps. He was just, kind and generous towards his subjects. Once while crossing Ganges, Humayun's horse sank under him and he was saved from drowning by a water carrier who lent him his inflated water skin. Humayun rewarded the water carrier afterwards by inviting him to sit on the throne and rule as a king for half a day.[99] In 1540 Humayun was defeated by Sher Shah. He was nearly drowned in the Ganges and this time was rescued by Shamsuddin Muhammad of Ghazni, whom he later honoured by appointing his wife as one of Akbar's wet nurses with the title of Jiji Ananga. Shamsuddin and his son Aziz Koka, both rose to be the Prime Minister under Akbar.[100] The troubles, which disturbed his reign, were the effect of the ambition of others; and his expulsion from the throne was "less a misfortune to him than his subjects" When he returned with victory, he left the mean passion of revenge behind. The people of India felt, by the benefit received from his presence, how much they had lost by his absence. Everyone without any discrimination was allowed to place his grievances before the king. A special drum was placed near the audience hall so that the aggrieved person could beat it; they were then allowed to lay their complaints before the king. Justice was delivered to all and culprits were not spared.[101] He was a scholar and promoted education in his kingdom. He established a college at Delhi appointing Shaikh Hussain as its Principal. During his reign "the population was happy as he patronised and protected all according to their respective stations or ranks. Desires of high and low were fully satisfied; and by the light of his judicial administration, he made the entire country of Hindustan as rich and prosperous as the garden of Iran".[102]

Akbar, the most secular and beloved emperor of India, imbibed in himself all that was good in Zainul Abidin, Mohammad-bin Tughalaq and Sher Shah. He was the first emperor who won over the hearts of all his people Hindus, Muslims, Sikhs, Christians and Parsis alike. The result was that the people of Hind united together along with their emperor in building a new India based on the principles of equality, freedom, and fraternity. The boundaries of the country were extended, economy flourished, amity prevailed, and orthodoxy declined and rational outlook had its hey day. It was, in fact, the golden period of Medieval India.

Akbar was the greatest ruler of his time. Elizabeth I of England, Henry IV of France and Abbas I of Persia were great monarchs of the 16th century but none excelled Akbar either in idealism or in the discharge of his duty or even in concrete achievements. He legislated not only for his own generation but also for those who were to follow. In the words of the historian V.A. Smith "He was a born king of men, with a rightful claim to rank as one of the greatest sovereigns known to history. He was the greatest ruler of medieval India and, in fact, one of the greatest in the country's entire history".[103]

Akbar took his duties as sovereign seriously. Abul Fazl gives a picture of his daily routine. At sun rise he showed himself to the people assembled in the outer court of the palace, listened to their complaints and held an open court lasting over four hours, where people could state their cases, which were decided on the spot. In each case he announced his decision and reason for it; if anybody had any doubts, he was allowed to express them and Akbar listened to their objections before he gave the definite order of what had to be done. Altogether, he used to devote about sixteen hours a day to state business.[104]

Akbar enjoyed immense popularity because he interacted and intermingled with his subjects as one of them. Rafiuddin Shirazi, a Persian who came to India in 1559-60 as a merchant, witnessed Akbar, who was at that time a youth of twenty years, intermingling with the crowds as an ordinary person. He also saw him"flying a kite on the roof of his own palace; his head was bare and he was wearing a loin-cloth. From this I was convinced that His Majesty was of an open bent of mind and extremely informal".[105]

He did not sleep more than four and half-hours and used to move incognito in the streets of Agra among the people, ascetics and faqirs to know the state of his subjects.[106] When he was born his father happened not to be at Amarkot. It was usual at such occasions, for the father to give presents to his friends; but Humayun, when the news reached him, had nothing but a pod of musk. This he broke up and distributed with a wish that his son's fame might be diffused through the world like that perfume. Humayun's wish was fulfilled, Akbar's policies won him a place in history as no other ruler of India could have.[107]

Like Sher Shah, Akbar treated his entire subject equal and recruited the best of talents irrespective of their race, religion, or caste to run the administration of the country. His ministers served him with total loyalty, ability, and devotion. Akbar treated them as their kith and kin and shared their sorrows and happiness by paying personal visits to their houses. Whenever, an officer died or was killed, Akbar visited the residence of the officer and as a consideration showered many favours.[108]

More than half of his army consisted of Hindus and the commander-in-chief of the army was Man Singh, upon whom he conferred the title of Farzand (son) and Mirza Raja Man Singh, throughout his life, fought and won many battles for his master. He subdued all those who stood against Akbar or refused to submit, even if they were Rajputs.[109] On the command of Akbar, Man Singh went to wage war with the Afghans in Kabul. He ordered his army after crossing the Indus, to take off their Janeo (sacred thread) telling them that the creed extended only so far as the Indus. On reaching Kabul, they were obliged to leave off their bathing etc. on account of extreme cold to which they were unaccustomed. Whatever they bought for their daily food, they received from the hands of the Muslims, as the country was a Muslim country. In winter the sepoys were given 'Posteens'to wear. (The Hindus do not like to touch the skin of dead animals). Man Singh did not join Akbar's Din-I-Ilahi yet he was the most favourite and trusted minister of Akbar.[110]

Raja Todarmal, a devout Hindu, was Akbar's Prime Minister. He was the son of a poor peasant, had first served under Sher Shah and was later employed by Akbar in the revenue department. Both Hindus and Muslims held him in high esteem. His unflinching loyalty towards the Muslim rulers like Sher Shah or Akbar did not mean that he was anti- Hindu or Hinduism. In fact Hindu pandits depicted him as the fish incarnation of Vishnu.[111] Akbar too respected Todarmal's religious feelings. Once at Amber, the Raja lost idols of his deities. He was very upset because of it and did not drink or eat without performing his devotion (puja) When Akbar came to know about it he spoke to the Raja, a few words of sympathy and it was only then that Todarmal recovered somewhat and attended to his duties.[112] On another occasion, the Raja was wounded in an attack by a person whom he had once punished for his behaviour. He could recover soon from his injury with the help of the emperor, who as the official historian records, applied giradam.[113] Akbar trusted Todarmal so much that the latter was put in charge of Bengal Mint. The closeness between the emperor and Todarmal and the latter's consequent growing powers, position and influence, roused jealousy of some of the nobles in the court. Badayuni's ire is expressed in the following verse:

"He who of Indian affairs made a Mull
Was the Raja of Rajas, Todarmal"[114]

They instigated Akbar against the Raja but the emperor refused to dismiss or to lessen his powers. So much so when Todarmal sent a petition to Akbar seeking permission to lay down his office and to spend the last days of his life in Hardwar on the bank of the holy Ganges, Akbar wrote back to Todarmal:

"It is immeasurably more virtuous to look after one's duties than to sit aimlessly on the bank of Ganges. Even Hindu Dharma enjoins the observance of one's worldly duties to the end. In our opinion it would be more beneficial for you to return to Lahore and derive Divine beneficence by continuing to work for the good of the people". [115]

The letter shows not only the affection of the emperor towards Todarmal but also his concern about the welfare of his subjects. The service of the subjects was not less than the service of God. Raja Todarmal like Man Singh did not join Din-I-Ilahi yet remained very close to the emperor and enjoyed his confidence.

Birbal, an orphan Brahman, was the hot favourite of Akbar. He became Raja Birbal because of his poetic talent, ready wit, humour and sagacity in political affairs. Akbar conferred upon him the title of Raja and the jagir of Nagarkot. He was the recipient of a mansab (military rank) of two thousand troopers. Akbar himself designed Birbal's residence and performed its opening ceremony. Birbal was, perhaps the only courtier whose residence was built within the royal compound.[116]

Akbar was very fond of him and always kept him near him and enjoyed his wit. Once he asked Birbal, if he knew of any man of ill omen in Delhi. "Yes I have heard of a man in the city" replied Birbal, "and it is said of him that if one were to look on his face early in the morning, one would not get a crust of bread the whole day". "Bring him here one morning and we shall make an experiment" said the emperor. Birbal brought the unlucky man to the emperor's palace and arranged matters in such a way that he was the first person, whom the emperor saw after rising from the bed. It somehow happened that the emperor was so busy that day about the business of the state, that he could not find time to eat till the evening. He sent for Birbal and observed "The man is surely of very ill omen, let him, therefore, be hanged". Birbal replied "O king of Kings, as you saw his face in the morning, you could not find time to eat, but he is to be hanged because he looked on your Majesty's face. Now, pray, decide who is the more ill-omened?" Akbar relished the wit of his favourite, saw the imprudence of his order and remitted the sentence.[117] To Akbar tobacco was a taboo but Birbal was addicted to it. One day Akbar and Birbal were seated on the terrace of the royal palace.

Opposite to them was a tobacco field on which an ass was standing. For amusement sake, the emperor diverting his attention to the field observed, "See Birbal, tobacco is such a bad thing that even an ass does not like to eat it". Birbal smilingly replied, "Only people who are like the ass discard the fragrant leaf".[118] This sufficiently shows the relationship of Akbar with Birbal.

Akbar twice saved Birbal's life. In the first incident, Birbal fell from his horse and became insensible. Akbar revived him with the kiss of life. On the second occasion, an elephant notorious for his ferocity suddenly disengaged itself from fighting the other elephant and charged Birbal. Unmindful of his own security Akbar spurned his horse and interposed himself between the angry beast and Birbal.[119] When Birbal was slain by the tribesmen after he had quelled their rebellion, Akbar was shocked and stricken with grief. He expressed himself as;

"Sab kuch dinan din, ik durayo dusah dukh I
Sou de hamhi parveen, nahi rakhyo kuch Birbar II"

(Birbal used to give away all that he had to the deserving people on the occasion of his birthday anniversary and he did the same when he left for the battlefield, where he fell).[120]

Akbar confined himself to his room for a week and did not take any food or drink for two days. "The emperor never experienced such grief' says Badayuni, "at the death of any amir (noble) as he did at that of Birbar".[121]

He punished Bairam Khan but assumed responsibility of bringing up his four-year old son Abdur Rahim. Under his care, Rahim grew up so well that he acquired a special place in the history of the country. Like his father, he served Akbar with total devotion and attained the same title and rank as his late father Khan Khanan and Prime Minister. Abul Fazal was also very close to the emperor. When the news of Abul Fazal's death was brought to Akbar, he uttered an anguished cry and lost consiousness.[122]

His nine jewels not only adorned his Court, but also co-operated with him in making India a land of plenty, prosperity and happiness. Poet Holarai wrote:

"Dilli tain na takht haweh, na bakhat na Mughal kaiso,
Haweh na nagar badi Agra nagar tain I
Gang tain na guni, Tansen tain na tanbaz,
Man tain na Raja aur na Data Birbar tain II
Khan Khan Khana tain na, nar Narhari tain na,

Haweh na diwan kou bader Todar tain I
Navo Khand sat deep; sat hu samunder par,
Haweh na Jalaluddin Sao Akbar tain.[123]

(There cannot be a throne like that of Delhi. There can't be a fortunate like a Mughal and no city larger than Agra. There can't be a versatile poet like Gang and musician like Tansen. No kings like Raja Man Singh, no generous like Raja Birbal. No Khan like Khan-I-Khanan (Rahim) There can't be a finance minister like Todar Mal. There can't be a monarch greater than Jalaluddin Akbar in nine continents, seven islands and seven seas)

The all round progress during his reign was the outcome of his non-discriminatory and humanistic approach. Favoritism or nepotism did not any place in the Court. Merit was given recognition and reward. Rai Patr Das, a Khatri who began as a Munshi (accountant) of the elephant stable was later made Diwan of Kabul, Bengal and Bihar, a rank of 5000 and the title of Raja Bikramjit.[124] Jagannath was asked to look after armour and roads along with Rai Shekhwat and Salih Aqil. "The management of the household, "which according to Abul Fazl"is equal to the administration of the kingdom" was assigned to Kachhawaha Rai Sal Darbari of Shekhawati. Raja Askaran Kachhwaha of Marwar, along with others was to watch over the property of the deceased to its conveyance to the heir. Raja Bir was associated with justice and complaints. He appointed to the twelve subas, eight of them were Hindus, all of them except a solitary Rajput, being drawn from the category of Khatris and Kayasthas.[125]

He always encouraged and rewarded his officers. He honoured an eunuch with the title of Khan and put him in charge of crown lands when the latter, who once had been in the employ of Islam Shah, the son of Sher Shah, told Akbar of the measures by which Sher Shah had checked embezzlement and regulated financial affairs.[126]

While at Amber Akbar decided to restore the ancient city. He laid its foundation with his own hands. He ordered his architects and engineers to build a fortress and other buildings and named the new city Manohar Nagar after the name of Manohar Das, son of Rai lun Karan.[127] (It is now known as Manoharpur.) During war with Chittor, Jai Mal and Patta, a lad sixteen years old died defending Chittor. Akbar appreciated their heroic sacrifices by erecting in his palace garden fine statues in honour of Jai Mal and Patta.[128] Du

Jarric rightly remarks "And indeed he was a great king; for he knew that the good ruler is he who can command simultaneously the obedience, the respect, the love and the fear of his subjects. He was a prince beloved of all, firm with the great, kind to those of low estate and just to all men, high and low, neighbour or stranger... so that every man believed that the king was on his side".[129]

He was not content with maintaining his rule and preserving the then existing system. He had a rational outlook and possessed the rare ability and courage to reform the system by discarding what was rotten and by retaining what was valuable and healthy. He did not believe in miracles. In his own words "The vulgar believe in miracles, but the wise men accept nothing without adequate proof" He respected Christianity but refused to believe that Christ possessed the supernatural powers. He remarked "Christ performed miracles such as giving sight to the blind, raising the dead and healing the wounded not because of any supernatural power but because he was a great man and wonderful physician". The same view was held by Raja Ram Mohan Roy three hundred years afterwards. He attacked the hypocrisy of those saints who pretended to be saints but were self seekers. He said: "To be a Pir (mystic guide) should mean to have the power of recognizing sorrow and providing its relief, not letting the beard grow, wearing out the rob and raising a tumult through worldly talk".[130]

Guided by reason and humanistic approach, Akbar sought to reform the entire social structure. In the words of Dr. P. Saran: "In the comprehensiveness of his reforms-religious, social, political, educational, cultural, eugenic-history can hardly show a parallel to Akbar among the crowned heads of any age or country".[131]

To enlighten the people and to change their outlook he laid emphasis on rational and scientific education. In Ain-I-Akbari, there is a directive of Akbar, stating that education of people of heterogeneous elements, diverse creeds and conflicting religions, should be state controlled and absolutely secular in form and spirit.[132] Accordingly, religion was not part of education and the pupils were not required to learn either the elements of Hindu religion or Islam.[133] Akbar patronized the study of astronomy, mathematics, history, medicine and diverse other subjects. For his own son Salim, Akbar himself drafted an unconventional syllabus where special care was taken to exclude all learning not based on rationalism.[134]

He passed many regulations to rescue Indian women, both

Hindu and Muslim from all kinds of exploitation. He paid special attention to save them from inhuman customs and worked for ameliorating their condition. He suggested Muslim women to be given more share in the property of their father. He stated: "In the Muslim religion, a smaller share of inheritance is allowed to the daughter, though owing to her weakness she deserves to be given the larger share". He was against the custom of Sati. He opined: "It is an ancient custom in India for a woman to burn herself on her husband's pyre, however much unhappy she may have been with him, and to give up her priceless life with a cheerful countenance, conceiving it to a means of her husband's salvation. It is a sad commentary on the magnanimity of men that they should seek their deliverance by means of their lives".[135]

He took strong exception to a woman being forcibly made Sati. He ordered that a Hindu girl, whose husband had died before the marriage was consummated, should not be burnt. Instructions were given to all the Kotwals that they should not suffer a widow to be burnt against her will. He was not satisfied with merely passing promulgation against forcible Sati. He personally intervened to stop the pressure on the unwilling women. When Jai Mal, a cousin of Raja Bhagwan Das, died, his widow, daughter of Udai Singh of Jodhpur refused to be Sati. But she was being pressurized to perform the Sati rite, Akbar hearing the matter, decided to intervene and rushed to the spot just in the nick of time, and had those, who were forcing the widow to burn arrested.[136] He also personally persuaded those women who had small children not to perform the rite. The widow of Birbhadra, the son of Ram Chandra, desired to be Sati but Akbar persuaded her not to throw away her life, as she had children, who needed her maternal care.[137] When Rai Singh's son-in-law died, Akbar personally went to Rai Singh's house to console him and dissuaded her daughter from committing Sati on the account of the tender age of her children.[138]

However, he had a very high regard for the Hindu women's sacrificing spirit. One day, he told Jesuit Fathers:

"Since you reckon the reverencing of women as a part of your religion and do not allow more than one wife to a man, would it then not be a wonderful thing if such fidelity and lifelong sacrifice were also to be found among your women?. The extraordinary thing is that it occurs among the women of the Hindu religion. Here there are numerous concubines and many of them are neglected and unappreciated and spend their days unfrutuously in the private chamber of chastity, yet in spite of such embitterment of their lives, they die as flaming torches of love and fellowship".[139]

He was also concerned with the plight of the prostitutes and regarded men responsible for their pitiable condition. He took steps for the upliftment of these unfortunate women and punished the culprits. He himself called some of the principal prostitutes and asked them who had deprived them of their virginity. After hearing their replies, some of the principal and most renowned grandees were punished or censured or confined for a long time in fortresses.[140] He got made a separate locality for prostitutes called Shaitanpura and for its supervision, a Daroga and a clerk were appointed who maintained a record of patrons of prostitutes.[141]

Thus like a father he acted and ensured that no wrong was done to his children. He was regarded as a holy man. Abul Fazl writes in Ain that women used to bring their sick infants for his benediction.[142] He had so much concern for the feelings of his subjects that when Dussehra happened to fall on the day after his mother's death, he suspended mourning for that day and celebrated the festival as usual. He made a public appearance at the palace window as usual and distributed shawls to numerous officials as a part of the festivity.[143]

People, not only loved their kind hearted monarch but also regarded him a holy man, a reincarnation of a saints. Songs and stories were written eulogizing Akbar. One such folk song of Oudh describes the emperor as following:

"He is Akbar Padshah, the kind hearted monarch,
Who looks after Hindus and Muslims with equal love
He is a Rishi, a holy man who looks upon his
Subjects with the eye of impartiality. Akbar is great.
Let us praise him with our heart and soul."[144]

In an another song he is called Chakravarti. People prayed for his long life.

"Oh Lord Krishna, give our Akbar long life,
He is just, he is kind, he is generous,
Our hearts are aflutter with joy."[115]

For the well being of his people he worked to build a new happy society Akbar endeavoured to weed out evil wherever he found it. From 1580 onwards, came a spate of reforms in quick succession, in the shape of census of population, liberation of all slaves in the realm, marriage laws, prohibiting marriage between boys and girls below the age of 16 and 14 respectively, prohibiting second marriage unless the first one had proved barren; marriage between cousins was forbidden; in matters of marriage, the consent of both the parties as well as their parents had to be obtained before the ceremony; circumcision before the age of 12 was forbidden and then was left to the will of the boys; use of wine was also regulated and it could be purchased only on medical prescription. To discourage involuntary conversions a regulation was issued specifying "Should a Hindu woman fall in love with a Mussalman and be converted to the Islam, she should be taken away by force and handed over to her family; but so should also a Mussalman woman, who had fallen in love with a Hindu, be prevented from joining Hinduism.[146]

All these regulations made the orthodox sections of both the Hindus and Muslims restless.

They made efforts to restrain and malign him. In his own court Badayuni was his most vocal critic. But Akbar could not be restricted. In fact he restrained the orthodoxy by acquiring the final interpretation of the Muslim Law.[147] Akbar, thus was the first one to place the state above religion. Hobbes, who is also regarded as the father of liberalism, suggested one hundred years later that the state should be above the church. Thus Akbar was a hundred years ahead of his time.

During his reign, state patronage to artisans and industries made India an El Dorado. No wonder that the Dutch, the Portuguese, the French and the English traders besought to trade with India. The emperor encouraged trade by an exemption of duties through the interior provinces; and by the invariable protection given to merchants of all communities. Lahore, Delhi, Agra, Ajmer Allahabad and Banaras were the prominent trade centres. Chanderi, now in Gwalior, was famous for its fine cloth, Masulipatam for its prints, Surat for its borders, and Banaras for its rich brocades. Kashmiri shawls, carpets, and silk weaving trade too had developed. Cloth of every quality was woven, as India was the sole supplier of cotton clothes to many countries.[148] Akbar took interest in Chakman and shawls. Chakman was made of woolen stuff or wax cloth; which according to Abul Fazal used to be very light and pretty and even rain could not go through it.[149] Fancy Bazars were arranged every month which provided special opportunity for the merchant class to lay their grievances before the emperor without being prevented by mace-bearers.[150] Tales of inexhaustible wealth and priceless collection of pearls and diamonds became current in the whole of Asia and Europe. The British Queen heard of the splendor of India and she wrote to Akbar a respectful letter, introducing some of her merchants who wanted to trade with India.[151] Ralph Fitch, the first envoy of the English merchant bourgeoisie, who arrived in India during the last days of Akbar's reign, was greatly impressed by the big towns and lavish wealth of the empire, compared to which his own country appeared to him as poor and underdeveloped.[152]

Akbar took interest in making ships. He invented a gun and a large cart drawn by one elephant.[153] Akbar perhaps without realization prepared the ground for the advent of capitalism. He introduced payment in currency in place of payment in kind in most transactions. Akbar also sanctioned the charging of interest, a practice against Islamic principles.[154] He however made it clear that if a good Muslim did not want to receive interest, he could avoid it. But if their Hindu creditors wanted a return for their money they could secure it. This makes it clear that the state was secular and the subject was treated impartially and none enjoyed superiority over others on the basis of race or religion. He also issued an edict that the rents should not be increased upon those who improved their lands. This regulation encouraged industry and became a source of wealth to the state.

Akbar also ensured that none was deprived of justice and culprits were punished adequately. People fearlessly placed their cases before the emperor, as they knew that he was just and belonged to everyone. The emperor showed himself at the window at least twice a day and listened to everyone who wished to speak to him.[155] A contemporary Jesuit observer remarks on Akbar's sense of justice and writes;

"Towards his fellowmen he was kind and forbearing, averse from taking life and quick to show mercy. Hence it was that he decreed that, if he condemned anyone to death, the sentence was not to be carried into effect until the receipt of his third order. He was always glad to pardon an offender, if just grounds for doing so could be shown."[156]

In delivering justice, Akbar was always impartial. In 1577 Shaikh Abdur Nabi, the chief Sardar put an influential Brahmin of Mathura to death for latter's indiscreet remarks about Prophet Mohammad.

Akbar invited the opinion of the ulema on the question and came to the conclusion that capital punishment was unwarranted and should not have been inflicted. On Akbar's order Abdur Nabi was put to death.[157] The Chief Trade Commissioner was remorselessly strangulated to death by the emperor's order for violently debauching a Brahmin girl. Thus, how so ever powerful, no one could escape punishment for his offence.[158]

Akbar advised his sons to protect the feeble from the strong and to work for the progress of the country. When prince Murad was leaving for Ahemadabad, Akbar exhorted him as:

"It is important that action is taken after careful thought. In eating, clothing, sleeping and walking, men should seek to increase wisdom and not the fattening of the body or pleasure. In governing the idea should be to protect the feeble from the strong arms of oppression. Improvement of the country and the army should be advanced. Company should always be kept with the good...Do not turn away from the bitter disposition of the truthful and be not angry with them.... Be not offended by diversity of religion. Struggle hard to sit in the shade of peace with all. Do not stain your soul with revenge."[159]

This letter speaks of his patriotism, humanism and secularism. He was not only a great emperor but also a great man. In the words of John Thronton:

"His life (Akbar) was a life of a truly great man. Viewed in relation to the age, in which he flourished, he may justly be regarded as one of the finest characters in all history. Indeed it is hardly necessary to impose even this restriction upon our judgement of him. Viewed even in relation to the present time and judged by our modern standard of what a great ruler should be in himself and towards his people, Akbar must still be confessed full worthy of the name, he bore-a name signifying, "The Very Great".[160]

If a king cared for his people, he commanded respect, loyalty and obedience of his subjects. One such ruler was Jani Beg Arghun of Sindh. When Akbar tried to annex lower Sindh, the people resisted him under the leadership of Jani Beg who had been completely Sindhized by his Sindhi mother and who had come to be known as Sindhi Bacha (son of Sindhi). He was extremely popular with his subjects and during his reign Sindh came to be known as "Wilayat-Dil-Pasand-Sindh"(The pleasant province of Sindh).[161] Baz Bahadur of Malwa was equally popular with his subjects. His love for Rupmati was famous throughout Malwa. When the Imperial forces defeated Baz, Rupmati committed suicide in agony. The people however immortalized their love by composing folk songs and ballads. When Baz died he was buried by the side of Rupmati at Ujjain (Their tomb located in the middle of a lake, is a popular rendezvous for lovers all over the country).[162]

Ibrahim Qutubshah of Golkonda who ruled from 1550 to1581 A.D was deeply loved and respected by his subject. One of Chatu verses, curses Brahma of stupidity and says "Instead of taking away useless and miserly kings you have taken away Malikbharama, Who will hereafter look to the poor and helpless? Can you create such a one again?"[163] Thus the spirit of liberalism and feeling of oneness radiated in all the parts of the country.

After Akbar, Jahangir became the emperor and he like his illustrious father, wanted to see his countrymen flourishing and happy. He too wanted to be remembered as a benevolent and just ruler. He wrote in his Memoirs:

"Neither would I neglect, so far as compliance rests within my power, to fulfil the just expectations of any man, without distinction of infidel or true believer. This age stricken ruin of a world has survived hundreds of thousands such as I am; what then can be more desirable than to do something in the fleeting present, of the merit of which we may avail ourselves in an eternal thereafter? Even in this world, the advantages of a benevolent action, of gaining to ourselves the attachment of mankind, are beyond all price; and for my part, I should derive a greater satisfaction from rejoicing the heart of a single individual, than from leaving behind me jewels and gold by the horse-load, to be squandered by a profligate heir".[164]

The regulations made by Akbar continued during Jahangir's reign also. No woman, who was the mother of children, was allowed to be Sati. Besides a slight degree of pressure on the widow by her relative for the performance of Sati was a crime and was met by severe punishment. Permission for voluntary Sati had to be obtained. At Agra Jahangir himself decided all the cases. He also forbade in 1620, the practice of female infanticide. Concerning these two evils he "gave an order that hereafter they should not do such things and whoever was guilty of them, should be capitally punished".[165] He issued a Farman prohibiting the horrid practice of making and selling eunuchs which was especially prevalent in Sylhet in Bengal. Capital punishment was to be inflicted upon the violator of this regulation.[166]

He also made war on certain evils. Public sale of intoxicants, bhang and wine was forbidden. No one was allowed to drink wine without permission. Roe records some cases where certain nobles were punished for drinking. He also ordered total suppression of gambling.[167]

He opened schools, for all irrespective of race or religion. He had himself been taught by the Jain Monk Bhanuchandra as a child and later asked the same Monk to teach his son Shahryar. A large number of public hospitals were opened and the physicians were appointed for the healing of the sick at the state expense. Not only this, after the recovery, the patient was discharged after being provided with sufficient sums of money for his exigencies.[168]

He was just, generous and kind and people used to pray for his long life. As was the emperor so were his ministers. Ram Das did not disappoint any beggar or seeker of favours. He used to distribute money freely at the ghats of the Jamuna where he took his daily bath. One day in severe winter amidst a storm and shower of hail, he was returning from his daily bath when he found a shivering mute old man. He immediately took off his woolen shawl, put it on his body and went home bare bodied. On hearing this Jahangir conferred upon him the title of Karan.[169]

Jahangir was a lover of justice. After becoming the emperor, he made it known to all his nobles that as all mankind, both high and low, were equal in his contemplation, his love of justice did not permit him to overlook an act of oppression in any man. He also stated that if there occurred the slightest proof of oppression or injustice, the punishment would be exemplary. He writes in his Memoirs:

"The very first ordinance which issued from me, on ascending the throne of my ancestors, was that which related to the chain of justice, one of which I caused to be fastened to the battlements of the royal tower of the castle of Agrah, and the other to a stone pillar near the bed of the river Jumnah; to the end that, when at any time the dispensers of law under my authority might fail in the administration of justice, the injured party by applying his hand to the chain would find himself in the way of obtaining speedy redress. The chain was of gold, one hundred and forty guzz in length with eighty small bells attached at different distances..."[170]

The purpose was to prevent the intervention of the courtiers. As the chain was pulled, a bell was sounded and a petition was promptly pulled up and provision made for its satisfactory disposal. Once it is said that the bell was sounded during the night and on inquiry, it was discovered that there was no man but only an ass. Jahangir soon summoned its owner and ordered him to provide proper fodder to it on pain of punishment. Thus the emperor redressed even the wrong to an ass.[171] Jahangir, himself inspected the cases and conditions of the prisoners in Gwalior and Ranthambore fortress whenever he happened to pass by. In 1618 he inspected the Ranthambore fort. With the exception of those convicted for murder, he freed all of them and to "each one in accordance with his circumstances gave his expenses and dress of honour".[172] He maintained the administration of justice as part of the Jharokha Darshan. His audience was given to any one bringing a written petition. He kept Tuesday exclusively for the administration of justice. None was spared for misusing office. Once returning from the chase, he saw the officers of justice carrying away a Rajput to be hung. The king asked what offence he had been guilty of. They replied that he had forced a Mohammedan woman, then present and demanding his execution. The king called the woman before him and asked her if the Rajput's body was hairless, like he was in the face. 'Yes', answered the woman. She supposed that as it is the fashion of the Rajputs to shave their beards, they must also be accustomed to remove the hair from all the rest of their body. The king ordered an examination. It turned out that the woman had raised a false complaint; whereupon he ordered that the woman should die and the Rajput be released. He also fined the officials for their negligence. In the execution of impartial justice he did not forgive anyone even his kith and kin. The story of Seif Alla remains as a monument of his savage justice. Alla was the son of empress Nurjahan's sister and from his tender years had been brought up at the Court. The empress regarded him as her own son and even Jahangir was fond of him and often seated him upon his throne. When Alla grew up, Jahangir appointed him as the governor of Burdwan (Bengal). One day, when Alla was riding on an elephant, a child got crushed and died. When the parents of the child approached Alla and demanded exemplary punishment on the driver, Alla, considering it an accident refused their request. He even expelled them from the district of Burdwan. The disappointed parents met Jahangir who at that time was residing in Lahore. The emperor immediately wrote a letter to Alla with his own hand and ordered Alla to provide justice to the parents of the child. The pride of the Alla was hurt and instead of obeying the order he threw them into prison till they made submission to him for their conduct. But as soon as they were released, they travelled again to Lahore. Alla was alarmed and wrote letters to the empress and Asaf Jahan to prevent the petitioner from being admitted into the presence. As a result they were denied the access to the emperor, till one day, that he was taking his pleasure in a barge upon the river. They pressed forward through the crowd and called out aloud for justice. Jahangir ordered the barge to be rowed and heard their complaint. He said not a word, but commanded Alla to appear immediately at Court. Alla obeyed the imperial command but knew nothing of intentions of Jahangir. The emperor gave orders for one of his elephants to be ready, by the dawn of the day; and he at the same time asked the parents of the child to attend. He himself was up before it was light and having crossed the river, he came to the camp of Alla and commanded him to be hound. The parents were mounted upon the elephant; and the emperor ordered the driver to tread Alla to death. But the driver afraid of the resentment of the empress, passed over him several times, without giving the elephant the necessary directions. The emperor however by his threats obliged him at last to execute his orders. He retired home in silence and issued out his commands to bury Alla with great pomp and magnificence and that the Court should go into mourning for him for two months, "I loved him" said Jahangir, "but justice like necessity, should bind monarchs".[173] He was an invariable protector of the people against the rapacity and tyranny of his own officers. The subas of provinces avoided oppression as the poor had a determined avenger of their wrongs, in their sovereign. Rustom Khan, the Governor of Sind was found oppressing some persons, and Jahangir immediately dismissed him and appointed Rai Singh Valan, the chief jailer of the state prison, in his place. Once he wrote to Sayeed Khan, the Governor of Punjab, warning him as: "I have heard that your personal servants oppress the people. Beware, if I hear such a report once again, I will punish you severely".[174]

Poet Usman eulogized the emperor's love for justice in the following verses:

"Puni kali adal umar sab kinah, dhann so purush jo yeh jas lina l

As bha adal mate hari bani, chana nava purana pani ll.

Puhmi pare na pave kanta, hasti chapi sake nahi chanta l
Gai, Sinh gavnahi ek gali, bal bha adal, abal bha bali ll.
Sahs khat kanchan ke saje, pat daur tehi bar biraje l
Dukhiya chuat hoi jhankara, uthe kanpi saktak khandhara ll.
Patshah suni nikat bulave, darsan paye dad puni pave l
Jahangir ke adal par, puri raha jag chain l
Sarvan suna nauservan, Sah so dekha nain ll.

He instituted twelve special regulations, to be applied by the different functionaries of the empire as rules of conduct. He remitted altogether three sources of revenue, the Zekhaut, Sermohary and Tumgha, which yielded no less than sixteen hundred mauns of gold to the state treasury. To ensure the free movements of goods throughout his empire, he took steps to ensure safety to the merchants and travellers. If the property of anyone was wrested either by highway robbery or any other act of violence, the inhabitants of the district were compelled to produce either the property or the depredator. Merchants travelling through the country were not to have their bales or packages of any kind opened without their consent. A large number of sarais or stations were erected for the accommodation of travellers at the expense of the state treasury.[175] In the fourteenth year of his reign, he directed that wells should be dug at every kroh.[176] He also directed that if a person died, leaving no children then his property should be spent on making religious place or watertanks, so as to secure perpetual blessings on the soul of the departed.[177] Though he was addicted to wine yet in public he maintained a strict appearance of sobriety and never allowed any person whose breath smelled of wine to enter his presence.[178]

Nurjahan, the empress was the chief advisor of Jahangir. She used to appear before the public and had her name struck along with that of Jahangir on the coins as well as on the imperial seal. Jahangir was so much enamoured of her that he allowed her to conduct all affairs of the state. She also had a large heart and provided out of her private purse dowries for the marriage of poor girls. By her acts of benevolence, wise administration of the state, she won the golden opinions from all quarters.[179]

People lived in harmony and used to join enthusiastically in celebrations when hostilities ceased and concord made between the warring kings. After the war of Mewar, prince Khurram and Prince Karan Singh, son of Rana concluded an agreement and then both went to the shrine of Hazrat Moinuddin Chishti for prayers. The people of the whole city were delighted at the show of unity. They gathered in thousands to welcome them at the Dargah. Old and young women (Hindu) did the tilak ceremonial as the two princes entered the precincts of the shrine on foot. 'The day ended with the feeding of the poor at all chowks 'of the city and display of such firework as had seldom before seen in Ajmer' [180] For their beloved king, the people willingly sacrificed their lives. Pelasaret mentions in his Remonstranti how a Rajput horseman named Anup Rai jumped upon a lion to save the life of Jahangir and was seriously mauled.[181]

Della Valle, who visited India in the time of Jahangir observed that Hindu and Muslims "live all mixed together and peacefully because the grand Mughal, although he be a Mohammadan, makes no difference in his dominions between the one sort and the other and both in his court and armies and even amongst men of high degree, are of equal account and consideration".[182] Of the twelve provincial Finance Ministers in 1594-95, no less than eight were Hindus.[183] This amity ushered in the country prosperity which dazelled the eyes of all the foreign travellers. An account of the celebration of King's birthday makes us know of the magnificence of Jahangir's court. "On the king's birthday, a rich tent was pitched for the monarch, and the ground around to the extent of two acres was covered with the carpets of silk and gold and hangings of velvet embroidered with gold and pearls and precious stones. The king was weighed in golden scales against gold and silver and perfumes & c., which were afterwards distributed among the spectators. The nobility also displayed all their magnificence and diamonds and other jewels blazed on every side. Richly caparisoned, elephants, lions. Tigers and other wild beasts were led past the throne, where were the king and his nobles "in cloth of gold".[184]

Shah Jahan, the successor of emperor Jahangir, according to Tavernier "reigned not so much as a king over his subjects but rather as a father over his family and children"[185] Like his father and grandfather, Shah Jahan used to show himself at Jharokha to his subjects at 6.45 am and listened to their complaints. He used to sleep only for six hours and devoted all his time working for the well being of his people. He kept himself well informed about the affairs of the state and happiness of his subjects. He inflicted exemplary punishments on the officials guilty of oppression. One day, Shah Jahan, while inspecting the revenue records of the empire, found that the revenue realised from a certain village in that year was a few thousand rupees more than that the realised from the same village in the preceding year. He forthwith summoned the head of the department, Diwan-I-Ala Saadullah Khan and demanded an explanation for the increase in the revenue. On the investigation, it appeared that the river adjoining that village had somewhat receded in that year and so there was some increase in the area under cultivation in that village. Consequently, the land revenue assessment of the village had also been increased. The emperor again wanted to know whether the increase in area had been to the ordinary revenue paying land or to Maafi, i.e., revenue free land. On being informed that it was revenue free land whose area had increased by the recession of the river, the emperor became furious and exclaimed:

"The lamentations of the poor, the widows and the orphans of that village had dried up the waters and side turned the river. The resulting accession was God's gift to them and you have dared to usurp it for the State. Had my compassion for God's creatures not restrained me, I would have ordered that the Devil of the Faujdar, who had exacted revenue for the accession to the Maafi land, be hanged until dead. As it is, his dismissal will be enough punishment for him and will also serve as a warning for others, not to do such evil acts of injustice. Let an order be issued that the excess revenue thus collected from the people be immediately refunded to them"[186]

In 1662, Mohammad Hashim, the Diwan of Orissa, employed a few new Karories (revenue collectors) because they had undertaken to collect more revenue from the same lands than the old Karories had been doing. As soon as the news reached the ears of the emperor, he at once ordered the dismissal of Mohammad Hashim.[187] He ensured that his people should get relief during natural calamity. During the early part of his life a famine occurred. Shah Jahan "in his gracious kindness and bounty directed the official to Burhanpur, Ahmadabad and the country of Surat, to establish soup kitchens or alm-houses such as are langar... for the benefit of the poor and destitute". He also remitted taxes amounting to nearly seventy lakhs.[188]

Nasir Khan, the governor of Gujarat, was a tyrant who had bribed the news writers so that the emperor should not get any information about his misdeeds. The oppressed merchants managed to arrive in Agra to stage a play before Shah Jahan, which showed the misgovernment in Gujarat. The emperor was astonished and made enquries. Having found the truth, he ordered the confiscation of Nasir Khan's property and his imprisonment in the fortress of Rohtasgarh.[189]

Such attitude of the emperor led to the path of prosperity of the country. The European travellers, who visited India during the reign of Shah Jahan, had all testified to this. Bernier, appreciating the prosperity of Bengal under Shah Jahan's rule says "The rich exuberance of the country together with the beauty and amicable disposition of the native women has given rise to a proverb in common use among the Portuguese, English and Dutch, that the kingdom of Bengal has a hundred gates open for the entrance but not one for departure".[190]

Moreland, a well-known historian, writes in his book 'A Short History of India' about the economic development of the empire during Shah Jahan's rule as:

"During Shahjahan's reign the splendour of the court was famed throughout the world. Extensive workshops were maintained, not only at the capital but in the chief industrial centres of the empire, where carpets, shawls, muslin and other luxury goods were produced of a quality unknown and at a cost which nowadays sound fantastic."[191]

Shah Jahan had a peculiar fancy for the Peacock which was considered a sacred animal. Sidney Owen writes:

"Under Shah Jahan the empire reached its zenith. At no other period was it so tranquil, well ordered and thriving in its older Indian provinces, never were the feudatory princes of Rajputana more zealously devoted to the Imperial service, never was the Court so splendid or the emperor more powerful, wealthy, or generally respected. Nor was the conventional idea of the great Moghul- as the sovereign of India, and of India alone- ever so near being realized"[192]

None was deprived of justice as the emperor regarded it as the most important duty of the state. The emperor himself used to see that it was delivered without any bias. Manucci recorded that Shah Jahan made all efforts to ensure justice to everyone including the foreigners living in the country. When Shah Jahan's patron Bellamont (ambassadors of Charles II to the Mughal court) died, two English imposters pretending to be imperial officers wanted to appropriate to themselves all the belongings of Bellamont. When Shah Jahan came to know of this, he ordered all the property to be restored to the rightful assignee of the dead envoy with the exception of an Arab horse which he kept for himself, giving an order to pay to the said John (Young) one thousand pataca (Rs 2000) the price at which it had been valued.[193] Manucci writes further "His laws for purging his dominions of Highway men are commendable above all the rest... The means he made use of for clearing his country of 'em,' was to render the Civil Magistrates accountable for all the robberies committed within their districts. Thus the Hollanders storehouse at Surate, being plundered in the Night, Cha-Jahan made the governor pay the sum, which their Effects amounted to".[194] He was impartial while delivering justice. There are many cases to describe to prove how anxious he was that none was deprived of justice in his realm. Once a soldier took wrongfully the slave girl of a Hindu clerk. The latter brought a complaint before the courts. The soldier said the slave girl was his, and so likewise said the girl herself, as she wanted to live with the soldier. The charge was transferred to the king's tribunal and he ordered the slave-girl to be placed in his palace. When he wanted to write he directed the girl to pour a little water into the inkstand, and this she did most dexterously. This proved to the king that she was the slave of the scribe, from whom she had learnt how to pour water into an inkpot. The soldier was expelled from the service and banished the country. Not only did Shah Jahan do justice against those guilty of great crimes: he also dealt with the nobles whenever he found an opportunity, in order to terrorize the rest. One day, going out to hunt, there came before him a servant complaining that for months his master had not paid him and he was in great distress. On hearing the complaint, the king, without advancing a single step, ordered the man's master to be brought, whereupon he presented himself. He acknowledged the wrong done to the servant. The king ordered the gentleman to dismount, and the servant to get upon the horse of his master, while the master should remain running in front, in the servant's place, where he (Shah Jahan) could see him. This continued till the master, unable to run any longer, fell to the ground, whereupon the king said to him: 'I do not fail to pay you, because you serve me, it is equally just that you should pay those who serve you.' Fidal Khan, the governor of Bengal was removed by Shah Jahan because lots of people complained against him. He banished Haji Sultan of Thaneshwar on account of accusation of cow killing brought against him by Hindus.[195] Not only was Shah Jahan prompt in chastising the great; he was equally grateful in every matter even the smallest. It happened that one day on his way to hunt he became separated from his men. Worn out and very thirsty, he went into a village lying on the king's highway from Agra to Delhi, and arrived at a helmet where as a charity a Brahman was giving water to the wayfarers. The king came up to him, and requested him to give him water. The Brahman, seeing that Shah Jahan was drinking greedily owing to his great thirst, threw into the vessel a little grass, thereby forcing him to drink slowly. The king in anger asked him why he had put in the grass. The Brahman not knowing to whom he was speaking, said: 'It is what I do to my asses when they are tired, so that they may not get colic pains'. The king took a rest at the edge of the village, beneath a tree. His retinue arrived, when the Brahman in a fright, recognising that it was the king, prostrated himself on the spot and asked for pardon. But Shah Jahan rewarded him with a gift of the said village which came to be known as the 'Brahman's village.[196] Emperor was followed by the officers, who ensured that the culprit whosoever he was, should not go scot-free. Manrique mentions a litigation in which a Muslim was accused of killing of peacock belonging to a Hindu. The Muslim pleaded that he could not be accused of killing an animal, which was sanctioned by Islam. But the Shikder-in-charge retorted: "The emperor who conquered these lands from heathens had given his word that he and his successors would let them live under their own laws and customs; he, therefore, allowed no breach" Manrique further says that this spirit of liberalism in a subordinate officer (during Shah Jahan's reign) in the matters of personal rights of the non-Muslim subjects must have radiated from the centre.[197]

If a man had clear title, his rights were respected. When Shah Jahan settled on the site for Tajmahâl, he gave raja Jai Singh four mansions in Akbarabad for his land and buildings.[198] The Hindu chronicler of Shah Jahan's time, Rai Bhar Mal remarks "It was owing to the great solicitude evinced by the king towards the promotion of the national weal and the general tranquility that the people were restrained from committing offences against one another and breaking the public peace."[199] People lived without any fear of theft or injustice. Shah Jahan himself wrote;

"For when he (Shah Jahan) directed the empire, officials walked so uprightly that inspite of the daily beating of the big drum to call in to his presence (those persons) wanting to complain of having received an injustice, months and months would pass without anyone coming to lodge a petition".[200]

There was religious freedom as voluntary conversions took place and new cults were formed. When Guru Hargobind captured Kiratpur, the entire village was converted to Sikhism. When the Mugahls recaptured it, there is no reference that the converts were brought back to Islam. The author of Dabistan-I-Mazahib, writing in the reign of Shah Jahan mentions several cases of the conversion of the Muslims to Hinduism. Hindu teachers taught the Muslim disciples and the Muslim teachers had Hindu disciples. Gosain Chaturapath, a Brahmin from Gujarat taught the author of Dabistan. His son Ganesh taught him the elements of Hinduism.[201]

The harmonious co-existence and the consequent peace and progress of the country under Shah Jahan's rule was highly praised by all the poets of his time.[202]

When Aurangzeb captured the throne, Shah Jahan had to pass his remaining years of life under detention. He died as an unhappy man. Manucci narrates an interesting incident, which took place at that time. Shah Jahan's elephant, called Khaliqdad grew fierce and restless, hearing a great noise being made in the tomb of Taj Mahal in preparation for the burial of his master. When the driver who had charge of him came up and said to him, 'Unhappy Khaliqdad! What will become of thee now that he who was thy master is dead? What is there for thee now but to die too? For no one will take the trouble to look after thee!' On hearing these words, the elephant began to gather dust with his trunk and throw on his head. Then with groans and cries he fell on the ground and died. [203]

People cursed and sometimes killed those who betrayed their beloved kings. Dara Shikoh was one such Prince. He was liberal, just, generous and inclined towards Sufism. The would be successor of Shah Jahan, Dara after losing the war of succession at Dharmat, planned to escape to Persia. On the way his wife fell seriously sick. Dara took shelter at Jiwan Malik, a tribal chief's territory, whom he had saved thrice from being killed by his father Shah Jahan. Dara's wife died there and her body was sent to Lahore for burial. Dara and his eight-year-old son Siphir Shikoh stayed with Jiwan who betrayed them and informed Aurangzeb. When Dara and his son were asleep, their legs and arms were chained and the two were taken to Delhi.

When Dara's elephant approached the vicinity of the fort, an old time faqir of Delhi called out aloud " thou son of the illustrious emperor Shahjahan, O generous Prince, in the days not long ago you never passed by this humble servant of God without a show of your benevolence. I know today your august hand has nothing to give to me. I will be more than content with a smile and a prayer. Do oblige me my saintly Prince". On hearing this plaint, Dara looked up, recognized the familiar face and threw to him the shawl he carried on his shoulders. "Here" he said, "this is all I possess. Keep it as a momento. We may meet again". The faqir blessed him. The crowd gathered round the mendicant. They touched the shawl with respect and awe. A precious gift had never been given by any king to a seeker of alms. Dara's face lit up in a mysterious happiness at the sight of faqir scampering away with his newest possession.[204]

The crowd gathered on the occasion was immense writes Bernier. He observed people weeping, lamenting the fate of Dara in the most touching language and cursing Aurangzeb. Bernier writes further that "Gian Khan (Jiwan Malik) rode near the wretched Dara; and the abusive and indignant cries vociferated as the traitor moved, were absolutely deafening. I observe some fakirs and several people throw stones at the infamous pathan."[205]

Aurangzeb watched the scene from a balcony. This exhibition of sympathy for Dara scared Aurangzeb who made up his mind to execute Dara. Jiwan was asked to come to the court through the main street of the city. A contingent of the imperial bodyguard and seven mansabdars of the order of two thousands were deputed to escort him to the royal presence. Despite this, Jiwan faced the wrath of the people enroute. The people of Delhi pelted him with dirty shoes and animal dung mixed with stinking concoctions of urine and foul herbal brews. Efforts by the city Kotwal Mirza Abdul Rahim, to stop the demonstrations failed completely. Men and women gathered on the roofs of their houses sang traditional songs in condemnation of treachery..."[206]

Historian Jadunath Sarkar gives the following account of the incident:

"On 13th of August, as he was going to court with the Afghan followers, the populace of Delhi; instigated by Haibat, a gentleman trooper of the imperial army and joined by the ruffians, beggars and other desperadoes of the city and workmen from every lane and bazar, besides Dara's friends mobbed the party. From abuse, they quickly passed to hurling stones, clods of earth and sweeping at the traitors and finally growing bolder assailed them with sticks. From the housetops on both sides the women showered ashes and pots of filth on the heads of the Afghans and spectators mingled in the melee below. The tumult and noise were very great. Some of Jiwan's followers were slain outright and some wounded; and if the prefect of the city police had not come to the rescue with his men, not one of the Afghans could have escaped from the crowd with life. The newly created Khan, going to his first audience at Court, was brought away in safety under cover of a wall of shields formed over his head".[207]

In the Court Jiwan was rewarded and enriched with presents. He was appointed a commander of 1000 horses and raised to the peerage under the title of Bakhtiar Khan, as the price of treachery.[208] Passing through the city of Delhi, he was pointed out to the mob, who falling upon him near the gate which leads to Lahore, killed seven of his attendants. He himself escaped; but the country people rose upon him everywhere. They hunted him from place to place; till at length he met with his deserts, and was slain when he had almost reached the boundaries of his own government.[209]

Aurangzeb in dread of a general revolt called a council of his nobles. He began for the first time to show symptoms of political fear. The demonstration of public sympathy for Dara made Aurangzeb to eliminate his brother forever. Aurangzeb himself confessed that the popular support and sympathy for Dara led him to execute him:

"The fate of Dara Shikoh excited the passions of the misguided citizen of Delhi. They wept in sympathy with him and pelted the loyal Malik Jiwan who had brought him to Justice with pots full of urine and excreta".[210]

After Dara's death common people, says Manucci, an eyewitness, composed a song in the memory of their beloved Prince Dara. The words ran as:

"Fate turned the Fakir's (Aurangzeb) bowl in to a crown and took a Prince's head away"

When Aurangzeb heard about this ballad, he ordained by public proclamation that anyone caught singing it, would have his tongue cut out. But the song was so pitiful that almost everybody sang it in private.[211]

About this time, the Rajah of Srinagar was induced to deliver up Dara's son Sulaiman Shikoh. Like his unfortunate father, he was paraded through the city in chains on an elephant and then presented before Aurangzeb. His gallant presence moved many to tears. He was sent to Gwalior where he died due to slow poisoning.[212]

Aurangzeb had other side of his character too. Aurangzeb in his normal dealings with his people was quite humane and considerate. Once his private secretary Wali Ram felt insulted, as Aurangzeb did not notice his presence in the Court though he was waiting for an audience for nearly an hour. In umbrage Wali Ram left the country. When Aurangzeb came to know about this, he sincerely regretted the incident, went all the way himself walking on foot to persuade his secretary to resume his office.[213] Soon after his accession he found that the late devastating movements of the contending armies, combined with the drought, had produced a famine in the land. He at once established houses for the distribution of free meals and ordered the remission of eighty taxes.[214]

He formally banned the practice of Sati. During his rule it was a penal offence. He banned drinking of wine. The cultivation of hemp (bhung) was forbidden. Public women and dancing girls were commanded by Aurangzeb to marry or to leave the realm.[215] He also projected himself as impartial in delivering justice. The instrument of instructions issued to Qazis at the time of their appointment under Aurangzeb's rule was as; "Be just be honest, be impartial. Hold the trial in the presence of the parties and at the courthouse and the seat of the government. Do not accept presents from the people of the place where you serve, nor attend entertainment given by anybody and everybody... Know poverty to be your glory".[216]

Even in his old age, he personally accepted petitions from his subjects and issued orders on them with his own hands. He prohibited strictly the system of darshan, but there was a general permission for an oppressed one to send afloat his petition through the string. He held open court twice or thrice a day, where there was no check for even an ordinary man to come and say anything he liked. He heard each and all of them attentively and did not make any distinction between a relation and a stranger, high and low, friend and foe. Shibli Nomani cites many instances, which show Aurangzeb's love for justice. In the 17th year of his accession, in his journey to Hasan Abdal, Aurangzeb halted one day in a garden, which had a house of an old woman close to its wall. The old woman had a watermill, which received water through the garden. The royal servants stopped water, as a result of which the watermill could not work. When Aurangzeb heard of this, he ordered at once to make the water run. And when he sat for dinner he sent Shaikh Abdul Khair to the old woman with two plates of food and five ashraffis apologising for the hardship, which she had to undergo. When it was morning, he called for her. It was learnt from her that she had two unmarried daughters, and two young children. Aurangzeb gave her ample money along with jewellry for her daughters' marriage.[217]

He took strong action even against his own sons for their complacency in matters of justice. They were turned out of their office upon the least well founded complaints; and when they appeared in the presence, the nature of their crime was put in writing in their hands. Stripped of their estates and honours, they were obliged to appear every day at Court, as an example to others and were punished according to the degree of their crime. When Aurangzeb learnt from the newsletter of the Province of Gujarat that Janaji Dalvi, a Maratha general had robbed some traders on the road to Surat and on that matter being reported to the Prince, he had remarked "It has taken place within the limits of the faujdari of Amanat Khan, collector of Surat; it does not concern me" Aurangzeb wrote across the sheet in anger "Reduce Azam's rank by 5000 and take from him the value of what the traders have lost...Bravo for your Princeship, that you consider yourself lower than the Amanat Khan! In my lifetime you have a claim to inherit my empire, why then do you not make Amanat Khan a sharer of your heritage".[218] Mirza Kam Baksh was his very dear son. Kam Baksh's foster brother was accused of murder. Aurangzeb ordered to make a thorough investigation of the case. Kam Baksh showed sympathy with his foster brother. Aurangzeb ordered Kam Baksh to be brought to the Court. Kam Baksh would not part with his foster brother. Aurangzeb sentenced Kam Baksh to undergo imprisonment along with the accused and the royal order was executed accordingly.[219]

In letters, written to his sons, Aurangzeb advised them to devote themselves to the task of protecting the poor and chastising the oppressors, promoting ministers and nobles of sound judgement. He wrote to his grandson Azim-us-Shah "You should consider the protection of the subjects as the source of happiness in this world and the next".[220] He refused to send money for the needy at Mecca. In a letter written to the Shrif-I-Mecca, Aurangzeb remarked; "Why should it (that is money) not be distributed among the poor of this country (India) because manifestation of God is reflected in every place".[221] He himself used to devote most of his time to state matters and slept for only three hours. To an officer who suggested to

Aurangzeb that for considerations of health, he should spare himself, he said "I was sent to this world to live and labour, not for myself but for others...It is my duty not to think of my own happiness, except so far as it is inseparably connected with the happiness of my people. It is the repose and the prosperity of my subjects that it behoves me to consult; nor are these to be sacrificed to anything besides the demand of justice, the maintenance of the royal authority and the security of the state".[222]

He led a simple life and earned his livelihood by making skullcaps. However he was not loved by all his subjects. The killing of his brothers, imprisonment of his father and destruction of Hindu temples had completely alienated him from the Hindus and the liberal elements of the Muslim community. The economy was shattered. The supply of men and money was exhausted in wars. Production fell off and the artistic handicraft decayed as the Court offered no patronage. Unemployment increased sharply. Aurangzeb's own son Akbar wrote him some verses depicting the state of affairs in Aurangzeb's reign:

"In Aurangzeb's reign vile and low are favoured;
They pass by in mighty state and arrogance,
They are his companions and consellors; they govern all;
The noble and learned are undone, he uses not such,
They have no place in his Court
The whole world wonders at seeing such misrule;
Behold to what conditions we are reduced!
Asses plant kicks on noble horses, great men ride in fear,
Not a soul pays any attention to the king's orders;
The officials trade, buying and selling officers at Court
Today, when done eating, they break their salt-cellar and
Pay him with ingratitude"[223]

People disliked Aurangzeb but the harmony at the social level continued. The imposition of Jaziya was not resented by the Hindus alone, the unorthodox minded Muslims both commoners and the nobles, criticized Aurangzeb. When Aurangzeb imposed a duty on the Hindu merchants alone in A.D.1667, the Muslims passed the goods of the Hindu merchants in their own names.[224] Even the Muslim masses cursed Aurangzeb for his insatiable lust for expansion of empire. Sikandar Adil Shah, a beloved king of Bijapur, also became the victim of the emperor's political ambition. When Sikandar's coffin passed out the cities of his kingdom, there were heart-rending lamentations of his subjects. Women wept bitterly, broke their bangles in grief and cursed Aurangzeb.[225]

Thus Aurangzeb was deprived of love not only of his subjects but also of his kith and kin. After his death, his body was hurried through empty streets and none of his subjects mourned his passing away. He was buried in a simple grave in the little town of Ranza.[226]

The successors of Aurangzeb did not follow his religious policies. They adopted the path of religious liberalism and tried to conciliate the annoyed sections of the Indian society. Emperor Jahandar Shah appointed Zulfiqar Khan his Chief Minister. Zulfiqar on the other hand left the affairs of the state in the hands of his favourit, Raja Sobha Chand. During the reign of Farrukh Siyar, the state affairs were in the hands of Diwan Ratan Chand.[227]

Ahmad Nizam Shah, the founder of Nizam Shahi dynasty, was a popular Sultan. He founded the city of Ahmednagar and made it as famous as Baghdad or Cairo. He was wise, gentle and forward looking person. He established a college for the training of military officers; so much so, that the people of Deccan came to be reputed for swordmanship. During the reign of Hussain Nizam Shah, the famous gun of the Deccan was cast weighing 40 tons and it was regarded as the world's heaviest gun. This gun is now in Bijapur. [228] Sultana Chand Bibi was an efficient and popular ruler. When Murad, Akbar's son attacked Ahmadnagar, she fought heroically. In the battlefield, she in full armour, with a naked sword in her hand checked the assailants. The Mughal, though superior in number, had to accept the terms Chand Bibi had proposed.[229] In Golkonda Sultan Ibrahim Qutub Shah and Mohammad Quli were popular among their subjects for their catholicity and concern for the welfare of their kingdom. Ibrahim, the son of Sultan Subhan Quli Qutub Shah was placed on the throne with the help of the residents of the state both Hindus and Muslims. Rai Rao, the close confidant of the late Sultan played an important role in providing power in the hands of Ibrahim. Even the ruler of Vijaynagar, Ram Raj, offered Ibrahim a massive escort of ten thousand cavalry and twenty thousand infantry.[230] Ibrahim never forgot this support and reigned as a secular king and accorded equal respect to all the religions of the land. He constructed numerous tanks. The Hussain Sagar tank of Hyderabad is one of them. Telangana was the centre of commerce.[231] Muhammad Quli, his successor followed the tradition of harmony set by his father. He founded the city of Hyderabad.There is a legend relating to the prosperity of Hyderabad. It is said that one day in the evening Goddess Lakshmi came to see the Charminar, constructed by Sultan Mohammad Quli. When the Sentry (guard) asked her name, she replied "I am Lakshmi, the Goddess of wealth". The Sentry had the future well being of Hyderabad at heart. So that Lakshmi would remain in Hyderabad forever and thus bring prosperity to the city, he made her promise to wait there until he returned. Then he departed. When he was out of sight, he killed himself. True to her vow, Lakshmi waited-and is still waiting. That is how Hyderabad became famous around the world as a centre of wealth.[232] Abul Hasan, king of Golkonda, was looked upon as the father of his subjects. Religion was no barrier between people and the two communities lived in complete harmony. Madanna, a Telugu Brahmin was the Prime minister and his brother Akkanna, a Peshkar and later as the Commander-in-chief of the kingdom of Golkonda. The two served their master Abul Hasan loyally and along with him worked for the welfare of the people. Abul Hasan, along with his ministers personally made himself acquainted with the condition of his people. He used to visit different localities, making inquiries into their life, righting wrongs and devising ameliorating measures. This made Abul Hasan's name a revered and dear one in every heart of Telingana. He was called Tanashah with affection and legend began to weave around it, which bears witness to the king's liberality and generosity. People prayed for his welfare while he lived and long after his death prayed for his spiritual welfare.[233]

Impartiality was the cardinal principle of his administration. There is a tradition relating to Gopanna, nephew of Akkanna, who spent the money of the state in the construction of a temple at Bhadrachalam and did not pay arrears in payment of the dues. He was promptly arrested and was released only when the money was recovered. When Abul Hasan came to know of this incident he scolded his ministers. He liberated Gopanna, put him on an elephant and sent him back to the village. As a further compensation, the Sultan even endowed the temple in question with a substantial annual grant. The king was seen as the Protector of Dharma because of his impartiality and protection of all faiths.[234]

Even Aurangzeb was impressed by the popularity of Abul Hasan. The loyalty of Abul's officers towards their king made the emperor envious. One such officer was Abdul Razak Lahiri. When Aurangzeb's troops captured Abul's palace, the ladies of the royal family started screaming. Abdul Razak, hearing the screams of woe, could not restrain himself. He snatched up a sabre and a buckler, and throwing himself upon a horse that had a bridle but no saddle, he with only twelve men that were at hand, advanced towards that part whence he heard the scream. Without caring for his own life, he rushed in the very middle of thousands of unsheathed sabres, with so much eagerness that his little troop was lost in a moment. Without being dismayed by that disaster, he cried with all his might, that so long as he was alive, he would prove a friend to Abul Hasan. Seid Gholam gives an interesting account of the incident in his work "The Seir Mutaqherin"as following:

"He (Razak) said and kept advancing to the gate, making his way with his own blood. He was aimed at all sides, struck on all sides, and he received so many wounds, from the top of his head to the nail of his toe, that he looked like a shrub of full blown roses. Such feats of prowess were that day exhibited by that undaunted man, as are most past belief, and past the human power; and such as would have excited the wonder, and exhorted the admiration, of Rostom and Sohrab, two ancient heroes, who would have gladly taken upon their shoulders the trappings of submission, and followed him as his friends to the end of the world. He was now arrived close to the gate; but had received twelve large wounds. Here he received another, which blinded one of his eyes, and by throwing the skin of the forehead over the other, blinded him totally. Here he assaulted again, received many other wounds, and his arm was disabled; his body, weakened by so much loss of blood, was seized with an universal trembling. In this extremity, he had presence of mind enough to turn the bridle about, and to abandon himself to his own horse; and the animal, although much wounded, carried him back to his house, where four men took him down, and laid him upon his carpet. Hashem-aaly-qhafi, who enjoyed then a high command in the imperial army, as well as in the Court; and was present in all this amazing affair, writes that all those that aspire to raise a character for valour and attachment, ought to have their minds illuminated from the beams emitted by that incomparable gem of a sea of prowess and fidelity, if they intend to serve their Lords and masters with zeal and truth, that may entitled them to applause of their contemporaries, and to the secret and public favours of their Maker in this world and the other".[235]

Aurangzeb, when told about the incident, highly appreciated

Razak's heroical prowess and unshaken fidelity, sent two Indian and two European physicians with orders to take the utmost care of him and to report daily about his condition. The emperor also remarked: "Had it been Abul-Hassen's good fortune to have had such another servant, or at least another General as faithful and as zealous as Abdol-Rezac, the conquest of the palace would have taken up a great deal more time, and possibly might have become impracticable at last".[236] When Razak recovered, Aurangzeb felt pleased and sent him a message in these words:

"I have forgiven your conduct. Send your son, Abdol-Cadyer, to Court, with such of your other children as shall think most deserving, that I may raise them to dignities, offices and honors; and let them humble themselves in their father's name, and thank me for having forgiven your conduct, and for my being inclined to promote you to high commands suitable to your rank".[237]

The valorous Rezak, after hearing the massage answered:

"I acknowledge His Majesty's goodness for all the kindness shown to me; but although this deformed soul of mine is not yet gone out of this mangled body, yet in the condition in which it now chances to be, it is not in the nature of things that life should hold out. Nevertheless, should He that can resuscitate the dead, think proper to exhibit a token of His plentitude of power by restoring life to this body, of what use shall it be then to His Majesty or to me, with both hands and legs disabled? But admitting that I ever shall be able to serve again, a man that owes this flesh and this blood to Abul-hassen's nursing and care, cannot consent to serve the Emperor Aoreng-zib".[238]

In Delhi, Farrukh Siyar was another most popular emperor. His amiable qualities and liberality had him endeared to his subjects. The main reason of Farrukh Siyar's popularity among the common people was his extraordinary generosity. Rustom Ali Khan records one instance to prove this particular virtue possessed by the emperor. One day the emperor came to the great mosque and saw a large number of persons in a most wretched condition,. With eyes full of tears he asked Abdullah Khan, the wazir, to give alms to them. The wazir immediately distributed a few lakhs of rupees among the poor persons. [239] Farrukh was imprisoned and blinded when his father-in-law, Ajit Singh betrayed him and joined hands with the Sayyid brothers who conspired against him. For killing Farrukh Siyar, the Sayyid brothers sent for Sidi khan and after promising him a reward said: "Farrukh Siyar took your father's life without cause. You have a legal right of retaliation. Put your hand on your dagger and slay him." The young man refused. As no one was willing, Sayyids got Farrukh brutally murdered.[240]

When the body of Farrukh Siyar was brought to Akbarabad's Mosque, 15,000 to 20,000 men from the camp and bazars received it. Gholam Hussein Khan writes in his book the Siyar-ul-Mutakherin about the pain and anger of the people when they saw the body of their beloved emperor as;

"There were weeping and wailing from the crowd. As the procession passed, lamentations arose from every roof and door. Men and women, old and young, rich and poor, shed tears for the departed emperor and cursed his oppressors. The streets and lanes were rendered impassable by the crowds. The rabble and the mendicants who had received alms from Farrukh Siyar followed his bier, rending garments, throwing ashes on their heads and as it passed, the women on the roof raised their cry of mourning and flung stones and bricks upon the servants and officers of Sayyids.... The bread and the copper coins, brought for distribution to the poor were rejected by the crowd with scorn; and on the third day, the rabble and professional beggars assembled on the platform where the body had had been washed and there cooked and distributed a large quantity of food and until day dawned sang funeral laments".[241]

He Writes Further

"For many a day, no beggar deigned to appeal for charity to any passing noble who had been concerned in Farrukh Siyar's death. Zafar Khan's liberal gifts of bread and sweetmeats were far famed; but these too were refused. The beggars said that in their mouth was still the flavour of the kindness bestowed by the martyred emperor 'May he be poisoned who takes a morsel bearing upon it the mark of those men'. They made collections from artisans and shopkeepers and distributed alms of food every Thursday at Humayun tomb (where Farrukh was buried) If any great noble passed along the road or through the bazars, they pursued him with the shouts and harsh reproaches. Especially was this the case with regard to Maharaja Ajit Singh and his followers, so that they were forced to reach Darbar by the most out of the way routes. The Rajputs raged inwardly and fiercely laid hand on sword or dagger. But who can fight a whole people".[242]

There was popular outcry against Ajit Singh. When he passed the bazars, he was followed by the cries of "slayer of son-in-law" (Damad-Kush) Insulting words were written on pieces of paper and stuck upon the door of his house and one day cow-bones were thrown down among the vessels he used in daily worship".[243] Ajit Singh, in order to escape these insults hastily quitted Delhi.

Emperor Mohammad Shah, who ascended the throne in 1719 at the age of 17 years, was kind and cared for his subjects. An anecdote given in Chahar Gulzar speaks of his inner being. "One night a Baksari foot-soldier placed as guard over the imperial jewel house, dug a hole in its roof, entered it, and stole a jewelled necklet (kanthi), when trying to creep out of the hole, he fell down on the floor, broke his leg, and lay there helpless. Next day he was discovered there and taken before the emperor. Mohammad Shah asked him, "O shameless wretch! You committed theft where you were appointed watchman. Could you not find any other place more appropriate for stealing?" The Baskari replied "My salary for 12 months is due from the Government. It is not fair that my salary should remain in this room and I should commit theft elsewhere. I also thought that there could be no better place than the emperor's palace for stealing" The emperor smiled at the reply, paid the man his arrears of salary and retained him in service as a watchman!".[244] "He never gave his consent to shedding blood or doing harm to God's creatures. In his reign the people passed their lives in ease and the empire outwardly retained its dignity and prestige."[245] He could not see his subject suffering at the hand of Nadir Shah. Instead of fleeing to Bengal as advised by his friends, he voluntarily went forth into Nadir's captivity in order to save his people and capital from the horrors of a violent assault and forcible subjugation to incensed victor.[246]

Many of the Muslims kings were progressive and ahead of their times. Giyasuddin, the king of Gujarat, had a regular Brigade of 500 women dressed in the male guard and equipped with bows and arrows and other requisites of a fighter. Likewise another brigade consisted of African women, was equipped with muzzle guns, an unheard thing in those days.[247]

Zakariya Khan, the governor of Lahore and Multan, who contributed a lot to the peace and prosperity of the province was popular among his subjects. He was a very strong and just ruler, vigilant in supervising the administration and protecting the people from oppression-for which his fame spread throughout the land

and he was idolised by his subjects in a degree unequalled in that age.[248] Elliot writing about Zakariya's sense of justice states:"In those days, the bigoted Mullas of Lahore used to dispute with the Hindus on religious points and prosecuted them; but the Khan always tried to adjust their quarrels amicably"[249]. Once a Muslim claimed that a wife of Khattri had converted to Islam and had married him on her own will. On the denial of such a happening by the woman, the matter was placed before Zakariya Khan, who deferred his decision to the next day. In the night time, he disguised himself as a faqir and made his own inquiry and found that the Muslim was telling a lie. Next day, the Muslim and a washerwoman who had conspired with him in this affair were put to death. Many stories like this of the justice of Zakariya khan were related in Lahore.[250]

Zakariya Khan's crowning act of nobleness was done for the relief of humble sufferers who had none else to befriend them and who could not do him any benefit in return. Nadir Shah highly appreciated him, and when passing by Lahore on his withdrawal from India he pressed Zakariya Khan to ask for a personal favour, but the only boon that he asked of the world conqueror was the liberation of the artisans and other people of Delhi whom Nadir was dragging away with him to Persia. Nadir agreed and thousand of Indian homes, far away from Punjab were rendered happy by this nobleman's unselfish generosity. [251]

After promoting the peace and prosperity of Punjab Zakariya Khan died in 1745. " There was so much grief for him among the people, especially in the city of Lahore that for three nights in succession, no lamp was lighted in any house. Thousands and thousands followed his coffin through the streets, lamenting aloud, beating their breast and heaping flowers on his bier, till at last not a handful of flowers was left in the city.[252]

No wonder in such harmonious co-existence, the social relations were governed not by religion but by mutual friendly interests, and understanding. History cites numerous instances when a Hindu willingly sacrificed his life for the sake of his Muslim friend and a Muslim did not betray his Hindu friend. One Adina Beg Khan was a revenue collector of village Kang in Sultanpur. He had a Hindu friend named Lala Sri Niwas of Dhir caste, a banker of Sultanpur. The Lala was a very influential man, who in few years obtained for Adina Beg many villages and later all the villages of Kang passed to Adina's charge. When the district officer of Sultanpur died, Adina met the Viceroy Zakariya Khan and requested to be given the post of district officer. Zakariya Khan demanded the security for his good behaviour, which was immediately provided by Lala Sri Niwas and Adina became the district officer. He showed his gratitude by appointing Lala Sri Niwas his immediate assistant, while his elder brother Bhawani Das, who knew Persian, was given the post of Superintendent of his office. Later Adina was appointed Nazim (Governor) of Jullundur. In course of time Adina failed to pay revenue to the Lahore Government, as he could not have realised revenue from the people on account of their having suffered during Nadir Shah's invasion. Adina met Diwan Lakhpat Rai, who did not listen to his entreaties. Adina Beg and his two assistant Bhawani Das and Nidhan Singh were consequently imprisoned. One night Adina Beg escaped from the prison. Bhawani Das then was ordered by the Diwan to render account of the income and expenditure. He respectfully replied that he would disclose the account only in the presence of his master, Adina Beg Khan. He was at once put into a large pot and was half boiled, but even then he did not yield. Lakhpat Rai was so much impressed with the loyalty of Bhawani Das that he took him out of the boiling pot, ordered his physicians to treat him so that he may be able to beg for a favour. Bhawani Das requested the reinstatement of Adina Beg, which was granted. After a warning Adina was awarded a robe of honour (khillat) and was appointed to the post of Deputy Governor of Jullundur.[253]

Diwan Kauramal was the most trusted and the most capable officer of the Viceroy of Punjab Moin-ul-Mulk. The Viceroy was so pleased with the valour, diplomacy and loyalty of Kauramal that he appointed him the Governor of Multan province after conferring upon him the title of Maharaja. Moin always sought his advice on all-important matters. In 1752 during war with Abdali, Kauramal sacrificed his own life to save that of his master Moin-ul-Mulk.[254]

In fact religion did not stand as a barrier between the rulers and the ruled. A generous ruler, whether Muslim, Hindu or Sikh was loved by his subjects. One such ruler was Maharaja Ranjit Singh of Punjab. Not only the prominent Hindus Muslims and Sikhs played an important role in placing him on the throne of Punjab, they all joined him in making the state a land of peace and prosperity. In Ranjit Singh, the people found a monarch, who belonged to all and did not discriminate against anyone or favour anyone on the ground of religion. The Golden Mosque (Sunaheri Masjid) which had been in the possession of the Sikhs was restored to the Muslims of Lahore.[255] When some Sikhs complained to the Maharaja that they were disturbed in the early morning by the loud azan given by the Muslim priest, he told them that he would stop it if the Sikhs took the responsibility to awaken the Muslims.[256] The Maharaja on a few occasions was even present at Id-ul-Fitr and during Muharram, young princes used to make offerings (Nyaz). When Holi was celebrated his Muslim officers and ministers participated in the revelry of colours.[257] In the year 1803 he went on a pilgrimage to the Ganges at Hardwar-the sacred city of the Hindus. In the year 1815, he presented a gilded roof to the Jawala Mukhi temple at Kangra. When the present Visvanath temple at Benares was built in eighties of the eighteenth century, Ranjit Singh gave a golden gilt to the spire of the temple.[258] In 1839, he ordered that the Kohinoor should be sent to the temple of Jagannath at Puri.[259] His Hindu Muslim and Sikh subjects equally reciprocated his respect for their religion by remembering him in their prayers on important occasions-when he launched a new campaign or when he won a victory or when he was ill. He was just and impartial and sought to build an egalitarian state. He had a petition box placed in a part of his palace accessible to everybody and kept the key of the box in his own possession. The petitions put in the box were read out to him and he used to take suitable action.[260]

Faqir Nur-ud-din, the governor of Lahore was so much respected by Maharaja that he had orders to remonstrate even with the Maharaja if the latter were found doing any act of injustice. These orders were given in writing and are still preserved by the descendants of the Governor Nur-ud-din.[261]

While reorganising the state's administration he ensured that none was deprived of justice. Since the majority of the population was of Muslims, the Maharaja set up separate courts for them under Qazis who administered justice according to Shariat Laws. But for those Muslims, who like the Hindus and Sikhs preferred to be governed by the customary law of the district, there were other courts under judicial officers appointed by the state.[262] None escaped punishment if found guilty. Once Sardar Hukum Singh Chimni, a brave general and a favourite of the Maharaja, got one Said Khan of Kot Hasan Ali, assassinated on the score of personal enmity. When Maharaja came to know about it, he dismissed the Sardar and fined him one-lakh twenty five thousand rupees to be paid as compensation to the deprived family.[263] During his reign of forty years he did not sentence even one man to death.[264]

Ranjit Dev, the Raja of Jammu (1750 to1781) had made Jammu, a veritable paradise on earth. George Forester, a secret agent of Warren Hasting in Jammu, wrote a long account about Ranjit dev's administration as;

"He avowedly protected and indulged his people, particularly the Mohametan to whom he allotted a certain quarter of the town which was then denominated Moghulpur and that no reserve, might appear in his treatment of them, a mosque was erected in the new colony...He was so desirous of acquiring their confidence and esteem that while he had been riding through their quarter during the time of prayer, he never failed to stop his horse until the priest had concluded his ritual exclamations. The Hindoos once complained to this chief that the public wells of the town were defiled by the vessels (made of leather) of the Mohametans and desired that they might be restricted to the water of river; but he abruptly dismissed the complaint saying that water was a pure element, designed for the general use of mankind and could not be polluted by the touch of any class of people".[265] During his reign, both the Hindus and Muslims lived in harmony and supported their Raja.

In Oudh, Asaf-ud-daulah commanded love of all his subjects. He was proverbially known for his munificence to the people as the saying goes:

"Jis ko na de Maula,
Tis ko de Asaf-ud-daulah"
(To whom the Lord does not give, Asaf-ud-daulah will).[266]

Nawab Sirajuddaula in Bengal commanded the love and affection of his subjects. During his short reign, he protected the interests of his people and tried to restrict the rising interference of the East India Company in the State matters. The Nawab was put to death as the people of the state were on his side and could rebel to rescue their Nawab. Clive himself stated in a letter to the Select Committee that they, "thought his death necessary for the peace of the country, as on his approach to the city, the Jemidars grew mutinous".[267]

The Muslim rulers in Rohilkhand, called Ruhelas were liberal and wise and ruled the state in an efficient manner. They protected the peasants and the traders in their lands from unauthorised oppression and were eager to drive away robbers from their own preserves. In this they formed an honourable contrast to Marathas, who extorted their chauth and then went, without recognizing any moral obligation to protect the people whom they had robbed or whose regular Government they had overthrown. The Ruhela chieftains left the revenue collections in the hands of the Hindu ministers (diwans) and their household accounts and correspondence in charge of Hindu sectaries (munshis), who were generally very capable men of business and faithful to their master's interests. The result was that both the rulers and subjects prospered. George Forester, who was travelling through Rohilkhand in the disguise of a Georgian merchant, wrote in February [1783] that "the Ruhelas by their salutary system of government had enriched their country and had made their name respected.... had made the country populous and opulent".[268]

Mysore also witnessed benevolent, efficient and impartial monarchs in Haider Ali and Tipu Sultan. In the words of Upendranath Ball. "It was Hyder Ali, who realised that India was in danger of losing her freedom in the hands of English and tried to organise the Indian powers in league against them. He was outwitted by the English who separated his allies by offering flattering terms. Till the end of his life he was a dread to the English. The inhabitants of the territories conquered by him were happy under his rule. He was a born soldier, bold in the execution of his plans and skilful in tactics. He was farsighted as a statesman. He failed because he overshot the mark. It was impossible in those days for any ruler to remain disentangled. In trying to develop a comprehensive plan he was not honestly served by his allies. Although illiterate he carried on the government with regularity and dispatch. He could make accurate calculations and could check the accounts without keeping notes. He was a genius and a man of remarkable abilities".[269] He respected the religions and customs of his subject. Haider was kind to the prisoners of war and even arranged disposal of the enemy's corpses according to their customs. Tipu also respected the old traditions of Mysore and allowed his Hindu subjects to be governed by their own laws. "The Mysore Government", wrote Munro to his father on January 17,1790 "is the most simple and despotic monarchy in the world, in which every department, civil and military, possesses the regularity and system communicated to it by the genius of Hyder and in which all pretensions, derived from high birth being discouraged, all independent chiefs and zamindars being subjugated or extirpated, justice severely and impartially administered, a numerous and well disciplined army was kept up and almost every department of trust or consequence conferred on men raised from obscurity, gives the government a vigour hitherto unexampled in India".[270] Major Terror wrote: "Of all the states in India, the state of Tipu seems to be the most prosperous state and her people the most happy".[271] Another official of the East India Company Moor, wrote on the basis of his personal experience as "When a person travelling through a strange country finds it well cultivated, populous with industrious inhabitants, cities newly founded, commerce extending, towns increasing and everything flourishing so as to indicate happiness, he will naturally conclude it to be under a form of government congenial to the minds of the people. This is a picture of Tipoos country and this is our conclusion respecting its government".[272]

Tipu was particularly friendly to the rural population. Forced labour in villages was totally abolished and oppressive methods of collecting rents or revenue were strictly banned. If any official, however highly placed, was discovered to have been guilty of such practices, Tipu punished him severely. For further development of agriculture, he had in 1793 started the construction of a dam on the Kaveri River to store water for irrigation. He himself laid its foundation, which bore an inscription in Persian.[273]

According to a French officer, "Tipu made the cultivator happy and protected the Indian merchant".[274] Influenced by Europeans, Tipu also tried to promote the trade of his kingdom by establishing factories both in Mysore and abroad. As a result the development and progress achieved in trade and industry during his reign was unprecedented. In 1789, he established two factories in Cutch. A factory was established at Ormuz to purchase mainly pearls, and other at Jeddah. The factory set up at Masqat in 1785 was the most important, because it was through this that export from Mysore kingdom were distributed over the Persian Gulf and imports from the Persian Gulf were brought in to Mysore. His chief broker at Masqat and Bushire was Seth Mao.[275]

During his reign prosperity flourished. He connected all the parts of his kingdom by making a chain of roads. This facilitated the movements and increased trade activities.

He looked after his people like a father. Once some Hindu Nairs of Malabar Coast sought his advice about their conversion en-masse to Christianity. Tipu said to them: "The Raja is the father of his people and as such my advice is that you stick to your ancestor's religion".[276] He banned prostitution and intoxication and administered justice fairly. He allowed the age-old panchayats to function without hindrance. Each town had a qazi and a pundit who decided cases for Muslims and Hindus respectively. But in case of dissatisfaction with the judgements of these courts, an appeal could be made to the High court at Sringapatam, which consisted of a Muslim and a Hindu judge. The highest court of appeal was the Sultan himself.[277]

Tipu was extremely popular with his subjects admit even the English writers. Mackenzie, who was with the English armies during the third Anglo-Mysore war, wrote: "Nor have we to boast of many instances when his people were induced by our flattering prospects of success to throw his yoke and shelter themselves under the benign influence of Christian rule.[278] He lived a simple, clean and disciplined life. He never touched liquor or any other intoxicant and had great respect for women and did every thing to safeguard their honour and virtue. In his battle he took every possible precaution against molestation by his soldiers of the women of the vanquished foe and came down with a heavy hand on any one found misbehaving in this respect. Twice in his battles with the Marathas, a number of Maratha women, some of them wives of Maratha Sardars, fell into his army's hands. On both the occasions, he treated them with respectful consideration and handed them over to their men-folk.[279]

Tipu was accustomed to tie a white handkerchief over his turban and under his chin. In the use of spear, he had no equals.[280] He possessed great personal courage. He was fearless and fair in dealing with the soldiers of his army. His military commanders under his instructions, looked after the wounded. The soldiers were given rest after a long march. If they fell in a battle, inams were granted to their families. Dirom and Wilks testify Sultan's army was loyal towards him till the last. According to Moor, "there were such instances of attachment and fidelity as to excite our admiration and perhaps can scarcely be equalled".[281] His bravery and patriotism inspired his soldiers also who stood behind him like a rock against English. Tipu exhibited his valour even at the last moment of his life. He fell fighting. When the English found him, he was almost dead. When an English soldier made an attempt to detach his sword-belt, then Tipu with all his remaining strength made a cut at him and wounded him on the knee.[282] The English were so scared of his name that they decided to wipe out his memory. An English official confessed later " If one of Tipoo's sons was reinstated, it was feared that the British dominion would never be secure. Hatred of the English having been instilled into him from his birth, he would probably be for ever plotting against them...It was therefore resolved to set Tipoo's family aside".[283] Tipu's family was removed to Bengal, and their allowance diminished. [284] Historian Sinclair writes that with the fall of Tipu, the weavers of Sringapatam came to the British commander and told him that they might take away all the wealth which they possessed, if only they could leave the state to the family of the Tipu. Thus his people showed a great attachment to him and his family. They did not forgive the betrayal Mir Sadiq, who after perpetrating the foul deed, tried to escape and joined the English, Tipu's soldiers killed him. They mangled his body in a shocking manner. Even after he was buried, his body was dug up and for over two weeks it was treated with insult by men, women and children who assembled around it and threw filth on it. Strong measures were taken by the English to put a stop to this. Even now, people, who revere Tipu's memory, while visiting Sringapatam, throw stones towards the spot where Mir Sadiq was killed.[285]

Thus religion did not stand as a barrier between the king and his subjects as all religions existed amicably on the Indian soil. Both the Hindus and Muslims alike respected Bahadur Shah Zafar, the last Mughal emperor. He was anxious to do justice to all classes and ranks of people and with this object in view, he personally received petitions from the aggrieved. He never supported the royal princes in connection with any complaint that happened to be filed against them. Zakatullah an opponent of Zafar and supporter of English testifies: "It is still remembered that whenever the Hindu waited on him and complained against any of Mussalmans, he warned the latter saying 'If you Musalmans are to me like one eye, verily the Hindus are dear to me like another eye". Zafar was like a father to his subject. Though his treasury was empty yet he used to give fixed allowances on the Ist of every month unasked for, to almost all the disabled persons known to him.[286] He observed all the festivals ceremoniously in the royal court. He built his palace called Zafar Mahal and from there he used to watch the annual Hindu-Muslim fair called Phool Walon Ki Sair which he had inaugurated.[287]

The rulers of Medieval India contributed greatly to make the country a land of wonders and enriched it in every sphere and this surely could not have been possible, had there been no peace in the social sphere. Feeling of oneness and amiable relations among the people belonging to different religions or regions made India a nation, where unity existed in diversity. It is only in the later period that both the British and the Hindus as well as Muslim communalists joined hands in presenting the false picture where Muslims rulers were portrayed with dark paints. Their negative aspects were highlighted and the entire period of their rule was characterized as dark ages. If it was so then how could the foreign companies including the English came to India after crossing seven oceans and fought among themselves to acquire more and more Indian goods for the European market. In fact it were the Britishers who during their rule of about two hundred years converted India from a land of prosperity to a land of poverty. Not only this, they communalised the entire social structure. It is because of their policies and encouragement that the Hindus, Muslims, and Sikhs who had lived together as brothers for centuries thought in separatist terms. The British drained Indian wealth to their own country and divided India on communal lines but presented their rule in the historical works as the age of enlightenment and progress in India. If this is not the falsification of history than what else it is.

REFERENCES

1. Dr. Syed Mahmud, *India of Yesterday*, Indo-middle East Cultural Studies, Hyderabad, 1957, p. 201.

2. *Ibid*. p. 22.

3. Ibid p. 31 Also see Syed Moinul Haq, *A Short History of the Delhi Sultanate*, S.Chand, Delhi, p. 11.

4. *Ibid*.

5. Alexander Dow, *History of Hindustan, Today* and *Tommorrow*, New Delhi, 1973, Vol. I, p. 79, 80.

6. W.W. Hunter, *Brief History of the Indian People*, Morrison and Gibb, Edinburg, 1881, p. 103.

7. S.R. Sharma, *India As I see Her*, Lakshmi Narayan Aggarwal Agra, 1956, p. 148.

8. Stanley Lane Poole, *Medieval India Under Mohammedan Rule*, London 1912, p. 63, 64.

9. Syed, p. 47.

10. S.M. Ikram, *Muslim Civilization in India*, Columbia University Press, New York, 1964, p. 17, 18, Also see Alexander Dow, Vol. I, p. 172.

11. S.M. Ikram, p. 15.

12. Rafiq Zakaria, *Raziya : Queen of India*, Popular Prakashan, Bombay 1966, p. xix.

13. Thomas Keightley, *History of India*, Whittaker and comp London, 1847, p. 12, Also see Dow, p. 172.

14. Rafiq Zakaria, p. 86.

15. *Ibid*, p. 124.

16. Syed Mahmud p. 50.

17. Thomas Keightley, p. 12, Also see Dow, p. 191.

18. Dow, p. 190.

19. Syed, p. 49.

20. Stanley Lane poole, p. 18.

21. Dow, p. 195. Also see S.M. IKram, p. 71.

22. Syed, p. 64.

23. *Ibid*. p. 62.

24. Herman Kulke Dietmar, Rothermund, *A History of India*, Manohar, New Delhi, 1987, p. 174.

25. Dow, p. 265, Syed, p. 67.

26. B.N. Luniya, *Evolution of Indian Culture*, Lakshmi Narayan Aggarwal, Agra 1955, p. 153.

27. Michael Edwards, *A History of India*. Thames and Hudson, England 1961, p. 99.

28. Hem Chandra Rai, *Romance of the Fort of Gwalior*, Marathi Press, Delhi 1931, p. 15-16.

29. V. Raghvendra Rao, *Indo-Muslim Culture*, p. 31 Vichara Sahitya, Banglore, p. 31.

30. A.B.M. Habibullah, *The Foundations of Muslim Rule in India*, Central Book, Allahabad 1971, p. 352.

31. *Ibid*, p. 328.

32. Mahdi Husain, *The Rise and Fall of Mohammad Bin Tughlaq*, Orient, London, 1938, p. 320.

33. *Ibid*.

34. *Ibid*. p. 313.

35. *The Delhi Sultanate*, ed. by R.C. Majumdar, Bhartiya Vidya Bhavan, Bombay, 1967, p. 82.

36. Syed, p. 77.

37. *The Delhi Sultanate*, p. 82.

38. Syed, p. 77-78, 181

39. Ziyauddin Barani, *Fatwa-i- Jahandari*, p. 2.

40. *Journal of Bihar Reserch Society*, Vol. IV, Parts 1-4, 1968, p. 253.

41. Stanley Lane Poole, p. 113, 116.

42 .Luniya, p. 415.

43. Stanley Lane Pool, p. 113.

44. Yusuf Husain, *Glimpses of Indian Culture*, Asia, Bombay, 1957, p. 83.

45. Syed, p. 83.

46. K.S. Lal, *Theory and Practice of Muslim State in India*, Aditya Prakashan, New Delhi 1991, p. 203.

47. Syed. p. 181.

48. Flora Annie Steel, *India Through the Ages*, George Roultedge London, 1908, p. 121-22.

49. Sir George Dunbar, *British History of India*, Ivor Nicholson and Watson, London, 1936, p. 119.

50. Shafat Ahmad Khan, *School History of India*, Longman Green Comp. Calcutta, 1928, p. 118, 19

51. Stanley Lane Poole, p. 111. Also see Alexandar *History of Hindustan*.

52. K.S. Lal *Twilight of the Sultanate*, Asia, New Delhi 1963 p. 261.

53. Murry T. Titus, *Islam in India and Pakistan*, YMCA, Calcutta, 1957 p. 16.

54. K.S. Lal p. 261. Also see Mohibbul Hasan, *Kashmir under the Muslim Sultans*, Iran Society, Calcutta, 1959, p. 54, 59.

55. Mohibbul Hasan, p. 83, 88.

56. *The Delhi Sultanate*, p. 382.

57. Mohibbul Hasan p. 84.

58. Mohibbul Hasan, p. 90, Also see G.M.D. Sufi *Kashmir*, Light and Life, New Delhi, 1974, p. 347-348.

59. Mohibbul Hasan, p. 92, 93.

60. *The Delhi Sultanate* p. 382.

61. Mohibbul, p. 83.

62. G.M.D. Sufi, p. 664.

63. Parmu, p. 171, Mohibbul p. 80.

64. S.R. Sharma, *India As I See Her*, p. 161.

65. M.L. Bhagi, *Medieval India*, The Indian Publication, Ambala 1965, p. 348.

66. Syed, p. 88.

67. Lane Poole, p. 36.

68. Yusuf Husain, p. 63.

69. K.S. Lal, *Twilight of the Sultanate*, p. 247.

70. Niamatullah's *History of the Afghans* trs. by Nirodhbhusan Roy, Shanti Niketan, Bengal 1938, p. xxv. Also see Pandey, p. 235.

71. Syed, p. 91.

72. Rahul Sanskrityana. *Akbar*, Kitab Mahal, Allahabad 1957, p. 3.

73. Sir, George Dunbar, p. 174.

74. P. Saran, *Islamic Polity*, Allahabad, p. 81.

75. Dunbar, p. 173.

76. Manucci, *Storia Do Mogor* trs. by Irvine Vol. I John Murry, London, 1908, p. 116.

77. Lane Poole, p. 193.

78. Ram Krishna Mukerjee *Rise* and *Fall of the East India Company*, Popular Prakashan, Bombay 1973, p. 193.

79. S.V. Venkateshwara, *Indian Culture Through the Ages* Longman, Green and Company, London 1932, p. 146.

80. M.L. Bhagi, p. 139.

81. S.R. Sharma, *India As I see Her*, p. 171.

82. S.M. Jaffer, *Cultural Aspect of Muslim Rule,* Published by Mohd. Sadiq. Peshawar, 1939, p. 35.

83. Syed, p. 97.

84. Michael Pradwin, *The Builders of the Mughal Empire,* George and Allen and Unwin Ltd, London 1963, p. 117, 118.

85. K.S. Lal, p. 205.

86. Sufi, p. 622, 23.

87. Father Francois Catrou, *History of the Mughal Dynasty*, Published by J.M. Richardson, London 1820, p. 67, 70. Also see Manucci, p. 115.

88. Rahul Sanskrityana, p. 5.

89. Pradwin, p. 118.

90. H.G. Keene, *History of India* Vol-I Research Co, Delhi 1972 p. 98-99.

91. *Ibid.*

92. *History of Mughal Dynasty in India,* Founded on the Memories of Signour Manucci, Published by, J.M. Richardson, London, 1826, p. 56.

93. William Ersqine Esq. *History of India,* Vol. I Longman, Brown and Green, London 1854, p. 468.

94. *Ibid*, p. 524-25.

95. *Ibid*, p. 455.

96. *History of Mughal Dynasty in India*, p. 468.

97. Father Francois, *History of the Mughal Dynasty*, p. 55.

98. *History of Mughal Dynasty*, p. 55.

99. S.M. Burke, *Akbar, The Greatest Mughal,* Manohar, Delhi, 1989. p. 13.

100. S.M. Jaffar, p. 29.

101. Pradwin, p. 85. Also see Dow, p. xxiv.

102. S.S. Kulshrashta, *The Development of Trade* and *Industry under the Mughals*, Kitab Mahal, Allahabad, 1964, p. 43.

103. A.L. Srivastva, *Akbar the Great,* Vol. I Shivalal Aggarwal Agra 1962, p. 529-530.

104. *Ain-i- Akbari, Abul* Fazl Allami trs. H, Blochmann, Printed for Asiatic Society of Bengal, Calcutta,1873, p. 205.

105. *Episodes in the Life of Akbar*, trs. by Shireen Moosvi, NBT. Delhi, 1994, p. 31.

106. R.P. Tripathi, *Rise and Fall of the Mughal Empire,* Central Book Depot. Allahabad, 1956, p. 229.

107. Thomas Keightley, *History of India*, Whittaker and Com, London 1847, p. 20.

108. C.M. Aggarwal, *Akbar and his Hindu Friends,* ABS. Jullundhar 1986, p. 141.

109. *The Journal of Bihar Research Society*, Vol. XXIVI 1950, p. 100.

110. *Ibid.*

111. Kumud Ranjan Das, *Raja Todarmal*, Sarswati Library, Calcutta, 1970, p. 17.

112. A.L. Srivastva, p. 228.

113. Kumud, p. 198.

114. *Ibid.* p. 16.

115. *Ain-i- Akbari*, p. 352.

116. *Ibid*, p. 404. Also see Muni Lal, p. 82.

117. *Modern Review*, Jan 1969, p. 38.

118. *Ibid*, p. 37.

119. S.M. Burke, p. 200.

120. Ambika Prasad Vajpeyi, *Persian Influences on Hindi*, University of Calcutta, Calcutta, 1936, p. 29.

121. Srivastava, p. 342.

122. S.M. Burke, p. 44, 206.

123. Ramchandra Shukla, *Hindi Sahitya ka Itihas* (Hindi) p. 119.

124. *Ain-i-Akbari*, p. 469.

125. Satish Chandra, *Mughals Religious Policies*, Vikas, New Delhi 1993, p. 30.

126. Pradwin, p. 135.

127. Srivastava, p. 228.

128. S.R. Sharma, *Mughal Empire in India*, Lakshmi, Agra, 1934 p.120.

129. Srivastava, p. 529.

130. *Ain-i- Akbari*, Vol. I, p. 9.

131. P Saran, *The Spirit of the Age of Akbar*, in *the Indian History Congress*, 1946, p. 272.

132. *Ain-i-Akbari*, p. 219.

133. *Visva Bharati Quarterly*, 1963, p. 356.

134. *Episodes in the Life of Akbar*, p. xiv.

135. *Akbar's Sayings.*

136. *The Indian Historical Quarterly*, Vol. XXIV, No. I March, 1953, p. 50.

137. *Modern Review*, April 1969, p. 267.

138. Satish Chandra, p. 32.

139. Pradwin, p. 161.

140. *Ain-i-Akbari*, p. 192.

141. *Ibid.*

142. *Ibid.* p. 165.

143. S.M. Burke, p. 122, 208.

144. Muni Lal, *Akbar*, Vikas, New Delhi 1980, p. 226.

145. *Ibid.*

146. *Ain-i-Akbari*, p. 288.

147. *Ibid.*

148. K.M. Panikkar, *A Survey of the Indian History,* The National Information New Delhi 1947, p. 220. Also see Dow, p. xxv.

149. U.N. Day, *The Mughal Government,* Manohar, Delhi, 1970 p. 63.

150. S.M. Burke, p. 138.

151. H. Kabir, *Our Heritage,* Popular Prakashan, Bombay 1946, p. 86.

152. Ram Krishna Mukherjee, p. 140.

153. Ain-i-Akbari, p. 275.

154. *Ibid,* p. 47.

155. S.M. Burke, p. 138.

156. S.R. Sharma, *India As I see Her,* p. 172.

157. Srivastava, p. 232.

158. G.M.D. Sufi, *Kashmir,* p. 626.

159. Muni, Lal, p. 273.

160. John Thronton, *The Story of India,* Henry J. Drane, London, p. 38.

161. K.R. Malkani, *The Sind Story,* Allied, New Delhi 1984, p. 45.

162. Muni Lal, p. 100.

163. *Proceedings of India History Congress,* Allahabad, 1945, p. 295.

164. *Memoirs of Emperor Jahangueir* trs. by Major David Price Rare Book, New Delhi 1904, p. 48.

165. Ellison Banks Findly, *Nur Jahan,* Oxford University, New York, 1993, p. 118.

166. Beni Prasad, *History of India,*. p. 411.

167. *Indian Culture,* 1937 (4), p. 316.

168. *Memoirs of the Emperor Jahangueir,* p. 8.

169. *Proceedings* of *Indian History Congress,* 1953, p. 257.

170. *Memoirs of the Emperor Jahangueir,* p. 8, 3, 12, 27.

171. A.B. Pandey, *Society and Government in Medieval-India,* p. 164.

172. *Proceedings* of *Indian History Congress,* 1964, p. 47.

173. Alexander Dow, p. 106, 107.

174. Manucci, Vol. I, p. 174, 75. Also see Syed, p. 107.

175. *Memoirs of Emperor Jahangueir,* p. 7, 8.

176. *Tazuk-i- Jahangiri* trs. by Rogers and Beveridge, Vol. II, p. 100.

177. *Memoirs of Emperor Jahangueir,* p. 7-8.

178. W.W. Hunter, *Brief History of India,* p. 128.

179. Upendra Nath Ball, *Modern India,* p. 169. Doaba House, Lahore, 1939.

180. Muni Lal, *Shah Jahan,* Vikas, New Delhi, 1986, p. 40.

181. M.L. Roy Choudhry, *The State and Religion in Mughal India* Indian Publicity Society, Calcutta, 1951, p. 265.

182. Yusuf Husain, p. 70.

183. M.L. Roy Choudhry, p. 266.

184. Thomas Keightley, *History of India*, p. 21.

185. S.R. Sharma, *Mughal Empire in India*, Lakshmi, Agra 1934, p. 258.

186. Pt. Sunderlal, *How India Lost Her Freedom*, Popular Prakashan, Bombay 1970, p. xciv.

187. *Ibid.*

188. S.R. Sharma, *Mughal Empire*, p. 259.

189. Manucci, Vol. I, p. 198.

190. S.R. Sharma, p. 259.

191. W.H. Moreland and Atul Chandra, *A Short History of India* Longman, London, 1936. p. 242.

192. Sidney J. Owen, *India on the Eve of the British Conquest*, H. Allen and Comp. London 1872, p. 39, 40.

193. S.R. Sharma, *Mughal Empire in India*, p. 126.

194. Ram Krishna Mukherjee, p. 194.

195. Manucci, Vol. I I, p. 201. Also see Raghavendra Rao, *Indo-Muslim Culture*, p. 49.

196. Manucci, Vol. I, p. 214.

197. M.L. Roy Choudhry, p. 25.

198. Stephen P. Blake, *Shahjahanabad*, New York, 1991, p. 50.

199. S.R. Sharma, *India As I see Her*, p. 173, 74.

200. Manucci, Vol. II, p. 20.

201. Sidney J. Owen, *From Mahmud Ghazni to the Disintegration of the Mughal Empire*, p. 131.

202. Asad Ali, *Bhaktikaleen Sahitya par Muslim Sanskriti ka Prabhav* (Hindi), Asia, New Delhi 1971, p. 36

203. Manucci, Vol. I, 354.

204. Jadunath Sarkar, *History of Aurangzeb*, M.C. Sarkar and Sons, Calcutta 1916, p. 943. Also see Manucci, Vol. I, p. 355.

205. Francois Bernier, *Travels in the Mughal Empire*, Humphrey Milford, Oxford University, Press, 1914, p. 98, 99.

206. Muni Lal, *Shahjahan*, p. 403.

207. Jadunath Sarkar, p. 547, 48.

208. *Ibid.*

209. *Ibid.*

210. K.S. Lal, *The Legacy of Muslim Rule in India*, p. 219.

211. Manucci, Vol. I, p. 362.

212. *Ibid*, p. 378.

213. *Ruka 'at-i-Alamgir*, p. 60. Also V. Raghvendra, p. 41.

214. Lane Poole, p. 68.

215. Manucci, p. 7, 9 and 97.

216. A.B. Pandey, *Society* and *Government in Medieval India*, p. 165, 66

217. *Alamgir* of Maulana Shibli Nomani trs. by S. Rahman, Idara-i-Adabiyat, Delhi 1981, p. 219.

218. *Maasir-i- Alamgiri of Saqi Mustad Khan* trs. by Jadunath Sarkar , Asiatic Society, Calcutta, 1947 p. 80. Also see Dow p. 397.

219. *Ibid.*

220. Satish Chandra, *Mughal Religious Policies*. p. 220.

221. *Ibid.* p. 206.

222. S.R. Sharma, *The Crescent in India, Hind Kitab*, Poona 1954, p. 660.

223. Manucci, Vol. IV, p. 166.

224. *Proceedings of Indian History Congress*, 1946, p. 267.

225. Z. Faruki, *Aurangzib* and *His Times*, Idara-i- Adibiyat, Delhi, 1972 p. 345.

226. David Kincaied, *Shivaji The Founder of Maratha Empire*, Discovery, New Delhi 1984, p. 312.

227. William Irvine, *The Later Mughals*, p. 126.

228. Syed Mahmud, p. 144.

229. See for detail, *Memoirs of Chand Bibi*, S.A. Qadiri pub-Tarikh-i-office, Hyderabad, 1939, p. 90-98.

230. Ian Austin, *City of Legends*, Viking Calcutta 1992, p. 10.

231. Syed Mahmud, p. 145.

232. Ian Austin, p. 25.

233. *Proceedings of Indian History Congress*, 1956, p. 282, 85.

234. *Ibid. Also see Ian Austin*, p. 25.

235. Seid Gholam Hussein Khan,*The Seir Mutaqherin* Vol. IV, Calcutta 1789, p. 216- 217.

236. *Ibid*, p. 220.

237. *Ibid.* p. 221.

238. *Ibid.*

239. Zahir-uddin Malik, *The Reign of Muhammad Shah*, Asia, Aligarh 1977, p. 34.

240. Irvine, *Later Mughals*, p. 389.

241. *Ibid.* p. 393.

242. *Ibid.* p. 394.

243. *Ibid*, p. 408.

244. Jadunath Sarkar, *The Fall of the Mughal Empire*, Vol. I Orient Longman, Calcutta 1971, p. 6.

245. *Ibid.*

246. *Ibid.*

247. Syed Mahmud, p. 153.

248. H.M. Elliot, *History of India As Told by its Historians*, Vol-viii. Low Price, New Delhi, p. 346.

249. *Ibid.*

250. *Ibid.*

251. Jadunath Sarkar, *Fall of the Mughal Empire*, Vol. I, p. 118.

252. *Ibid.*

253. Hari Om Gupta, *Later Mughal History of the Punjab*, Minerva Book, Lahore, 1944, p. 59, 63.

254. *Ibid.* p. 75.

255. R.L. Ahuja, *Maharaja Ranjit Singh-A Man of Destiny*, Punjab Writers Co-operative Society, Delhi 1983, p. 26.

256. Teja Singh, *Essays in Sikhism*, Sikh University Press, Lahore, 1944, p. 105.

257. R.L. Ahuja, p. 86. Also see Faqir Syed Waheeduddin, *Real Ranjit Singh*, Oriental, New Delhi 1976, p. 23.

258. A.S. Atlekar, *History of Banaras*, The Cultural Publishing House, Hindu University, Banaras, 1937, p. 57-58.

259. Abdul Ali, *Notes on the Life and Times of Ranjit Singh*, p. 14.

260. R.L. Ahuja, p. 35.

261. Teja Singh, p. 102.

262. Khushwant Singh, p. 202.

263. R.L. Ahuja, p. 58.

264. Teja Singh, p. 103.

265. Hari Om Gupta, *We Are One*, Director Public Relations, Haryana 1973, p. 42.

266. S.N. Chandra, *1857 Some Untold Stories*, Sterling, New Delhi 1976. p. 3.

267. Upendra Nath Ball, *Modern India*, p. 582.

268. Jadunath Sarkar, *Fall of the Mughal Empire*, p. 35.

269. Upendra Nath Ball, p. 582.

270. Mohibbul Hasan, *History of Tipu Sultan*, The World Press Calcutta, 1951, p. 332.

271. Syed, p. 165.

272. Mohibbul, p. 332.

273. Pt. Sunderlal, p. 172.

274. Mohibbul, p. 368.

275. *Ibid.* p. 345-46.

276. Surendra Nath Sen, *Studies in the Indian History*, University of Calcutta, Calcutta 1930, p. 172.

277. Mohibbul, p. 338.

278. *Ibid*, p. 374.

279. *Ibid.* p. 173.

280. Kirmani, *History of Tipu Sultan*, Calcutta 1864, Published by Sushil Gupta, p. 133.

281. Mohibbul, p. 332.

282. Hugh Murray, *History of British India*, T. Nelson and Sons, London, 1854, p. 436, 38.

283. Thomas Keightley, p. 138.

284. *Ibid.*, p. 152.

285. Mohibbul, p. 329.

286. Mahdi Husain, *Bahadur Shah* II, M.N. Publication New Delhi 1986, p. 39, 65.

287. *Ibid.*

5

Composite Indian Culture

The finest product of Medieval India was Indian culture. Close-cooperation between communities culminated in to a common outlook, which in turn gave emergence to common culture. All the people of the land, jointly contributed in evolving and enriching a culture, which was neither Hindu, nor Muslim but truly Indian, the core of which was the communal harmony.

Literature

The process of assimilation was started as early as the establishment of the Muslim rule. Though the Sultans were primarily military persons, some of them however took keen interest in belles-letters and under their liberal patronage, literature of high order was produced during the Sultanate period. The Court of Delhi Sultans was well attended by writers, poets, scholars, philosophers, logicians and chroniclers. Similarly celebrated writers, poets and scholars adorned the Courts of the provincial dynasties, under whose patronage, provincial literature and language too got a stimulus. Thus a new renaissance of Indian literature ushered in India. The Muslims with their introduction of paper, calligraphy and the system of illumination of manuscripts provided a boost to the art of literature.[1] Numerous new works were composed and translations from Sanskrit to Persian and from Persian to other languages were made of the then existing literature. Hindu scholars learnt Persian and the Muslims learnt Sanskrit. The knowledge of each other's literature fascinated the literary minds and contributed greatly in breaking all sorts of barriers between the two communities and bringing them closer to each other.

Mahmud Ghazni patronized scholars like Al-Beruni and

Firdausi and did not object to the study of Sanskrit literature, philosophy and science. C.V. Vaidya writes:

"At any rate the galaxy of learned men, poets and philosophers of unique ability, like Firdausi and Al-Beruni which illuminated the court of Mahmud should make him renowned as Akbar of Modern and Vikramaditya of ancient fame"[2]

In India Al-Beruni studied Sanskrit which was called as Devbani (holy language) under Hindu Pandits to acquaint himself with its vast literary treasure. He wrote about twenty books on Indian themes. His writings contain citations from Ramayna and Mahabharta.[3] Perhaps under his influence, Mahmud issued a silver coin from Lahore in the tenth-century, bearing a Sanskrit legend in Devanagri to replace his Dinar in India. The rendering of the Muslim concept of Allah by the word Avyakta imperceptible, is very happy and shows genuine understanding of each other's philosophical concepts.[4] Mahmud had a number of persons well-versed in Indian languages at his disposal. One such person translated the Hindi verse composed by Ganda, the Raja of Kalinjar, in praise of the Sultan.[5] When Mahmud invaded Gwalior, the ruler Raja Nand Rai, composed a poem and sent it to him. The poem was so fine and of so high a quality that Mahmud, his companions and all the poets that were with him were wonder-struck. He was so pleased with the poem that he not only gave up the idea of attacking his capital but he also presented him with fourteen fortresses and two serais.[6]

Thus Indianization of the Muslim rulers began with the very beginning of their rule in India. Amir Khusrau (1253-1325) the Toot-i-Hind or Parognet of India, who still shines like a moon among the literary figures of the sub-continent, wrote his works influenced and inspired by the Indian environment. In one of his Persian Masnavis called Nur-Sipher (Nine skies) Amir says: "Why some one may ask me all this zeal and admiration for India? It is because India is land of my birth and is my own country. The Prophet has said that 'the love of one's country is part of the faith'. It is my country. I am going to speak about it within the limits I have set to myself".[7] Amir wrote about one-lakh stanzas. His riddles, songs on rainy season and dholak are still sung on festive occasions. During the same period (1295 A.D.) Mulla Dawood wrote Prem Katha Chandyan and Sheikh Rahim, his Prem Ras.

Hinduism and Islam came to be regarded two different ways of reaching the same God. The Muslim writers wrote about Hindu gods with as much devotion as for Prophet Mohammad. These writers were not prosecuted or punished by Sultans, speaks of the liberal outlook and approach of the rulers. Mahmood Shabistri (1317 A.D.) the well known writer of Gulshan-e-raz, writing on the theme of idol worship, explains the difference and similarity between Hinduism and Islam as:

"The idol is the expression of love and unity in this world and to wear the sacred thread is to take the resolve of service. As both faith and unfaith are founded in existence, unity of God is the essence of Idol worship. As things are the expression of existence, one out of them must at least be the idol. If the Muslims knew what the idol is, then he would understand that religion consists in idolatry and if the idol worshipper understood the idol, he would not go astray in his faith".[8]

A Muslim theologian Sheikh Rizqullah (1491-1581) wrote lyrics on the love of Krishna in Hindi under the title of Wujub-Jap-Niranjan.[9] Mir Abdul Wahid Bilgrami, a saint and scholar, wrote a treatise entitled Haqaiq-i-Hind in 1566 in which he sought to reconcile more than fifty symbols of the Vaishnavites and a large number of terms and expressions used in other devotional songs.[10] The Hindus too did not remain unaffected. A Brahmin of Sultan Sikandar's reign, who was also a poet, used to give instructions in the books of Islamic learning.[11]

Keenness to know each other's philosophies also led the Sultans to get the existing works translated into different languages. Under the patronage of the provincial Muslim rulers, literature in regional languages also flourished. The Brahmins were displeased with the development of regional languages They were against the translations of the Sanskrit works in to any other language as it was believed that, "if a person hears the eighteen Puranas of the Ramayana recited into Bengali; he will be thrown into the hell called Rourava hell".[12] Muslims were free from this taboo and hence freely encouraged the languages of the people. The literary upsurge engulfed the entire country from Kashmir to Kanyakumari.

In Kashmir, Sultan Zainul Abidin established a translation department where competent scholars translated Sanskrit works in to Persian and Persian works in to Sanskrit. He further got them translated in to Kashmiri. Srivara began the translation of Jami's Yusuf Zulaikha into Sanskrit and named it Katha Kautuka. Thus Mulla Ahmad, the Court poet translated the Mahabharta, Dasavtara and Rajatrangini into Persian. Jonaraja continued the Rajatrangini into Sanskrit verses and brought down to 1458. Srivara and Soma Pandit too worked on this project. Yudha Bhatta composed the Zaina Prakasa, the biography of the Sultan Zain into in Kashmiri verses.[13] A Kashmiri Brahmin named Bodi Bhatt rendered Firdausi Shahnama, a book of 60,000 verses into Hindi.[14] Zain, who himself knew Sanskrit, Kashmiri, Tibetan and Persian, realized that one could receive the best instruction in his own mother-tongue and hence introduced mother-tongue as the medium of instruction in educational institutions.[15]

In Bengal, the Muslim kings were the great patron of art and literature and it was through their encouragemnt that the Bengali language, which had been neglected under the Hindu kings, was elevated to a literary status.[16] Ramayna and Mahabharta were translated into Bengali.The first Bengali rendering of Mahabharta was ordered by Nasir Shah (1282-1325). A Maithali poet Vidyapati has showered praises on Nasir Shah and Sultan Ghiasuddin in this connection. Sultan Husain Shah and his son Nusrat Shah patronized poets like Vipradas, Piplai, Vijaya Gupta etc. and during their reign Vaishnava literature developed.[17] Many works of Hindu religion were translated into Bengali because of their encouragement. For his liberal ideas and non discriminatory attitude, Husain Shah was regarded as the ideal king, comparable to Arjuna and the incarnation of Lord Krishna in the Kali age.[18] Chhotey Khan, the son of Parangal Khan, who was the Governor of Chittagong got the translation of the Ashwamedha of Mahabharat done by Shri Krishna Nandi.[19] Muslim poets and writers greatly contributed into the development of the regional literature. One Daulat Kazi wrote in Bengali, Sati Meenavati. Alau'l, Syed Murtaza and Syed Sultan, wrote a large number of Vaishnavite songs. Syed Sultan also wrote books on Islamic religion like Gyan Pradeep, Hazarat Mohammad Charit, and Nabi Bangash. In Nabi Bangash, he counted all Brahma, Vishnu, Shiva, and Shri Krishna as Nabis and showed great respect towards them. Lal Mahmud a Vashnavite poet wrote; "Janam niyya Musalmane, wanchit hove Shricharne" Sabit Khan wrote Vidya Mandir, Ali Raja is known for his book Gyan Sagar and Dhyanmala in which his devotion for Hindus gods reflects.[20]

Muslim Sultans thus rendered a great service to Bengali language and literature by granting recognition to Bengali in their Court. Dinesh Chandra writes:

"When powerful Muslim Kings of Bengal accorded such a high place to Indian languages in their Darbars, naturally the Hindu Rajas also followed their example...Thus the practice of appointing Bengali poets in the Darbars of Hindu Rajas had its origin in what the Muslim kings had done and were doing."[21]

In Oudh, the rise of Awadhi literature was due to the stimulus of the Sharqi Kings of Jaunpur. Qutb Ali composed the story of Mrigavati at the instance of Sultan Husaain Shah Sharqi (1469-79). In this he compared Hussain Shah with the heroes of Hindu mythology and not with Rustom or Hatim. Praising Shah's liberalism Qutb wrote:

Shah Hussain aahe badd raja1 Chhatra singhasan unko saja[11]
Pandit o budhwant siana1 Padhe Puran arth sab jana11.[22]

(Shah Hussain is a great king who adorns the throne. He has acquired the knowledge of Vedas from pandits and other learned men.)

Under the patronage of Sher Shah, Malik Mohammad Jaisi, who was affectionately called as Jaisi Das by the Hindus wrote his immortal work Padmavat in Awadhi. It was about Allauddin Khalji's love for Padmini. Mir Manjhan wrote Madhumalti in pure Awadhi during Adil Shah Sur reign.[23]

In South, the Bahmani kings greatly contributed to the development of the local literature. Their liberal patronage to the poets and writers and their non-sectarian outlook gave emergence to a revolutionary upsurge in the literary field. Adil Shah I (1558-1580) was a learned scholar. Sanskrit Vaman was his favourite and was incharge of his large library. As the Court language was Marathi, a lot of literature in this language was produced. Ibrahim Adil Shah II who became the ruler of Bijapur in 1580 was himself a literary figure. He had command over many languages and wrote Nauras, the work in which he wrote many devotional poems on Hindu gods and goddesses.[24] Qutb Shah Dakkhini too was a Marathi poet. During his reign, a poet named Adil wrote a large number of devotional poems on Lord Krishna:

"Nand ke Kishore, Chitchor, Morepankhware,
Bansiware, Sanvare, Piarey, et aao re.
Adil sujan roop gun ke nidhan Kanha,
Bansuri bajai tan tapin bujhao re."[25]

(Son of Nand, who adorns, feathers of peacock and flute, an epitome in beauty and quality. Please play your flute and make me happy)

And

Nand ju ka piara, jin Kans ko pachhara,

Wh Brindaban vara, Krishna Sahib hamara hai.[26]

(Who is the beloved of Nand, who defeated Kans, who lives at Brindaban, is our Lord Krishna)

Khwaja Banda Nawaz Gesu-daraz, who lived in Deccan, wrote an inspiring work, The Miratul Ashiqin in Deccani. In the works written during this period words of both Hindi and Persian language freely entered the Marathi language.[27]

Qutb Shahi rulers of Golkonda were patrons of Telgu language and literature. The famous Telgu poet, Gangadhara Kavi was amongst a number of others who adorned the Court of Ibrahim Qutb-Shah. (1550-1580) Ibrahim's cordial relations with his people of Golkonda won him the popular name Malikbrahma. He generously rewarded the poets of his kingdom. One-verse states that Ibrahim used to give princely gifts to poets, not in thousands but in lakhs.[28] His son Sultan Mohammad Quli promoted Hyderabad as a centre of culture. Writers and scholars from around the world were encouraged to visit the city and share their talents. The Sultan embarked upon an almost passionate patronage of Telugu literature, which stimulated an intellectual awakening throughout his realm. He also pioneered the use of Urdu in contemporary Deccani writing. He eulogised his homeland thus:

Daccan hai nageena, angoothi hai jug;

Angoothi ko hurmath, nageene sai jug.

(The Deccan is the gem and the world is the ring. The gem is the dignity of the ring.).[29]

He was also a well-known scholar. His most famous work, the Kulliyat, gives a glimpse of social life of that time. Its subjects include Hindu and Muslim festivals, dress daily ceremonies, food drink and games such as polo and kabbadi.[30] In Madras, the ruler, Nawab Walajah was a great patron of learning. He held a magnificent Court at South and honoured the literary talents. He built a mosque at Madras and invited the poets of his Court to compose chronograms to be inscribed on that edifice. Of all the compositions presented before the Nawab, those composed by Lala Mukkhan Lal, (born in 1177A.D) whose poetic name was Khirad, were selected as the best and were inscribed on the edifice.[31]

In Sindh, Sindhi Language developed and though written in

Arabic script, over seventy-percent of the Sindhi words were taken from Sanskrit. Sufi saints during the Sultanate period greatly contributed to the development of the local dialects and the literature In Punjab, Punjabi dialect which was called as Lahori was developed by Baba Farid who is also considered as the first poet of Punjabi. Khatib Ali and Baba Nanak were also great writers of Punjabi.

Thus it was due to the encouragement, patronage and liberal outlook of the Muslim rulers which led to the development and enrichment of the local languages and literature which played an important role in integrating and beautifying the diversity of India. They rendered a great service to the entire Hindu society by translating the Hindu religious works and thereby enabling all the Hindus to know about their religion as these, prior to their rule, were known only to the higher castes. Common literature and common language also promoted feeling of oneness among the inhabitants of a region. People of a region, whether Hindus or Muslims looked alike, had a common outlook and were treated alike by their rulers.

Thus before the Mughal period, the seeds of common identity and harmony had been sown by the Muslim rulers which blossomed during the Mughal rule and caused a literary ferment which India had never experienced before.

Babar himself a poet and a writer, had Hindi poets in his Court. When he defeated Ibrahim Lodi, an unknown poet wrote:

Nau se ooper hota vatia-Panipat mein Bharat diya 1
Satu rajab avat daba-Babar jita Ibrahim hara II 23
(In 932 A.H, India was made over at Panipat
On the 7th Rajab Babar won Ibrahim lost)

Narhari, another Hindi poet, wrote:

Babar brober Badshah digar na didam na suni.[32]
(We neither seen nor heard about a king like Babar)

However, it was during the reign of Akbar, which witnessed unprecedented growth and development in the Indian literature. His court was like a pilgrimage for all the poets and writers who vied with each other to produce works which are the precious heritage of that age. The religious literature written by the Hindu and Muslim Saints makes all Indians proud of that period. Tulsi Das wrote his Ramayna, Surdas his Sursagar and Mirabai her devotional songs in praise of Lord Krishna. The religious harmony prevalent in the society reflected in the literature also. Hindu poets wrote in praise of Prophet and the Muslims poets composed verses praising the Hindu gods. They not only had cordial relations but sought each others help in composing verses and helping the deserved. Sanskrit was not the monopoly of the Hindus as the Muslims had acquired equal proficiency. If Rahim, a Muslim, was adept in Sanskrit than Surdas knew Persian and made use of the Persian words in Hindised form in his verses.[33] Rahim authored Madanashtak, Barbai Naika Bhed, Sahitya-Sutra and Rahim Satsai.[34] The liberty with which Rahim sang in praise of Brahma, Rama and Krishna clearly explains that gods of both the communities were revered with equal devotion by the followers of both the religions. In a beautiful sloka, of which any Indian devotee could be proud of, Rahim sings of Vishnu:

Your abode is the jewel-laden ocean;
You have for wife, the lotus deity.
What can I give O Lord of universe?
Well since Radha stole Your mind,
Mindless you are, I offer you my mind.
Here take it.
Ratnaakro asti

Rahim's songs of Krishna were sung by him with as much devotion as that of an ardent Vaishnava.

Thou as Krishna appeared, as Rama, Lakshman
Without stain thyself took form,
Thyself Mahadev, art a shining beam,
Thyself art Brahma, who established Vedas,
Thyself the three Vedas, Thyself the three worlds
Thou, the tapas, Thyself the Yogi who established.
Thyself became fish of the sea,
Thyself took the form of Narsimha.[35]
Again
Tain Rahim man aapno kinho Chas chkor I
Nisi vasar lagyo rahe Krishanchandar ki aur II [36]

(Rahim your heart is like Chakore who always looks at Moon. Likewise you always think and pray Lord Krishna.)

Rahim was thus a representative of composite Indian culture. Bhartndu Harishchandra has paid a glowing tribute to the secular spirit of Rahim by saying that he could sacrifice crores of Hindus for one such Muslim.[37] Rahim had intimate relations with saint Tulsidas, who wrote Barvai Ramayana as a tribute to Rahim. It was

Rahim's admiration of Tulsidas that led to this reciprocal gesture. According to the Gosain Charita by Beni Madhav Dasa, Rahim lent some Barvais to Tulsidas to compose Barvai Ramayna. The following couplet shows:

"Kavi Rahim Barve rache, pathey Munivar pass I
Lakhi teyi sunder chhand mein, rachna kiye prakas. II [38]

(Rahim wrote Barve in praise of Lord Rama and sent it to Tulsi. He composed it beautifully and enlightened the entire world)

Both had great respect and regard for each other. Once Tulsidas sent a poor Brahmin, who was in dire need of money for his daughter's marriage, to Rahim with the following line:

Surtiye nartiye nagatiye yeh chahat sab koi.[39]

Rahim gave the Brahmin a lot of money with the following line, which completed Tulsidas's doha (couplets): Goud liye Hulsi Phire, Tulsi so sut hoi.11.[40]

(All women desire that they should, like Hulsi, mother of Tulsi, have a son like Tulsi)

This spirit wrote new chapters in the Indian glorious past. Hindu Rajas did not remain behind. Once a person came to Rahim for financial help, as the latter was famous for his generosity. Rahim, who at that time was not in a position to help, sent the person to Rivanaresh with the following verse:

"Chitrakoot mein Ram rahi, Rahiman Awadh Naresh I
Japar vipda parat hai so aawat yahi des II [41]

(Chitrakoot, where Lord Ram lived during exile, is now the kingdom of Riva king. Whosoever is in trouble comes to him and the king helps everyone.)

Riva Naresh gave Rupees one lakh to the petitioner. Mutual rivalries or exclusiveness had no place in this atmosphere. Tansen, who was also an accomplished poet, wrote verses in praise of Allah:

Pak Mohammad Allah Rasul tero he noor-Zahoor
Dhan-dhan parvardigar, gunahgar Tu, Krisan Tu he jag mein ramyo bharpur.[42]

(Both Allah and Prophet have enlightened the universe. God you are very kind. You are lord Krishna. You are omnipresent)

Thus Krishna did not remain God of Hindus alone. The religious literature composed during this period makes it evident that Muslim too had deep devotion for Him. Raskhan, a Muslim, who (Sayyid Ibrahim Pihani) belonged to a royal family worshipped Krishna. His spiritual quest took him to the Braj bhumi i.e., Brindaban where he became the disciple of Goswami Vithaldas, son of Swami Vallabhacharya. He wrote Sujan Raskhan' and Pembatika'. His verses reflects his bhakti towards Krishna:

"Manus hoin to vahin Raskhan, Bason mili Gokul Gavn ke gavaran I

Jo pasu hon to kaha bas mero,
Charon nit Nand ki dhenu manjharan II
Pahan hoin to wahin giri ko,
Jo kio kar Chhar purander dharan I
Jo khag hoin to Basera karon
Va Kalind ja kool Kadamb ke daran II [43]

(Poet Raskhan says that if I were to be man in next life, then I would prefer to live in Gokul, the place of Lord Krishna. If I were to be an animal then I should be one of the grazing cows of Nand, father of Lord Krishna. If I were to be stone, then I should be of that mountain which once was prevented by Krishna to fall. If I were to be a bird then I should stay on Kadamb tree on the side of Kalindi River.)

The ruler of this period, Akbar was above any kind of sectarianism. The best literary talents illuminated his Court. Among the prominent poets were Rahim, Narhari, Holrai, Jagannath, Raja Mukand Singh Hada, Gobindhatt, who was honoured by the title of Akbariya Kalidasa, Keshavdas, Tansen, Raja Todarmal and Manohar Taswani who called himself Mirza Mohammad. These poets and writers produced a valuable literature, which leaves no doubt that it was the age of enlightenment. Manohar Taswani wrote a panegyric in praise of Imam Ali. Urfi, another contemporary poet of Akbar, too echo the ideal of unity and fraternity between the Hindus and Muslims. In one of his poems, he stated that a man should live with others in such a manner that when he dies, the Muslim may wash his body in the zamzam water and the Hindus may burn it according to their own rites.[44]

Akbar greatly respected, honoured and rewarded the literary personalities. Once Akbar held poet Narharis palanquin on his own shoulder. It is said that once on the request of Keshavdas, Akbar cancelled Rupees one crore fine on Inderjit brother of Raja Ram Singh of Orchha.[45] The emperor offered gold and silver coins for lyrics composed by Surdas and read them in their Persian translation.[46] Akbar also composed verses in Braj bhasha, which was also called Badshahi boli,(King's language) in which he signed himself as Akbar

Rai.[47] For his skill in the poetry he earned the title of Kaviraj.[48] He wrote the following verse;

"Jo ko jas hai jagat mein, jagat sara hai jahi,
Ta ko janam safal hai kahta Akbar Sahi.
Sah Akbar aik samy chale I
Kan vinod bilochan balahi II

(One who has fame in the world and is praised by all. His life alone is successful, says Akbar Shah. Shah Akbar went once for seeing the sporting Krishna.) [49]

On another occasion when Kunwar Man Singh was ordered by Akbar to lead the army to Kabul on pursuit of his stepbrother Mirza Hakim, Man Singh refused to march beyond Attock on religious ground. Akbar then sent him the following verses, which changed Man Singh's views. These were:

"Sabai Bhumi Gopal ki,
Ta mein attak khan II
Ja ke man mein attak hai
Soi attak raha. II

(The entire universe belongs to Gopal (Lord Krishna). The man in whose mind is obstruction has become obstructed).[50]

Akbar poured out his feelings in the form of verses. In his old age he wrote the following couplets in honour of his intimate friends who had all passed away:

"Pithla so majlis gai Tansen so rag,
Hansio, ramio, bolio gayo Birbal sath."

(With Pithlas, Prithviraj of Bikaner; the assembly has departed; with Tansen Musical modes have gone; and laughter and pleasantries and conversation have gone with Birbal).[51]

The royal family too contributed in the enrichment of the literature. The Queens, princes and princesses also penned poems. The liberal spirit, which had encompassed the entire country, also engulfed the life inside the palace. Taj, a wife of Akbar was a devotee of Krishna. She composed many verses in the admiration of the Hindu God:

"Jagat ko jivan jahan which nam sunyo,
Radha ke Vallabh Krishna Vallabh hamare hain".[52]

(The Maker of the entire universe, whose name is known to everyone is Radha's Lord Krishna, is also our Lord)

His Court presented a picture of complete harmony. If there was Badayuni, a die-hard orthodox, a broadminded Abul Fazl was also in the service of the emperor. It seems that Akbar was inspired by Sultan Zainul Abidin's ideas and cosmopolitan outlook. According to Abul Fazal, the Court historian, the emperor ordered him to re-write the history of Kashmir in easy style. (The original work on Kashmir was translated by Mulla Shah. Akbar, however was not satisfied with this work) Fazal translated it and it was read to the emperor.[53] Like Zain, Akbar too set up a translation bureau under Abul Faizi to get Sanskrit works translated in to Persian. Some of them were Ramayna, Bhagwad Gita, Yoga Vashishta, Lilavati, Atharveda, Nala Damyanti, Singhasan Battisi and Panchtantra.[54] About the translation of Mahabharta, Abul Fazal writes: "For two nights, His Majesty himself translated some passages of the Mahabharta and told Naqib Khan to write down the general meaning in Persian; the third night he associated me with Naqib Khan".[55] After translation, it was profusely illustrated and caligraphed at a cost of 40,000 pounds.[56] One of the copies of Mahabharta made for the Imperial Library was in possession of the Maharaja of Jaipur.

Badayuni translated Ramayana in to Persian and for this the emperor liberally rewarded him.'Kishanjoshi', the 'Gangadhar' and the 'Maheshanand' were translated in to Persian by Abul Fazl.[57] After translation, all these works were read to Akbar by the poets and scholars. Thus Akbar's regime presents a picture of enlightenment, a golden period in the history of Indian literature.

Like his father, Jahangir also provided patronage to the poets and writers. Composition of the composite literature continued. Jahangir is said to have great respect for Saint Surdas, whose Sursagar is reputed to have been compiled under Jahangir' patronage.[58] Like Akbar, Jahangir also used to give one gold coin for every verse of Surdas. Many Sanskrit writers flourished during his reign; their works being recognized and accepted as authority even today.

Jahangir himself was a literary figure. He wrote his memoir, which provides us knowledge about the emperor as a person and of his reign.

Translation of literary works too continued. Two Persian renderings of the verses of Ramayna were made during his reign. Girdhar Das a Kaystha of Delhi, rendered Valmiki's Ramayna in to verses, called it Ram-Nama and dedicated it to Jahangir. Masihi, a Muslim, made another Persian translation of Ramayna in which he also wrote in praise of the Prophet.[59]

Shah Jahan was a poet himself. He used to express his experiences and feelings in the form of verses. When Aurangzeb killed his brothers and imprisoned him, the emperor wrote:

"Janmat he lakh dan diyo aur nam dhryo navrangbihari,
Balhinso pratipal kiyo aur des mulakk diyo dal bhari,
So sut bair bujhe man mein dhari hai diyo bandhsar mein dari,
Shahjahan bin be harison bali rajivnain rajai tihari"[60]

(When you (Aurangzeb) were born I donated a lot of money and also gave you a kingly name. Love was showered and responsibility of governing the state was assigned. The same son nurses enmity for his father and has interned him. Oh God if this is your will then Shah Jahan is helpless)

Kavindrachrya Sarswati, a Sanskrit poet, enjoyed Shahjahan's patronage. He was a Brahmin of Benaras. He also wrote a Hindi poem of 160 stanzas, entitled Kavindra-Kalplata in which he described the splendor of Shahjahanabad and happiness of its people. Another favourite of Shahjahan was the son of Akbar's Court poet, Narhari Mahapatra. He once received a reward from Shahjahan one horse, one elephant and one lakh of Dams. It is said that while Harinath was returning from the Court with these gifts, a Brahmin beggar recited an extempore couplet in his praise and asked for reward. The poet gave him a lakh of Dams.[61] Poet Chandar Bhan flourished at the Court of Jahangir as well as Shahjahan. He used to write under the name of Brahman. He hailed from Lahore and served also as a private secretary of prince Dara. He was the incharge of the Dar-ul-Insha (the Secretariat) during Shahjahan's reign. The first line that the poet recited before Shahjahan was; "My heart is so bound to kufur that each time I took it to Kaba, every time it came back as Brahman".[62] He wrote the famous work Chahar-Chaman. Sunar Kavi, Siromani Misr and Banarsi Das were other prominent poets of Shah Jahan's Court.

Prince Dara Shikoh was a great scholar. He wrote Sirr-ul-Asrar, a translation of fifty Upanishads; Majmua-ul-Baharain, a treatise on the technical terms of Hindu Vedanta with Sufi Equivalents; Dialogue with Baba Lal; Sakinat-ul-Auliya contains lives of the Muslim saints and a Persian translation of the Athervaveda. His untimely death deprived the Indian literature of a literary luminary.[63]

Like the harmony, literature also suffered during the reign of Aurangzeb. The emperor was not only orthodox but also launched campaigns one after another, which blocked the development in the literary field. However, the emperor was not devoid of interest and capability in the literature and had a number of Hindi poets in his Court. Poet Virind was his favourite. He appointed the poet to teach Hindi to the royal princes and princesses.[64] Motiram and Chintamani were prominent poets of his Court, upon whom he also conferred robes of honour and other gifts.[65] Aurangzeb was very fond of Hindi poetry and himself used to write poems. One of his poems is in praise of his favourite Hindu wife Udaipuri:

"Tuv gun Ravi udai kino yahi te kahat tumko bai Udaipuri,
Anginat gun gayan ke alap vistar sur jot dipak
Jo to loin vitha haitduri
Jab jab gavat tab tab ras sumandar lahrain upjavat,
Aysi Sarswati kaun ki Puri'
Jat naman jan Shah Aurangzeb reejh rahe,
Yahi te kahat tumko vitharoop chaturi.[66]

(You shine like sun that is why your name is Udaipuri. You are an epitome in matters of beauty, singing and music. You are incomparable. Aurangzeb is deeply impressed and beholden by your manifold qualities.)

Zaibunisa, a daughter of Aurangzeb was a scholar. She not only patronised men of learning but herself wrote verses full of rare pathos under the pen name of Makhfi (the concealed one). Her poems having been collected and published acquired wide celebrity under the title of Diwan-I-Makhfi.[67] Outside the Court, the saints and writers continued writing their works. Shah Barkatullah Pemi, a contemporary of Aurangzeb, wrote his famous Hindi poetic work Pem Prakash in which he emphasised over oneness of God:

Pemi Hindu Turk mein har rang raho smay,
Deval aur Masit mein deep ek hi bhai.[68]

(As there is same God in both the temple and the mosque so there is no difference between Hindu and Mussalman)

His continuos military campaigns did not let any art to grow. The state during his reign faced severe financial crisis and in this state no art could develop.

After the death of Aurangzeb, the splendor of the Mughal Empire was on the decline. There was no progress as there was no political stability. Emperor Mohammad Shah's rule witnessed some growth in the literary field, as the emperor himself was a noted poet.

He used to play Holi with his courtesans and enacted the role of

Krishna. He also penned many poems under the name of Sadarang and Mohammad Shah:

"Aao baalam ji hamare dere, abir gulal, malo mukh mere"[69]

(Oh beloved come to my place and apply red colour on my face)

Shah Alam used to compose poems in Sanskrit.[70]

In Kashmir, Sukhjivan Mal was a patron of literature. Once every week, he used to hold a poetical gathering. All the well-known poets attended it. At the end of it, he used to embrace every one of them. He engaged five best scholars to compile a history of Kashmir from the earliest times. Each writer was provided with ten assistants. The head of these historians was Muhammad Taufiq.[71]

Wajid Ali Shah, the ruler of Awadh (1847-56) was a man of many accomplishments. He wrote poems and plays of great value. In Delhi, the last emperor, Bahadur Shah Zafar was a gifted poet. His pen name was Zafar. He composed five diwans of mixed Urdu, Punjabi and Persian poetry, one of which running to 8,000 verses. He used to recite his own compositions to his courtiers. During his reign Urdu replaced Persian. Ghalib, the great Urdu poet and Zauq, the emperor's favourite contributed immensely to the growth of Urdu poetry.[72]

Urdu language was the outcome of the Hindu Muslim entente. It contains words from Arabic, Persian, Turkish, Punjabi, Purbi, Sanskrit, Braj and many other dialects spoken in India. It grew in north, nourished in Deccan, reached to its full development in north in the eighteenth and nineteenth century but later became a victim of the communal divide.

The love of learning of many of its Muslim kings also led to the establishment of Libraries. From the Sultanate times, they always maintained a state Library and every king added to the volumes therein. Scholars were appointed to write books and translate books from different languages. In those days there were no printing presses and consequently the works were all written in fair handwriting. Amir Khusrau was the Librarian of the State Library during Mohammad Bin Tughlaq's reign.[73] It was not only the kings and princes who collected rich store of literatures for their enlightenment, but noblemen of all classes vied with one another in owning such collections. Humayun was a man of literature. His fondness for books was unbounded and he carried a fine collection of books wherever he went. He took delight in the company of the scholars and had converted the pleasure house of the palace into a library wherein he used to spend most of his time. He died at the step of the library while descending.[74] Akbar maintained a grand library. It was located in the big hall in the fort of Agra. Rahim also had a very big and rich library at Ahmedabad. The library staff totalled to ninety-five. The Hindu painters illustrated most of the books in his library. Sheikh Faizi too had a library, which contained 4600 books. Nur Jahan too had her personal library. Jahangir is said to have always carried with himself a library of selected books while on a journey or expedition. In fact all the Mughal emperors were great collectors of books and the nobles both Hindus and Muslims followed the fashion of the Court. It is interesting to note that the great private manuscript Libraries of north India were set up during their reign, the Anup Library of Bikaner, the Potha Khana of Jaipur and the great collection of Jaisalmer.[75] Tipu Sultan had a large number of books in his library most of which were taken to England by the Englishmen. In his Library was found a large collection of state papers, which revealed his incessant activity to raise up enemies to the English; for it contained his correspondence with the French, the Afghans, the Marathas, the Nizam and his officers and even with Mohammad Ally of Arcot. Such patriotic correspondence could ignite the natives against the English, hence they sent the entire collection to their homeland, far away from the people of Tipu Sultan.[76]

Music

In the field of music, the conquerors were conquered by its splendor. They thus not only patronized it but also learnt it and contributed to its development. The liberal grants made by the rulers made both the Hindus and Muslims to join together in producing fresh melodies and inventing new tunes and instruments. Not only the Court musicians but the Sufi saints and the commoners too contributed in its growth and enrichment.

Raziya Sultana was also fond of Indian music and patronised them openly much to the annoyance of the orthodox. She was particularly fond of open-air music, appropriate to a procession or military display. At her court the military band played an important part. She allowed the Amirs to have their own bands, the size of which depended on their rank.[77] During her rule Indian music made a considerable progress. Sultan Balban was a great patron of music. He spoke of music in the highest terms and regarded it as superior to the music of any other country. He is credited with the invention of several new melodies compounded of Iranian and Indian tunes.[78] His son Prince Bogra Khan founded a dramatic society whose members included musicians also.[79] Amir Khusrau, the greatest poet-singer, is the representative of the spirit of the Sultanate period. He was a musicians in Alauddin's Court, who himself had fascination for Indian music. It is said that the Sultan found South more advanced than North in the field of music. He brought both male and female singers of the South to Delhi. The great singer Gopal Nayak was one of them. Musical competitions were held in the Court and the Sultan rewarded richly the winners. Amir Khusrau's talent in this field flourished during his reign.[80] He wrote songs on all aspects of life and seasons in the language understood by the masses. Amir liked India to the Garden of Eden where Adam resided before his fall. For him India was a paradise on earth. He had a great genius for synthesis and was the first one to thought of combining Persian and Indian tunes and thus enriched Indian music. He invented Sitar by combining the old Indian Vina and the Iranian Tambura. He is said to have modified the old Mirdang and to have given to it the shape of Tabla. Besides Qwwali mode of singing, several rags like Zilaph, Sazagiri and Sarpada were introduced by him.[81] Music being the language of the soul, the changes brought by Khusreau had far reaching social consequences in bringing together people of divergent creed.

Firoz Tughlaq was a lover of music. His succession to the throne was celebrated by entertaining the public for twenty-one days with music.[82] During his reign, he got a number of books on music and dance translated into Persian. A collection of Indian melodies was compiled during Sikandar Lodi's rule entitled Lahjat-I-Sikandar Shahi, which is also considered the first book in Persian on Indian music.[83]

However music prosper with greater vigour in the case of regional Muslim kingdoms during the [15]th and [16]th centuries. Sultan Husain Shah Sharqi of Jaunpur is credited with having invented seventeen Indian ragas (musical tunes) of which twelve were Shyam, four todi and one asawari geners which are almost purely Indian. Another regional Muslim ruler of Gujarat was also a composer of such purely Indian musical varieties as Suramba, dhya, Chhand and dohra. Bakshwa, a musician at the Court of Bahadur Shah of Gujarat (1526-37) is credited with the authorship of a very large number of Indian Dhrupad melodies.[84] Zainul Abidin of Kashmir was an accomplished musician. He patronised singers and musicians of repute. Buddi Datta, an author of an excellent treatise on music, which he called Zain, enjoyed his favours. Srivara played on the lute and was a good singer with a sweet voice. Yodhbhatta was a well-known musician. In all there were twelve hundred musicians in Zain's court.[85]. In Deccan, Firoz Shah Bahmani had a great liking for the music because it helped him to think of God. Mahmud Shah Bahmani was too much devoted to music to think of anything else. He neglected state duties for music and lost the crown. Yusuf Adil Shah of Bijapur (1490-1510) was a votary of music. He could successfully play on two or three kinds of musical instruments and in his delightful mood he sang songs extempore. It is said "His skill in it was superior to that of many a master musician of the time, whom he encouraged to attend his Court, by handsome rewards".[86] His son Ismail (1510-1539) was also passionate for music. The famous Chand Bibi was a great musician of the 16th century. She was the daughter of Sultan of Ahmednagar and was married to the prince Ali Adil Shah of Bijapur. She was a master of art as well as of war. She could play on Vina and Sitar as well. She was an admirer of Indian music and appreciated Dhrupad style of music.[87]

The music developed outside the Courts also. The Sufi saints too gave importance to music. Both the Chistiya and the Qadriya schools sanctioned Sama' musical rhythms, that enhanced the effect of the devotional poetry. They enabled the devotees to be plunged into a state of trance called Haal. The effectiveness of Sama can be gauged by the fact that many a Sufi embraced death while listening to devotional songs which intensely affected their hearts. Khwaja Bakhtiyar kaki and Shah Latif were among them.[88]

Thus during the Sultanate period in the field of music, a perfect harmony of taste and sentiments between the Hindus and the Muslims had developed. The Mughals found a common musical art an accomplished fact. They further enriched it by providing liberal patronage and promoting harmonious co-existence. No wonder, the music acquired its perfection and reached its zenith in the Mughal period. Babar loved music and practised it. He also wrote a treatise on it. During Humayun's reign a large number musicians and singers were dependant wholly on the patronage of the emperor for their maintenance While raiding Mandu Humayun came to know about Bachchu, a musician amongst prisoners. He asked him to sing something. Bachhu was especially skilled in Persian sentimental dittis; he began to sing one of these. When Humayun heard it he was immensely pleased. His fury disappeared and having bestowed a dress of honour on Bachhu, said to him, "Bachhu ask whatever you wish, I will not deny it to you" Bachhu replied that many of his kinsmen had been made prisoners, and he desired their release. The emperor bound his own quiver about Bachhu's loin and put him on one of his own horses and desired that no one was to interfere with them. Bachhu rode off and whenever he saw any of his acquaintances he declared them to be his kinsfolk and released them. This was reported to the emperor and complaint was made that Bachhu released not only his kinsmen but those who were perfect strangers and did this purposely, making no difference between those who were akin to him and those who were otherwise. The emperor said, " Let it pass. If to-day he had asked me to restore the kingdom of Bahadur I should not have refused his request" Humayun employed him in his Court. One day Bachhu ran away and went to Sultan Bahadur. The emperor remarked, "Bachhu has done very foolishly. I was so fond of him, and I should have treated him so well, that he ought to have forgotten Sultan Bahadur" It is said that when Bachhu came to Sultan Bahadur, the latter exclaimed: "Today I have regained all I have lost! And the sight of Bachhu had banished all grief and sorrow from my heart. I have now no desire unfulfilled. God has given me all that I have asked of Him".[89]

The Surs too patronised the art of music. Islam Shah and Adil Shah were lovers of music. About Adil, it has been said that he granted to Bhagat boy, Mansab of 10,000 who was a skilled musician.[90] One day a famous Deccani musician came to the darbar with a gigantic pakhawaj and challenged the court musicians, who comprised dome of the leading lights of the day, to play on the instrument, which could not be enveloped by the arms of a single person. The Court musicians were confounded by the huge size of the instrument and hung down their head in shame. The Deccani was exulting in triumph when Adil, perceived a way to get over the difficulty. With a pillow under his head, he lay down full length on his musnud and laid the pakhawaj alongside him. To the wonder of onlookers then Adil passed his right hand under the instrument and began to play, beating time with his foot. The music produced was splendid and the darbar hall rang again and again with shouts of genuine applause. An idea of Adil's refined sense of smell can be gathered from the fact that the sweeper scrapped over two seers of purest camphor every morning from his privy room. Adil kept on enjoying music and dispatched his general Hemu to drive out the Mughals. The battle of Panipat, which followed, struck the deathblow at Afghan Empire in India ".[91] Akbar took special delight in music and song and had a considerable knowledge of the technicalities of these arts Abul Fazl writes in Ain-I-Akabari that Akbar was the master of such knowledge of the science of music as trained musicians do not possess and he was likewise an excellent hand at performing, especially on the Nakkarah. He had a troupe of thirty-six excellent musicians at his court. Baz Bahadur, the ruler of Malwa in the early years of Akbar's reign and later as mansabdar under him, was a great musician himself and so was his beloved Rupmati. Baz Bahadur was not only a noted vocalist but also a great rank instrumentalist and used to perform on tabla. He composed a volume of love songs in Hindi, which became popular throughout in central India. He wrote Dhrupad:

"Tu he shaktiman jag mein virajat
Surjan karat jeev nirakh acharj lagat
Baz Bahadur nit hi gun gavat
Aur annad magan rahat"[92]

(You are all-powerful and omnipresent. Baz Bahadur is amazed to see your creation. Baz Bahadur always praise You and remains happy)

Baiju, the famous singer, was also adorned his Court. Before that he was in the service of Sultan Bahadur Shah of Gujarat in whose honour, he invented a todi, and named after him as Bahadur Todi. Tansen, one of the nine jewel of Akbar's Court was, however the greatest musician of his times. In the words of Abul Fazal: "A singer like him has not been produced in India for the last thousand years."[93]

Tansen, like Baiju was the creation of swami Hari Das, a Brahmin saint and musician. Tansen, a son of a Brahmin was brought up by a Muslim saint named Ghaus who also taught him the art of music. After Ghaus's death, Tansen went to Riva where he served in the Court of Riva Naresh, Raja Ramchandra and from there he came to the Court of Akbar. It is said that when Akbar heard Tansen's Basant Rag, he was so much impressed that he not only gave Tansen Rupees one crore but also married him to one of his daughters.[94] Akbar is also said to have visited Swami Hari Das and Mira Bai along with Tansen.

Tansen had very intimate relations with saint Surdas. He greatly appreciated Surdas's religious literature and wrote the following lines for the Saint:

"Kidhon Sur ko Sar lagyo, Kidhon Sur ki pir
Kidhon Sur ko pad lagyo, tan man dhunat Shrir"

Surdas wrote back to Tansen;

"Vidhna as jip jan ke, sheshi diye na kaan
Dhra meru sun dolti Tansen ki tan.[95]

(Praising Tansen's music, Surdas stated that his music had captivated the entire world. Brahma has deliberately not given ears to the Sheshnag who is holding the earth on his head otherwise hearing your music he too, would have danced and had thus shaken the earth. The mountains and occeans are also charmed with your music)

Tansen invented twelve new ragas. He is credited with the power of stopping the flow of Jamuna by his singing, just as his rival Baiju is believed to have split a rock with a single powerful note.[96] The bewitching sweetness of his voice is said to have set the Jamuna on fire and at his charming tunes and household utensils dance. It is also said that Sufi Saint Salim Chisti gave up his life after hearing Tansen's music.[97]

The liberal atmosphere at the Court encouraged and provided opportunities to everyone to present their composition and to get recognition and reward. He honoured the merit and so were his courtiers. Rahim once gave rupees thirty-six lakhs to poet Gang, one lakh to his musician Ramdas and one lakh to Tansen.[98]

When Tansen died, Akbar deeply mourned his death. On Akbar's order, Tansen was given a state burial. All the prominent musicians formed a procession and accompanied his dead body to the graveyard, singing as in a marriage party. He was buried in Gwalior by the side of the mausoleum of Sheikh Mohammad Ghaus. Akbar raised a fine building over his grave which became a pilgrimage for the musicians all over India.[99] Popular tradition believes that the neem leaves, growing by his grave will improve the human voice if eaten.[100] Jahangir and Shahjahan were fond of Hindi music and patronized the musicians. Jahangir was fond of Ghazals having Indian background Damodar Misra wrote Sangita Darpan in about 1625 AD He described in it twenty rags and dhayanas or prayer-formulas for the most of the melodies.[101] Shah Jahan delighted in Tansen's son-in-law, Lal Khan. He conferred upon him the title of

Gunasmundra. He was particularly fond of Dhrupad. Among the Hindu musicians at his court, the most distinguished was Pandit Jagannath, who was both a composer and a singer and had received from him the title of Maha Kavi Rai.He was also once weighed against gold and Shahjahan gave him the amount as his fee. Another musician Darong Khan was weighed against silver and Shahjahan gave the whole amount to him in reward.[102] Sukhsen and Sursen, the renowned instrumentalists also adorned his Court. Shahjhan himself was a renowned singer. It is said that his voice was so sweet and attractive that many Sufi and holy men who attended the evening assemblies lost their senses in ecstasy produced by Shahjahan's singing.[103] He also played on several musical instruments. The emperor refrained from music for two years after the death of his beloved wife Mumtaz Mahal.[104]

In Aurangzeb's time music was banned and the musicians observed the event by taking a funeral procession of music. Aurangzeb who was seeing this asked what was meant by such a show. The musicians and the dancers replied that they were carrying the corpse to the grave. "And so they may", replied the emperor, "but let them take care lest in contrariety to the law of God, the dead should seem to move in his grave or pretend to speak or sing" Inspite of this, the nobles did not cease to listen to the songs in secret.[105]

Perhaps to project himself as puritan, Aurangzeb showed his averseness to music. There are instances, which indicates that he too loved music. Once he went to the shrine of Saint Moin-ud-din Chisti to pay his respect. The musicians in the shrine as usual sang in the praise of the saint. Aurangzeb expressed his displeasure and did not allow them to sing in his presence. In protest, the authorities did not accept any royal gift. Perturbed by this Aurangzeb went to the shrine again and this time he not only let the singers sing but also gave double the normal gifts.[106] However, the lack of patronage during Aurangzeb's reign arrested the growth of music.

In Deccan, music reached its zenith during the reign of Adil Shah II. He not only provided state patronage to this art but also himself was a master of Indian music. Large numbers of both Hindu and Muslim students learnt music from him. In Bijapur, he built the Anand Mahal, in his new capital, which he named Nauraspur the Sangeet Mahal for his dancers and musicians.[107] He was the author of Nauras' a work which is considered a unique contribution to literature and music. In his songs collected in Nauras he invokes

Hindu deities Sarswati and other Hindu god and goddesses as well as the Prophet and the Sufi saint Gesu-daraz. Paying his respect to Sarswati, he says:

Sursati swacch sundari maha uttam jat nirmal

Aik hast pustak, duje panri sugiran, tije Shankh chhothe kar Kamal.

(Sarswati is perfect pure, holding book in one hand, in second a book, in third a counch and in fourth, flower Kamal)

Again:

"Nauras sur jug jag joti anur sarve guni,
Yosit Sarswati Mata Ibrahim Prasad bah duni"[108]

(O my mother Sarswati, you are kind to Ibrahim. Songs of Nauras will prevail for long and will enlightened the wise-men)

He also composed verses in praise of Shiva:

"Bhairon ka soor gaura bhal tilak chandra,
Trinature jata mukat Ganga dhra,
Aik hast rund Trisul jugal Kara
Vahan Bailo disat jat Gusai Ishwara"[109]

(There is chandra Tilak on the fair forehead of Shiva. He has three eyes and a crown of tangled hair. He is holding a human head in one hand and in other Trishul. He is riding on a bull. He is God.)

The tradition of patronising music survived in Deccan till the age Tipu Sultan under whom in 1785 Hasan Ali Izzat compiled his Mufarrih-al-qulub, an interpersed with Persian and Urdu verses. In Awadh, Wajid Ali Shah, was himself a musician and expert in dancing. He invented several tunes such as Jogi-Kuntur, Shah Pasand, and Johi.[110]

In Delhi, emperor Mohammad Shah was a poet and a gifted musician. He patronized musicians like Ghananana, Guman Mishra, Surti Mishra, Yugak Kishore Bhatt etc. He used to sing his own compositions:

"Yak gavat yak been bajawat abir gulal liye bhar jhori,
Sadarang (his poetic name) barsat Gokul mein khelat Nanad Kishori"[111]

(In Gokul, the Gopis celebrate Holi in great enthusiasm. Some time they sing and some time they dance, showering colours upon others.)

Thus melodies, music and dance, captivated the hearts and enthralled all its lovers Hindus, Muslims and others. No wonder, Nadir Shah fell under the spell of the Indian music during his stay at Delhi and he is said to have expressed himself saying, "Let Mulk (country) go away, but less not miss the Tori" (Tori ragini was being sung at the time of his departure).[112]

The Art of Painting

The fusion of two sets of art ideals in the field of painting gave emergence to a style of wondrous beauty. Muslim rulers evinced a great interest in this art and provided all opportunities, encouragement and facilities, which were essential for its development. They did not pay any heed to the orthodox Mullas who were hostile to the art of painting. There is said to be a painting of Sultana Raziya's period in which she appears riding on her favourite horse. She had liked this work immensely and rewarded the painter handsomely. So long as she reigned, it remained displayed in the hall of her Darbar.[113] It was however in Mughal period that this art reached its zenith. Babur was very interested in the art of painting. He brought with him the entire fine and choicest specimens of painting which he could lay hands upon in the library of his ancestors. Such paintings gave an inspiration to the Indian painters who flourished during the Mughal rule.[114] Humayun was also like his father interested in the art of painting. He came in touch with the Persian School of painting during his exile in that country. He brought in India two master painters who contributed to the development of this art. The progress of painting under Akbar is depicted by Abul Fazl in the following words:

"His Majesty from his earlier youth has shown a great predilection for the art, as he looks upon it as a means both of study and amusement. Hence the art flourishes and many painters have obtained great reputation. The works of all painters are weekly laid before His Majesty by the Daroghas and the clerks; he then confers rewards according to the excellence of workmanship, or increases monthly salaries. Much progress was made in the commodities required by the painters and the correct prices of such articles were carefully ascertained. The mixture of colours has especially been improved. The pictures thus received a hitherto unknown finish... The minuteness in detail, the general finish, the boldness of execution etc., now observed in pictures are incomparable; even inanimate objects look as if they had life".[115]

With regard to orthodoxy's opposition to the art of painting, Akbar remarked:

"There are many that hate painting; but such men I dislike. It appears to me as if a painter had quite peculiar means of recognizing God; for a painter sketching anything that has life and devising its limbs, one after the others must come to feel that he cannot bestow individuality upon his work and is thus forced to think of God, the Giver of life and will thus increase in knowledge".[116]

This attitude of Akbar led this art to grow and develop. Reputed painters from Persia and Central Asia were invited to the Mughal Court. He founded and endowed a state gallery where Painters used to assemble from different parts of the country to emulate one another. He made a provision for dividing the painters into different groups according to their special aptitudes and provided them intensive training in only one branch or aspect of the painting so that at least in that aspect they might acquire maturity with in a short time. Akbar personally examined their work every week and gave them rewards in proportion to the extent of their progress. He took one other step to help Indian painters. He acquired a collection of masterpieces of foreign painters and displayed them on the walls of the college of painting to serve as models to the Indian artists.[117]

When the Jesuits Misssion brought with them a picture of Madona, Akbar not only showed it to his mother and wives but also have it copied by his painters.[118] Of the painters of Akbar's Court mentioned by Abul Fazal, thirteen were Hindus and four Muslims. Baswan, Kesu Lal, Mukund, Mushkin, Madhu, Jagan Mahesh Khemkaran and Daswanth, Tara Sanwlah, Haribans Ram and Jagannath were prominent painters. They were entrusted with illustration of important works. The best painters illustrated Mahabharat, Ramayna, Nal Daman and Panchtantra and a huge amount of money was spent on decorating these epics. The inventory of his library at his death had 24,000 such manuscripts.[119]

During Akbar's reign, the art of painting not only made a great advance but was also Indianized. Indians animals appeared along with the familiar animals of Persian paintings. Indian flowers replaced Persian flowers. The mural decorations of Fatehpur Sikri are splendid specimen of the art of painting.[120]

Jahangir was the prince of Artists and carried the art of painting to perfection. Like his father Jahangir encouraged talents and liberally provided all facilities for their growth. He provided good education to the son of a well-known painter of his father's Court named Aka Raza. Under his care Abul Hasan, became so perfect in this art that he had no match in his time. Jahangir conferred upon him the title of Nadiru-z-zaman. He drew a picture of Jahangir's Court and attached it as a frontispiece to the Jahangirnama.[121] He has stated in his Memoirs that he could distinguish between the style of all living and dead painters and could say that who the painter was. Mansur, Manohar, Govardhan and Bishandas, Tulsi, Keshava and Madhava were unequalled in their art of drawing and painting. He himself was an excellent art critic Under him painting reached its highest watermark. Bishandas was sent to Persia and he brought from there the portraits of the Shah and his principal courtiers drawn by himself.[122]

About Jahangir, Bernier writes, "All artists were in the pay of the Court or some noblemen, and could not exist apart from patronage" The Indian painters were proficient in the art to such an extent that they drew admiration from Roe and Terry who were struck with wonder and amazement at the skill of the Court painters. Thomas Roe presented a picture to the Emperor, who gave him back six in the evening and the Ambassador Roe found it difficult to distinguish and confessed himself to be unable to pick out the original.[123]

Shah Jahan maintained the high tradition of his farther. S.M Jaffar writes "Under Shah Jahan, who himself was a good painter and a past master in the art of illuminating books, miniature and portrait painting underwent a great deal of elaboration, so much so that a picture or a portrait, however, elaborate and exquisite, was considered to be wholly incomplete if it was not provided with a beautiful border of the birds and butterflies, flowers and foliage".[124] Eminent artists continued to be employed at the Court and by the great nobles who treated them well and appreciated their work. The houses of the nobles were decorated with the master pieces of paintings Shah Jahan had a peculiar fancy for peacock. The walls of his palace were decorated with peacock design. His Peacock throne was designed in the similar way. The great Hindu painters of his reign were Bishandas and Bichittar. His son Prince Dara Shikoh was also great patron of painting. His album is still preserved in India Office Library and bears an inscription: "This album was presented to his nearest and dearest friend, the lady Nadira Begum, by Prince Mohammad Dara Shikoh, son of Shah Jahan in the year 1051.[125] Nadir Shah was so deeply impressed by the elegant arts of India that he chose to take with him a number of artists, poets and scholars, musicians and architects.[126] However, with Shah Jahan, decline in this art began as his successor Aurangzeb was averse to this art also. So much so that when he visited Akbar's mausoleum at Agra, and saw drawings of human figures on its walls, he ordered a coat of whitewash to be applied so that the drawing might not be seen. He regarded such things as prohibited by Islam.[127]

Architecture

The mingling of Hindu Muslim art in the field of architecture produced a style, which was Indian, a mixture of beautiful elements of both the arts. The buildings designed by the kings and constructed by the joint efforts of artisans of both the communities made India a centre of splendour, a dreamland for travellers all over the world.

The Sultans were great builders. The beauty of the then Indian architectural structures impressed them. The Jain arrangements of pillars, the colonnaded Courts of the Jain temples, were imitated in the designing of Mosques. Pierced stone screens were also borrowed from the indigenous tradition by the Muslim architects.[128] The design of Jama Masjid of Ajmer was taken from the Jain temple on Mount Abu. In the buildings of Gujarat, all the elements except the dome and the pointed arch are Hindu.[129]

The Hindus too, impressed by the Muslim architecture began to construct Mausoleums over their dead, i.e., samadhis and chhatris. The use of arches in buildings, vaulted roofs and the art of gardening were borrowed from Muslims. The great palaces that the Hindu Princes built in their capitals imitated the Diwan-I-Khas, Diwan-I-Aam, Shish-Mahal and the Baradari and the resultant architecture differed from the earlier Hindu mansion.[130] Qutub Minar, a masterpiece in architecture, makes evident the taste of the early Muslim rulers of the Delhi Sultanate. In this field Firozshah's name surpassed all other Muslim Sultans. He built many buildings and cities and named them after him. Firozshah Kotla, the multistoried citadel of his capital still exists in Delhi. He founded his capital Firozabad, which was burnt by Timur, when he invaded India in 1398-99.[131]

Sultan Sikandar Lodi built a new capital at Agra, Sikandra near Agra is named after Sikandar. In the Lodi gardens in New Delhi, the stern edifice tombs of Lodi Sultans are last monuments of the Sultanate. Sher Shah, after defeating Humayun in 1540, built a new city called Shergah (Sher's palace) known later as Purana Qila.[132]

The Deccan Sultans too contributed to the development of the art of architecture. The Osmani rulers of Bijapur were great builders. The Gol Gambez whose dome is larger than that of pantheon at Rome; Ibrahim Rauza, the tomb of Taj Sultana; and the palaces of Relic, gave to the city of Adilshahis, a glory which was greater than that of Agra and Delhi. Ibrahim Rauza is in its dream like beauty is considered equal to Taj Mahal and the tomb of Sultana, the architect himself had it inscribed with blasphemous pride that heaven itself stood astounded at this building. The palace of Relic, which housed two hair of the holy Prophet, bore witness to the cosmopolitan taste of the monarchs of Bijapur.[133]

The Jami Masjid of Jaunpur, the Mosque and palaces in Mandu and Ahemadabad were a harmonizing of Hindu and Muslim traditions. The great palace of Bir Singh Bundela, the old fort at Bikaner, the palaces of Udaipur, Jodhpur and Amber are among the surviving example of great period of architecture.[134] The Surs were the rulers till Humayun regained power. The Mosque known as Qila-I-Kunha Masjid is a structure of admirable architectural qualities built in the Purana Qila. It reflects its Persian influence in its recessed portal, small minarets, round the dome, though in other respects it is Indian. The tomb of Sher Shah is "one of the best designed and most beautiful buildings in India unequalled among the earlier buildings in the northern provinces for grandeur and dignity...."It is constructed on a high plinth in the centre of a lake at Sasaram in Bihar The design is a mixture of both Hindu and Muslim architectural elements. According to Qanungo, "His noble tomb at Sasaram still brings home to the mind of the beholder the grandeur of the empire, severe yet graceful; externally Muslim but Hindu inside".[135]

The Mughal period was an age of continuation and culmination of the processes that had been initiated and promoted during the preceding period under the Sultans. However, during the Mughal period the art of architecture attained its magnificence. The red-sand-stone and marble blended buildings in the words of Tavernier "were built like titans and finished like jewellers"or as Abul Fazl puts it, "These clever craftsmen chiselled marble more skillfully than carpenters carved wood". V.A. Smith writes, "The buildings of Akbar's time, as a rule obviously combine both Hindu and Mussalman features, and so may be described correctly as being designed in an eclectic or mixed Hindu Muslim style. Sometimes the Hindu, sometimes the Muhammadan element predominates" His architecture speaks for his statesmanship aiming at Hindu Muslim unity. The emperor himself took a keen personal interest in architecture. "His Majesty" writes Abul Fazal, "Plans splendid edifices and dresses the work of his mind in the garment of stone and clay".[136] Akbar himself designed the palace of Birbal. Akbar's own palace combined features of both Muslim and Rajput palaces. The vast army of the architects, which was employed in Fatehpur Sikri, was recruited from all over the Mughal Empire. The Emperor carefully laid out himself its design himself. His own special suite was in the palace so well planned that he could view the Government offices and all the principal buildings from it and by a covered way could reach, quite unobserved, the places which interested and pleased him best.[137] Jodhbai's palace at Agra Fort, Panch Mahal and Akbar's tomb at Sikandara borrowed the structural design of Buddhist Vihara.8 The Hindu temples and palaces also borrowed from the Muslim style. The temple of Ahalya Bai, the palace of Raja Jai Singh of Jaipur and of Raja Surajmal of Dig and a temple at Kantanagar in Bengal all exhibited the synthesis in their architecture.[138]

The spirit of the age was to produce in every field, which was the best, eloquent and incomparable. Perfection in every art was the principle followed by artisans. Jahangir was the lover of gardens, some of them laid out in patterns like Persian carpet. He built paradises in Srinagar (Nishat and Shalimar), Udaipur, Fatehpur Sikri and Lahore. The Kohinoor and the Peacock Throne are the symbols of the age of magnificence "If there is a paradise on earth, it is here, it is here, it is here!" So reads an inscription in Persian in the Diwan-I-Khas (chamber of private audience) of Shah Jahan at Delhi Red Fort.Taj Mahal which is also known as Taj-bi-ka-Roza, depicts the crowning glory of the Mughal period. 'A dream in marble', 'Romance in stone' or 'a tear drop on the cheek of Time' still remains unrivalled in the world. Not content with enriching his grandfather Akbar's capital with these and other architectural glories, he planned re- transfer of the seat of government to Delhi and adorned that city with buildings of unrivalled magnificence. The palace at Delhi, now the fort, covered a vast parallelogram, 1600 feet by 3200 with exquisite and sumptuous buildings in marble and fine stone. The magnificence of Shahjahan's court was the wonder of the European travellers. His Peacock throne, with its tail blazing in shifting natural colours of rubies, sapphires and emeralds was not only the costliest but also incomparable in its beauty. Even Tipu,s throne was so artistic, elegant and of such a huge size that the English, who took it away to England had to disjoint it into many parts in order to take it in one ship.[139]

Hindu Rajas and nobles of the Court too built numerous beautiful buildings. Man Mandir in Gwalior, the Govind Deva temple at Brindaban, Hawa Mahal at Jaipur speaks about the taste of the time.

Medicine

Before the introduction of Unani system, Ayurveda was reigning supreme in India.

Interaction between Ayurveda and Unani system influenced and enriched both the sciences. History relates that when Arab carried on trade with India they also carried Indian drugs and introduced them to other countries. In those days Unani system was developing in Greek. The Greek physicians incorporated Indian drugs into their own medicine. However, in India, the Unani system made inroads in the 14th century when the Mongols ravaged the Persian and Central Asian cities like Shiraz, Tabrez and Alam. The scholars and physicians of Unani medicine fled to India. The Delhi Sultans and later the Mughal emperors provided state patronage to the scholars and even enrolled some of them as state employees and court physicians. These physicians subjected Indian drugs to clinical trials and as a result of their experiments, added numerous drugs to their own system. Ayurvedic Medicine was also translated into Persian. A book entitled "Madan-us-Shifa Sikandar Shahi was written by Hakim Bahwa Khan in the reign of Sikandar Lodi which is an epitome of the works of Sushruta, Charaka, Vaghbhatta, Rasratnagar, Sarangdhar, Bang Sen, Chintamani, Chakradutta, Madhonidan and other Ayurvedic books.

If Ayurvedic Medicine influenced Unani Tibb, the latter influenced the former. Sixty years after Sikandar Lodi, Bhavamisra mentions several drugs in his Bhav Prakash, which were borrowed from Unani medicine. Some of these drugs are ajwain kursani (henbane) aqarqarha (pyrethrum) podina (mint) gulab (rose) chobchini (china roots).

The Unani system was at its peak in India during 14th to 18th century. It found favor not only with the rulers but was also popular among the Indian people all over the country. However during the

British rule in India, the Unani medicine suffered. Its development was hampered due to the withdrawal of Government patronage. But since masses had complete faith in the system, it still continues to be practised in the sub-continent.[140]

Social Life

Living together for centuries resulted in producing a new social system, which was the mixture of both Hindu and Muslim way of life. Similar way of living, beliefs, customs and practices were evolved and followed by the inhabitants of a region, made it difficult to distinguish between Hindus and Muslims except in mosque or temples.

The Muslim rulers in Sind influenced by the locals adopted their practices. They started wearing dress similar to that of a native Kings. They also started wearing pagdi (headgear) keeping long hair and let their beard grow. Islamic law prohibits the use of gold and silver ornaments for Muslim men. But due to their close contacts with Hindus all the Muslim rulers and elites adorned themselves with all kinds of jewellery and precious stones in their daily life and on important festive occasions.[141] The Hindu kings too influenced by the Muslims, adopted Achkans and tight fitting trousers (churidar pyjamas). Brocades printed silk and muslin were the common dress of the upper classes of both the Hindus and the Muslims. The manner of clothing, with the passage of the time became so similar that it was difficult to distinguish Hindu noble from his Muslim counterpart. The Album of emperor Jahangir preserved in the Berlin Museum shows that even the rulers of distant Kutch and Nawanagar had began to put on the Mughal dress and the portraits of Rajput nobles from the time of Man Singh shows that apart from the caste-mark which distinguished the Hindu, the dress both Hindu and Muslim nobles was practically identical.[142] So similar were their appearances that it was not easy to make out the identity of the person. As a matter of fact, Husain Khan, Governor of Punjab greeted a Hindu with the Islamic mode of salutation in his Court and on discovering his mistake, issued an instruction asking the Hindus to wear a particular badge on the sleeves of their garments.[143] The common people comprising both the Hindus and Muslims looked so similar that it was not possible to detect their identity. Jahangir writes in his Memoir that in Kashmir, he could not distinguish between a Hindu and Muslim. Aurangzeb, it is said had tried to bring reforms in the Muslim society in the manner of dress after his accession to throne. He posted barbers and tailors at the gate of the royal castle to cut of the extra length of beard and pyjamah but failed in this venture.[144]

The Muslim rulers borrowed Court ceremonies from the Hindus. The royal custom of nyochawar, passing over of the gold and silver coins thrice over the head of the ruler and offering them to the menials and the poor persons, was a Hindu Court etiquette followed by the Muslim rulers. Another ceremony was the Tula Dan, weighing the ruler in in precious metal or goods and then distributing among the poor was also adopted by the Muslim from the Hindu rulers.[145]The Hindu rulers also copied many practices of the Muslim Courts. Persian words like Peshwa, daftardar, Jagtan-Mulk, Hukumatpanah, Mukhtyara, Kayda were used. The Muslim Names like Shahji, Piraji, Sultanji, Sabhanji, Haibatrao, Sahebrao etc were common in Hindus also.[146] Muslims, on the other hand adopted Hindu Names. Even the high born Muslims of Turkish descent kept Hindu names as Chajju, Kachchan, Hamidraja etc. In Bengal, the names of innumerable families bear the stamp of Muslim influence. The names suggesting the position which their forbears used to occupy in the states of Muslim Kings, for instance, Tarfdar, Mahal, Navis, Chitnavis, Majumdar, Khastagir, Viswas, Nakhal, Motamad etc.[147] In Muslim Courts, the official language was Persian and there used to be particular seat arrangement for different categories of orders. The non-Muslim rulers imitated the Mughal Court and it was difficult to find out the dissimilarities. Even in Maharaja Ranjit Singh's Court, the title of the Order of Merit or Star of Punjab or of gold medal was Persian. In fact the whole of the Court was a Punjabi version of the Persian Court. The Courtiers looked like feudal lords of Persia or Persian officers of the Mughal emperors. The coin which the Maharaja struck was in Persian legend;

"Deg O, Tego, fateh Nusrat Bedarang
Yaft Az Nanak Guru Gobind Singh"[148]

(Through hospitality and the sword to unending victory granted by Nanak and Guru Gobind Singh.)

In Rajasthan Persian words were used in the Rajasthani language. The royal seal of Swai Jai Singh bore on the reverse Nagari characters and on the obverse Persian characters. Technical terms used in all the states of Rajasthan were Persian though the script used was Devanagri.[149]

Polygamy was common both among the Hindu and Muslim nobles and kings. The number of wives that a Hindu or Muslim chieftain possessed usually depended on his economic status. Their amusement, games and exercises were common. The virtues which they esteemed and the vices which they condemned were the same. Their manners of dealing with the superiors, equals and inferiors were similar. People respected not only their teachers but also their sons. Teacher was addressed as Ustad and his son was addressed, even by older students as Ustadzada. In their domestic life and household arrangements, arms and armours, it was difficult to distinguish the one from the other.[150]

There are instances of Rajput custom jauhar adopted by the Muslims. Kamaluddin, the Governor of Bhatnair and his followers advanced to fight Timur after burning their women-folk and property.[151] In [1734] the Marathas attacked Sambhar in Malwa region. Finding it difficult to defend, the Chief, Fakharuddaulah slew his women after the manner of Rajputs and the fought with the Marathas.[152] The practice of taking out a man from his bed before he breathes his last was also common. On the death of her husband, the Muslim women in imitation to her Hindu sisters gave up wearing of certain ornaments and coloured clothes.[153]

Hindus and Muslims both had superstitious veneration for odd numbers. "It is remarkable," observes Howell, "that a Gentoo never gives or receives an obligation for an even sum, if he borrows or lends a hundred, a thousand, or ten thousand rupees, the obligation runs for a hundred and one, a thousand and one, ten thousand and one etc. The Mohammedans, in conformity only, have adopted this custom".[154] The nobles gave money in the form of nazar to the emperors on festive occasions in odd figures. This custom is still prevalent among both the communities.

Early marriages were current among both the communities. Dowry, a Hindu practice too became widespread among the Muslims. The simplicity of Muslim marriage was given up in favour of growing pomp and expensive display including music dancing and drinking. Girl's engagement (mangani) and her decoration for marriage, corresponding to Hindu bride's solah singar as well as some other ceremonies like ubbatan and mehndi, singing of wedding songs all were observed by both the communities. Keeping of iron weapons by the bridegroom, the bridegroom's mounting the horseback while going to the house of the bride and gifts showered on the laps of the bride etc, were borrowed by the Muslims from the Hindus.[155] Widow remarriage sanctioned by Islam was frowned upon by the Indian Muslims under Hindu influence.[155] Both Hindu and Muslims regarded the birth of a girl child as burden and many Muslims like Hindus killed their daughters "to save the expenses and trouble of rearing them"[156] Both cherished an ardent desire for a male child. Like the Hindus, delivery was usually effected on the ground, the mother being made to lie on the quilt. Chhatti or the celebration of the sixth day after the birth of the child was common among both the communities. Caste system too crept in among the Muslims. Besides social distinction, there also grew occupational caste distinctions as among Hindus.[157]

Muslims also influenced Hindus dietary habits and preparations. Prejudice against onion which was called Malechcand by Hindus as it was brought in India by Mahmud, was given up. Biryani, Pulao, Korma, kofta became popular and so were Baloo-Shahi, Gulab Jamun, Barfi, Halwa, Qala Qand, Khurma Babar-bari, Murabba, Khursasani-khichri and the use of earthen oven (tandoor) and so on. Chewing the betel leaf, a Hindu habit was prevalent among Muslims both the nobles and the common people. 'In the houses of Hindu nobility the great feast were in imitation to the manner of the Persian and the Central Asian Amirs'. [158]

Islam has prohibited the use of wine but in India its use in Muslim community was prevalent from kings to common masses. Even the women used to drink it. Aurangzeb made a frantic effort to banish its use but had to acknowledge defeat in the long run. Once in despair, he cried, "In all Hindustan no more than two men could be found who did not drink, namely himself and Abdul Wahhab, the Chief Qazi, appointed by him." But Manucci humorously adds that "with respect to Abdul Wahhab, he was in error, for I myself sent him every day a bottle of spirits (wine) which he drank in secret, so that the king could not find it out."[159]

Except the small orthodox section, both the Hindus and Muslims participated in each other's festivals without inhibitions. Both the communities celebrated their fairs, feasts and festivals in the same way. Holi, Diwali, Dussehra, Shivratri, Id and Bakrid were national festivals. These were not only celebrated with pomp and show in the Courts but also by the common people with great enthusiasm. These were the occasion for enjoyment and paying reverence to God. On the occasion of Diwali, the Muslims particularly of rural areas, illuminated their houses and huts, and took part in gambling, an important feature of the festival. The Muslims women considered Diwali as their Id. On the day of Diwali, they sent pitchers full of red coloured rice as presents to the houses of their sisters and daughters. They observed all the customs associated with it. The Meos and Minas, living in the state of Alwar and Bharatpur celebrated not only Diwali and Dussehra but also Janamasthmi, the birthday of Lord Krishna. The Nawabs of Bengal and Awadh celebrated this festival in the royal fashion.[160]

In India, the Muharram festival drew some of its features like burying of the Taziyas and mimic attacks on effigies from the Ram-Lila of the Hindus .In celebrating Muharram Hindus number exceeded than that of Muslims. It was not only in the procession that the Hindus joined. "They actually observed Muharram as Muslims did in their homes as day of mourning and prayers when no festivity could be indulged in and no auspicious act such as marriage could be solemnized Many Hindus had their own Taziyas and spears and Hindus boys fully became Paiks Bahistis donning green dress and badge and carrying the water Mashak. Hindu Akharas vied with the Muslim Akharas in displaying their feat with sword and scimitar, Jutaku and lathi. Very often there were joint Akharas".[161] Daulat Ram Sindhia and his officers participated in Muharram procession in green dress like Muslims.[162]

Taziya processions were influenced by Durga Puja immersion or Rath Yatra processions. Even as late as 19th century Buchanan found that of the 1400 Taziya procession of Patna and Bihar Sharif area, 600 were conducted by the Hindus.[163] The preparation of Taziyas was carried with great religious fervour. The rich Hindus used to subscribed towards its expenses as the Muslims did to Durga image.[164] Basant Panchmi was celebrated with both the Hindus and Muslims with great enthusiasm. The celebrations which continued for seven days. The citizens of Delhi, including amirs and rich persons, dressed in costly robes used to visit the bank of Jamuna where the festivities of the festival were held.[165] The fair of Garh Mukhteshwar was an important fair in which thousands of people from different regions assembled for a dip in the holy Ganges Muslims in the company of their Hindu friends also visited the fair and used to have dip with devotion.[166]

Hindus took auguries from the Quran and the Muslim consulted Brahmins for the auspicious dates and days. The Churihars of U.P worshipped Kalka Sahja Mai (a Hindu Goddess) ; the Mirasis of Amritsar used to make offerings to Durga Bhawani, the Dudekulas Muslims of Madras worshipped tools as done by Hindus at Dussehra festival.[167] Like the Hindus, the Muslims had invented several imaginary female personalities, endowed with supernatural powers, called Bibis, in whose name they cooked and observed fasts. Common to both was the Goddess Sitla or Small Pox. When a Child was attacked with the dread disease, small pox medicine as rule was not given for the fear of offending the Goddess Sitla. Cholera was worshipped as Ola Devi by the Hindus and as Ola Bibi by the Muslims. The Serpent Godess was invoked equally by both, as Manasa [168] Similarly moon was believed to possess a decisive influence on human affairs. Common to both was a dread of the effect of the eclipse of the moon or sun on a pregnant woman. They used to lie quietly for the duration of the eclipse lest their child be born deformed.[169]

Belief in omens, witchcraft, sorcery was also common among both the communities. Evil spirit was avoided by the use of charm (tawiz) bound on the arm or the neck and the use of magic or Jhar-phoonk. The evil eye of the deformed or the mutilated person was especially feared. Lemon was considered a protection against the evil eye. A curious case of syncretistic demonology was Hawwa. Another malignant Hindu figure Mano (the cat) was called Nikki Bibi among Muslims. Hindu dread of the departed wandering soul Pret was accepted in popular Indian Islam. So was the Bhut, the malignant soul of the victim of a violent death and churel.[170]

A man's name is a part of personality and a recital of those of the deities has special influence in Hindu religion. Hence the name and the age are to be concealed, the reason being that the knowledge of the age coupled with that of the sign of Zodiac under which a person was born will give his enemies a chance of working black magic against him. Because of this belief "all the Mughal Emperors and other Muslim kings had at least three names; and accordingly the date of Akbar's birth was concealed and he was given a new name at his circumcision."[171]

The masses both the Hindus and the Muslims believed that the Pir possessed a supernatural power, e.g., curing diseases, assuaging the sorrow and pains of the poor, being present at the same time at different places or even reviving a dead man or causing rain to fall at a place. Both the Hindus and Muslims sang together to please the rain gods:

"Aulia! Maulia! Minh barsa'
Sadi Kothi Dana pa'
Chiriye de munh pani pa"[172]

(Aulia Maulia send rain, put grain in our house and water in the beaks of the bird)

Sectional or communal feelings had no place in such cordial environments. All the people of a village stood together in their thick and thin, shared their happiness and sorrows as one large family. Together they composed and sang songs praising the bravery and celebrated the victory of their village-lad. One such composition sung by both the Hindus and Muslims of village Bhatti was:

"Dulla Bhatti wala"

Dulla was a Rajput of Bhatti who fought bravely with the imperial troops and defeated them during Akbar's reign.[173]

Love stories too were popular and ballads were composed and sung by both Hindus and Muslims. Stories about love of Baz Bahadur-Rupmati, Sohni-Mahiwal, Sassi-Punnu, Baji Rao and Mastani, Heer-Ranjha, Mirza-Sahiban were favourite with everyone.

Thus medieval India presents a picture of harmony in every field. It was an age of enlightenment, advancement and peace and amity. Hindu Muslim scholars, poets, artists, artisan architects and musicians worked together in creating wonders in every art and made India a paradise on earth

REFERENCES

1. Jadunath Sarkar, *India Through the Ages*, S.C. Sarkar, Madras University, Calcutta, 1928, p. 89.

2. C.V. Vaidya, *History of Medieval Hindu India*, Vol-iii, Published by C.V. Vaidya Poona, 1926, p. 101.

3. S.R. Sharma, *India As I see Her*, Lakshmi Narayan, Agra 1956, p. 160.

4. *Proceedings of the Indian History Congress*, 1970. Vol. I p. 236.

5. Hakim Said and Dr. A.Z. Zahid, *Al- Beruni-His Life, Times and Works*, Karachi, 1981, p. 89.

6. Syed Mahmud, *India of Yesterday*, Indo-Middle East Cultural Studies, Hyderabad, 1957, p. 38.

7. Yusuf Husain, *Glimpses of Indian Culture*, Asia, Bombay, 1957, p. 119.

8. *Ibid.*

9. *Khuda Baksh Library Journal*, No. 44, 1987, p. 55.

10. K.S. Lal *Twilight of the Sultanate*, Manohar, New Delhi 1980, p. 246.

11. S.A.A. Rizvi, Muslim *Revivalist Movements* in *Northern India*, Balkrishna Book, Agra, 1965. p. 62.

12. Mohibbul Hasan, *Kashmir Under the Sultans*, Iran Society, Calcutta, 1959, p. 90.

13. R.K. Parmu, *A History of Muslim Rule in Kashmir*, P.P.H., Delhi, 1969, p. 162.

14. *An Outline of Cultural History of India*, ed Abdul Latif, Hyderabad, 1958, p. 185.

15. *Ibid*.

16. Tarachand, *A Short History of the Indian People*, Macmillan, Bombay, 1940, p. 193.

17. Pt. Sunderlal, *How India lost Her Freedom*, Popular Prakashan, Bomaby 1970, p. evi.

18. *The Delhi Sultanate*, ed R.C. Majumdar, Bharatiya Vidya Bhavan, Bombay, 1967, p. 220, 635.

19. Pt. Sunderlal, p. evi.

20. *Khuda Baksh Library, Journal* No. 44, 1987, p. 74.

21. Dinesh Chandra, *History of Bengali Language and Literature*. p. 13-14.

22. Asad Ali, *Bhaktikaleen, Hindi Sahitya par Muslim Sanskriti ka prabhav*, AIS Publication, New Delhi 1971. p. 25. (Hindi)

23. *Ibid*.

24. K.S. Lal, *Twilight of the Sultanate*, p. 246.

25. Parmanand Panchal, *Hindi ke Muslim Sahitykar*, Bharat Bharti, 1971, p. 47-48.

26. Uday Shankar Srivastva, *Madhyayaugeen Hindi ke Sufi*. Itr *Mussalman kavi*, Jawahar Pustkatya, Mathura, p. 225. (Hindi)

27. K.S. Lal. p. 254.

28.Fathullah Mujtabai, *Aspects of Hindu Muslim Cultural Relation*, NBB, Delhi 1978, p. 100.

29. Ian Austin, *City of Legends*, Viking, Calcutta, 1992, p. 35.

30. *Ibid*.

31. *An outine of Cultural History of India*, ed Abdul Latif, p. 197.

32. Niamatullah's *History of the Aghans*, trs. by Nirodhbhushan Roy, Shanti Niketan, Bengal 1938. p. xviii.

33. *Akbar* and *His Times*, ed by Irfan Habib, Oxford University Press, Delhi, 1997 p. 204.

34. Asad Ali, p. 26-27.

35. M.A. Jawed, *The Unknown Iqbal*, Kitab Publishing House, New Delhi 1996, p. 5.

36. Uday Narayan Tiwari, *Hindi Bhasha Tatha Sahitya*, Rajkamal Prakashan, Delhi 1953. p. 145 (Hindi).

37. Sivaram Krishna and Suniti Roy, *Poets-Saints of India*, Sterling New Delhi, 1996, p. 60.

38. Uday Shankar Srivastav, p. 227.

39. Ramchandra Shukla, *Hindi Sahitya ka Itihas* Nagri Pracharni, Kashi 1997, p. 120 (Hindi).

40. *Ibid.*

41. *Ibid.*

42. Narmdeshwar Chaturvedi, *Kavi Tansen Aur Unka Kavya* Sahitya Bhavan, Allahabad, 1956, p. 124, 25. (Hindi)

43. Ambika Prasad, *Persian Influences on Hindi*, University of Calcutta, Calcutta 1936, p. 32.

44. Fathullah Mujtabai, p. 125.

45. Uday Narayan Tiwari, p. 148.

46. *Akbar and this Times*, p. 204.

47. C.R. Naik, *Abdul Rahim Khan-i-Khanan*, Gujarat University, Ahmedabad 1966, p. 243.

48. V. Raghvendra Rao, *Indo-Muslim Culture, Vichara Sahitya*, Banglore p. 86.

49. Suniti Kumar Chatterjee, *Indo-Aryan and Hindi*, Gujarat Vernacular Society, Ahmedabad 1942, p. 181.

50. *Ibid.* Also see Sukhdev Bihari Mishra, *Hindi-Sahitya or Itihas*, p. 84.

51. Suniti Kumar, p. 181.

52. Uday Shankar, p. 173.

53. *Ain-i-Akbari*, Abul Fazl Allami, trs. by Blochmann, Asiatic Society, Calcutta 1873, p. 106.

54. *Ibid*, 105.

55. *Ibid.*

56. *Ibid*, p. 106.

57. Visva-Bharati Quartrly, Feb. April,1947, p. 309.

58. *Early European Travellers to India*, ed by Foster p.147, 48.

59. *Indian Culture*, 1937 (14) p. 318.

60. Ambika Prasad, *Persian Influenee on Hindi*, p. 33.

61. K.S. Lal, *Twilight of the Sultanate*, p. 183.

62. *An Outline of Cultural History of India*, ed by Abdul Latif, p. 185.

63. K.M. Panikkar, *A Survey of Indian History*, p. 105.

64. DR. Motilal Menarik, *Rajasthan ka Pingal Itihas*, Hindi Granth Ratnakar 1958, p. 97, 98. (Hindi)

65. *Proceedings of the Indian History Congress*, 1939. p. 896.

66. Asad Ali, p. 39.

67. M.L. Bhagi, *Medieval India*, The Indian Publication 1965, Ambala, p. 88.

68. Parmanand Panchal, *Hindi ke Muslim Sahityakar*, Bharat Bharati, p. 85 (Hindi).

69. Uday Shankar, p. 171.

70. See Muhammad Umar, *Islam in Northern India During Eighteenth Century*, Manohar, New Delhi 1993, p. 381.

71. Hari Om Gupta, *Later Mughal History of the Punjab*, Minerva Book, Lahore, 1944, p. 194.

72. Mahdi Husain, *Bahadur Shah II*, M.N. Publication New Delhi, 1986, p. 44.

73. Tarachand, *Society and State in the Mughal Period*, Publication Division, Delhi, 1961, p. 105.

74. B.L. Bhagi, p. 351.

75. Tarachand, *Society and State in Mughal Period*, p.105.

76. Thomas Keightley, *History of India*, Whittaker and Co., London 1847, p. 138.

77. Rafiq Zakaria, *Raziya: The Queen of India*, Popular Prakashan Bombay, 1966 p. 85.

78. *The History and Culture of the Indian People*, ed by R.C. Majumdar, Bhartiya Vidya Bhavan Bombay, 1967, p. 610.

79. M.L. Vidyarthi, *Cultural History of India*, Meenakshi Prakashan, New Delhi 1977, p. 221.

80. *Ibid.*

81. Yusuf Husain, p. 120, 124.

82. *The History and Culture of the India People*, p. 611.

83. K.S. Lal, p. 242.

84. Aziz Ahmad, *Intellectual History of Islam in India*, Edinburgh 1969, p. 147.

85. Mohibbul Hasan, p. 93, 105.

86. M.L. Bhagi, p. 256.

87. *Ibid.*

88. *Khuda Baksh Library Journal* No. 44, 1987 p. 76.

89. Sir Edward Clive Bayley, *Local Mohammadan Dynasties* of *Gujarat*, W.H. Allen, London 1846, p. 389, 90.

90. M.L. Bhagi, p. 258.

91. Hem Chandra Rai, *Romance of the Fort of Gwalior*, Marathi Press Delhi, 1931, p. 31, 32.

92. Uday Shankar Srivastav, p. 206.

93. Ain-i-Akbari, p. 681.

94. Narmdeshwar, *Kavi Tansen Aur Unka Sahitya*, Sahitya Bhavan, Allahabad Vikrami , 2013, p. 14, 15. Also see Ain-i-Akbari, p. 445, 681.

95. *Ibid* p.124-125.

96. Raghvendra Rao, p. 106.

97. S.M. Jaffar, *Some Cultural Aspects of Muslim Rule in India*, Published by Mohd, Sadiq Khan, Perhawar, 1939 p. 161.

98. A.L. Srivastva, *Akbar the Great*, Shivalal Aggarwal, Agra 1962, p. 360.

99. *Ibid.*

100. Raghvendra Rao, p. 106.

101. M.L. Bhagi, p. 260.

102. K.R. Qanungo, *Historical Essays*, Shivalal Aggarwal, Agra 1968, p.183.

103. M.L. Bhagi, p. 260.

104. Ibn Hasan, *The Central Structure of the Mughal Empire*, Oxford University Press, Lahore, 1967, p. 84.

105. Manucci, *Storia Do Mogor*, trs. by William Irvine, John Murry, London 1908, p. 8. Also see Seid Gholam Hossein, *The Seir Mutaqherin*, p. 140.

106. *Embassay of Sir Thomas Roe to India*, ed by Sir William Foster, Oxford University Press, London 1926, p. 199.

107. *Journal of Indian History*, 1940, Vol. XIX, p. 250.

108. Parmanand Panchal, *Hindi ke Muslim Sahityakar*, p. 46-47.

109. *Ibid.*

110. A.M.A. Shustery, *Outline of Islamic Culture* p. 220.

111. *Ibid*, p. 110.

112. *Visva Bharati Quarterly*, Jan 1951, p. 214.

113. Rafiq Zakaria, p. 85.

114. S.T. Garratt, *The Legacy of India*, Oxford, Britain, 1937, p. 296.

115. Ain-i-Akbari, Vol. I, p. 107.

116. *Ibid*, p. 108.

117. A.B. Pandey, *Society and Government in Medieval India*, Central Book Depot, Allahabad 1965, p. 273.

118. Pradwin, *Builders of Mughal Empire*, p. 108.

119. *Ibid.*

120. *Ibid*, p. 172.

121. *Tuzuk-i-Jahangiri*, p. 20.

122. *Ibid.* Also see Pandey, *Society and Government in Medieval India*, p.

123. *Embassy of Sir Thomas Roe to India*, p. 199.

124. S.M. Jaffar, p.135.

125. *Proceedings of the Indian History Congress* 1939, p. 216. Also see M.L. Bhagi, p. 249.

126. Zahiruddin Malik, *The Reign of Muhammad Shah*, p. 343.

127. Manucci, Vol. I, p. 141.

128. Aziz Ahmad, p. 131.

129. Abid Hussain, *National Culture of India*, Asia, New Delhi 1956, p. 94.

130. K.M. Panikkar, *A Survey of Indian History*, p. 208.

131. Stephen P. Blake, *Shahjahanabad: The Sovereign City in Mughal India*, Combridge University Press, New York, 1991, p. 11.

132. *Ibid.* p. 12.

133. Panikkar, p. 209.

134. *Ibid*, p. 208.
135. M.L. Bhagi, p. 318.
136. *Ain-i-Akbari*, p-
137. Isabel, F.K. Hunter, *The Story of India*. Aberdeen Milne and Hutchinson, 1928, p. 96.
138. M.L. Bhagi, p. 286.
139. G.T. Garratt, *The Legacy of India*, Oxford Press, U.K. 1937, p. 250. Also see W.W. Hunter p. 130.
140. Prof. Jamil Ahmed and Hakim Ashrar Qadeer, *Unani The Science of Graeco Arabic Medicine*, Rolli Book, New Delhi 1998, p. 17, 18 Also see Hakim Mohammad Said ed, *Hamdard pharmacopocia of Eastern Sciences*, Sri Satguru New Delhi, 1997, p. xii.
141. Muhammad Umar p. 431.
142. K.M. Panikkar, p. 209.
143. *Visva Bharati Quarterly*, Jan 1951, p. 215.
144. Manucci, p. 7.
145. B.N. Luniya, *Evolution of Indian Culture* p. 432.
146. *Indian Historical Congress*, 1970, Vol. I, p. 235
147. Syed Mahmud, p. 175.
148. R.L. Ahuja, *Maharaja Ranjit Singh*, p. 106
149. G.N. Sharma, *Social Life in Medieval Rajashtan*, Lakshmi Prakashan, Agra, 1968, p. 355.
150. Tarachand, *A Short History* of *India*, p. 368.
151. Luniya, p. 433.
152. Hari Om Gupta, *Maratha* and *Panipat*, Punjab University, Chandigarh,1961, p. 35.
153. Muhmmad Yasin, *Social History of Islamic India* p. 90-91.
154. Mohammad Umar, p. 437.
155. *Journal of Indian History*, April 1976, p. 485. Also see Tarachand, *A Short History of India*, p. 368.
156. *Ibid*, p. 486.
157. *Ibid*. Also see Muhammad Umar, p. 430.
158. K.M. Panikkar, p. 209.
159. Manucci, Vol. II p. 5.
160. Zahiruddin Malik, p. 352. Also see Mohammad Umar, p. 420.
161. Rajendra Prasad, *India Divided*, Hind Kitab Bombay, 1946. p. 36.
162. Zahiruddin Malik,,p. 353.
163. *History of Bangladesh* ed by Siraj-ul-Islam, Asiatic Society, Bangaldesh 1992, p. 89.
164. Azizur Rahman Mallick, p. 8.
165. Zahiruddin Malik, p. 352.
166. *Ibid*.
167. Murry T. Titus, *Islam in India* and*Pakistan* p. 172.

168. *History of Bangladesh*, p. 105, 116.

169. Aziz Ahmad, p. 49.

170. *Ibid.*

171. H.A. Rose, *Religious Life of the Indian People*, Amar Prakashan, Delhi, 1991, p. 629

172. M.R. Majumdar, *Cultural History of Gujarat*, p. 237.

173. *Ibid.* p. 849.

Conclusions

The study of the preceding chapters presents a different picture of the Muslim rule in India. The period was not 'dark ages' full of atrocities, oppressions and injustices as depicted by the British or British inspired historians. The Muslims, who came to India as conquerors were conquered by its great civilization. They adopted the land as their homeland and gave up all connection with the land they had come from. Living together with other inhabitants of the land in course of time indianised not only their outlook but also their religion Islam.

During the Sultanate as well as the Mughal period, the religion was more or less a matter of personal faith and not a source of strife in the society. Mutual aspirations, adjustments, admiration and understanding existed. The liberal religious movements in the form of Sufi, Bhakti and the numerous religious syncretistic cults, worked in a big way in creating and promoting harmonious co-existence of all Faiths. The teachings of the Saints, which were the combination of Vedanta and Islam, succeeded in convincing the masses that God was One, having two different names Ram and Rahim. The Saint's conviction that the way to reach Him was not through reading and reciting the Scriptures or renouncing the world but by true devotion and service of the needy made them popular and revered figures. Their followers both Hindus and Muslims flocked to their place for guidance, blessings and sometime for assistance during hard times. Gradually, exclusiveness or belief in superiority of one's own religion disappeared and respect for all religions became the norm of the day. Besides, the liberal religious movements had social significance too. The Saints opposed the orthodoxy, rigidity and divisions of every kind. They emphasised the principles of equality, freedom and fraternity. The common kitchens and common set of rules and regulations promoted brotherly feelings and broke all barriers among their followers. They came to regard themselves as members of one large family and in such cordial atmosphere feelings of hatred, distrust and disharmony had no place. The Sufis, the Bhaktas and the heads of various Orders were thus great integrators.

The teachings and the rapidly increasing influence of the saints irked the orthodox sections of both the communities. But they could not restrain the new wave of religious liberalism, which swept over the entire country, despite hard efforts.

However, the saints could not have succeeded had the then rulers been tyrant or bigot. The rulers because of their political compulsion or liberal outlook allowed religious freedom to their subjects. Not only Hinduism and Islam had evolved a healthy pattern of synthesis, the Sikh religion and the numerous cults founded by Hindus and Muslims, emerged and flourished during their reign. The rulers not only respected and revered the saints but many of them even became their followers. They visited their places for blessings, built tombs in their memory, wrote books, and composed verses in their honour.

Liberalism and not orthodoxy governed the public or private life of the rulers whether Hindu or Muslim. The Muslim rulers gave lands, jagirs and other presents for the construction and maintenance of temples and the Hindu and Sikh Rajas built mosques and tombs The Muslim rulers even built small temples within the palaces and forts for their non- Muslim wives and officials. Quran and Puranas were placed together and were read and revered alike. They respected religious feelings of their subjects and were impartial in religious matters. Emperor Shahjahan got demolished the minarets built on a temple which was converted in to a mosque by prince Aurangzeb, and handed over to the Hindus who were the rightful claimant of the place. Maharaja Ranjit Singh returned the Sunehri masjid in possession of the Sikhs to the Muslims and yet these rulers commanded highest respect and love of their subjects.

The Muslim rulers were not Jehadis. They did not impose their creed upon their subjects. Barring a few instances, conversions took place out of free will. Rulers like emperor Akbar and Sultan Zain-ul-Abidin, provided freedom to their non-Muslim subjects to renounce the religion, if it had been forced upon them, and to rejoin the one of their ancestors. Often conversions were the concomitants of war; as features of normal policy they were rare. Had it been the policy of the rulers, the Muslims would have out numbered the non-Muslims.

Even in Agra and Delhi, the centres of the Muslim power, the Muslims did not form even one-fourth of the total population. Even during the reign of Aurangzeb forcible conversion did not take place. He did not convert Shahu, the grandson of Shivaji, who along with his family remained, in his custody for many years. Aurangzeb even arranged his marriage with Hindu girls and with Hindu religious ceremonies. Under the prevalent religious freedom, one could choose the religion and join or formulate the cult of his choice. If Hindus joined Islam then a good number of Muslims became Sikhs and Vaishnavas. Rupa and Sanatna two Hindu Courtiers in Hussain Shah's Court were converted to Islam and then joined back Hinduism, speaks of the extent of religious freedom exercised by the people during the Muslim rule.

The state was not theocratic and the Ulemas were not allowed to interfere in the state matters. Even orthodox like Aurangzeb did not pay any heed to the Ulemas if it did not suit his designs. Temples or mosques were destroyed out of momentary fury during war. Aurangzeb is not the solitary example, Maharaja Ajit Singh and Banda too destroyed the mosques. However, in peacetime, the rulers not only visited the sacred places to pay their respect but also gave liberal grants and sought counsels and directions from the religious saints.

In the liberal religious regime, the Muslims kings and commoners alike-celebrated festivals like Diwali, Dussehra, Holi Shivratri, and Basant Panchami with as much enthusiasm as they celebrated Id, Bakrid or Shab-e-barat. These festivals were the national festivals and the state used to provide finances and made arrangements for the ceremonial pomp and show. Except Aurangzeb, all other Mughal emperors, the royal families and the nobles till the end of the empire, used to participate in the festivity with devotion.

Literature is the mirror of the age in which it flourishes. From this point of view the medieval period was the age of enlightenment of which any Indian can be proud of. The harmonious literature produced in this period is unprecedented. The liberal religious atmosphere devoid of fear, discrimination or prosecution ensured the freedom of expression. Saint Tulsi wrote Ram Charit Manas, Surdas the Sursagar, Guru Arjun compiled Guru Granth Sahib and Mira's immortal songs in devotion of Lord Krishna aroused the religious fervour all over the country. Had the rulers been fanatic, such great works could not have been written. Hindu writers wrote literature and composed poems on Prophet Mohammad, the Muslim writers wrote in praise of Rama Krishna and Sarswati and enriched the Vaishnav literature. Rahim Jaisi, Surdas, who wrote with great devotion for Hindu gods were patronised by the Muslim rulers .

It were the Muslim kings who made the Hindus to know their religion by getting the Hindu religious scriptures translated into local languages. Earlier only the Brahmins had the privilege of the knowledge of the Shashtras as all of them were written in Devbhasha, i.e., Sanskrit. Under the supervision and patronage of the Muslim rulers all the Hindu religious and non-religious works were translated not only in local languages but also in Persian thus enabling the foreigners to easily acquire the knowledge of Hinduism. The works were hugely decorated and preserved in the royal Libraries.

The rulers considered deliverance of justice to all without any bias as their religious duty. Even a commoner could drag a king or a noble to the court without any fear. None was deprived of justice as it was completely free of charge There was no animosity of any kind between Pandit and Qazi. Both used to sit together and decided cases of their respective community members if they desired so. The Muslim rulers had established a rule of law, which was in many ways w more humane than that administered in the contemporary Europe. The death sentence, which was inflicted for theft in England, was reserved for serious offences under the Muslim administration in India.

Many of the Sultans and Emperors had Hindu wives who exercised influence even in state matters. And who can say that the Rajput rajas and other Hindus who co-operated with the Muslim rulers and consented inter-religious marriages were not actuated by broader secular and patriotic outlook, rather than by a mere sense of their individual interest. Many Sultans and Emperors were born of Hindu mothers and were put on the throne, even bypassing the claims of those born of Muslim mothers. How could such rulers hate or prosecute their Hindu relatives and their religion.

The Muslim rulers ruled as national kings. They identified with all the sections of the Indian society and not with any particular section. They never attempted to impose the civil law of Islam on non-Muslims. They took care of the religious sentiments of their subject. Cow slaughter was banned and separate arrangements of cooks, Qazis and Pandits were made even in the sarais built on the roadside for the travellers. Their outlook was progressive and their rule was not oppressive. Raziya, a woman was nominated by Sultan Iltutmish as his successor. He did not find any of his sons possessing the qualities of an efficient ruler. Merit was the criterion for every job. Whosoever possessed the talent was richly rewarded and was provided with all state assistance in further development of the talent. Attempts were made to rescue the people from evil practices prevalent in the society. It were the Muslim rulers who banned the Sati practice though we give credit to British only. The Hindus were treated at par with the Muslims and were not discriminated on any ground. The Muslims rulers and the nobles not only recruited Hindus in the state services but also fully trusted them. So much so that the Hindus were entrusted to guard the state treasury and in the absence of the king even the fort and the palace. In fact they enjoyed hegemony in the financial field. Not only the Muslim nobles but the kings as well used to borrow money from the wealthy Hindus. Had they been hostile to Hindus, they would not have allowed the Hindus to grow economically The Hindus managed the finances of the state and they also acted as the confidential advisor to the Muslim rulers. It was thus impossible for a Muslim king to rule over his non-Muslim subjects who formed the majority and to manage the economy of the state, in an autocratic manner.

Though that was not the age of democracy yet the government was of the people and for the people. The desire to make a place for themselves in the history of the country and the memory of the people, made the rulers work for the welfare of the people and the development of the country. They built strong forts, colleges, libraries, students hostels, hospitals, rest houses for the trevellers, excavated tanks, laid down roads and gardens all over the country. The encouragement and patronage provided liberally by the state made Indian artisan manufacture goods of amazing beauty and quality. Tavernier refers to the white calicuts at sironj which was so fine that one appeared naked while putting it on. So fine was the cloth produced that a piece of thirty yards could easily be shoved in to the shell of a coconut. Artisans created wonders in every art. Taj Mahal was the crowning glory. To see this land of splendour and majestic magnificence, the merchants from far off countries, endangering their lives in crossing many unknown seas, came to this land to acquire Indian goods. The head of their respective Governments, including the British Queen wrote letters requesting the Muslim emperor to grant permission to the merchants for trade. India was the largest producer of the industrial goods in the entire world. Almost every nation was indebted to India for their supply in exchange for gold and silver The country was economically not only self sufficient but was exporting its products in large quantity to other counties and was getting gold in return. All parts of the country were flourishing in manufacture, agriculture and commerce. European travellers had testified that under the Mughals India was rich beyond compare. Bernier, who called this land as Al Dorado, wrote "It should not escape notice that gold and silver, after circulating in every other quarter of the globe, came at length to be swallowed up, lost in some measures in Hindustan".

The rulers were able to lay out vast surns of money for palaces, temples, mausoleums, gardens, canals, tanks and irrigation reservoirs. Even military disturbances and dynastic wars were absorbed without much difficulty in to the general prosperity The prosperity of the country could not have ushered in had there been no peace, amity and good will.

There was unity in diversity. The diverse religions, cultures and languages did not cause divisions but strengthened the harmonious co-existence and enriched the country in every field. People lived happily, as their kings were generous, just and benevolent. They stood on his side and fought for him even with their co-religionists. The Muslims professed a common faith yet they had no common centre of religious authority in India or outside India, like the Roman Catholic Church or later the national Churches of Europe which gave the feeling of belonging together. They were Indian Muslims and their loyalties were towards this land. So much so that Timur regarded most of the Indian Muslims no better than heathens. During Akbar's rule even Afghanistan was captured and was made a part of India. They regarded their country as sacred. The last wish of dyeing wife of Dara was that she should be buried in her homeland Hindostan. Emperor Bahadur Shah cried and lamented in agony for being away in Rangoon and longed to see and got buried in the lap of his motherland.

All the rulers whether Muslims or Hindus, committed inhuman crimes for the sake of power. Aurangzeb was not the exception. In the words of Sir Jadunath Sarkar. "There was no crime which a Rajput would not commit for the sake of land. Father killed the son and the son murdered father. Women of the noblest rank gave poison to their trusting kinsmen. Kings took the lives of loyal ministers. None, not even the highest born descendant of the God Rama, shrank from buying the aid of an alien plunderer to decide his domestic contest".

Though there were wars between Muslims and Hindus yet they were just as frequent or infrequent as those between Muslims and Muslims or Hindus and Hindus. Besides no war was ever fought on religious or communal issue. The rulers whether Muslims or Hindus fought with one another for their imperial designs but if the warring rulers belonged to two different religions, it was given a religious colour by the biased historians and sometimes by the rulers themselves. Akbar had no religious animosity with Pratap so was Shivaji with Aurangzeb but unfortunately their wars are characterized as religious wars fought for the defence of Dharma.

Conflicts and confrontation here and there but generally, the Medieval India was an age of enlightenment, elevation, eloquence, peace, progress and prosperity which made this land a paradise on earth, a golden sparrow and the Jewel of the East. It were the English, who caused an eclipse on this flourishing state. During more than hundred and fifty years stay as merchants in this country, they became familiar with the land, its people, kings and customs. After the death of Aurangzeb in 1707, and the weakening of the Empire, they started meddling with Indian political affairs. The merchants of the company became monsters. By playing one ruler against another and acquiring economic and political advantages thereafter, they acquired the position of dictating their terms. They fomented all disputes; allied themselves with rulers or rebels as suited their designs; hired out troops to fight a rival and then helped the rival when the other grew strong. The policy of pleading and pleasing the Indian rulers was given up and intrigues, conspiracies and purchase of loyalty of the nobles became the guiding principle of East India Company. Their first victory was over Nawab Siraj-ud-daula in 1757 and the train of success continued till1857 when their home country directly enslaved India They dethroned Emperor Bahadur Shah, cut off the heads of the princes and presented them as Nazar to the helpless emperor and later hung on Delhi gate, known as Khooni Darwaza. They mercilessly plundered India and carried its wealth to Britain. They looted not only the Indian treasury but also took away the rare manuscripts. Tipu's huge size throne, which the Sultan had constructed but could not ascend was disjointed and taken to

Britain as Nadir had taken the Peacock throne. Precious Kohinoor was studded in the British Queen's crown. They injected the virus of communalism in the Indian system and worked for its rapid spread in every aspect of Indian life. No wonder, under their patronage the communalists acquired ascendancy. The age of harmony, respect and reverence for each other's god disappeared. The literature written during this period depicts hatred, mutual jealousy and ill will. So much so that Guru Nanak was called Dhurt and Dhambhi and Prophet as Rangeela Rasool by the Hindu communalists. Muslims wrote literature maligning Hindu gods. Successful in their designs, the new rulers took over the task.of presenting themselves as civilized and their rule as an era of enlightenment. The English writers left no stone unturned to characterize the Muslim rulers as barbarians, orthodox, oppressive who caused unending atrocities upon non-Muslims. They also hired Indian historians, who for their vested self or community's interest wrote what suited the British rulers. In their hands the medieval age was painted black and the British rule as progressive, just and for the good of the country. These historians persisted with their view even when the British divided our country. If this is not the distortion and misrepresentation of our history then what it is.

Bibliography

Original Sources

Abul Fazl, Allami, *Ain-i-Akbari*, trs. Blochmann, Asiatic Society of Bengal, Calcutta, 1873.

Abul Fazl, Allami, *Akbar Nama*, trs. Henry Beveridge, Calcutta 1948.

Ziyauddin Barani, *Fatawa-i-Jahanrdari* trs. Afsar Begum, Published by Muslim University. Aligarh, in Medieval India Quarterly, July-Oct. 1957.

Abdul Qadir Badaoni, *Muntakhab-ul-Tawarikh*, trs. Kumud Ranjan Das, Sarswati Library, Calcutta 1970.

Ibn Battuta, *The Rehla of Ibn Battuta*, trs. Agha Mahdi Husain, Oriental, Baroda, 1953.

Zahiruddin Babur, *Memoirs of Babur Emperor of India*, trs. F.G. Talbot, ESS Publishers, Delhi, 1974.

Muhammad Nuruddin Jahangir, *Tuzuk-i-Jahangiri*, trs. Rogers and Beveridge, Royal Asiatic Society, London. 1914.

Ishwardas, *Futuhat-i-Alamgiri*, trs. T. Ahmad, Idara-i- Adabiyat-i-Delhi, Delhi 1978.

Niamatullah, Makhzan-i-Afghana, trs. Nirodh-Bhushan Roy, as *History of the Afghans*, Shantiniketan, Bengal, 1938.

Seid Gholam Hossein Khan, *The Seir Mutaqherin* or *Review* of *Modern* Times, Calcutta 1789.

Major David Price, trs. of *Tarikh-i-Salim Shahi* as *Memoirs of the Emperor Jahanguir* Rare Book, Delhi, 1904.

Ruka 'at-i-Alamgiri, trs. Jamshid H. Bilimoria, Idara-i-Adabiyat-i-Delhi, Delhi, 1972.

Maasir-i- Alamgiri of Must' Ad Khan, trs. Jadunath Sarkar, Royal Asiatic Society, Calcutta, 1947.

Futuhu's Salatin or Shah Namah-i-Hind of Islami trs. Agha Mahdi Husain,

Asia, Aligarh, 1977.

Maulana Shibli Nomani, *Alamgir*, trs. S. Abdur Rahman, Idara-i-Adabiyat, Delhi 1981.

Memoires of Chand Bibi, S.A. Qadiri, Pub-Tarikh-i-office, Hyderabad 1939.

Foreign Travellers Accounts

Bernier, Francois, *Travels in the Mogul Empire* Humphrey Milford, Oxford University Press, 1914.

Della Valle, *The Travels of Pietro Della Valle in India*. trs. by Edward Grey, Hakluyt Society, London, 1892.

Manrique, *Travels of Frey Sebastian Manrique*, trs. Eckford Luard, Hakluyt Society, London 1927.

Niccolao Manucci, Storia Do Mogor, trs. William Irvine, John Murry, London 1908.

Pelsaert, Franciso, *Jahangir's India*, trs. W.H. Moreland and P, Geyl, Cambridge. 1925.

Tavernier, *Travels in India*, trs. V. Ball, London 1925.

The Embassy of Sir Thomas Roe to India 1615-19 ed. Sir William Foster, Oxford University Press, London 1926.

A General Collection of the Best and *Most Interesting Voyages*, ed. John Pinkerton, London, 1811.

The Norris Embassy to Aurangzeb trs. Hari Das Mukhopadhyay, Calcutta, 1959.

Journals

The Journal of the Bihar Research Society.
The Hindustan Review and Kayastha Samachar.
Proceedings of the Indian History Congress.
The Visva-Bharati Quarterly.
Khuda Baksh library Journal .
Journal of Indian History.
The Indian Antiquary.
Iqbal [Lahore, Pakistan]
Medieval India Quarterly.
Modern Review.
The Indian Historical Quarterly.
The Aryan Path.
Indian Culture.
New Review.
Indian Studies Past and Present.
The Hindustan Times.
Dawn (1901) Calcutta.

Index